MULTINATIONAL BANKING

MULTINATIONAL BANKING

A study of certain legal and financial aspects of the postwai operations of the U.S. branch banks in Western Europe

by

STUART W. ROBINSON, Jr.

A. W. SIJTHOFF LEIDEN 1972

ISBN 90 286 0072 8

Library of Congress Catalog Card Number: 72-76419
© A. W. Sijthoff International Publishing Company, N.V. 1972

Printed in the Netherlands.

To
Stuart William Robinson and
Mary Buckley Robinson,
my parents.

PREFACE

The origins of the present study are twofold.

First, for several years the author had the privilege of serving on the staff of the Graduate Institute of International Studies at the University of Geneva, and more particularly of working as assistant to Professor Pierre A. Lalive, whose advanced seminar on "Les problèmes juridiques des entreprises internationales" involved a concentrated examination of many of the legal problems faced—and caused—by very large corporations operating simultaneously in several countries.

Second, the author also spent a number of years as a practicing attorney in a New York City law firm, as a result of which he had first-hand contact with certain aspects of the operations of banking corporations, including those of non-U.S. banking institutions established in the United States.

From these two strands there evolved a keen interest in the role of private (i.e., non-governmental) financial institutions operating in foreign host countries. Partly this concerned the way in which they are established abroad, whether as branches, subsidiaries, or otherwise. This might be called a static element.

More importantly it concerned their operations, which involve, broadly speaking, the transfer of purchasing power across national or political frontiers. This might be called a dynamic element, and is the more challenging of the two, although any examination of this latter aspect must necessarily be set in the context of the former.

Preliminary research suggested that an attempt might be made at analysing, from the jurist's viewpoint, the operations of major commercial banks in several foreign host countries. Little has been written on the subject; and it has not previously been explored in depth. It was decided that an initial examination should take home and host countries in stages of industrial development as nearly equivalent as possible so that the number of independent variables could be kept at a minimum.

This resulted in the choice of the major U.S. commercial banks' branch operations in three Western European host countries: France, Great Britain, and Switzerland. The factors underlying the various aspects of this particular choice are set forth at some length in Chapter One.

Hopefully the results of the present study might contribute to and encourage further exploration of this field, including the role of commercial banking and other non-governmental financial institutions in the economic. development of host countries. Also, increased East-West trade relations could call for a close look at the possible role of foreign banking establishments in host countries, both eastern and western.

As the Graduate Institute of International Studies stresses an interdisciplinary approach to problems, it has been possible to undertake this study primarily from the juridical point of view, but one which is aimed at financial operations. Some legal elements are therefore purposely excluded from the examination because they are not germane to the financial aspects, and vice versa. The result is a narrower approach, perhaps, than if either discipline were taken alone; but it has the advantage of permitting an analysis in that part of the stream where the two flows converge.

Terminology and Presentation

Several comments are in order concerning some of the terms used in the text and in the presentation of certain material.

As for the terms, the following should be mentioned:

Banker: The word "banker" is used to identify an individual in the management of a banking firm and responsible for taking and carrying out decisions of more than routine nature. Thus, as used herein this word is not limited to a person whose own personal fortune is at stake, e.g., a private banker whose assets are not shielded by corporate limited liability.

U.S. and American: Use of "U.S." does not imply any offical connection with the federal or state governments in the United States unless otherwise indicated. The same applies to the word "American". It is hoped that the infrequent use of the latter word, which in the English language has become nearly tantamount to "U.S.", will give rise to no offense to those—in particular some Latin Americans—who rightly claim that the United States and its citizens have no monopoly on things "American".

Great Britain: "Great Britain" refers to England and Scotland. (Cf. Union with Scotland Act, 1706). The term "United Kingdom" refers to Great Britain and Northern Ireland (Cf. Royal and Parliamentary Titles Act, 1922), and is used when a particular statute or practice so requires.

Host countries and monetary areas or zones: For exchange control purposes both France and Great Britain are in currency zones, the French franc area (now technically the "Operations Account countries") and the sterling area (officially referred to as the "Scheduled Territories"), respectively. In the present study we have concentrated on the U.S. branch banks' operations in the host countries themselves, because for most exchange control purposes residents of the respective zones are treated much like those of the particular host country itself. Moreover, U.S. commercial banks tend to use units or links other than the branch banks in the host countries for transactions in the outlying parts of these areas.

Indigenous institutions and practices—whether to use English language terms: Confusion sometimes arises if direct English language translations are used for certain indigenous institutions and practices in the foreign host countries. It would be convenient if, for example, *banques de dépôts* in France could simply be referred to as "deposit banks". This term is not helpful in the British or American context, however. Nor would it be advisable to proceed with a direct translation in the other direction and arrive at *"banques commerciales"* as a French term for commercial banks[1] in the United States. Indeed, as is pointed out in the text, even the term "foreign branch" does not have the same meaning in British and American banking usage. Accordingly, in the Chapters to follow we have attempted to avoid such misleading terms, pointing out the reasons, and sometimes using a host country term itself if necessary.

Longer-term transactions: Although it is generally agreed that short-term transactions are not expected to exceed one year, there is no common international standard for determining what should be called a "medium-term" transaction. In a single country one may encounter tacit agreements to roll over short-term credits, the trading of long-term securities in shorter periods, or window dressing operations, all of which make uniform classification difficult. When transactions derive from several countries matters can be further complicated when two countries' monetary or banking authorities treat differently the same type of operation. In this study it has therefore seemed appropriate to identify transactions as nearly as possible as they are called by the individuals and institutions involved with them, and to apply "longer-term" to those which do not conveniently fit into any particular rubric. As will become more apparent, this terminology is particularly helpful in connection with a metamorphosis which occurred in the operations of the U.S. branch banks during the two and one-half decades since the end of World War II.

Banks and holding companies: During the 1960's one-bank holding companies were formed by most of the major commercial banks in the

1. "The banks which, under a central bank régime, are brought into special relationship with the central bank—for example, for purposes of credit control—are frequently referred to as 'commercial banks'. However, whether these banking institutions are actually 'commercial banks' is a question of law and fact which requires special scrutiny in each particular instance." Hans Aufricht, *Comparative Survey of Central Bank Law,* London, Stevens, 1965, p. 10.

United States. Since the multinational banking operations of the foreign branches have not depended directly on this phenomenon, reference is made throughout to the bank itself (either the head office or the branch) and not to a holding company.

Currencies and amounts: Unless otherwise indicated, the U.S. dollar is meant when "dollar" (or the symbol $) is used. When necessary, amounts in French and Swiss francs or pounds sterling (FF, SF, £) are converted into their approximate dollar equivalents at the free rate of exchange then prevailing. The word "billion" is used in lieu of thousand million or milliard.

Much of the primary research has involved personal interviews with individuals in the home and three host countries, including bankers, corporate officers, government administrators, lawyers, academicians, and private consultants. The author has not included in the present study any private or confidential information to which he has been granted access. Accordingly, the hypotheses have been formulated and the conclusions are based on material that is available to the public. In this context it is worth noting that information sometimes thought to be private or confidential is actually available to the public at large, but in a foreign language or in another country, or sometimes in documents issued by governmental or other agencies or organs normally dealing with other aspects of a particular question.

Every effort has been made to indicate the current status of statutory and other materials to which reference is made. It is possible, however, that changes may have occurred despite extensive re-checking in the final stages of the preparation of the manuscript. If so, the author hopes for the comprehension of those who will appreciate the inherent complexities of the interrelationship among four bodies of law.

Finally, the author asks for the forebearance of individuals involved in the day-to-day intricacies of multinational banking. It is hoped that they will find his theoretical approach to the subject borne out by their own experience in this specialized and complicated field.

ACKNOWLEDGEMENTS

There is a long list of persons to whom acknowledgements are due.

Beyond any doubt, the person to whom I owe the greatest debt of gratitude in connection with this study, as in countless other ways, is Margareta Habicht Robinson, my wife, whose unfailing interest, patience, and welcome encouragement during the evolution of this work have been precious assets. Her lightening of this task deserves, and has, my heartfelt thanks.

I wish to acknowledge the guidance of Professor Pierre A. Lalive of the Graduate Institute of International Studies and of the Faculty of Law at the University of Geneva, as well as that of Professor Henri Schwamm of the Institut Universitaire d'Etudes Européennes in Geneva. Professors Lalive and Schwamm made helpful suggestions concerning the research that went into this study; and their comments on an earlier draft of the text proved extremely valuable. In the same vein I would also like to acknowledge the perceptive observations and criticisms of Dr. Nicolas Krul, who helped me clarify the theoretical interrelationships between some of the legal and financial elements under analysis.

In addition, I would like to thank Professor Jacques Freymond, Director of the Graduate Institute in Geneva, who encouraged and made it possible for me to undertake this task, and whose counsel in a broader context some fifteen years ago has remained with me.

The basic research for this study has led me into official archives and libraries and into the private collections of institutions and individuals in four countries on two continents. In addition to the libraries at the University of Geneva and at the Graduate Institute of International Studies, these have included the library at the Bank for International Settlements, in Basle; those at the United Nations European headquarters (Palais des Nations), at the Institut Universitaire d'Etudes Européennes, and at the Center for Education in International Management, all in Geneva; the library of the Institute of Bankers, in London; the Joint Library of the International Bank for Reconstruction and Development and the International Monetary Fund, in Washington; the library of the Association of the Bar of the City of New York; and the Harvard Law School library in Cambridge, Massachusetts.

Of the many persons associated with these libraries I wish to thank in particular Mr. Pierre Pagneux and his colleagues at the Graduate Institute library in Geneva, especially Mrs. Lydia Anhöck and Miss Irène Sauvin. At the United Nations' library at the Palais des Nations in Geneva Mr. Norman S. Field made it possible for me to consolidate many of the various countries' documents which had to be examined simultaneously. For this I wish to thank him and his associates, especially Mrs. Zerrin Polite and Messrs. Mikhail Glouchenkov, Peter Pjovic, Charles Pernoud, Julio Pommerenck, René Robert, and Basil Ross, as well as Miss Marcelle Soulier and Dr. Badr Kasme who were formerly members of this able staff.

A special debt of gratitude is due Mr. Peter Spiro in London for having more than once made available to me the valuable collection of the library of The Institute of Bankers.

I wish to express my gratitude to two outstanding authorities on the Euro-dollar market, which has an important bearing on this work. They are Doctors Paul Einzig and Julien-Pierre Koszul, in London and Paris respectively, who generously shared with me their views on an extraordinarily complex subject and who encouraged my attempt to analyse one aspect of it. I would also like to acknowledge the interest and kindness of the late Philip Cortney, who made it possible for me to explore some of the broader international monetary aspects involved.

Several hardworking young women have had close contact with different parts of the text. In this connection I wish to thank Miss Micheline Debbas, Mrs. Elisabeth Kaytar, Miss Brenda Randall, and Mrs. Jane Volkert Wilson for the chapters and drafts which they have typed for me. An extra measure of appreciation I owe to Mrs. Elisabeth Kaytar for her remarkable multilingual abilities and for her skillful rendition of fequently difficult manuscript, the final version of which she produced.

Finally, I wish to thank a great many individuals who have graciously taken the time to discuss with me various aspects of the postwar operations of the U.S. branch banks in Western Europe. Shared views and honest differences of opinion resulting from such interviews have been invaluable to me. The responsibility for any errors or omissions in this work is, of course, my own; but these individuals, whose anonymity is respected by mutual accord, have made it possible to bring forth the present study.

Geneva, 1972   Stuart W. Robinson, Jr.

TABLE OF CONTENTS

Chapter One

"INTRODUCTION"

I. ANALYSIS: ELEMENTS

This study attempts to examine certain operations of the U.S. branch banks in Western Europe after World War II and to analyse particular aspects of those operations. Accordingly, at the outset we shall introduce the analytical method that has been adopted as well as the particular elements employed in the analysis.

A. *Multinational Banking*

1. *Use of the Words "Multinational" and "Banking"*

Derived from the Greek *"multus"* (many) and the Latin *"natio"* (people, nation), "multinational" would signify a person or thing of, or pertaining to, many nations or peoples. Unlike "international", which implies something existing or carried on between or among two or more nations,[1] "multinational" would signify an identity with or a derivation from many nations or peoples. There would need to be no flow or exchange between them, but rather an affinity to them.

"Multinational" must also be distinguished from "multi-state" (and "inter-state") and from "multi-governmental" (and "inter-governmental"), which introduce respectively the notions of states as political or social systems, and of governments, either as the agents of nations or peoples or as the agents of states themselves. *"Natio"* refers less to politically drawn lines than to the existence of groups of people with kindred customs, heritages, and languages.[2]

For two reasons, the qualifying adjective "multinational" has proved to be more useful and meaningful than either "multi-state" or "multi-governmental" in the context of the present study. First, the

1. See *Webster's Third New International Dictionary of the English Language Unabridged,* Springfield (Mass), 1961, p. 1181, and *The Shorter Oxford Dictionary,* 3d ed.rev., Oxford, 1964, p. 1030.
2. See *The Shorter Oxford Dictionary,* p. 1311.

origins of many of the operations under scrutiny do not lie in actions taken by states or governments, but rather in banking concepts and practices that have evolved or atrophied because of stimuli or deterrents present in particular financial centers. Second, the most important operations, especially those in the Euro-dollar field, ignore many state or governmental barriers altogether. As will be shown, when certain barriers exist, such as particular types of foreign exchange control regulations, the operations do not occur at all. When the barriers are lowered sufficiently, or where holes or channels are provided (or discovered), these artificial boundaries cease to exist whereas national styles of operation often continue. The adjective "multinational" has been selected, therefore, to designate the operations on which our attention will be focused.[3]

"Banking" can be defined most simply as "the business of a banker",[4] or more elaborately as "the business of a bank, originally restricted to money changing and now devoted to taking money on deposit subject to check or draft, loaning money and credit (as by discounting notes and bills), issuing drafts, and any other associated form of general dealing in money or credit".[5] In either case "banking" is a broad concept, comprising all the various activities carried out by banks in Western Europe, the United States, and elsewhere. Some of these activities are conducted by nearly every institution normally referred to as a "bank", e.g., holding funds (on deposit or otherwise) for third parties, be they public or private. Other activities are by no means widespread. For instance, some banks lend funds to certain types of borrowers to which other banks will not or may not lend; some pay interest on funds held for third parties while others do not or may not. In any event, the broad spectrum included by the term "banking" includes all the various operations undertaken by banks, wherever situated.

2. *Use of the Term "Multinational Banking"*

For centuries some bankers have had occasion to deal with foreign customers, both depositors and lenders as well as borrowers, and to deal in foreign currencies. Many commercial banks today, in the United

---

3. Linguistic harmony might have been better respected by adopting the Latin equivalent of *"multus"* to give the term "polynational" banking. During the course of the research leading to the present study we have occasionally used this latter term, but always we have reverted—perhaps as much from habit as from logic—to "multinational" banking.

4. *The Shorter Oxford Dictionary*, p. 144.

5. *Webster's Third New International Dictionary of the English Language Unabridged*, p. 172.

States, Western Europe, and elsewhere have so-called "international" or "foreign" departments or divisions carrying out such activities, which range from the financing of foreign trade transactions to the sale or cashing of travelers cheques.

The degree of emphasis which any bank puts on this sector of its activities depends upon various factors, including the bank's location, its clientele, and its size, as well as the latitude—legal or other—permitted for its operations. The emphasis also depends upon the interests of a bank's owners (whether public or private), the expertise of its employees, and how profitable, directly or indirectly, or necessary this sector may appear to be. Some or all of a wide variety of such transactions might comprise "international" banking as some bankers and observers use that term. They do not, however, constitute multinational banking.

From the foregoing it is evident that "banking" is a broad concept which we have limited and qualified by the adjective "multinational." The term "multinational banking" is narrow, not broad, and is meant to designate only a part of the field of banking operations. We must now examine and define this term as it is used herein.

a. *Manifold Points of Attachment*

(1) Geographical

At the very least, multinational banking requires actual, physical presence outside the bank's national or "native" territory or sphere of operations. Resort to a foreign correspondent bank would not provide this; nor would the location of a representative office abroad, since this merely places one or more individuals there but would not constitute an extension of the bank itself onto foreign territory. Ideally, the extension would not be through a separate legal entity, such as a wholly— or partially—owned institution chartered or incorporated under the law of a foreign state, but would be accomplished by having an integral part of the bank itself located abroad. As we shall see, the establishment of a branch bank in a foreign "host country" is the clearest and most direct method of constituting this type of actual, physical presence of the bank itself on foreign territory.

Some of the legal and other differences between the various alternatives mentioned above, ranging from the creation of a correspondent relationship through the establishment of a branch bank abroad, are covered in greater detail in Chapter Two. Suffice it to state at this point that whereas operating a single branch bank abroad would not alone constitute multinational banking, the activities comprising multinational banking cannot be undertaken without the establishment of at least one

3

such foreign branch bank, which conducts its own affairs in collaboration with the head office bank in the home country, (here the United States) and with that bank's other foreign branches, banking subsidiaries, affiliated banks, or representative offices abroad.

(2) Conceptual

Multinational banking comprises more than the mechanical act of providing a framework by establishing one or more branch banks abroad. It requires conceptual points of attachment outside the native territory of the banking institutions involved. The ideas and techniques which make up multinational banking derive from sources in many national banking systems and sets of banking practices. Concepts from many host and other foreign countries are woven into and among those stemming from the institutions' home country, to produce a hybrid form of operation that cannot evolve out of any single national source.

Moreover, multinational banking operations involve many countries for their execution. Actively, this is so when banks or bankers transfer purchasing power across national boundaries; passively, this is so when they decide not to conduct certain operations, for legal or other reasons, across those boundaries.

b. *"Multinational Banking" Defined*

Both in its inspiration and in its execution, then, "multinational banking" requires a number of differing countries and banking systems. We would define "multinational banking" as operating a bank in, and conducting banking operations that derive from, many different countries and national systems.

B. *Structural Aspects*

Having defined multinational banking for the purposes of the present study, it will be our task to examine certain legal and financial aspects of the operations of the U.S. branch banks in three Western European host countries during the period following World War II, and to analyse the multinational banking aspects of these operations.

1. *Legal*

With regard to the legal aspects, we shall examine the relationship between these operations and the legal structures in or alongside which they are conducted. We shall attempt to determine whether—and if so, how and why—these operations have affected or have been affected by the legal and paralegal elements in the national banking systems of the home

4

and host countries. We shall investigate the hypothesis that multinational banking is favored by the absence of legal restraints, both as to the magnitude as well as to the type and complexity of the operations involved. In addition, we shall try to see to what extent the mode or method of applying the laws affects those operations, and vice versa. That is to say, we are interested both in the quantity and density of the laws, and in how and why they are applied in practice.

Also, we shall scrutinize the qualitative aspects of the laws, i.e., we shall attempt to determine whether some types of laws bear more heavily than others on multinational banking. For our analysis we have chosen to include banking, credit control, and exchange control laws and regulations. Further along in the present Chapter this choice is explained.

2. *Financial*

Not only are we interested in certain legal aspects of the postwar operations of the U.S. branch banks, but also in specific financial or operational aspects. We shall delve into three particular areas: first, the significance of the type and duration of the link or attachment between the U.S. bank itself and the host country banking sector; second, the role of non-indigenous banking institutions in general and that of the U.S. branch banks in particular; and third, the extent to which different U.S. commercial banks have used different approaches to their operations, and why some of these have come closer than others to the concept of multinational banking.

C. *Evolutionary Aspects*

We shall not be content with a static relationship among the structural aspects outlined above, principally because some of these relationships changed both in magnitude and in content over the course of the postwar years under study. Accordingly attention will be focused on certain evolutionary aspects.

1. *Legal*

We shall analyse the emergence of multinational banking in sectors— geographical and operational—where there have been, or have appeared to be, evolutionary paths or channels in the legal framework. The operations have evolved along certain of these, determined partly by where legal and paralegal aids or obstacles have lain or could be erected. As these paths or channels have been modified the evolutionary process has accelerated or decelerated, changing to include new techniques and to

5

reject or modify others. Paralegal aids and obstacles must be taken into consideration because in some instances accepted practices and unwritten (but binding) rules are no less effective than laws.

It is on the operations that we shall focus our attention, not on the legal structures which the U.S. commercial banks have chosen to use. Accordingly, in Chapter Two we shall examine only the basic static elements, principally the legal ones, so that in Chapters Three through Five we can deal with the dynamic elements. We are not examining "multinational" banks but rather multinational banking, as defined above.

In analysing the evolution of the legal aspects we shall concentrate upon the national laws of three host countries (France, Great Britain, and Switzerland) and of the home country (United States) rather than on the treaty law in the background. Primarily this is because the latter has not evolved during the period under study in the same fashion as have the municipal laws.[6] This is not to underrate the pertinence of treaty law. Indeed, as will become apparent further ahead, had there been no treaty providing for external convertibility of the principal Western European currencies, the Euro-dollar market, as we know it, would not have emerged. Once put into force, however, this and other treaties[7] have not evolved in a manner that has directly affected the multinational banking operations of the branches of the major U.S. commercial banks. Since we are interested in analysing a dynamic rather than a static phenomenon, the national legal and paralegal aspects are of greater importance to our study.

2. Financial

Just as we are probing into the evolution of the legal aspects of multinational banking, we are also probing into the evolution of the finan-

6. During the postwar period under study the Swiss-U.S.A. treaty relationship has shown signs of some evolution. In the late 1960's there were bilateral talks leading toward the drafting of a treaty that would affect certain aspects of the Swiss banking secret. See page 78, note 211. Otherwise there were no modifications in U.S. treaties with that country or with France or Great Britain. It is noteworthy, however, that certain informal agreements existed which affected the multinational banking operations of the U.S. branch banks in the host countries. For example, it was reported in 1946 that France and the United States had agreed to furnish reciprocally the names of citizens of the other country maintaining bank accounts within its territory. See New York Times, May 29, 1946, p. 12, col. 3 (late city edition).

7. Treaty obligations under the Articles of Agreement of the International Monetary Fund (especially Article VIII) lie in the background. Also, the O.E.C.D. has shed light on the reciprocal rights and duties involved in facilitating the flow of capital. See Organisation for Economic Co-operation and Development, *Code of Liberalisation of Capital Movements*, Paris, 1965. The O.E.C.D. published its *Code of Liberalisation of Current Invisible Operations* the previous year.

cial or operational aspects. Thus, referring back to the three elements noted earlier, it will be necessary to analyse the changing nature of the attachment (physical and conceptual) between the U.S. banks themselves and the host country banking sectors, the evolution of the role of the U.S. branch banks in their foreign environments, and the emergence of different styles of conducting multinational banking.

In order to do this, we shall investigate simultaneously four important developments:

First, we shall examine the changing concepts of competition and style of regulation in thé host country and U.S. banking communities.

Second, we shall test the two-way flow of ideas and techniques between host and home countries, and among host countries, through the medium of the U.S. branch banks.

Third, we shall delve into the gradual development of a relatively high degree of autonomy on the part of these U.S. branch banks, an autonomy that is unusual in several respects, notably in that (1) they are branches and thus integral parts of the U.S. banks rather than separate legal entities; (2) they differ from domestic branches of U.S. commercial banks by enjoying—and accepting the responsibilities involved in—the self-discipline imposed on banks operating in two of the host countries, as well as the agency status with respect to the host government or monetary authorities in all three; and (3) particularly during the latter years of the postwar period covered, this growing autonomy ran counter to a general trend toward greater concentration of the international operations of many U.S. corporations at their principal offices in the United States or at some single point overseas.

Fourth, we shall probe into the evolution of a special type of outlook or frame of mind which is essential to the conduct of multinational banking operations.

II. CHOICE OF ELEMENTS

It is now in order to explain the choice of the elements to be employed in the analysis.

A. *Major U.S. Commercial Banks' Foreign Branch Operations*

1. *Why* Banks' *Operations?*

Banks have been chosen because their activity abroad can have an impact that is quite striking compared to the cost of establishing operational facilities. Whereas manufacturing or selling operations abroad normally require significant fixed capital outlays, most service operations demand considerably less. Among the latter, the ability to provide financial services abroad usually necessitates a smaller physical investment overseas than, for example, the ability to provide transportation or communication services, which involve the use of rolling stock or transmission facilities. Of course, the entire assets of a bank are exposed when a branch bank rather than a banking subsidiary is established abroad; but this would not resemble exposure of fixed assets as much as inventory.[8]

At a bare minimum, banking services abroad can be provided by locating a single individual armed with adequate credit or placement facilities. Optimizing the operation will necessitate the hiring of personnel, the furnishing of office space, the installation of communication equipment, and in some banking operations, it must be added, the provision of a certain aura of substance—or lack thereof—depending upon the type of clientele sought and the services offered.

Neither warehouse facilities nor packaging machinery are required, however, for the banker deals in an intangible, twofold product consisting of credit and confidence. By choosing banks, one can examine a sector where the ease or difficulty of access depends relatively less upon the installation of major physical plant than would be the case with other possible choices.

Another reason for selecting banks, equally important analytically, is that until fairly recently the substance of their operations has been relatively little affected by technological innovations compared with some other service industries. Instruments such as computers and magnetic readers have been adopted to reduce the cost of handling checks and other documents. This adaptation has been ancillary, however, and has not changed the very core of the transactions involved,[9] unlike the impact of the reaction engine upon commercial air transport, the container upon land and ocean cargo handling, and solid-state components

8. Banking is not the only service activity where a relatively small fixed capital outlay is required. For example, the same holds true in the insurance industry. Likewise, legal or financial counseling services can be offered by establishing abroad with small fixed capital investment. Here it is worthy of note that many countries' laws strictly limit the extent to which foreigners can engage in certain of these service activities, notably the supplying of insurance protection or the practice of law. We shall have occasion to see various aspects of the limits on foreign-owned or -controlled banks' operations in the Chapters to follow.

9. Computers have in the last few years, however, permitted banks (and their large commercial clients) to obtain statistical information much more rapidly, so that amounts can be transferred from one unit to another—for extremely short periods, if necessary—on a global basis when exchange control or other laws do not block such operations. This may well prove to be a technological factor affecting the core of multinational banking operations.

and satellites upon electronic communication. Banks' operations, therefore, have remained "classic" or "traditional" in nature to a larger
extent.[10] This has allowed reference to a relatively more stable historical background in observing and analysing those changes that have occurred, particularly the ones which have constituted multinational
banking.

2. *Why* Commercial *Banks' Operations?*

Commercial banks' operations, rather than those of investment banks or
other types of banking institutions, have been chosen because the former
relate more directly and more immediately to nearly all segments of a
country's economy. The effects of investment banking transactions per-
colate eventually into those same segments, it is true, but by no means
as broadly or at the same velocity as those of commercial banking
transactions. Short-term credit, the primary area in which commercial
banks operate, is very sensitive to a country's overall economic outlook,
and itself acts in turn on other elements sensitive to it.

A second analytically important reason for choosing commercial banks'
rather than investment banks' operations is that there are more of the
former. Although every banking transaction—commercial or investment—
is ultimately separate and unique, the greater size and relative infrequency of investment banking transactions mean that to a much larger
extent they are "tailor made".

Accordingly, any change that occurs in commercial banks' operations
is easier to observe and to verify, since the change is set against a background comprising numerous elements. In social scientific terminology,
the "control" group is larger and more stable in the case of commercial banks' operations than in the case of investment banks' operations,
so that the "experimental group"—particularly those operations pertaining to multinational banking—can be more accurately observed and
analysed.

3. *Why* U.S. *Commercial Banks' Operations?*

The operations of certain foreign branch banks of the major U.S. com-

10. Of course, the U.S. branch banks' operations have been subject to the second
level impact of technological innovation in other service industries. Swift, regular
transatlantic air service, and rapid telephone or teleprinter communication among
branches or with the head office bank in the United States have contributed immen-
sely to the ability of these branch banks to function effectively. Also, credit cards
and various forms of computerized or electronic money have already made inroads
domestically in the United States. These will certainly affect the core of banking
operations in the future.

mercial banks, rather than those from other possible home countries, have been selected for two basic reasons:

Preliminary research indicated that although some banks in other countries had embarked on multinational banking ventures, the U.S. commercial banks had been most active as a group in the field of multinational banking. It must be emphasized in the nature of a *caveat*, however, that although this has been true in terms of the group as a whole, individual U.S. commercial banks display different operating traits, so that we are dealing with a bloc of homogenous but not identical institutions. Nevertheless, the group characteristic is strikingly apparent and is important in the analysis of some of the phenomena to be scrutinized in the Chapters ahead. By "major" U.S. commercial banks we mean those with deposits in excess of $1 billion at any time during the period in question.

Moreover, U.S. commercial banks' operations abroad comprise several elements that lend them a degree of uniqueness compared to the operations of many of the foreign branches of banks from other home countries. These are:

First, U.S. commercial banks have had no pressing need to establish branches abroad in search of profitable or interesting opportunities. During the postwar period the domestic U.S. market has offered ample challenge. Until the mid-1960's the decisions to establish and operate branch banks overseas, or new branches in the case of those banks already having branches abroad, were taken so as to engage in additional, supplementary activities outside the banks' normal domestic pattern of activities.[11]

Second, with one exception (the Philippines), the U.S. banks have not been establishing branches in former colonies. Seen from Western Europe, it is fair to say that in some respects Latin America resembles an area of special U.S. economic interest; but not even that area represents ex-colonial territory. Thus, unlike many of the overseas establishments of British and French banks, none of the U.S. branch banks has had the advantage of operating in areas where the local language, host currency, and style of banking are closely related or identical to those in the home country. In other words, U.S. branch banks abroad are bound to be operating in territory that is essentially unfamiliar to them.[12]

11. But see p. 266.
12. As will be shown in the analysis to follow in the following Chapters, however, the U.S. branch banks abroad have normally concentrated to a large extent in operations that are more "American" than "indigenous" and have dealt with large corporate customers that are either U.S.-controlled or are willing to transact business with U.S. branch banks along lines similar to those followed by U.S. corporations or their foreign subsidiaries.

10

Also, except for a short-lived trial in the interwar years, only a very few U.S. commercial banks set up overseas establishments. There has been no tradition among U.S.-trained bankers of residing and operating overseas.

Third, indigenous and other foreign banking establishments in the host countries may or may not have banking offices in the United States; but all the U.S. branch banks operating in the host countries have one thing in common, viz., a full-fledged banking facility (here, the head office bank) in a major U.S. financial center. To the extent that multinational banking requires a permanent banking establishment in the world's principal cities—and increasingly it does, as will be seen in the analysis—the U.S. commercial banks have an unquestionable advantage over many of their foreign counterparts.

Fourth, a concomitant advantage emerged in the latter part of the postwar period under study as Euro-currency operations became increasingly important to multinational banking. This lay in the fact that the primary currency in those operations—the Euro-dollar—is closely related to the national currency of the U.S. branch banks.

Fifth, from the point of view of the analyst, choosing commercial banks chartered in the United States has several practical advantages. Generally speaking, the major U.S. commercial banks are willing—and sometimes eager—to make their operations known to the public at large or to interested observers. This is not to imply that officers of these banks are keen on discussing confidential relationships or on providing information that management considers private. It is a fact, however, that these individuals are not reluctant to discuss, often with surprising frankness, the essential nature of their banks' operations, their successes and failures, their future plans, and how these are to be implemented.

Another advantage to the researcher has lain in the fact that information from private non-bank sources and from official channels can be used to cross-check that supplied by U.S. banks, and sometimes to elucidate material otherwise obscure or unobtainable. In this respect the reports filed with governmental agencies like the Board of Governors of the Federal Reserve System, and the U.S. Treasury Department's Office of the Comptroller of the Currency have proved to be of invaluable aid. In the same vein, information gleaned from the U.S. banks' annual reports to shareholders and proxy statements, as well as from the reports and statements issued by many of their U.S. corporate clients, have been of great help.

It would have been impossible to find another national group of commercial banks where information from differing sources thus lent itself to corroboration. Inevitably this has led to interpolative or extrapolative reasoning in the development of parts of the hypothesis; but as stated in the Preface, only information accessible to the public has been used to substantiate the thesis, although admittedly the interrelationship of some of this information has been made clearer by taking into account material from sources less readily available.[13]

4. Why U.S. Commercial Banks' Foreign Branch Operations?

Branch banks have been selected over other types of foreign banking facilities because juridically speaking they constitute maximum penetration into the host country banking sector. At the very least, multinational banking would require the establishment of a branch bank, since we have partially defined this as "*operating a bank* in ... many different countries and national systems", not as operating banks abroad. That is, the bank itself must be at least partially abroad. As will be shown in Chapter Two, *stricto sensu* only the branch bank fulfills this requirement.

An additional incentive has lain in the major U.S. commercial banks' practice of establishing branches rather than subsidiaries in the host countries, contrary to the practice of large U.S. corporations generally. We shall examine the reasons for this practice of the banks and test their validity insofar as they relate to multinational banking.

B. *Host Countries: France, Great Britain, and Switzerland*

Having attempted to explain why the branch bank operations of the major U.S. commercial banks have been selected, we must also show why France, Great Britain, and Switzerland have been selected as the host countries. There are several reasons behind this choice.

First, all three are industrialized countries with long established, highly developed banking systems. Thus, it is less likely that the presence of branch banks from another industrialized country will jar the local banking scene than in the case of economically less developed host countries.[14] Banking phenomena are relatively less influenced by non-banking factors and can be scrutinized in a more stable surrounding environment.

---

13. The choice of U.S. commercial banks for the present study has had an additional practical advantage in that the author previously spent several years as practicing attorney in the United States, where he dealt with some of the legal problems encountered by commercial banks there, including those of banks chartered abroad.

14. See p. 111, note 83.

To be sure, non-banking factors are not absent from the analysis, as will be seen in the Chapters to follow, where certain economic, political, social, and psychological factors are taken into account. It has been possible, though, by choosing industrialized host countries, to observe where these latter factors are genuinely related to the development of multinational banking.

Second, these three countries differ in many respects from one another as far as the host environment is concerned. For example, the banking sectors range from a highly structuralized system in France, where the government controls directly (and indeed, owns) the major deposit banks, to the British and Swiss systems, which are both much farther removed from the public sector of the economy. Also, the style of official regulation differs in each country; and in all three it is unlike that in the United States.

Too, the banking industry has a different marginal importance in each of the host countries. In all three it is a service industry to the extent that it provides services which are utilized by other industries. In Switzerland, however, banking is far more important locally as an industry in its own right than in either France or Great Britain. Moreover, during the latter years of the postwar period under study the British banking industry was more industrious and inventive than British industry in general appeared to be. Accordingly, if all three host countries have highly developed banking systems, each is quite unlike the others in important respects.

Third, these three countries have been chosen because all have banking systems unlike that in the home country of the branch banks whose operations are under study. The similarities between the U.S. banking system and that of the Federal Republic of Germany, for example, are not shared with the British, French, or Swiss systems. Of course many structural aspects are similar, such as the existence of the central bank as the (actual or theoretical) lender of last resort. One need only trace the path from the commercial bank to the ultimate lender, however, to be made strikingly aware of the significant differences in the systems. Or indeed, one can try to explain one of the host country banking systems to persons familiar with the U.S. system—or vice versa—to see how importantly they differ.

Fourth, these host countries have been selected because some indigenous commercial banks from all three (unlike the Federal Republic of Germany, for instance) have well-fixed banking facilities in the United States. This has meant that an element of reciprocity can be tested in different situations, with regard to a static right of establishment and, more importantly, with regard to a dynamic interchange of information and techniques.

C. *Legal Aspects*

Multinational banking has developed in an environment where the legal "density", so to speak, is relatively low. In an absolute sense, in all four (home and host) countries the banking laws and regulations are less numerous than those covering certain other areas, for example, taxation, social security, or immigration. It is also true in a relative sense, for even in France, where there are more banking laws than there are in Great Britain, the banking sector has fewer laws and regulations than many other French sectors. This relative paucity of laws facilitates the observation, identification, measurement, and interpretation of the effect of a new law or the modification of one already existing.

No attempt has been made to cover all the legal phases of a branch bank's operations abroad. Many of the important legal problems encountered by a U.S. branch bank, both in terms of day-to-day operations as well as with regard to long range planning, arise from regulations concerned with fiscal matters, unfair competition, restrictive business practices, and social welfare in the home and host countries alike. We have concentrated on three legal areas: banking, exchange control, and credit control. The other areas mentioned above are dealt with only when and to the extent that they are germane to the thesis.

This has allowed an analysis of phenomena peculiar to the operations of the U.S. branch banks abroad as such. Bankers, lawyers, corporate treasurers, and students of the field will recognize that much of their experience and daily work lies outside the scope of this study. It is within the ambits of the study, however, that the dynamic legal aspects of multinational banking are found; and this is why we have focused our attention on this area.

D. *Postwar Period*

The period from the cessation of hostilities at the end of World War II has been chosen because this was when the most interesting evolution was taking place in multinational banking. The interwar period offers little guidance to the events that were to occur during the postwar years in the host countries and elsewhere outside the United States, although they are of historical interest.[15]

Of course, for analytical purposes a terminal date must be set to permit the development and testing of the hypothesis. Through 1967 the evolution in the home country legal structure was in one direction, while it

15. See Clyde William Phelps, *The Foreign Expansion of American Banks— American Branch Banking Abroad*, New York, The Ronald Press Co., 1927.

varied in the host countries for reasons that will be shown. Then, on January 1, 1968 a fundamental change occurred when the United States began to apply mandatory capital movements controls. Accordingly, the developments through the end of 1967 have been used as the core of the analysis because they can be examined with the perspective made possible by the passage of intervening time.

Subsequent developments are introduced and dealt with as appropriate, and as will be demonstrated, they bear out the thesis set forth at the end of this Chapter. As a result, the present study carries well into the early 1970's but is based upon analytical elements that have been selected and evaluated in a tested medium.

III. U.S. BRANCH BANKS ESTABLISHED IN THE HOST COUNTRIES

Several of the major U.S. commercial banks had already established branch banks in London and Paris prior to World War II,[16] and either had been able to keep them open during the War, albeit under German surveillance in Paris, or reopened them as soon as possible after the cessation of hostilities in mid-1945.

In London these included the branches of the Bank of America, N.T. & S.A.,[17] Bankers Trust Co.,[18] the Central Hanover Bank and Trust Co.,[19] the Chase National Bank of the City of New York,[20] the Guaranty Trust Co. of New York,[21] and the National City Bank of New York.[22]

In Paris the Guaranty Trust Co.[23] had a branch. Other banks had offices that were not branches at the time but which eventually became

16. See Phelps, *supra.*
17. London branch established in 1932.
18. London branch established in 1922.
19. London branch established in 1925. The Central Hanover Bank and Trust Co. changed its name to the Hanover Bank in 1951, and then merged with the Manufacturers Trust Co. in 1961 to become the Manufacturers Hanover Trust Co.
20. London branch established in 1887. The Chase National Bank of the City of New York merged with the Bank of the Manhattan Co. in 1955 to become the Chase Manhattan Bank, a New York State chartered bank. In 1965 it adopted a federal charter instead, to become the Chase Manhattan Bank, N.A. (for "national association").
21. London branch established in 1897. The Guaranty Trust Co. merged with J. P. Morgan and Co. in 1959 to become Morgan Guaranty Trust Co.
22. London branch established in 1902 as a branch of the Equitable Trust Co. When the latter bank was acquired in 1937 by the Manufacturers Trust Co. (see note 19 *supra*) its London branch was taken over by the National City Bank of the City of New York, which merged with the First National Bank of the City of New York in 1955 to become the First National City Bank of the City of New York. In 1962 this bank shortened its name to become the First National City Bank.
23. Paris branch established in 1917.

15

branches of the head office banks in the United States. These were the Chase Bank,[24] the National City Bank of the City of New York (France), S.A.,[25] and Morgan et Cie, Inc.[26]

For the purposes of the present study we have called "first wave" branch banks those which were in operation during the period 1945-1958 (Chapter Three).

From 1959 until mid-1963, the U.S. branch banks' first Euro-dollar operating phase (Chapter Four), a "second wave" appeared in London. In 1960 the Chemical Bank New York Trust Co.[27] established a branch, followed in 1962 by the Continental Illinois National Bank and Trust Co. of Chicago.

From mid-1963 through the end of 1967, the U.S. branch banks' second Euro-dollar operating phase (Chapter Five), the tempo increased as a "third wave" moved into London. In 1964 the First National Bank of Boston and the Marine-Midland Grace Trust Co. both established branches, followed in 1965 by the Irving Trust Co. and The First National Bank of Chicago. In 1967 The Bank of New York[28] and the Mellon National Bank and Trust Co. began branch operations there.

In this same period the First National City Bank opened its first Swiss branch in Geneva in the latter half of 1963, and what we have termed a "second generation" branch in Zurich in 1967. Also in 1967 the

24. Paris branch established in 1930 as successor to the Equitable Trust Co. office, which dated from 1910.

25. This was a subsidiary chartered under French law. It later became a branch of National City Bank (International Banking Corporation), an agreement corporation (see p. 40, note 56), and then a branch of the head office bank in New York City.

26. Originally established in 1867 as Drexel Harjes et Cie, a French partnership. Morgan et Cie, Inc. was an agreement corporation organized under the law of New York State in 1941. After the 1959 merger between J. P. Morgan and Co. and the Guaranty Trust Co. (see p. 15, note 21) the resulting bank had a branch in Paris, but retained Morgan et Cie as an inactive entity. In the early 1960's Morgan et Cie, S.A. was the investment banking subsidiary of the parent New York institution, controlled through Morgan Guaranty International Finance Corporation, an Edge Act subsidiary (see p. 40, note 56) which held 70% of Morgan et Cie, S.A. voting stock. Morgan-Grenfell & Co., Ltd in London and Mees & Hope in the Netherlands each owned 15% of the voting stock. In December 1966 Morgan Stanley & Co. and Morgan et Cie, S.A. formed Morgan et Cie International, S.A., holding two-thirds and one-third of the voting stock respectively in the new institution. See p. 261, note 230. In 1971 Morgan and Cie International, Ltd. was set up in London.

27. This bank (which had resulted from the 1954 merger between the Chemical Bank and Trust Co. and the Corn Exchange Bank and Trust Co. to form the Chemical Corn Exchange Bank) was merged with the New York Trust Co. in 1959 and later shortened its name to the Chemical Bank.

28. In the same year The Bank of New York merged with the Empire Trust Co. The latter had established a London branch in 1913, which was closed prior to World War II.

Bank of America, N.T. & S.A. opened two second generation branches, one in Birmingham and the other in Marseilles.

In addition to establishing the branch banks noted above, many of the major U.S. commercial banks opened a second branch in London's West End during the period under study. These are sometimes referred to as sub-branches because for operational purposes they are linked with the head office banks in the United States via the main branch in the "City of London", i.e., the financial district. The second generation branches located in other cities are more independent. This is especially so in the case of Switzerland, where the existence of several main financial centers has made the U.S. branch banks' roles in different cities complementary in many respects.

By the end of 1967 the situation was as follows:[29]

Bank	France	Great Britain	Switzerland
Bank of America, N.T. & S.A. (San Francisco)	Paris Marseilles	London* Birmingham	
(The) Bank of New York		London	
Bankers Trust Co. (New York City)		London*	
(The) Chase Manhattan Bank, N.A. (New York City)	Paris	London*	
Chemical Bank (New York City)		London*	
Continental Illinois National Bank and Trust Co. of Chicago		London*	
(The) First National Bank of Boston		London*	
(The) First National Bank of Chicago		London	
First National City Bank (New York City)	Paris	London*	Geneva Zurich
Irving Trust Co. (New York City)		London	
Manufacturers Hanover Trust Co. (New York City)		London*	
Marine Midland Bank		London	
Mellon National Bank and Trust Co. (Pittsburgh)		London	
Morgan Guaranty Trust Co. of New York	Paris	London*	

*Also West End branch in London

---

29. After 1968 some of these banks established additional branches in the three host countries. Bank of America opened one in Zurich as well as second generation French and British branches in Lyons and Manchester respectively. Bankers Trust Co., and Continental Illinois National Bank and Trust Co. of Chicago, and Marine Midland Bank opened branches in Paris. First National City Bank established a suburban branch in Paris and a second generation French branch in Nice, plus additional second wave Swiss branches in Lugano and Lausanne. Chemical Bank

17

IV. INITIAL STATEMENT OF THE THESIS

Many of the postwar U.S. branch banks in France, Great Britain, and Switzerland have engaged in multinational banking. For certain reasons the major U.S. commercial banks have chosen to use branches rather than other types of foreign units. It is our contention that these operations have been possible because of the existence of certain types of laws and practices and the absence of others. Multinational banking has evolved within and alongside a legal framework that has itself evolved, partially causing and partially resulting from the operations which it entails. Some of the U.S. branch banks have different roles than others; and, taken collectively, their role has undergone modifications. There has been a transfer of technology in both directions, i.e., to and from the home and host country banking sectors. Finally, the development of multinational banking marks a new chapter in international finance in that it is the response of certain institutions—here some of the major U.S. commercial banks—to a particular combination of stimuli to which neither they nor their host country counterparts have previously been exposed.

---

and Morgan Guaranty Trust Co. of New York established branches in Zurich, The Chase Manhattan Bank, N.A. opened a second generation French branch in Lyons, and the First National Bank of Chicago opened branches in Paris and Geneva. While these branches were being added, other major U.S. commercial banks were setting up their first London branches. For the situation as it stood as of June 30, 1971, see Appendix.

18

Chapter Two

"LEGAL STATUS OF THE POSTWAR U.S. BRANCH BANKS"

I. TYPES OF FOREIGN BANKING ESTABLISHMENTS AND RELATIONSHIPS

There are different techniques by which a U.S. commercial bank can extend the scope of its operations directly or indirectly abroad. The various methods offer differing advantages or disadvantages from one foreign host country to another, depending upon local laws and practices in those countries as well as upon the overall policy of a particular U.S. bank with regard to its operations in this field. The choice of methods range from locating a representative office in a foreign country up through establishing a full-fledged branch bank, the degree of the U.S. bank's presence increasing from minimal presence in the case of the representative office to total presence in that of the branch bank. Intermediate degrees consist of acquiring a non-controlling interest in an affiliated bank in a foreign country, conducting a joint banking venture there with indigenous or other foreign interests, and establishing a banking subsidiary.

On the very lowest end of the scale—preceding even the minimal presence attached to the representative office—can be added the maintenance of a correspondent relationship with a foreign bank. In a sense, this constitutes absence from that country, and an election on the part of a U.S. bank not to engage in banking operations there. Historically, however, correspondent relationships have been important since they frequently lead to stronger ties or greater degrees of presence in foreign countries. Moreover, correspondent relationships still have a role to play even when a U.S. bank is present in a foreign country.

The range of possibilities is, then, as follows:
(1) maintaining a correspondent banking relationship,
(2) locating a representative office,
(3) acquiring a non-controlling equity interest in an affiliated bank,
(4) conducting a joint banking venture,
(5) establishing a banking subsidiary, and
(6) establishing a branch bank.

The last of these, the branch bank, is the type of establishment whose operations in France, Great Britain, and Switzerland form the core of the analysis in Chapters Three through Five. Before undertaking the task of delving into those operations, however, it is important that the branch bank be situated with regard to the other alternatives. Accordingly, in the sections to follow a brief description is given of these techniques, noting the most important distinguishing characteristics of each, both legal and operational. Where appropriate, some of the advantages and disadvantages of the various methods are compared.

The order of presentation, with an increasing degree of penetration into the host country banking community, is not to suggest that a U.S. bank would necessarily go from one step to the next in arriving at the establishment of a branch bank. In some cases there has been such a progression in a general sense, particularly when the location of a representative office was a preliminary step to the ultimate establishment of a branch bank. This has not always been the case, however. It is noteworthy, too, that some of the U.S. banks have used several methods simultaneously, for example carrying on operations via a branch bank or representative office while having an interest in an affiliated bank or using local correspondent banks in the same host country.

Since the order chosen follows an increasing degree of presence in the legal sense, it might lead to the erroneous assumption that a one-man representative office, for example, will always penetrate far less deeply into the local banking scene than a larger establishment with greater facilities and more numerous personnel. Examination has revealed that while this is certainly true in some instances, it is quite untrue in others.

Or again, the order chosen might seem to imply that a U.S. bank with its own name prominently displayed on the exterior of a large office building and in the local financial press will carry more weight in the host country's financial community than one which has, for example, only a minority equity interest in a local bank. In fact, local banking practices and customs in the host countries can render illusory the apparent importance of the more prominently displayed institution. The legal aspects of the U.S. bank's presence and the operational aspects of its penetration locally must be differentiated.

A. *Correspondent Banking Relationship*

When a U.S. commercial bank has only occasional transactions with banks, firms, or individuals in a foreign country, it normally chooses to call upon an indigenous bank in that country to act as its agent for the purpose of the particular transactions involved. The local foreign bank in such cases is referred to as the "correspondent bank" or "banking correspondent"; and as the term would suggest, the link between the two

20

banks is maintained primarily through telegraphic or postal correspondence. Most of the major U.S. commercial banks have one or more correspondent banks in each of the principal foreign cities of the world, and frequently in cities of lesser importance, depending upon the extent to which customers call upon these U.S. banks to act on their behalf in those cities.

Typical correspondent services are the acceptance of drafts, honoring letters of credit issued by the U.S. bank, and furnishing credit information. Ordinarily a service charge is deducted from the U.S. bank's funds on deposit with the foreign correspondent bank. Often the U.S. bank will in turn act as correspondent for the foreign bank, performing similar duties in the United States.

Although some correspondent banking relationships have long histories, dating from transactions arising in the Nineteenth Century, neither the U.S. bank nor the foreign correspondent bank normally has any of its personnel located on a quasi-permanent basis in the other country. Contact, if any, between individuals in the two banks is usually limited to occasional visits by senior members of the two banks' management.[1]

The importance of the correspondent type of relationship is not to be underestimated. There are activities, however, in which the U.S. bank cannot engage effectively without having someone physically present in the foreign country on a recurrent or permanent basis. For example, it cannot hope to take full advantage of first-hand information or to make direct contact with potential customers, borrowers and depositors alike, without involving itself in the daily activities of the foreign country and particularly in its financial community. In essence, it cannot expand its services—and outlook—sufficiently to satisfy the growing demands of its American and other corporate customers, who are themselves becoming increasingly active in a particular foreign country, by continuing to rely upon the services of a local correspondent bank.

As some of the major U.S. commercial banks have turned to or have augmented other arrangements to increase their capacity to engage in banking operations overseas, the transactions which they conduct via a correspondent have become relatively less important. Nevertheless, with the location of a representative office, correspondent banking relationships with local institutions usually remain intact. Moreover, it is not unusual for a major U.S. commercial bank with a branch bank or other establishment in a foreign host country to utilize the correspondent ser-

1. Some banks make an effort to maintain such personal contact by having their senior personnel make calls, often more social than professional, on their foreign counterparts. There can be little doubt that such contact proved helpful when some of the major U.S. banks decided to go beyond the correspondent relationship in their operations in Western Europe.

vices of an indigenous or other local banking institution for certain transactions as the need arises.[2]

B. *Representative Office*

As the term implies, a representative office is essentially one in which the U.S. commercial bank installs one or more individuals to represent the bank in the foreign host country and sometimes in nearby countries as well. In addition to handling the affairs of local and other clients of the U.S. bank, the representative office seeks new business for the latter and channels information to and from the country or area for which it is responsible.[3] The U.S. bank neither requests nor needs permission from the U.S. federal banking authorities to locate a representative office abroad.[4]

The representative himself is often but not invariably an American citizen, sometimes being a native of the country in which the office is located. He generally has one or more assistants and an office staffed by clerical personnel, located in quarters which often have little resemblance to those of a commercial bank in the United States or, for that matter, to those of a commercial bank in the host country. There are no tellers' windows or facilities for handling even the smallest cash transactions.[5] On the one hand, the U.S. bank makes no effort to underplay the existence of the representative office. On the other, it makes every effort to avoid carrying on any type of activity that might be considered banking business.[6]

Such an office in Western Europe offers certain advantages to the U.S. bank:

(1) As no banking business is transacted by the representative office,

2. See for example William Boyd, Jr., "The Development of United States Banking Services to Meet Customers' Needs Abroad", *in* National Foreign Trade Council, Inc., *Proceedings of the Fifty-Sixth National Foreign Trade Convention* [in New York City, November 1969], New York, National Foreign Trade Council, Inc., 1970, p. 54.

3. Some of the major inland U.S. banks maintain representative offices in New York City.

4. As a matter of courtesy, the attorneys of at least one U.S. bank have telephoned the office of the Comptroller of the Currency in Washington whenever a representative office was being located abroad.

5. For example, tourists or other individuals with travelers cheques, even those issued by the U.S. bank represented by the office, are sent to local institutions to cash these instruments.

6. The representative has no formal authority under U.S. law to bind the bank to any contractual obligation. Indeed, if it arises that documents need to be signed or transferred or payments made, the representative sometimes leaves the host country temporarily so that nothing of this nature transpires within its boundaries.

its existence usually does not damage friendly correspondent relationships that the U.S. bank has built up in the past with local indigenous banks. In fact, the representative is in a position to put U.S. corporate clients in touch with local banks who can furnish banking services in the host country.[7] Also, the ties with local correspondents are often strengthened by the existence of a more direct link for communicating with the U.S. head office bank.

(2) Under host country law the representative office is not considered to be an establishment,[8] and the head office bank itself is not "present" for purposes of being sued or taxed in the host country on its global earnings. This is true even though the name of the U.S. bank appears on the office door, in the local telephone and business directories, and unofficially on the lists of foreign banks having offices in the host country. The bank can thus be present without being "present".

(3) The representative office can gather and forward to the head office bank in the United States information of use to the U.S. bank itself or needed by a U.S. corporate client.[9] In return it can provide American data and information to individuals and companies in the host country. A correspondent bank can perform these functions to a certain extent; but the representative office is generally in a better position to interpret quickly and accurately the needs and demands for information, from both sides of the Atlantic, because of greater familiarity with operating conditions in both places.

(4) It can channel customers to the head office bank or to a branch

---

7. The representative office can also put U.S. clients in touch with local firms which may be interested in marketing or servicing a product in the host country. In the latter part of the specific period under study, corporate acquisition and merger partners were sometimes introduced through the representative office of a U.S. bank, which has later handled the financial arrangements at one or more of its foreign branch banks or other units abroad.

8. For example, representative offices in France and Switzerland are not required to be inscribed in the *registre de commerce* of the localities where they are situated. Note, however, that representative offices of foreign banks in Switzerland are specifically made subject to Swiss law and are assimilated for many purposes to branch banks or banking subsidiaries. See (Swiss) Federal Banking Law of November 8, 1934, *Recueil officiel des lois et ordonnances de la Confédération suisse* [hereinafter cited as *Recueil officiel suisse*] 1935, pp. 121-41, art. 2 (1) and Federal Banking Commission, Ordinance of February 15, 1936, *Recueil officiel suisse* 1936, pp. 102-105, art. 4 (2), this ordinance having been replaced by Federal Banking Commission, Ordinance of January 18, 1968, *Id.* 1968, vol. 1, pp. 362-66, arts. 1 and 6. The 1971 amendment to the (1934) Federal Banking Law kept the relevant provision in article 2 of the amended Law.

9. This is usually limited to studies too small to be requested from one of the consulting firms operating in the field. Information forwarded by a representative office is frequently used to determine whether a more comprehensive study is warranted.

bank in a third country. When necessary, someone from the representative office can leave the host country to meet with the U.S. bank's correspondents or customers in third countries where the bank has no representative offices or banking establishments.

(5) If and when the head office bank decides that a branch bank or other type of arrangement is needed in the host country, there is already someone present to supervise and arrange the process.

The ultimate establishment of a branch bank does not ipso facto terminate the need for a representative office. Upon the establishment of a branch, some of the U.S. banks have retained a representative with an office in the same or an adjoining building, whose function is to act as liaison with correspondent banks in the host country and in nearby countries where the bank has neither a branch nor representative office. Such a representative office can also act in coordinating the bank's relations with correspondent banks in outlying provincial cities in the host country, thus taking charge of a task that otherwise would fall to the branch bank staff.

Nor does the presence of a representative office necessarily mean that a branch will automatically follow in due course. Some U.S. banks have opened representative offices in the host countries that have been followed by branch banks,[10] while others have preferred for various reasons to keep the representative offices rather than to establish branch banks.[11]

The representative office is not without certain disadvantages. For example:

(1) Since it cannot conduct a banking business in the host country there arise occasions where the U.S. bank operates at a handicap with respect to local banks, both indigenous and foreign (including other U.S.) banks. The need to rely on local institutions means that transactions are sometimes unwieldy. Moreover, the representative is supposed to refer many decisions to the head office bank, which also delays matters. The inability to transact a banking business has the further serious disadvantage that the representative office cannot take or place Euro-dollar deposits.

(2) The goodwill of local banking institutions is sometimes strained, even by the presence of a representative office, if it is thought to be the precursor of a branch bank that will ultimately be established in its place.

10. For example, Bank of America, N.T. & S.A. in Zurich, Bankers Trust Co. in Paris, The First National Bank of Chicago and Crocker-Citizens National Bank in London.

11. For example, The First National Bank of Boston in Paris. Continental Illinois National Bank and Trust Co. of Chicago shifted its Zurich representative office to Geneva and some time later (in 1971) established a banking subsidiary in the former city.

(3) The representative office is usually a rather small operation in terms of personnel and facilities. Accordingly there are physical limitations to the demands which can be placed upon the time and energy of its staff. This means, for example, that research provided by a representative office often lacks the breadth and depth that a larger establishment could furnish.

(4) Non-banking activities in some instances threaten to occupy more of the representative office's facilities than can be justified. Particularly this is the case when extensive courtesies are provided to customers, especially those from the United States who are temporarily in the host country on business or otherwise. Some banks' representative offices shun offering non-banking services; others consider these as among the public relations functions of a representative office.

Some of the major U.S. commercial banks find that the disadvantages of a representative office are clearly outweighed by the advantages. For them, the representative office has been an advanced outpost of great importance, ideally suited to their style of multinational banking.

C. *Affiliated Bank*

Some U.S. commercial banks have found it desirable in certain circumstances to hold an equity interest in a Western European bank. When this interest is not large enough to permit the U.S. bank to control the activities of the European bank, the latter is variously referred to as an "affiliated bank", a "banking affiliate", or occasionally an "associated bank".[12]

The equity interest can be acquired either by purchasing voting shares of a bank already in existence or by setting up, alone or in conjunction with others, a new bank and then retaining a minority voting stock interest. If the U.S. bank uses the first method, the controlling interest usually remains with the person, corporation, or group that has held control prior to the U.S. bank's purchase. Normally this party or group is indigenous to the host country. If the U.S. bank acquires its minority interest by the second method, i.e., by setting up a new bank, the controlling in-

---

12. There are variations in the definition and usage of the terms "affiliate" and "affiliated". In one part of the U.S. federal banking law the term "affiliate" includes any "corporation, business trust, association or other similar organization" controlled by a member bank. 12 U.S.C. § 221a (b). An "affiliate" is defined as "a company effectively controlled by another or associated with others under common ownership or control". *Webster's Third New International Dictionary of the English Language Unabridged,* Springfield (Mass.), 1961, p. 10. In practice, the terms "affiliated bank" or "banking affiliate" are usually applied when the U.S. bank does not have a controlling interest, the term "subsidiary" being used when it does.

terest may or may not be in local hands. For example, it can rest with another U.S. bank or with interests from a third country.

An affiliated bank is, then, a local bank, usually with a local name, which is either a previously existing bank continuing under its former local management or is a newly-formed institution dominated by interests which are probably but not necessarily local. The U.S. bank with a minority voting interest often sends one or several officers from the United States to the foreign bank; and the latter sometimes reciprocates.

Legally the affiliated bank is a local institution existing under host country law and being non-local only in the sense that some of its voting stock is directly or indirectly[13] controlled by a commercial bank in the United States. The activities undertaken by the affiliated bank are those normally permitted to banks in the foreign country. Usually the affiliated bank performs all or the major part of the correspondent services needed there by the U.S. bank. Also, the presence of the U.S.-trained bankers taking an active interest in the functioning of the affiliated bank often encourages the local management to undertake operations in which the American affiliation can be helpful.

An affiliated bank offers certain advantages for a U.S. bank's multinational banking operations. One of these is that the institution is not foreign in the host country, and hence turns a native face toward the local populace. If the affiliation has resulted from the acquisition of shares in an already existing local bank rather than from the creation of a new institution, the affiliated bank can present a familiar face as well. Also of great importance is the fact that a U.S. bank immediately gains easier access to a source of local deposits if the institution has existed prior to the affiliation. Particularly in host currency operations this is a great benefit.

Affiliated banks have their disadvantages, too. Although the general public may not be aware of the U.S. presence in the institution, the local banking community is better informed. Even when a U.S. bank has been careful not to make its weight unduly felt, some local banking interests have frequently resented the intrusion. An even more serious disadvan-

13. Until 1967 U.S. banks could not acquire the stock of foreign banks directly, but were required to utilize an "Edge Act" corporation or "agreement" corporation (see page 40, note 56) whose activities are subject to Regulation K issued by the Board of Governors of the Federal Reserve System. 12 C.F.R. § 211.8. This reflected the aim of keeping banks' domestic and foreign operations separated. In 1966 section 25 of the Federal Reserve Act was amended by the addition of a new paragraph which provides for the direct acquisition of the stock of foreign banks. United States, Pub. Law 89-485, July 1, 1966, § 12 (b), 80 Stat. 241; 12 U.S.C. § 601. This amendment was reflected in the March 15, 1967 amendment of (Federal Reserve) Regulation M, which renumbered the sections and added the provision entitled "Acquisition and Holding of Stock in Foreign Banks". 12 C.F.R. § 213.4. See 12 U.S.C. § 615 (c). See also pp. 224-25.

tage lies in the frustration which the U.S. bank management, and especially the U.S. members on the affiliated bank's board of directors feel whenever their ideas or recommendations are overruled or simply ignored by the local interests represented. In some cases, such frustration can be avoided; but in others it has led to a delicate and awkward state of affairs.

D. *Joint Banking Venture*

The next type of arrangement which warrants mention is the joint banking venture. As usually defined[14] the joint venture connotes an association for a finite time period, sometimes renewable, and implies the application of joint efforts toward a particular task or group of tasks either lying somewhat outside the scope of the participants' principal activities, or a project too large or too risky for any one of them to undertake alone. Typical international joint business ventures are those formed for the construction of highways, bridges, and irrigation dams.[15]

Although the term "joint venture" is frequently encountered in the reports of the Western European operations of some U.S. commercial banks, particularly in press releases, these banks appear to have engaged in few joint ventures, strictly speaking. Often the label "joint venture" is convenient for describing an arrangement whereby banks provide technical or other services for one another, or explore new areas or operations together. Sometimes it is used when, in fact, an affiliated bank is the outcome, albeit one whose non-local characteristics are prominent.

The major U.S. banks have frequently been called upon to participate in foreign lending operations so large that only a group of banks could, or would, provide the necessary credits. The resulting consortia or pools

14. In Anglo-American jurisprudence, the term derives from "joint adventure" which reflects the element of risk that normally has been associated with such arrangements. "Joint adventure" has been defined in courts in the United States as "a commercial or maritime enterprise undertaken by several persons jointly; a limited partnership—not limited in the statutory sense as to the liability of the partners, but as to its scope and duration"; and "an association of two or more persons to carry out a single business enterprise for profit, for which purpose they combine their property, money, effects, skill, and knowledge"; and "a special combination of two or more persons, where, in some specific adventure, a profit is sought jointly, without any actual partnership or corporate designation". Henry Campbell Black, *Black's Law Dictionary,* 4th ed., St. Paul, West Publishing Co., 1951, p. 73, citing cases from New York and Texas tribunals. In amplifying the definition, it is noted in that dictionary that a joint adventure "is ordinarily, but not necessarily, limited to a single transaction". *Ibid.* The same dictionary in defining "joint venture" refers to the definition quoted above with no further notation. *Id.,* p. 973.

15. See generally Wolfgang G. Friedmann and George Kalmanoff (eds.), *Joint International Business Ventures,* New York, Columbia University Press, 1961.

doubtlessly have implied joint endeavour for particular purposes, and for time periods delimited in advance. Rarely, however, has there evolved an arrangement which would justify the appellation "joint venture" as the term is normally used. Notable exceptions are entities set up for the coordination of research and lending or for the handling of medium-term lending via arrangements for sharing *tranches* or slices of private placements and maintaining a secondary market for borrowers' notes.[16]

The major U.S. commercial banks have tended to enter into more permanent arrangements in France, Great Britain, and Switzerland, and generally to engage in activities which, though foreign to their normal domestic operations in the United States, are not far removed from the expertise which they already possess or which they acquire rather rapidly as their operations get underway.

E. *Banking Subsidiary*

The selection of one of the foregoing methods of operating in a foreign country, i.e., locating a representative office, acquiring a non-controlling equity interest in an affiliated local bank, or engaging in a joint banking venture there, produces increasing degrees of presence in that country.

Minimal presence in the case of a representative office, and limited presence in the quality of a stockholder in an affiliated local bank or participant in a joint venture operation, are not, however, tantamount to presence as an established banking concern bearing the name and many of the distinguishing characteristics of the U.S. bank itself. If this greater degree of presence is sought, the U.S. bank has the alternatives of establishing a banking subsidiary or a branch bank in the host country.

The banking subsidiary is similar to the affiliated bank in that both are locally-chartered banking institutions in the host country. Seen locally, however, the foreign (here American) character of the banking subsidiary, normally emphasized by its non-local name, sets it apart from most affiliated banks, whose indigenous nature is at least superficially apparent. Accordingly the banking subsidiary has a different type of attraction for potential depositors and borrowers alike, depending upon who they are and the type of services they seek.

An important legal difference between the banking subsidiary and the affiliated bank is that the U.S. commercial bank directly or indirectly[17]

16. For example, the Société Financière Européenne, established by five major European banks and the Bank of America, N.T. & S.A. in Paris and Luxembourg, and the Compagnie Internationale de Crédit à Moyen Terme, S.A., which was established in 1967 in Lausanne by Bankers Trust Co. along with American Express Co. and thirteen European banks. See pp. 266-67.

17. See p. 26, note 13.

28

has a controlling interest in the banking subsidiary. For the U.S. bank this has the distinct advantage that its wishes will not be ignored by local management, one of the potential difficulties observed in a minority interest in a local affiliated bank.

The U.S. bank's policies and directives are thus directly applicable to the banking subsidiary to the extent compatible with local banking laws and practices. It is not necessary that the subsidiary be wholly-owned. *De facto* control is, of course, possible with 50% of the voting shares plus one additional share, or in certain instances with a smaller holding if the other shares are not bloc voted. 100% ownership has the advantage, however, that there are no dissenting minority shareholders' interests to contend with under the host country corporation laws.[18] Accordingly, the U.S. bank has a strong incentive to obtain control through total equity ownership rather than only a controlling block of shares.[19] Deciding whether to set up a banking subsidiary as a new corporate entity, taking all the issued voting stock, or through the acquisition of all the outstanding shares of an already-existing concern may depend upon whether there is a limited number of banking permits or licenses in the host country.

The choice between establishing a banking subsidiary or a branch bank is sometimes dictated by local host country laws. In some countries foreign branch banks are not permitted by local law.[20] Nonetheless, even in other countries a banking subsidiary may have its advantages, such as benefits accorded to indigenous firms by double taxation or other treaties to which the host country is a party.

Also, it is not necessary that the U.S. commercial bank's subsidiary be a commercial bank or the host country equivalent. Indeed, although some

18. Even a majority U.S. interest does not, however, ensure the compliance of a dissident minority in all cases. See *Fruehauf* v. *Massardy,* Cour d'Appel de Paris, 1965, *Juris classeur périodique* 1965, II, 14274, where minority French directors were able to compel a U.S.-controlled French subsidiary to comply with a contract calling for the delivery of truck-trailers to another French company for eventual shipment to Mainland China. The U.S. parent corporation had been ordered by the U.S. Treasury Department not to allow the French subsidiary to execute the contract on the grounds that it was a violation of the U.S. Transactions Control Regulations, 31 C.F.R. § 505.01 *et seq.* An English language summary of this case is found in American Society of International Law, 5 *International Legal Materials* 476 (1966). See W. L. Craig, "Application of the Trading with the Enemy Act to Foreign Corporations owned by Americans—Reflections on *Fruehauf* v. *Massardy*", 83 *Harvard Law Review* 579-601 (1970).

19. For the degree of control considered necessary in another context, see J.-P. Béguin, *Les entreprises conjointes internationales dans les pays en voie de développement; Le régime des participations,* Geneva, Graduate Institute of International Studies, University of Geneva, Switzerland, 1972.

20. See United States, Congress, Joint Economic Committee, *Foreign Government Restraints on United States Bank Operations Abroad,* Washington, 1967, p. 24.

of the major U.S. commercial banks whose operations are treated herein have had commercial banking subsidiaries in countries other than France, Great Britain and Switzerland, their banking subsidiaries in the three host countries have until recently consisted of the so-called "nominee companies" in London, which hold securities and handle the trust business of the branch banks there, and a single banking subsidiary in Paris which is a *banque d'affaires*.[21]

The U.S. commercial banks have established comparatively few banking subsidiaries. Partly this can be explained by the fact that until (Federal Reserve) Regulation M was modified in 1967,[22] shares in the subsidiary had to be held through the intermediary of an Edge Act or agreement company.[23] More importantly, however, the U.S. commercial banks which sought to establish their presence in a foreign banking community through the operation of a full-fledged bank, certainly in the three host countries, had little reason to refrain from passing to the highest degree of penetration and extending their own presence directly by establishing a branch bank. It is to this last form of establishment that we now turn.

F. *Branch Bank*

In many respects, a foreign branch bank is treated operationally by the head office bank in the United States like any branch unit located in the bank's home city or state. Geographical considerations aside, the branch bank established abroad is an integral part of the U.S. bank itself and constitutes, as the term implies, an extension of that bank rather than a separately constituted, locally-chartered corporation.

Legally this difference is of great significance, for the branch bank does not possess what civil jurists refer to as its own legal or juridical personality. That is, the branch bank is not a legal entity distinct from that of the U.S. bank. No separate shares of stock are issued, nor is a separate board of directors formed. Although the branch bank maintains a separate set of books for internal purposes,[24] it does not have assets and liabilities of its own. The staff of the branch bank has the same internal

21. Morgan et Cie, S.A. and Morgan et Cie International, S.A., French subsidiaries of Morgan Guaranty Trust Co. of New York. For the concept of *banque d'affaires*, see p. 51. It is noteworthy that Chase Manhattan Bank, N.A. (Geneva-1969), Bankers Trust Co. (Zurich-1971), and Continental Illinois National Bank and Trust Co. of Chicago (Zurich-1971) have established banking subsidiaries in Switzerland.

22. See p. 26, note 13.

23. See p. 40, note 56.

24. Additional sets of books are usually kept by the foreign branch bank. For example, French and Swiss laws specifically require that a separate set of books be maintained, covering the U.S. branch bank's operations (see pp. 59 and 84) and the British laws implicitly impose a similar requirement (see p. 69).

status with respect to the U.S. bank as the personnel at a branch bank in the United States or at the head office itself. Any corporate officers at the branch bank are officers of the U.S. bank and not of the branch bank. By establishing a branch bank, the U.S. bank itself is present in the host country.

One disadvantage to this resides in the fact that the U.S. bank can be subject to suit under local law for the debts contracted by the branch as well as for torts or other acts committed by the locally established unit. Even more serious, the bank itself can be sued in the host country by service of process against the branch bank there. Most U.S. commercial and industrial corporations, desirous of establishing abroad, create subsidiaries rather than branches in order to avoid this disadvantage. By setting up a separate corporate entity locally, they seek to isolate, as much as possible, the parent corporation and units located elsewhere from the laws in the host country.

A notable exception has been the practice of the major U.S. commercial banks in establishing foreign branches. The reasons most frequently given for this choice are as follows:

(1) to put the entire asset structure and net worth of the U.S. bank behind deposits as a guarantee,

(2) to attract large corporate borrowers by promoting the idea that greater sums can be made available for advances than if sole reliance were to be placed on local deposits and money market funds,

(3) to maintain the maximum degree of control over the establishment's operations, and

(4) to follow a "traditional" pattern of overseas expansion.

In analysing the operations of the U.S. branch banks we shall have occasion to scrutinize each of these reasons.

Whereas a foreign banking subsidiary can be a merchant bank or other type of banking institution, the branch of a U.S. commercial bank is itself ipso facto a commercial bank or the closest host country equivalent. In France it is classed as a *banque de dépôts,* in Great Britain as a non-clearing commercial bank or joint-stock bank, and in Switzerland simply as a bank, albeit as a branch institution in each instance. The range of activities engaged in by the host country counterpart institutions form the general framework within which the U.S. branch banks operate. In the local laws and regulations applying to this sector of the local banking community are found the points of departure for analysing certain of the legal aspects of the U.S. branch banks' operations in the three host countries.

Before turning to the laws applicable to the establishment of the U.S. branch banks, a note must be added as to terminology. The U.S. branch banks in the three host countries are sometimes variously referred to as "branch offices", "branch banking offices", or simply as "branches".

The difficulty with the term "branches" is that it is equally applicable to branch units of commercial and industrial firms which, though similar in some respects, are unlike those of banking concerns in many others. The term is too broad.

The alternatives of "branch offices" and "branch banking offices" suffer from their connotation of a branch unit offering some banking services but not functioning as fully constituted institutions offering a complete line of banking facilities. In fact, the U.S. branch banks whose operations are treated herein have in each case been full-fledged banks in the host countries, being branches in the corporate rather than the operational sense. For this reason, they are referred to as branch banks in the present study.

Another type of overseas banking unit deserving mention is the "agency". This institution, peculiar to a few jurisdictions, is like a branch bank in many respects except that it cannot take deposits. Foreign banks establishing in New York State, for example, could not maintain branches prior to 1961 but were permitted to establish agencies.[25] The term "agency" should not be confused with the term *"agence"* used in the French-speaking region of Switzerland by the major Swiss banks to designate a secondary banking facility other than a bank's branch or head office in that city.[26] Also, in France an *"agence"* is a local branch of a foreign bank.

II. LAWS APPLICABLE TO THE ESTABLISHMENT AND CONTINUING EXISTENCE OF U.S. BRANCH BANKS ABROAD

The purpose of the present study is to analyse certain legal and financial aspects of the operations of the U.S. branch banks in the host countries, and not their establishment as such. Nonetheless, in order to make such an analysis, it is necessary to examine their legal status as institutions.

In the preceding section of this Chapter we have seen how the foreign branch bank compares generally with other types of overseas banking units or relationships. We now turn to a consideration of certain of the legal aspects of this question. First we shall treat briefly the international law background, which has remained static in terms of our analysis. Then we shall treat at some length the national legal framework in which the U.S. branch banks have been established. This latter element demon-

25. See New York, Banking Law § 200 (5) prior to amendment by L. 1960, chap. 553, § 17, effective January 1, 1961.

26. The West-End sub-branches in London are roughly comparable to these Swiss units. See also United States, Congress, Joint Economic Committee, p. 29, note 20, at pp. 19-20.

strates dynamic tendencies closely correlated to the evolution of the U.S. branch banks' operations.

A. *Treaties*

The right to establish a U.S. branch bank can arise either from customary international law or from comity[27] between the home (United States) and host states or from treaties entered into between them. In the case of France, there is the Convention of Establishment of 1959, which provides as follows:

> Art. V. "1. Nationals and companies of either High Contracting Party shall be accorded national treatment with respect to engaging in all types of commercial, industrial, financial, and other activities for gain within the territories of the other High Contracting Party, whether directly or through the intermediary of an agent or of any other natural or juridical person. Accordingly, such nationals and companies shall be permitted within such territories:
> (a) to establish and to maintain branches, agencies, offices, factories and other establishments appropriate to the conduct of their business;
> (b) . . .
> (c) . . .
> Moreover, the enterprises which they control, whether in the form of an individual proprietorship, of a company or otherwise, shall in all that relates to the conduct of the activities thereof, be accorded treatment no less favorable than that accorded like enterprises controlled by nationals and companies of such other High Contracting Party.
> 2. Each High Contracting Party reserves the right to determine the extent to which aliens may, within its territories, create, control, manage or acquire interests in, enterprises engaged in communications, air or water transport, banking involving, [*sic*] depository or fiduciary functions, exploitation of the soil or other natural resources, and the production of electricity."[28]

As for Great Britain there is the Convention of Commerce and Navigation of 1815, Article I of which provides:

> Art. I. "There shall be between the territories of the United States of America, and all the territories of his Brittanick [*sic*] Majesty in Europe, a reciprocal liberty of commerce. The inhabitants of the two countries, respectively, shall have liberty freely and securely to come with their ships and cargoes to all such places, forts and rivers, in the territories aforesaid, to which other foreign-

---

27. See L. Oppenheim, *International Law,* 8th ed. (H. Lauterpacht, ed.), London, Longmans, 1955, vol. 1, pp. 33-35. See also Ernst Rabel, *The Conflict of Laws,* Ann Arbor, University of Michigan Law School, 1947, vol. 2, p. 173.

28. Convention of Establishment, signed at Paris, November 25, 1959; entered into force December 21, 1960. 11 U.S.T. 2398; T.I.A.S. 4625; 401 U.N.T.S. 75. This is one of the U.S. treaties of "friendship, commerce, and navigation". See generally Milton Katz and Kingman Brewster, *The Law of International Transactions and Relations,* Brooklyn, The Foundation Press, Inc. and London, Stevens, 1960, chapter 3 ("Engaging in Economic Activity within a Foreign Country"), pp. 122-70.

ers are permitted to come, to enter onto the same, and to remain and reside in any parts of the said territories, respectively; also to hire and occupy houses and warehouses for the purpose of their commerce; and, generally, the merchants and traders of each nation respectively shall enjoy the most complete protection and security for their commerce, but subject always to the laws and statutes of the two countries respectively."[29]

The pertinent treaty with Switzerland is the Convention of Friendship, Commerce, and Extradition of 1850, under Article I of which:

> Art. I. "The citizens of the United States of America and the citizens of Switzerland shall be admitted and treated upon a footing of reciprocal equality in the two countries, where such admission and treatment shall not conflict with the constitutional or legal provisions, as well federal as State and cantonal, of the contracting parties. The citizens of the United States and the citizens of Switzerland, as well as the members of their families, subject to the constitutional and legal provisions aforesaid, and yielding obediance to the laws, regulations, and usages of the country wherein they reside, shall be at liberty to come, go, sojourn temporarily, domiciliate or establish themselves permanently, the former in the Cantons of the Swiss Confederation, the Swiss in the States of the American Union, to acquire, possess, and alienate therein property, ... to manage their affairs; to exercise their profession, their industry, and their commerce; to have establishments; ... No pecuniary or other more burdensome condition shall be imposed upon their residence or establishment, or upon the enjoyment of the above-mentioned rights, than shall be imposed upon citizens of the country where they reside, nor any condition whatever to which the latter shall not be subject."[30]

The different treaty law bases on which U.S. commercial banks can establish branches in the three host countries emerge strikingly clear from these quoted passages. In the case of the treaty with France, a U.S. commercial bank (which is a "company" as defined in Article XIV of the Convention of 1959) can establish a branch on the condition that it complies with the special rules and regulations applicable to the banking field.[31] In addition, the application of these rules and regulations is to be

29. Convention of Commerce and Navigation, signed at London July 3, 1815; entered into force July 3, 1815. 8 Stat. 228; T.S. 110; I Malloy 624. This Convention was continued in force for ten years by a subsequent treaty and then extended indefinitely by the Convention signed August 6, 1827; entered into force April 2, 1828. 8 Stat. 361; T.S. 117; I Malloy 645.

30. Convention of Friendship, Commerce, and Extradition, signed at Bern November 25, 1850; entered into force November 8, 1855. 11 Stat. 587; T.S. 353; II Malloy 1763.

31. "Thus, under existing French law, American corporations may establish branches in France (article V, paragraph 1) but only on the condition that such branches are registered with the Commercial Register." Georges R. Delaume, *American-French Private International Law,* 2d ed., New York, Oceana Publications (Columbia University, Parker School of Comparative and Foreign Law), 1961, p. 48, citing *inter alia* French *décrets* of August 9, 1953 and May 20, 1955. See also Serge Dairaines, *Les étrangers et les sociétés étrangères en France; statut juridique, fiscal et social immunités,* Paris, Editions de Villefort, 1957.

"no less favorable" than in the case of French banks; i.e., the U.S. bank is accorded "national treatment" by the Convention.[32]

In the cases of Great Britain and Switzerland, however, the issue is less clear. The British treaty deals with "inhabitants" and with "merchants and traders", giving the equivalent of most-favored-nation treatment although the term is not explicitly used. The Swiss treaty deals with "citizens" and accords national treatment with regard to establishment. Neither of these conventions is addressed to companies or corporations. Moreover, the British treaty makes no mention of "establishment" as such.

The question can be raised, therefore, whether corporations can benefit from these international agreements. In fact, the issue did arise in the 1930's in connection with the Swiss treaty when the U.S. Department of State declared that in its opinion the "use of the word 'citizen' did not contemplate that the term should include corporations".[33] The Swiss government acquiesced to the U.S. government's interpretation in that particular instance;[34] and an authority on the subject considers that where a convention is silent on the point, corporate bodies and business firms should not be assimilated to individuals, following a theory of strict construction of treaties.[35]

In the absence of a clearly defined right of establishment derived from a treaty, customary international law would apply to the issue. Presumably this would be so in the case of the British and Swiss treaties, and was so in the case of France prior to the entry into force of the Conven-

32. This Convention is discussed at some length by Thomas L. Nicholson, "The Significance of Treaties to the Establishment of Companies", in Eric Stein and Thomas L. Nicholson (eds.), *American Enterprise in the Common Market; a Legal Profile*, Ann Arbor, University of Michigan Law School, 1960, vol. 2, pp. 155-64.

33. Note from the Acting U.S. Secretary of State to the Swiss Minister, January 3, 1934, quoted at Green Haywood Hackworth, *Digest of International Law*, Washington, U.S. Government Printing Office, 1942, vol. III, pp. 431-32.

34. In his reply the following year, however, the Swiss Minister stated that it was "clear that the only reason for their omission [from the treaty] must have been the fact that corporations did not yet play an important part in the economic life of the time", *id.*, p. 432, and that "there was certainly no intention of depriving citizens of both parties of their treaty rights in such cases where they do not act personally but through means of a corporation", *id.*, pp. 432-33.

35. Paul Guggenheim, "Traités d'établissement", *Fiches juridiques suisses*, no. 662, Geneva, 1943, p. 4. Professor Guggenheim comments that the Swiss Federal Tribunal in the past would seem to have been in favor of a more liberal interpretation, and cites one case where that court, in *obiter dictum*, noted that in practice the assimilation is made with regard to the treaty in question. See also Arthur Nussbaum, *American-Swiss Private International Law*, 2d ed., New York, Oceana Publications (Columbia University, Parker School of Comparative and Foreign Law), 1958, pp. 32-33. *Cf.* Marjorie M. Whiteman, *Digest of International Law*, Washington, U.S. Government Printing Office, 1967, vol. 8, pp. 353-54.

tion of 1959.[36] In this event the host countries can decide whether or not to allow foreign corporations to establish on their territories and would be justified in setting conditions thereon, since the U.S. banks are clearly intent on "doing business" there.[37] There are two schools of thought on the limits which customary international law places on the host state in the absence of treaty-derived rights. One alternative is that the host state may not treat aliens any less favorably than its own nationals; the other opinion is that there is a minimum international standard to which it must adhere.[38]

In the cases at hand, as will be seen later in this Chapter, the three host countries have treated the U.S. branch banks as favorably as indigenous banks. Accordingly, let us now turn to the national banking sectors and laws of the three host countries and examine the conditions in and under which the U.S. branch banks have been established.

B. *National Laws*

The municipal laws of the U.S. branch banks' home country as well as those of the three host countries bear directly upon their establishment in the latter. We now turn to these laws, considering in turn the banking sector of each country in which the head office banks and the branch banks are situated, then examining the pertinent laws and regulations themselves. In Chapters Three through Five we shall be concerned with the operations of the U.S. branch banks. In the present Chapter we are treating the establishment itself. The distinction between the two concepts, one dynamic and the other static, is important.

1. *U.S. Law*

a. *Establishment of Foreign Branch Banks*

In the United States there are four categories of commercial banks, as follows:

1. *National banks.* These banking corporations are organized under the federal banking statutes and are automatically members of the Federal Reserve System. Their deposits are insured in accordance with the

36. *Cf.* United States, Department of State, *The Department of State Bulletin*, vol. 43, no. 1120, December 12, 1960, p. 902, and *Id.*, vol. 41, no. 1067, December 7, 1959, pp. 828-35, especially p. 829.

37. On "doing business" in this sense, see Rabel, *supra,* at pp. 175-76.

38. Paul Guggenheim, *Traité de droit international public,* Geneva, Librairie de l'Université, Georg et Cie, S.A. 1953, vol. 1, pp. 343-44. (A revised second edition of this work is being published.) See also William W. Bishop, "General Course of Public International Law, 1965", in Academy of International Law (The Hague), 115 *Recueil des cours* 393-95 (1966).

rules of the Federal Deposit Insurance Corporation (F.D.I.C.).[39] As of December 31, 1970 there were 4,621 national banks, comprising 33.8% of the commercial banks in the United States.[40]

2. *State member banks.* These are banking corporations chartered under the banking laws of the various states, which have chosen to become members of the Federal Reserve System. By virtue of such membership these banks' deposits automatically come under the F.D.I.C. rules and protection. There were 1,147 state member banks as of December 31, 1970, representing 8.4% of the total.[41]

3. *State non-member insured banks.* These banking corporations organized under the state banking statutes either have not sought or have not been granted membership in the Federal Reserve System. Nonetheless, they have obtained F.D.I.C. protection for their depositors and are subject to the rules thereof. As of December 31, 1970, there were 7,735 state non-member insured banks, comprising 56.5% of the total.[42]

4. *State non-member non-insured banks.* As the title implies, these state chartered institutions are neither members of the Federal Reserve System nor are their deposits under the F.D.I.C. rules and protection. There were only 185 such banks as of December 31, 1970, representing a mere 1.4% of the total number of commercial banks in the United States.[43]

Of the four types outlined above, by far the most important are the first two. As of June 30, 1970, national banks' total deposits ($254 billion) represented 58.7% of all deposits in commercial banks ($433 billion) and state member banks' total deposits ($92 billion) represented 21.2%; i.e., 79.9% of the total deposits were with banks falling into these two categories.[44]

The fourteen major U.S. commercial banks whose branch bank operations are analysed in this study comprise all those with total deposits of $ 1 billion or more and which maintained one or more branch banks in France, Great Britain, or Switzerland during the period from mid-1945 through 1967. All of these fell into the first two categories. They were:

---

39. United States, Federal Deposit Insurance Corporation Act of September 21, 1950, Pub. Law 81-797, chap. 967, § 2 (3), 64 Stat. 873, 12 U.S.C. § 1813 (m). Originally set at $2,500 per depositor in 1933, the insurance limit has been successively raised to $5,000 in 1934, to $10,000 in 1950, to $15,000 in 1966, and most recently to $20,000 in 1969 by Pub. Law 89-695, title I § 7(a); 83 Stat. 371. See page 121, text cited to note 102.

40. Computed from data contained at 57 *Federal Reserve Bulletin* A 96 (1971).

41. *Ibid.*

42. *Ibid.*

43. *Ibid.*

44. 57 *Id.* A 21-22 (1971).

National banks:
1. Bank of America, N.T. & S.A.[45] (San Francisco)
2. (The) Chase Manhattan Bank, N.A. (New York City)
3. Continental Illinois National Bank and Trust Co. of Chicago
4. (The) First National Bank of Boston
5. (The) First National Bank of Chicago
6. First National City Bank (New York City)
7. Mellon National Bank and Trust Co. (Pittsburgh)

State member banks:
1. (The) Bank of New York
2. Bankers Trust Co. (New York City)
3. Chemical Bank[46] (New York City)
4. Irving Trust Co. (New York City)
5. Manufacturers Hanover Trust Co. (New York City)
6. Marine Midland Bank[47] (New York City)
7. Morgan Guaranty Trust Co. of New York

Also deserving mention is American Express Co., a corporation organized under the laws of New York State, whose wholly-owned subsidiary American Express International Banking Corporation (a Connecticut corporation) conducts certain types of banking operations abroad.[48]

(1) Federal Law

The statutory basis under which national banks have received authority to establish branch banks overseas was enacted in 1913 as Section 25 of the Federal Reserve Act, which provides as follows:

> "Any national banking association possessing a capital and surplus of $1,000,000 or more may file application with the Board of Governors of the

---

45. National banks are required to use the word "national" or the designation "national association" (commonly abbreviated "n.a.") in their names. N.T. & S.A. stands for "national trust and savings association".
46. Called the Chemical Bank New York Trust Co. before the present name was adopted.
47. Called Marine Midland Grace Trust Co. before the present name was adopted.
48. American Express Co. is not a commercial bank in the United States. It nevertheless deserves mention for two reasons: (1) many of its overseas offices, including the principal ones in the three host countries, have banking departments which conduct many of the banking operations transacted by the branch banks of the fourteen major U.S. commercial banks listed above; and (2) the "float" which American Express Co. obtains through the issuance of travelers cheques, combined with its customers' deposits, has totalled over $1 billion since 1965. Some of the banks listed above also issue or have issued travelers cheques in the past.

Federal Reserve System for permission to exercise, upon such conditions and under such regulations as may be prescribed by the said board, ... the following powers:

... To establish branches in foreign countries or dependencies or insular possessions of the United States for the furtherance of the foreign commerce of the United States, and to act if required to do so as fiscal agents of the United States. . ."[49]

With regard to establishing branch banks abroad, state member banks are subject to the same regime as national banks in accordance with Section 9 of the Act, which states:

"That nothing herein contained shall prevent any State member bank from establishing and operating branches in the United States or any dependency or insular possession thereof or in any foreign country, on the same terms and conditions and subject to the same limitations and restrictions as are applicable to the establishment of branches by national banks except that the approval of the Board of Governors of the Federal Reserve System, instead of the Comptroller of the Currency, shall be obtained before any State member bank may hereafter establish any branch ... beyond the limits of the city, town, or village in which the parent bank is situated."[50]

Thus, although national banks are for most purposes under the supervision of the Comptroller of the Currency while state member banks are under that of the Board of Governors of the Federal Reserve System,[51] both classes of banks are assimilated into one category with respect to the establishment of branch banks overseas.

A bank seeking permission to establish a foreign branch is required to file an application with the Board of Governors[52] in accordance with Section 25 of the Federal Reserve Act, which states that:

"Such application shall specify the name and capital of the banking association filing it, the powers applied for, and the place or places where the banking or financial operations proposed are to be carried on. The Board of Governors of the Federal Reserve System shall have power to approve or to reject such application in whole or in part if for any reason the granting of such application is deemed inexpedient, and shall also have power from time to time to in-

---

49. United States, Federal Reserve Act of December 23, 1913, chap. 6, § 25, 38 Stat. 273; 12 U.S.C. § 601.

50. Act, § 9, 38 Stat. 259 as amended June 16, 1933, chap. 89, § 5 (b), 48 Stat. 164 and August 23, 1935, chap. 614, § 338, 49 Stat. 721; 12 U.S.C. § 321. Prior to this modification some states' laws permitted overseas branches for banks chartered under the laws of those states.

51. See Howard H. Hackley, "Our Baffling Banking System", 52 *Virginia Law Review*, 565 and 771 (1966).

52. In practice the application is filed with the Federal Reserve Bank of the District in which the bank is situated.

crease or decrease the number of places where such banking operations may be carried on."[53]

In exercising its "judgement on application by banks ... to establish foreign branches" the Board of Governors has stated that:

"On each such application, the Board, in granting or withholding its permission, takes into consideration, among other things, the conformity of the proposal to the provisions of law and regulation, the condition of the applicant bank or Corporation and the capacity of management, and the general appropriateness of the proposal in the light of the broad public purposes the relevant statutes are intended to serve."[54]

Under the authority of the Federal Reserve Act the Board of Governors issued Regulation M[55] which deals with the foreign branches of national banks (and ipso facto of state member banks) and of Edge Act and "agreement" corporations.[56] Despite the power of the Board to issue

53. Federal Reserve Act, § 25, *supra. Cf.* Board of Governors, Federal Reserve System, Regulation H, 12 C.F.R. Part 208, which deals with membership of state-chartered banks in the Federal Reserve System. Pursuant to that Regulation, "with prior Board approval, a member State bank having capital and surplus of $1,000,000 or more may establish branches in 'foreign countries', as defined in ... [Regulation M] ..." 12 C.F.R. § 208.8 (d). 17 Fed. Reg. 8006, September 4, 1952 as amended at 28 Fed. Reg. 8361, August 15, 1963. Formerly this section was much more detailed. After specifying that the bank "must have a capital and surplus of $1,000,000 or more", 12 C.F.R. § 208.8 (d) (1949 edition), it provided that the bank's request "should be accompanied by advice as to the scope of the functions and the character of the business which are or will be performed by the branch and detailed information regarding the policy followed or proposed to be followed with reference to supervision of the branch by the head office; and the bank may be required to furnish additional information which will be helpful to the Board in determining whether to approve such a request". 12 C.F.R. § 208.8 (e) (1949 edition). Banks applying for permission to establish a foreign branch supply additional information including indications as to the amount of capital to be allocated to the new branch bank, whether quarters are to be rented or purchased, and a statement to the effect that the host country authorities have already authorized or will not oppose the establishment of the branch bank. Since the inauguration of the U.S. Voluntary Foreign Credit Restraint Program (see Chapter 5), banks have also been expected to state that there will be no adverse effect on the U.S. balance of payments as a result of the proposed foreign branch bank's establishment.

54. United States, Board of Governors of the Federal Reserve System, unpublished *Report* entitled "Foreign Operations of U.S. Banks and their Supervision," dated June 30, 1967, forwarded to the Committee on Banking and Currency of the House of Representatives, p. 10. "The Board obtains the views of the Federal Reserve Banks on all such applications." *Id.,* p. 9.

55. Board of Governors of the Federal Reserve System, Regulation M, 12 C.F.R. Part 213, 2 Fed. Reg. 1686, August 17, 1937.

56. In 1916 the Federal Reserve Act was amended to permit any national bank with a capital and surplus of $1 million or more "to invest an amount not exceeding in the aggregate 10 per centum of its paid-in capital stock and surplus in the stock of one or more banks or corporations chartered or incorporated under the

a multitude of provisions in this Regulation, it was not until 1963 that Regulation M dealt with anything other than the procedure to be followed in the event of a "suspension of operations during disturbed conditions".[57] Regulation M was substantially revised and enlarged in 1963, and thereafter has contained a new provision to the effect that if a bank has already established a branch in a foreign country it may, "unless otherwise advised by the Board, establish other branches in that country after thirty days' notice to the Board with respect to each such branch".[58]

It was noted above in connection with the establishment of branch banks overseas that national banks and state member banks are assimilated into one category, both types of bank coming under the authority of the Board of Governors of the Federal Reserve System. In 1964 the Bureau of the Comptroller of the Currency issued an International Operations Regulation specifying that:

---

laws of the United States or of any State thereof, and principally engaged in international or foreign banking, or banking in a dependency or insular possession of the United States either directly or through the agency, ownership or control of local institutions in foreign countries, or in such dependencies or insular possessions." Federal Reserve Act, *supra,* amendment of September 7, 1916, chap. 461, 39 Stat. 755; 12 U.S.C. § 601 as amended. The same law simultaneously added a new paragraph to Section 25 of the Federal Reserve Act, specifying that the corporations mentioned above would be required to "enter into an agreement or undertaking with the Board of Governors of the Federal Reserve System to restrict its operations or conduct its business in such manner or under such limitations and restrictions as the said Board may prescribe. . ." 12 U.S.C. § 603. Such corporations were thenceforth known as "agreement corporations", organized under the laws of the various states. The 1916 amendment did not, however, provide for the federal chartering of corporations to engage in such activities. This was remedied by the 1919 amendment to the Federal Reserve Act sponsored by Senator Walter Edge of New Jersey, which added a new Section 25 (a) to the Act and provided for what came to be known as "Edge corporations" or "Edge Act corporations". *Act,* § 25 (a), as added December 24, 1919, chap. 18, 41 Stat. 378; 12 U.S.C. §§ 611-631. For Edge Act and agreement corporations generally, see Frank M. Tamagna and Parker B. Willis, "United States Banking Organization Abroad", 42 *Federal Reserve Bulletin,* 1284-99 (1956), especially pp. 1287-94 and tables on pp. 1297-99. See also Terrence M. Farley, "The 'Edge Act' and United States International Banking and Finance", New York, Brown Brothers Harriman & Co., 1962 (unpublished thesis, The Stonier Graduate School of Banking); Don L. Woodland, "Foreign Subsidiaries of American Commercial Banks", 10 *University of Houston Business Review* 1-80 (1963); and J. Herbert Furth, "International Relations and the Federal Reserve System", *in* Herbert V. Prochnow (ed.), *The Federal Reserve System,* New York, Harper & Brothers, 1960, pp. 273-94. Some of the major U.S. commercial banks now have Edge Act subsidiaries in cities other than New York City. For instance, Chase Manhattan Bank in Los Angeles, Bank of America in Chicago, and Irving Trust Co. in Miami.

57. (Federal Reserve) Regulation M, 12 C.F.R. § 213.1 (1949 edition).

58. Regulation M, revised, 12 C.F.R. § 213.3, 28 Fed. Reg. 8361, August 15, 1963. Other effects of the 1963 revision of this Regulation are treated at pp. 47-48 and pp. 184-85.

"Prior notification to the Comptroller of the Currency shall be required before a national bank may engage in any of the following international operations:

(1) The establishment of a branch of a national bank in a foreign country, or in a dependency or insular possession of the United States or a foreign country."[59]

The basis for this Regulation was stated as follows:

"National banks which are long-established in the international field have been extending their foreign activities. Some national banks are undertaking, or are planning to undertake, their first international ventures. The expansion of international financial activities enhances their importance to the sound condition of a bank. These are matters which fall within the supervisory responsibilities of the Comptroller of the Currency for national banks."[60]

The Comptroller of the Currency was reported to have proposed earlier the "comprehensive regulation" of the international operations of national banks, which was to include the requirement that they obtain prior permission from the Comptroller before establishing a branch bank overseas.[61] The issuance of the Regulation quoted above was a step away from such "comprehensive regulation" but nevertheless underlines the interest which the Bureau of the Comptroller of the Currency has taken in the subject.[62]

59. United States, Treasury Department, Bureau of the Comptroller of the Currency, International Operations Regulation, 12 C.F.R. § 20.3 (a) (1), 29 Fed. Reg. 11333, August 18, 1964, redesignated 29 Fed. Reg. 13073, September 18, 1964. The other operations covered by this requirement of prior notification are those carried out by means of Edge Act and agreement corporations. The same Regulation also provides that the relocation of an overseas branch bank must be reported to the Comptroller of the Currency within thirty days. 12 C.F.R. § 20.4 (a) (1).

60. 12 C.F.R. § 20.1 (b) (2). Prior notification was deemed necessary because "actions of this nature, which may involve substantial risk, are not easily reversed, and hence, there is a need for advance knowledge by the Comptroller of the Currency". 12 C.F.R. § 20.1 (b) (3).

61. See New York Times, August 3, 1964, p. 31, col. 6 (late city edition).

62. The move by the Bureau of the Comptroller of the Currency towards sharing the supervision of the international activities of national banks was part of a larger dispute between that office and the Board of Governors of the Federal Reserve System with regard to regulation of national and state member banks generally. The disagreement was particularly heated in the area of branch banking and mergers. An indication of the position of the Comptroller of the Currency is seen in that part of the above-cited International Operations Regulation which states that "the prior notification and reporting procedure was chosen as the least burdensome means of supervising these important activities of national banks, considering the licensing authority over foreign branches and Edge Act corporations which rests with the Federal Reserve Board. This aspect of bank regulation would be greatly simplified if the licensing authority were lodged with the supervisory agency, rather than separated as it is at present". 12 C.F.R. § 20.1 (b) (4).

(2) State Law

Like national banks, state member banks seeking to establish a branch bank outside the United States are required to obtain permission from the Board of Governors of the Federal Reserve System. State member banks must also comply with the laws of the states in which they are chartered. Since all the state member banks listed on page 38 have been chartered under the laws of New York State, it is to these laws that we now turn.

The pertinent New York statute is Section 105 (3) of the Banking Law, which originally stated that:

> "Any bank or trust company having a combined capital stock and surplus fund of one million dollars or over, may with the written approval of the superintendent, open and occupy a branch office or branch offices in one or more places located without the state of New York, either in the United States of America or in foreign countries."[63]

In 1966 an additional paragraph was added to this Section providing that:

> "If any bank or trust company has opened and occupied a branch office in a foreign country pursuant to ... [the above-quoted statute] ... it may, unless otherwise advised by the superintendent, open and occupy an additional branch office or branch offices in such country without having to apply for the approval of the superintendent and the banking board, provided that it gives the superintendent notice of at least thirty days (or such shorter period as the superintendent in individual cases may approve) before opening and occupying any such additional branch office."[64]

The banking statutes of most other states in which major U.S. commercial banks are situated contain a variety of provisions with regard to the establishment of an overseas branch bank by a state-chartered institution. Examples are found in the statutes of California,[65] Massachusetts,[66] and

---

63. New York, Banking Law § 105 (3). On February 23, 1960 this statute was amended to require in addition "the approval of the banking board by a three-fifths vote of all its members." New York (183d) Session Laws, 1960, chap. 76, p. 216.

64. New York (189th) Session Laws, 1966, chap. 324, § 11, p. 965 (effective May 10, 1966). The new paragraph was designated § 105 (3) (b) and the statutory text cited in the preceding note, as amended by the 1960 addition, became § 105 (3) (a). It will be noted that this resembled the 1963 change to Federal Reserve Regulation M indicated at p. 41.

65. California Financial Code, chap. 4, art. 2 (Foreign Branches), § 530 states that "a bank having a paid-up capital and surplus of one million dollars ($1,000,000) or more may establish branches in foreign countries or in dependencies or insular possessions of the United States for the furtherance of the foreign commerce of the United States upon obtaining the approval of the superintendent and upon such conditions and other regulations as he may prescribe". (Stats. 1951, chap. 364, p. 845, § 530).

66. Massachusetts General Laws, chap. 172A (Banking Companies) § 12 permits a state-chartered bank to "establish and operate one or more branch offices in the

Pennsylvania.[67] Worthy of particular note is the banking law in Illinois, which forbade the establishment of foreign branch banks altogether during most of the period under study.[68] It seemed unlikely, however, that the Illinois banking authorities would rely on that statute to block the request of a state-chartered bank for permission to establish a branch bank overseas. In the event, the bank would have had the alternative of seeking a federal charter, i.e., becoming a national bank.[69] As such it then would have needed only federal permission to establish a foreign branch bank.[70]

---

city or town in which it is authorized to do business... or in any other city or town within the same county". No mention is made of the establishment of an overseas branch. Massachusetts General Laws, chap. 172 (Trust Companies) § 11 (c), on the other hand, provides that "with the approval of the commisioner and under such conditions and regulations as may be prescribed by him, any such corporation having a total capital stock and surplus account of five million dollars or more may establish and operate one or more branches in foreign countries or dependencies of the United States".

67. In Pennsylvania the Banking Code of 1965, § 907 (Branches outside Pennsylvania) provides, *inter alia,* that "an institution may maintain an office outside the states of the United States with the prior written approval of the department and subject to an agreement satisfactory to the department providing for the times, method, and reimbursement of expenses of examination of such branch". 7 P.S. § 907 (b). Prior to the 1965 amendment of the Code, foreign banking business was permitted "through a subsidiary with the approval of the department". The provision for foreign branch banks was added in 1965.

68. "No bank shall establish or maintain more than one banking house, or receive deposits or pay checks at any other place than such banking house, and no bank shall establish or maintain in this or any other state, *or country* any branch bank, nor shall it establish or maintain in this state any branch office or additional office or agency for the purpose of conducting any of its business". Illinois Revised Statutes, chap. 16$^{1/2}$, § 106 (emphasis added).

69. As provided by 12 U.S.C. § 35 ("Organization of State banks as national banking associations") and 12 C.F.R. § 4.3, ("Conversions of state banks into national banks"), 29 Fed. Reg. 7413, June 9, 1964. Two national banks in Chicago, Illinois are among the banks listed on page 17.

70. The Illinois statute was modified by a general election in 1968 to read "... and no bank shall establish or maintain in this or any other state of the United States any branch bank, nor shall ..." Illinois Revised Statutes, chap. 16$^{1/2}$, § 106 as amended July 30, 1968, Laws 1968, H.B. No. 2825, § 1. Section 3 of the amendment described the need for the change as follows: "The purposes for which ... [the subject portion of the statute] ... was adopted are not served by extending such prohibition to foreign countries and such prohibition was not the intention of the legislature and if it should be so interpreted by the courts there would be an intolerable burden on Illinois state banks by making them non-competitive with national banks and with banks chartered by other States which either expressly permit or do not prohibit branch banks in other countries ... therefore an emergency exists and this amendatory Act shall take effect upon its becoming law". Accordingly in the postwar period under study (and shortly after this change in the Illinois law) two Illinois

b. *Continuing Existence of the Foreign Branch Bank*

(1) Legal Status Generally

From the point of view of U.S. law the overseas branch bank is in some respects treated as an integral part of the U.S. bank itself and in others as a separate entity.[71]

As we have had occasion to state earlier, a branch bank is not a separate corporate entity, unlike the foreign banking subsidiary, which is a separate corporation organized under the laws of the host country.

On the other hand, American banking law and theory treat a branch bank as a separate entity for certain operations. The Uniform Commercial Code, for example, treats a branch bank as a separate bank for many purposes.[72] Moreover, a customer's deposit at a branch bank is considered to be a debt[73] payable at that branch and not at the head office or at another branch[74] unless payment has been wrongfully refused at the branch bank in which the deposit was made.[75]

The branch bank maintains accounts in the head office bank and frequently in other branches of the same bank for clearing purposes, and vice versa. In the case of branch banks overseas, the head office bank's accounts are in the host currency and not in U.S. dollars. Moreover, in the case of certain arm's length transactions between a foreign branch bank and the head office, each is treated as a separate institution.[76]

The separate status of the U.S. branch bank abroad is emphasized by Section 25 of the Federal Reserve Act which states that:

---

state-chartered banks in Chicago established branches in London. These were The Northern Trust Co. and the Harris Trust and Savings Bank, which were followed by the American National Bank and Trust Co. of Chicago in 1970.

71. See Jefferson B. Fordham, "Branch Banks as Separate Entities", 31 *Columbia Law Review* 975-95 (1931).

72. Uniform Commercial Code, § 4-106. For helpful commentary on this provision see Robert Braucher and Arthur E. Sutherland, Jr., *Commercial Transactions,* Brooklyn, Foundation Press, 1958, pp. 369-71.

73. "An ordinary bank deposit constitutes a debt of the bank to the depositor". Arthur Nussbaum, *Money in the Law, National and International,* Brooklyn, Foundation Press, 1950, p. 104. See Generally *Id.*, pp. 103-107.

74. It is helpful to consider that the deposit is "located" at the branch bank. Lalive points out, however, that "even if it is agreed that debts have a locality or a quasi-locality . . . it must be realized that this is merely a convenient way of stating that the debt is connected with a particular country and its legal system". Pierre A. Lalive, *The Transfer of Chattels in the Conflict of Laws,* Oxford, Clarendon Press, 1955, p. 70.

75. *Cf. Sokoloff* v. *National City Bank,* 130 Misc. 66, 224 N.Y. Supp. 102; 223 App. Div. 754, 227 N.Y. Supp. 907; 250 N.Y. 69, 164 N.E. 745 (1928).

76. *Pan American Bank & Trust Co.* v. *National City Bank,* 6 F. 2d 762 (2d Cir. 1925).

"Every national banking association operating foreign branches shall conduct the accounts of each foreign branch independently of the accounts of other foreign branches established by it and of its home office, and shall at the end of each fiscal period transfer to its general ledger the profit or loss accrued at each branch as a separate item".[77]

In Chapter Four we shall have occasion to return to this question as it affects the accessibility of the records of U.S. branch banks overseas,[78] and in Chapters Four and Five as to the payment of funds on deposit in such branch banks.[79]

(2) Inspection and Regulation

(a) Federal Law

With regard to federal control over the U.S. branch bank once it is established abroad, we must take account of two important aspects of its continuing existence, namely the periodic examination of its condition (i.e., of the accounts) and the regulation of certain phases of its operations.

The continuing surveillance of the U.S. federal banking authorities over the foreign branches of U.S. commercial banks arises out of the provisions of Section 25 of the Federal Reserve Act which, in the language of a Federal Court of Appeals deciding a 1959 case, shows "not an intent to insulate the records of foreign branches from official scrutiny but, on the contrary, ummistakeable intent that the branches shall report to the Comptroller of the Currency and shall at all times be subject to examination by the Federal Reserve Board".[80]

Section 25 of the Federal Reserve Act provides that:

"Every national banking association operating foreign branches shall be required to furnish information concerning the condition of such branches to the Comptroller of the Currency upon demand, ... and the Board of Governors of the Federal Reserve System may order special examinations of the said branches ... at such time or times as it may deem best".[81]

By virtue of this statute, the Bureau of the Comptroller of the Currency periodically examines the foreign branches of national banks, usually every three years. These examinations are in addition to the annual reports of condition which national banks file with the Comptroller with

77. United States, Federal Reserve Act of December 23, 1913, p. 39, note 49; 12 U.S.C. § 604.
78. See pp. 169-70.
79. See pp. 170-71 and pp. 202-204.
80. *First National City Bank of New York* v. *Internal Revenue Service,* 271 F.2d 616, 619 (2d Cir. 1959). See p. 169.
81. Federal Reserve Act of December 23, 1913, *supra;* 12 U.S.C. § 602.

respect to their branches overseas. In 1964, when the Bureau of the Comptroller issued the International Operations Regulation referred to on page 42, the following statement was included therein:

"In furtherance of the effort to pursue the overall improvement of supervisory methods and tools, this office has undertaken a stepped-up program of examination and supervision of the international operations of national banks. A special corps of national bank examiners has been assigned to a newly-established Department of International Banking under a Deputy Comptroller of the Currency. These examiners will be based in Washington, and will make periodic on-the-spot examinations in foreign countries of the international operations of national banks. This Office is also expanding its economic research in the international field to lay the groundwork for more intensive supervision in this area".[82]

In describing the international supervision conducted by his Office, the Comptroller has noted that:

"Although basic examining techniques are similar, international examiners must be familiar with many practices not usually encountered in domestic banking—for instance the Euro-dollar market, multi-currency credits, foreign exchange, and acceptance financing. The different banking laws, standards, and central bank policies of the host country must be considered as well as the many non-banking factors, including local and international political and economic conditions."[83]

With regard to the supervisory practice of the Board of Governors of the Federal Reserve System, the foreign branches of state member banks were examined periodically (every 3 to 4 years) until the end of the 1950's, since which their affairs have been "mainly scrutinized on the basis of the records of their head offices and in connection with the examination of the parent bank".[84]

In addition to periodic surveillance of the condition of the U.S. branch banks abroad there is also the aspect of continuing federal regulation of certain phases of their operations. We have had occasion to refer earlier to (Federal Reserve) Regulation M, which is directly applicable. In analysing its thrust one must take into account an important evolution in this regulation. When Regulation M was modified in 1963 two new paragraphs were added, as follows:

82. (Comptroller of the Currency) International Operations Regulation, p. 42; 12 C.F.R. § 20.1 (b)(1).
83. William B. Camp, U.S. Comptroller of the Currency, "Comptroller Emphasizes International Supervision", *The American Banker*, August 1, 1967.
84. Board of Governors of the Federal Reserve System, unpublished *Report*, p. 40, note 54, at p. 10. As in the case of the examinations under the aegis of the Comptroller of the Currency, this is in addition to the annual reports of condition filed with the Board of Governors for each foreign branch.

"§ 213.5

(a) . . .

(b) The continued or prospective exercise of any power under § 213.4 shall be subject to any notice interpreting or applying the terms of this part that a national bank may receive from the Board, and such bank *shall cause its foreign branches to comply* therewith; such branches may, however, unless the Board specifies otherwise, complete transactions undertaken prior to receipt thereof by the national bank.

(c) The Board may from time to time require a national bank to submit information regarding compliance with this part."[85]

These new paragraphs were subsequently revised and renumbered, effective March 15, 1967, to read as follows:

"§ 213.6

(a) The continued or prospective exercise of any power under this part shall be subject to any notice interpreting or applying it that a national bank may receive from the Board, and such bank *shall immediately comply* therewith.

(b) The Board may from time to time require a national bank to make reports at such time and in such form as the Board may prescribe regarding the exercise of any power hereunder and to submit information regarding compliance with this part."[86]

It is noteworthy that since the 1967 revision a U.S. bank has no longer been directed to "cause its foreign branches to comply" with notices which might be issued by the Board, but has been told that the bank itself shall "immediately comply. herewith". This has removed *ab initio* any argument that the head office bank might be powerless to force its branch banks overseas to comply with a notice from the Board. It also indicates clearly that the intended recipient of such notices is an institution chartered under U.S. federal or state law and located within the territorial jurisdiction of the United States.

(b) State Law

It was noted earlier that all the state member banks listed on page 38 have been chartered under the law of New York State. With regard to inspection of the foreign branch banks once established, the New York State Banking Department conducts periodic examinations of the condition of overseas branch banks.[87] During most of the postwar period, ex-

85. (Federal Reserve) Regulation M, revised, p. 41, note 58; 12 C.F.R. § 213.5 (b) and (c) (emphasis added). § 213.4 referred to in paragraph (b) was entitled, "Further Powers of Foreign Branches." See p. 184.

86. (Emphasis added). The 1967 revision caused the paragraphs in question to be redesignated 12 C.F.R. § 213.6 (a) and (b). In August 1967 the Board of Governors made it known by letter that it might in the future "publish the year-end statements of the foreign branches of United States banks on a bank-by-bank and country-by-country basis. . ."

87. The New York Superintendent of Banks is required to examine state chartered banks at least once each calender year. New York, Banking Law § 36 (2).

aminations were conducted jointly with the Federal Reserve Bank of New York when the latter was examining directly the overseas branches of member banks. So-called "desk reviews" were held at irregular intervals by the New York State examiners during interim years, these taking place at the head office banks in New York City. Reports were not consolidated; banks showed a brace of figures showing "due from" and "due to" their branches abroad.[88]

The state's examination has reflected a primary responsibility as the chartering authority. The examination has constituted no burden to the banks, however, since the information required was and still is essentially that made available to the federal examiners.

As for continuing state regulation of the foreign branch banks' operations, the New York State Banking Law sets forth the general powers of banks and trust companies. No specific mention of overseas branches was included in that Law until 1958 when it was amended to include the following provision:

> "§ 96. *General powers.*
> . . .
> 10. To exercise, subject to such regulations as may be issued from time to time by the banking board, through any foreign branch office opened and occupied with the approval of the superintendent and the banking board as provided in section one hundred five of this chapter, such further powers as may be usual in connection with the transaction of the business of banking in the place where such foreign branch office shall transact business, provided that no such foreign branch shall engage in the general business of producing, distributing, buying or selling goods, wares, or merchandise, nor, except with respect to securities issued by any foreign nation or any agency thereof, engage or participate, directly or indirectly, in the business of underwriting, selling or distributing securities."[89]

The regulations issued by the Banking Board are principially aimed at operations inside the state. The only specific reference to overseas branch banks' operations is one exempting branches outside the state from the prohibition against the payment of interest on demand deposits.[90]

As in the case of periodic examination, federal rather than New York State regulation is the important factor in the state chartered banks' foreign branch operations. For this reason we shall concentrate on U.S. federal rather than on state law in the ensuing Chapters of the present study.

---

88. In 1969 the New York State Banking Board Regulations were amended to require call reports (part 23) as well as annual reports (part 24). Banks with foreign branches have thereafter been required to file fully consolidated reports.

89. New York, Banking Law § 96 (10) as added by New York (181st) Session Laws, 1958, chap. 79, § 1, p. 100, (effective February 27, 1958).

90. New York State Banking Board Regulations (part 3, later part 20).

2. Host Country Laws

a. France

(1) Banking Sector

(a) Banks

Legal control of banking activities in France dates from a law or *loi* enacted in 1930 when persons convicted of certain crimes were barred from engaging in banking operations.[91] During the 1930's attempts were made to clarify the legal position of banks and bankers; but it was not until 1941 that banks were defined in the French statutes. A law of June 13, 1941 sets forth that "banks" are firms or establishments whose usual function is to receive from the public, as deposits or otherwise, funds which they use for their own account, either in discounting or in credit transactions, or in financial operations.[92] The 1941 law further provides that all banks will be inscribed on a list,[93] giving rise to the term *"banques inscrites"* or "inscribed banks" in France.

Subsequently, the 1945 law which nationalized the Banque de France[94] and divided all banks into three categories states that any bank seeking inscription on the list of banks must select the category in which it seeks to be placed.[95] The categories are:

a. *banques de dépôts,* or deposit banks, which are essentially takers of short term deposits and correspond in a great many respects[96] to commercial banks in the United States and in Great Britain.

91. France, *Loi* of June 19, 1930; *Journal officiel,* June 20, 1930, p. 6754.

92. France, *Loi* no. 2532 of June 13, 1941, art. 1; *Journal officiel,* July 6, 1941, p. 2830. The French language text of the first paragraph of this article is: "Sont considérées comme banques, les entreprises ou établissements qui font profession habituelle de recevoir du public, sous forme de dépôts ou autrement, des fonds qu'ils emploient pour leur propre compte, en opérations d'escompte, en opérations de crédit ou en opérations financières." This measure of the Vichy regime was later confirmed by the post-war French government. An English language translation of this law as amended through February 1, 1966 is found at International Monetary Fund, *Central Banking Legislation,* Washington, 1967, vol. 2, pp. 211-23.

93. *Loi* no. 2532 of June 13, 1941, art. 9.

94. The Banque de France is frequently referred to in English as the "Bank of France". Many other French institutions, however, do not have names which lend themselves so readily to translation. Accordingly, when reference is made in this study to French institutions their local names, without italics, will be used. Where the names are not English language cognates, an explanatory note will be supplied.

95. France, *Loi* no. 45-015 of December 2, 1945, art. 4: *Journal officiel,* December 3, 1945, p. 8001. An English language translation of this law as amended through February 1, 1966 is found at International Monetary Fund, *Central Banking Legislation, supra,* at pp. 199-209.

96. But not in all. Accordingly, in this study the French *banques de dépôts* will be referred to as such.

b. *banques d'affaires,* whose principal activity consists of acquiring and holding interests in already established or newly created firms, and of providing credit of any duration for public or private enterprises.[97] The *banques d'affaires* more closely resemble U.S. investment banking houses and British merchant banks than any other institution in those countries.[98]

c. *long- and medium-term credit banks,* which are primarily engaged in providing credit for durations of at least two years, and are forbidden to take deposits for shorter periods without authorization.

In addition to the three categories of banks listed above, there are other institutions in France taking deposits from the public. These include the state-owned and private savings banks known as *banques* or *caisses d'épargne,* the postal checking (giro) system, and institutions serving particular groups such as the Crédit Agricole, the Crédit Maritime, and the Crédit Artisanal. France also has specialized public and semi-public credit institutions created at different times to perform specific functions. For example there is the Caisse des Dépôts et Consignations, which has played a major role in the financing of local governments, the Crédit Foncier de France, which has been the most important institution in the long-term mortgage lending field, the Crédit National, whose initial task was to assist in the financing of the reconstruction of war-damaged enterprises after World War I, and the Caisse Nationale des Marchés de l'Etat, which originally was established to extend credit to firms with government contracts to fulfil and which eventually has become an official unit whose signature facilitates the rediscounting of certain bills at the Banque de France.

The principal focus of our examination is on the sector occupied in France by the *banque de dépôts.* Until 1966, that is during the major part of the specific period under study, a *banque de dépôts* was prohibited from taking deposits for periods exceeding two years,[99] and could not hold interests in other enterprises in excess of 10% of the capital of the latter, an exception being made in the case of holdings in other banks, financial establishments, or building societies when a greater percentage was necessary for their management.[100] Also, until 1967 a *banque de*

97. *Loi* no. 45-015 of December 2, 1945, *supra,* art. 5; and *Loi* no. 46-1071 of May 17, 1946, art. 2; *Journal officiel,* May 18, 1946. p. 4271. See pp. 207-208.

98. As with the *banques de dépôts,* the French *banques d'affaires* will, for the same reason, be referred to herein by their native designation.

99. *Loi* no. 45-015 of December 2, 1945, *supra,* art. 5 and *Loi* no. 46-1071 of May 17, 1946, *supra,* art. 1. By the terms of a ministerial decree or *décret* issued on February 1, 1966 a *banque de dépôts* is now permitted to take deposits for longer periods. See p. 208, note 28. But see also note 101, *infra.*

100. *Loi* no. 45-015 of December 2, 1945, *supra,* art. 5 and *Loi* no. 46-1071 of May 17, 1946, *supra,* art. 1. Since late 1966 this figure has been set at 20%. Minis-

dépôts could not have more than 75% of its own capital so invested or firmly committed without the permission of the Conseil National de Crédit, nor could it so invest any of its depositors' funds without such permission.[101]

The 1945 law which nationalized the Banque de France and defines the different categories of French banks also nationalized the four largest and by far most important of the six principal *banques de dépôts,* known collectively as the *grands établissements.* The *banques de dépôts* which were nationalized were the Crédit Lyonnais, the Société Générale pour favoriser le Développement du Commerce et de l'Industrie en France (now the "Société Générale"),[102] the Comptoir National d'Escompte de Paris, and the Banque Nationale pour le Commerce et l'Industrie. In May 1966 the latter two institutions were merged to form the Banque Nationale de Paris.[103] Like the "Big Five" (now "Big Four") clearing banks in Great Britain and the principal Swiss banks in their own respective countries, these four (then three) of the French *grands établissements* have carried on their commercial banking business by means of a multitude of branches scattered throughout France.

The remaining two *grands établissements,* which were not nationalized in 1945, were the Crédit Industriel et Commercial[104] and the Crédit Commercial de France.[105] In addition to the *grands établissements* there are

---

tère de l'Economie et des Finances, *Décret* no. 66-1053 of December 23, 1966; *Journal officiel,* December 31, 1966, p. 11763.

101. *Loi* no. 45-015 of December 2, 1945, *supra,* art. 5, and *Loi* no. 46-1071 of May 17, 1946, *supra,* art. 1. In September 1967 this limit was raised to the sum total of the capital of a *banque de dépôts* instead of the 75% figure. Since then it also has been allowed freely to invest funds taken on deposit for periods of two years or more. Permission is still needed for investment of funds taken on deposit for periods of less than two years if they are destined for *participations* (i.e., for investments where the bank exercises some influence on the firm in which it holds an equity interest) or for real estate investments. Ministère de l'Economie et des Finances, *Décret* no. 67-757 of September 1, 1967; *Journal officiel,* September 6, 1967, p. 8999.

102. Not to be confused with the Société Générale de Belgique, the oldest bank in Belgium.

103. See p. 264, note 234.

104. The Crédit Industriel et Commercial differs from the *banques de dépôts* mentioned above in that it is mainly a group operation with a number of subsidiaries, most of which are smaller *banques de dépôts* of regional importance. The Crédit Industriel et Commercial resembles a U.S. type bank holding-company in that the coordination of the activities of these regional banks has allowed it to extend their activities into other parts of France. One author has concluded that this structure, unusual in France, accounted for this particular bank's having been left under private ownership. Henry Germain-Martin, "France" *in* Benjamin Haggott Beckhart (ed.), *Banking Systems,* New York, Columbia University Press, 1954, p. 235.

105. Originally founded as the Banque Suisse et Française, the present name

other *banques de dépôts*. The Crédits du Nord would rank among the *grands établissements* if size alone were the criterion, and has several hundred branches in the northern industrialized zone in France.

Since the 1966 and 1967 *décrets* noted just above there has been a blurring of the distinction between *banques de dépôts* and *banques d'affaires*. Thus, for example, the Banque de Paris et des Pays-Bas, the Banque de Suez et de l'Union des Mines, the Banque de l'Union Parisienne, the Banque Worms, the Banque Lazard Frères, and the Banque Neuflize Schlumberger et Mallet have come to resemble one another in many respects despite their origins, which include both types, some being private banks or *banques privées*.

(b) Regulatory Institutions and Bodies

(1') The Banque de France

Founded by Napoleon Bonaparte in 1800 as a privately owned bank, the Banque de France was originally given the primary function of discounting bills and issuing its own notes in return. It did not acquire a monopoly of the note issue in France until the middle of the Nineteenth Century; and although it gradually became a "bankers' bank" where credit instruments could always be converted into cash or the equivalent, it was not until relatively recently[106] that the Banque de France became a central bank as this term is generally understood.

Since 1945, when it was nationalized,[107] the Banque de France has acted as a regulatory body in addition to maintaining the note issue, performing certain fiscal tasks for the Treasury, and acting as lender of last resort for the banking sector. It serves as an agent of the Conseil National de Crédit, making the Conseil's recommendations known to the banks. Also it maintains the Service Central des Risques, receiving detailed information on all bank advances in excess of a certain amount and trans-

---

having been adopted in 1917. The activity of the Crédit Commercial de France has been concentrated primarily in Paris and in the major French cities. Although large, it appears that this institution was not considered large enough to warrant its being taken into the nationalization program. See Germain-Martin, *supra,* at p. 235. With regard to the decision whether to nationalize, one contemporaneous observer noted at the time that it appeared "that the extent of the national character of the banks' network was the guiding line". J. Grahame-Parker, "The Nationalization of the French Banking System", 77 *The Banker* 18-21, 20 (1946).

106. France, *Loi* of July 24, 1936; *Journal officiel,* July 25, 1936, p. 7810. Thereafter the Banque de France has been directly controlled by the French government although its ownership remains technically in private hands. The French *"Front populaire"* is said to have had a strong influence on this legislation.

107. *Loi* no. 45-015 of December 2, 1945, p. 50, note 95, arts. 7-10.

mitting periodic reports to the banks in France with regard to borrowers' total outstanding credits with all lending institutions.[108]

The Banque de France plays a major regulatory role in the French exchange control system. Although until 1960 the administration of this system lay primarily with an exchange control office, the Office des Changes (whose chairman was the Governor of the Banque de France), the central bank has from July 1949 onwards been able to influence exchange rates by virtue of its financing of the exchange stabilization fund. Of direct importance to the present study, it is only upon the recommendation of the Governor of the Banque de France that the Ministre des Finances[109] accords to a bank the status of *banque agréée* or authorized bank for exchange control purposes. When the Office des Changes was abolished as of January 1, 1960[110] certain of its direct administrative functions were assigned to the Banque de France while others were put under the supervision of the Ministère des Finances.[111]

(2') The Conseil National de Crédit

The bank nationalization law of 1945 provided for the creation of a national credit council, the Conseil National de Crédit, which has been the keystone of the French regulatory machinery.[112] Presided over by the Ministre des Finances with the Governor of the Banque de France serving as vice-president, the Conseil National de Crédit is composed of 43 other members drawn from industry, the labor organizations, the banks (both nationalized and non-nationalized), the Cabinet Ministries, and the major governmental and government-controlled financial institutions. It has a wide mandate in controlling the quantity and distribution of credit in France. The powers of the Conseil range from deciding how a particular bank should be classified on the list of *banques inscrites* to controlling interest rates and charges for commercial banking operations. As noted above the Conseil makes its recommendations to the banks through the

108. The outstanding loans for each borrower is an aggregate figure. No individual bank's share of the total is made known to other banks.

109. I.e. the Finance Minister, later designated the Ministre des Finances et Affaires Economiques and still later the Ministre de l'Economie et des Finances. In the text of the present study the Minister or Ministry will be referred to in abbreviated form simply as the Ministre or Ministère des Finances, respectively. In footnotes the appropriate contemporaneous designation is indicated.

110. France, Ministère des Finances et des Affaires Economiques, *Décret* no. 59-1438 of December 21, 1959; *Journal officiel,* December 22, 1959, pp. 12195-96.

111. See International Monetary Fund, *Twelfth Annual Report on Exchange Restrictions,* Washington, [hereinafter cited as I.M.F., *(Number) Exchange Restrictions*], 1961, p. 131.

112. *Loi* no. 45-015 of December 2, 1945, *supra,* art. 12; Ministère des Finances et des Affaires Economiques, *Décret* no. 62-16 of January 11, 1962; *Journal officiel,* January 12, 1962, pp. 372-73.

Governor of the Banque de France, appeals from its decisions being taken directly to the Conseil d'Etat, the highest administrative tribunal in France.

(3') The Commission de Contrôle des Banques

Created in 1941[113] the Commission de Contrôle des Banques was in 1945 charged with additional duties with regard to the nationalized and non-nationalized banks as well as to the Banque de France.[114] Susequently the Commission was specifically given investigative, control, and disciplinary powers[115] with which it has generally set the rules for banking operations in France. Presided over by the Governor of the Banque de France (except with regard to surveillance of the central bank's own operations), the Commission is composed of the senior officials from the Conseil d'Etat and Ministère des Finances, as well as a representative from the banks and a representative from among the banks' employees, the latter being an individual recommended by the appropriate employees union. Decisions of the Commission de Contrôle des Banques are made known to the Conseil National de Crédit, it being possible to take appeals from the Commission's decisions directly to the Conseil d'Etat.

(4') The Association Professionnelle des Banques

Loi no. 2532 of June 13, 1941 also provided that all banking institutions in France would thereafter be required to become members of a professional association, the Association Professionnelle des Banques.[116] Far more important than its name might suggest, the Association serves both as a coordinating body for the banking industry and as an intermediary between the banks and the Commission de Contrôle des Banques.[117] Decisions of the Conseil National de Crédit and of the Commission de Contrôle des Banques are passed by the Governor of the Banque de France to the President of the Association, who is charged with communicating with the banks affected.

An additional function of the Association Professionnelle des Banques consists of advising the Commission de Contrôle des Banques on requests, both French and foreign, relative to the establishment of banks, branch

---

113. *Loi* no. 2532 of June 13, 1941, p. 50, note 92, art. 48.
114. *Loi* no. 45-015 of December 2, 1945, *supra*, art. 15.
115. France, *Loi* no. 50-586 of May 27, 1950, art. 34; *Journal officiel*, May 28, 1950, p. 5805; and Ministère des Finances et des Affaires Economiques, *Arrêté* of June 5, 1950; *Journal officiel*, June 7, 1950, p. 6096.
116. *Loi* no. 2532 of June 13, 1941, *supra*, art. 24. French banks had for many years been grouped professionally, but not on an obligatory basis. The new Association was constituted under a public law of July 1, 1901 and placed under the direction of a permanent organization committee created by *Loi* no. 2532, arts. 27-47.
117. Art. 25.

banks, or banking subsidiaries in France.[118] It is the Association that transmits such applications to the Conseil National de Crédit. Likewise, the Association can recommend that a bank be removed from the list of *banques inscrites.* With the approval of the Ministre des Finances, disciplinary functions can be assigned to the Assocation by the Commission for violations of banking regulations as well as for failure to observe the agreements concluded among the banks.[119]

(2) Establishment of a U.S. Branch Bank in France

Under the sub-heading "regulation of foreign banks in France" the pertinent French statute states that banks which are directly or indirectly controlled by foreigners are to be considered foreign banks regardless of where their *siège social*[120] may be situated.[121] By virtue of this same article, foreign banks can seek permission to operate in France provided

---

118. Art. 10.
119. Art. 26.
For a more complete description of the French banking sector see Henri Ardant, *Technique de la banque,* Paris, Presses Universitaires Françaises, 1953; Jean Marchal, *Monnaie et crédit,* Paris, Editions Cujas, 1964; Jacques Branger, *Traité d'économie bancaire,* vol. 1, revised, Paris, Presses Universitaires Françaises, 1968; and H. Fournier, "Les institutions et mécanismes bancaires en France", *in* Institut d'Etudes Bancaires et Financières, *Institutions et mécanismes bancaires dans les pays de la Communauté économique européenne,* Paris, 1969, pp. 67-194. Useful English language works are Germain-Martin, "France", *supra,* pp. 225-310; J. S. G. Wilson, *French Banking Structure and Credit Policy,* London, G. Bell and Sons Ltd. (University of London, The London School of Economic and Political Science), 1957; and J. S. G. Wilson, "France", *in* Richard Sidney Sayers (ed.), *Banking in Western Europe,* Oxford, Clarendon Press, 1962, pp. 1-52. A short but informative article is Jacques Branger, "The French Banking System", 85 *Journal of the Institute of Bankers* 184-95 (1964).
120. Literally, the "social seat" of the banking corporation, which is roughly equivalent to what Anglo-American jurists would refer to as its principal or head office. In French law the *siège social* of a foreign corporation is normally the main criterion used in determining its national character or nationality, unlike the situs of its incorporation which is given greater weight by Anglo-American jurisprudence. See generally Georg Schwarzenberger, *A Manual of International Law,* 5th ed., London, Stevens & Sons Ltd., 1967, pp. 144-45; R. Y. Jennings, "General Course on Principles of International Law", *in* Academy of International Law (The Hague), 121 *Recueil des cours* 469-70 (1967); Yvon Loussouarn, "La condition des personnes morales en droit international privé", 96 *Id.* 476 (1959), and Lucius Caflish, "La nationalité des sociétés commerciales en droit international privé", 24 *Annuaire suisse de droit international* 119-60 (1967). Adopting the criterion of control in the case of banks constitutes a significant departure from the usual French practice. See P. Dupont, *Le contrôle des banques et la direction du crédit en France,* Paris, Dunod, 1952, p. 81. In the case of a French branch of a foreign chartered banking institution there is, of course, no question as to the foreign nature of the U.S. head office bank.
121. *Loi* no. 2532 of June 13, 1941, *supra,* art. 15.

56

they are registered on a special list of foreign-controlled banks, the list being published in the official gazette. This list is divided into two categories, one for foreign-controlled banking corporations organized under French law, i.e., foreign banking subsidiaries in France, and the other for French branches of banking institutions chartered elsewhere.

Like any French *banque de dépôts*, a U.S. commercial bank seeking registration, in this case for a French branch, must obtain the favorable recommendation of the Association Professionnelle des Banques, which, as previously noted, acts as the applicant bank's intermediary.[122] Without first having been registered, a bank or foreign branch bank cannot engage in banking operations and/or use the terms "bank, banker, or credit institution" in its name or in any phase of its activities.[123] Once inscribed, the bank or foreign branch bank is assigned an identifying number which must appear on all its documents and letterheads. Inscription in this case is in addition to the mandatory registration in the local *registre de commerce*.[124]

The inscription on a special list of foreign banks might seem discriminatory in the sense that foreign banks and branch banks are thus segregated from other banks in France. In fact, however, all the various types of banks in France are separated into different categories on other similar lists. In any event, such segregation in the absence of other measures discriminating against foreign-controlled banks would certainly seem justified, even if, as one authority has put it, no purpose is served other than to bring to the attention of the public the non-French character of the institutions in question.[125]

---

122. *Loi* no. 2532 of June 13, 1941, *supra,* art. 10. "Certain types of [foreign] corporations, like banking institutions... must file a special registration with specified professional organizations as a condition of doing business in France..." Delaume, page 34, note 31, at pp. 48-49. But see France-United States Convention of Establishment, page 33, note 28, art. V(3).

123. *Loi* no. 2532 of June 13, 1941, *supra,* art. 12. Violation of this prescription carries penalties, of either a fine ranging from FF 360,000 to 3,600,000, or imprisonment from one month to two years, or both. Art. 21.

124. France, *Code de Commerce,* art. 48(3), *Décret* no 53-705 of August 9, 1953; *Journal officiel,* August 10, 1953, p. 7047, replacing the law that had evolved from a *Loi* of March 18, 1919. Subsequent modifications brought this requirement under *Code de Commerce,* art. 70, Ministère de l'Industrie et du Commerce, *Décret* no. 58-1355 of December 27, 1958, art. 1(2); *Journal officiel,* December 29, 1958, p. 11971; and then Ministère de la Justice, *Décret* no. 67-237 of March 23, 1967, art. 2(2); *Journal officiel,* March 24, 1967, p. 2870 (France, 64th ed. Dalloz 1968).

125. "Tant que des mesures spéciales ne seront pas édictées à l'égard des banques étrangères—et rien n'indique que l'on s'oriente dans cette voie—le classement d'une banque dans la catégorie des établissements non français n'aura qu'un effect psychologique, non négligeable d'ailleurs, mais qu'il importe, dans certains cas, de provoquer, ne serait-ce que pour avertir le public." Dupont, *supra,* at p. 82. Note that

In addition to its inscription on the special list of foreign banks, the U.S. branch bank also needs permission to deal in foreign exchange in order to perform many of the transactions required by its customers and certainly for multinational banking operations.[126] In France, as noted earlier, this permission is obtained from the Ministre des Finances upon the recommendation of the Governor of the Banque de France, and takes the form of an *agrégation* by which the branch bank becomes an *intermédiaire agréé* or authorized bank. Like any other *intermédiaire agréé,* the U.S. branch bank is expected to perform certain regulatory tasks with regard to customers' accounts and foreign exchange transactions. There is no evidence to suggest that any special treatment, favorable or unfavorable, has been accorded to the U.S. branch banks with regard to their *agrégation;* and in fact, all the U.S. branch banks in Paris have become *intermédiaires agréés.*[127]

Again, like any French *banque de dépôts,* the U.S. commercial bank maintaining a branch in France must conform to certain capital and accounting standards. All banks in France must to adhere to minimum capital requirements,[128] a foreign banking subsidiary established in France being obliged to maintain a minimum capital equal to that required of an indigenous bank, as measured by its operations.[129] In the case of a for-

---

proposed Swiss measures aimed at the same purpose have not yet been put into effect. See p. 85, note 249.

126. One observer notes that although exchange control authorization is not required for the establishment of a branch in France it might still be necessary where it involves the acquisition of the assets of a going concern. See Fernand Charles Jeantet, "Exchange Control Regulations in France", *in* Stein and Nicholson, p. 35, note 32, at pp. 189-233. See also p. 61.

127. For example, France, Office des Changes, *Avis* (i.e., Notice) no. 321; *Journal officiel,* May 8, 1948, p. 4433, listed the following U.S. branch banks in Paris as *intermédiaires agréés:* Chase Bank, Guaranty Trust Co. of New York, and National City Bank of New York. Also listed was Morgan et Cie., the French chartered subsidiary of J. P. Morgan & Co. By mid-1958 the list had been modified to include Bank of America, and listed Chased Manhattan Bank and First National City Bank of New York as the merger successors to banks included on the 1948 list. *Avis* no. 656; *Journal officiel,* June 20, 1958, p. 5763. As of December 31, 1967 the U.S. branch banks figuring among the current list of *intermédiaires* were Bank of America, N.T. & S.A.; The Chase Manhattan Bank (N.A.), First National City Bank of New York, and Morgan Guaranty Trust Co. of New York (as well as Morgan et Cie., S.A.). Ministère de l'Economie et des Finances, *Avis* no. 791 of August 13, 1966; *Journal officiel,* August 14, 1966, pp. 7175-77, which was extended in force by Ministère, *Arrêté* of May 30, 1968; *Journal officiel,* May 31, 1968, p. 5309.

128. *Loi* no. 2532 of June 13, 1941, p. 72, note 1, art. 8.

129. France, Ministère des Finances, *Décret* no. 46-1247 of May 28, 1946, art. 9; *Journal officiel,* May 30, 1946, p. 4732. The French language text of this portion of the article is: "Les banques étrangères ... doivent: 2° Justifier de l'affectation à l'ensemble de ces opérations et de l'investissement en France d'un capital minimum égal à celui exigé des banques françaises."

58

eign branch bank, which is not considered to be a separate legal entity, the foreign bank itself is required to allocate an equivalent portion of its own capital to the branch bank in France. As for accounting requirements, a separate set of books must be maintained, reflecting operations on French territory.[130]

Since the U.S. (or other foreign) branch bank in France is considered legally to constitute an integral part of the bank itself, it is not treated as a separate legal entity for corporate law purposes. For example, in order to obtain its enrollment in the local *registre de commerce* the U.S. branch bank files certified copies of the U.S. bank's corporate charter with the clerk of the Tribunal de Commerce in the district where the branch bank is to be established,[131] not its own charter as in the case of a banking subsidiary organized under French laws, since as a branch it has none. Also, in the event that the manager of the branch is a French national, the French *carte de commerçant* is issued to the head of the U.S. bank itself, even though he does not reside in France.[132]

Although not considered to be a separate entity for certain corporate law purposes, as illustrated above, the branch bank is none the less treated like a separate bank with regard to its banking operations. For example, on the annual tabulation of the balance sheets of banks and foreign branch banks in France prepared by the Commission de Contrôle des Banques, U.S. and other foreign branch banks are required to show their own local balance sheets as well as their respective banks' overall figures. This is a logical extension of the requirement that they maintain minimum reserves and separate books in France, as noted above. Also, the obligation to join the Association Professionnelle des Banques falls equally on foreign branch banks as on French chartered institutions, no exception being made for the former.[133] The member of the Association is the branch bank in France, not the bank itself in the United States.

The only requirement applying to non-French banks establishing themselves in France that does not have a counterpart relating to indigenous

130. *Décret* no. 46-1247 of May 28, 1946, *supra,* art. 9. The French language text of the pertinent portion of this article is: "Les banques étrangères, telles quelles sont définies à l'article 15 de l'acte dit loi du 13 juin 1941, qui exercent leur activité en France, doivent: 1° Tenir, dans l'un de leurs sièges, une comptabilité spéciale des opérations qu'elles traitent sur le territoire français. . ."

131. The charter has to be filed in French language translation. France, Ministère de l'Industrie et du Commerce, *Décret* no. 55-653 of May 20, 1955; *Journal officiel,* May 22, 1955, p. 5172. The branch bank is also obliged to deposit with the clerk documents showing that the branch has been properly constituted by the U.S. bank and that it has been accorded internally the powers needed for branch operations.

132. See generally Marcel Colomès, *Comment fonder et gérer une entreprise en France,* Paris, Editions J. Delmas et Cie, 1966, especially chapters Q, R, and T.

133. *Loi* no. 2532 of June 13, 1941, *supra,* art. 24.

banks is the necessity to obtain special permission, set forth in the pertinent statute as follows:

> "No one may habitually engage in banking operations or in any capacity head, serve on the board of, or manage a company or a branch of a company that engages in banking operations, or by virtue of an authorization sign documents connected with banking operations:
>
> . . . .
> 2. if he is not a French national . . .; however, individual exemptions may be granted by the Minister of Finance. . ."[134]

This requirement gives the French government a method whereby foreign banks or bankers can be prevented from establishing themselves in France. There is no evidence to suggest, however, that it has constituted any hardship whatsoever in the case of the U.S. branch banks. Moreóver, this French rule reflects a practice common to many countries whereby certain sectors of the national political and economic life are restricted to nationals outright or are, as in the present case, opened to foreigners only on special conditions. Limitations on activities such as the manufacture and possession of arms, the practice of law or medicine and the prescription or production of drugs, the ownership of real property, the dissemination of news or other information, as well as the conduct of banking operations[135] are found in the laws of many countries for a host of different reasons.

There are, then, three types of French requirements which the U.S. branch banks must meet in order to effect their establishment in France. First, those with a counterpart requirement for indigenous banks, such as the minimum capital and accounting rules. Second, the one with a counterpart requirement which is equivalent to, but as Dupont has implied, psychologically unlike the one imposed on foreign-controlled banks, namely the segregation by means of a special list. Third, the special requirement that bars foreigners from the banking sector unless they obtain prior permission. In themselves, these French rules do not appear unfair. Examination has revealed no case in which they have been used to discriminate against a U.S. branch bank, which should expect to receive equal treatment with indigenous and other foreign-controlled banking in-

---

134. *Loi,* art. 7.

135. For an informative discussion of this subject, see the section entitled "Attitudes of Foreign Countries toward U.S. Banks" in *Foreign Government Restraints on United States Bank Operations Abroad,* p. 29, note 20, at pp. 8-14. A comparison of the legal status of foreign banking establishments under the laws of several host countries (Argentina, Brazil, Czechoslovakia, England, Italy, Poland, Spain, Switzerland and the United States) with that under French law during the early inter-war period is found in P. Barazzetti, *Le régime des banques étrangères dans les principales législations,* Paris, Rousseau & Cie, 1923. See also Phelps, page 14, note 15, at pp. 176-91.

stitutions with regard to its establishment in France.

With the French exchange control system revision effective January 31, 1967 a new and different requirement has been imposed on a U.S. commercial (or other foreign) bank seeking to establish a branch bank in France. Under the terms of *Décret* no. 67-68, any proposed direct investment in France must be preceded by a declaration made to the Ministère des Finances, which has two months within which to object to the proposed direct investment.[136] If no objection is raised, the foreign investor, here a U.S. commercial bank, can proceed as before, but still is required by the new rules to file a report with the Ministère once the branch bank is established. Although this new procedure could serve as a discouragement to potential investors in certain sectors of the French economy, there is reason to believe that generally speaking it does not. In any case, no evidence appears to suggest that the new requirement hinders the potential establishment of a U.S. branch bank in France.

b. *Great Britain*

(1) Banking Sector

(a) Banks

In the words of one authority, "English banking law, not unlike English constitutional law and central bank law, is governed by a multiplicity of statutes . . ."[137] Another observer sees the British system in quite a different light, which is perhaps more significant in the context of the present study. For example, when comparing British banking regulation with that of other countries, he notes that some countries have unusual banking systems in that they are unregulated or in any event do not have written regulations, and states that among the present day major banking systems only that of England falls into this category.[138]

These two appraisals reflect different viewpoints on a system where various statutes bear directly or indirectly on different aspects of banking, while at the same time there is no separate banking act as such.[139] More-

136. France, Ministère de l'Economie et des Finances, *Décret* (sur les relations financières avec l'étranger) no. 67-78 of January 27, 1967; *Journal officiel*, January 29, 1967, pp. 1073-74. The terms of this decree apply as well to direct investment from other member countries of the European Communities. Compare with article 71 of the Treaty of Rome, p. 158, material cited to note 10.

137. Hans Aufricht, *in* International Monetary Fund, *Central Banking Legislation*, Washington, 1961, vol. 1, p. 201.

138. Samy Chamas, *L'Etat et les systèmes bancaires contemporains*, Paris, Sirey, 1965, p. 35.

139. Cf. Bank for International Settlements, *Eight European Central Banks*, London, George Allen and Unwin Ltd., 1963, p. 108, n. 1.

over, unwritten conventions determine or guide many of the activities that are dealt with in the banking acts or codes of other countries. In the absence of satisfactory statutory definitions of "bank" or "banker", one is inclined to agree with the conclusion that in Great Britain "it is probable that a person cannot claim to be carrying on the business of banking unless he receives money or instruments representing money on current account, honours cheques drawn thereon, and collects the proceeds of cheques which his customers place into his hands for collection"[140]

There are four categories of banks in Great Britain, namely:

a. *commercial or joint-stock banks,* which are the nearest British equivalent to the commercial banks in the United States. In 1964 there were nineteen such banks in Great Britain, several being much larger than the others as a result of mergers and consolidations, particularly during the first two decades of this Century. During the period under study eleven of the joint-stock banks made up the London Bankers' Clearing House and were known collectively as "clearing banks" or "clearers". Subsequent mergers have reduced this group to six.

b. *merchant banks,* consisting of two types of institutions. There are the accepting houses, so named because of their long experience in financing foreign trade transactions by accepting bills of exchange. The other type of merchant bank consists of the issuing houses, which sponsor and underwrite their customers' securities issues. In London there is an Accepting House Committee as well as an Issuing House Association, with some merchant banks belonging to both groups.

c. *discount houses or bill brokers,* which play an important role because the commercial banks do not have direct access to the Bank of England as a lender of last resort Although small in size, these banking houses wield large sums, much of which is borrowed from the commercial banks, for acquiring Treasury and other bills. When the commercial banks or other lenders seek additional liquidity, they call their loans in the discount market, causing the discount houses to discount their bills at the central bank. When money is more easily available, these houses provide a ready outlet for the commercial banks' excess funds. An institution peculiar to the City of London, the discount house or bill broker has no counterpart in France or Switzerland or in the United States. The London Discount Market Association groups the twelve houses.[141]

140. Herbert Percival Sheldon, and C. B. Drover, *The Practice and Law of Banking,* 9th ed. rev., London, Macdonald & Evans, Ltd., 1962, p. 184.
141. See "The London Discount Market: Some Historical Notes", Bank of England, 7 *Quarterly Bulletin* 144 (1967). This extremely valuable source dates only from 1961. The manifold U.S. and (especially) French publications of official regulations and notices do not—unfortunately for research purposes—have British counterparts. In the field of banking regulation, where even the French and U.S. mate-

d. *savings banks,* a group which includes the Post Office Savings Bank which operates throughout Great Britain, and the eighty trustee savings banks which together form the Trustee Savings Banks Association.[142]

Along with the banking institutions briefly described above there are other organizations performing operations important to the functioning of the British banking mechanism taken as a whole. There are the insurance companies, the hire-purchase houses specializing in consumer finance, the building societies (roughly comparable to the savings and loan associations in the United States), the investment trusts and unit trusts (which resemble U.S. closed- and open-end investment companies, respectively), and other institutions designed to pool savings or spread risks among their members or participants, such as the so-called friendly societies, cooperative societies, and trade unions.

In addition to these privately-controlled entities, there are public bodies such as the Industrial and Commercial Finance Corporation Ltd. and the Finance Corporation for Industry Ltd., whose funds come from private sources as well as from the Bank of England, and whose functions are to provide medium- and long-term credit. The Air Finance Ltd., Ship Mortgage Finance Company Ltd., Commonwealth Development Finance Company Ltd., and Agricultural Mortgage Corporation Ltd. are public bodies whose principal sectors of interest are reflected in their names. Particularly noteworthy is the Export Credits Guarantee Department of the Department of Trade and Industry,[143] which provides insurance in the form of guarantees for exporters.[144]

For the present study, the most important British banking sector is that in which the commercial banks operate. Whereas the operations of their French equivalents, the *banques de dépôts,* are outlined rather sharply in the statutes of that country, there is no such legislative description of the activities of commercial banks in Great Britain. The most authoritative statement concerning the clearing banks is that their primary business is "the receipt, transfer and encashment of deposits

---

rials tend to be less multifarious than in other sectors (e.g., taxation, health, social welfare), the British equivalents are even rarer. An interesting description of the functioning of the London discount market is found in *This is Bill-broking,* London, Allen, Harvey & Ross Ltd., 1966.

142. In October 1968 the National Giro system was put into operation by the Post Office, and has since expanded its activities to offer many services that formerly were available elsewhere, including personal loans in collaboration with a hire purchase (personal loan) company, and provisions for having account holders' salaries and wages deposited automatically into their postal giro account. Both these activities are an encroachment on the clearing banks' terrain. (Clearers have provided personal loans indirectly via so-called "backdoor" subsidiaries.)

143. Formerly the Board of Trade.

144. See page 136, note 168.

repayable on demand".[145] In describing commercial banks generally, the British government has stated that their "traditional role" is to "provide working capital, and to a certain extent the temporary financing of longer-term capital requirements pending the raising of finance through other channels".[146] The commercial banks base their lending on customers' deposits in current accounts payable on demand, or in deposit accounts payable on seven days' notice by the depositor. Unlike the case in France prior to the 1967 change in the law affecting French *banques de dépôts*,[147] these banks have not been limited by statute to lending exclusively in the short-term market.

Before the 1968 mergers the five largest clearing banks, then commonly referred to as the "Big Five", were Barclays Bank Ltd., Lloyds Bank Ltd., Midland Bank Ltd., National Provincial Bank Ltd., and Westminster Bank Ltd.[148] Together with the remaining clearing banks[149] these institutions have usually held approximately four-fifths of the total bank deposits in Great Britain.[150] In addition to smaller non-clearer joint-stock banks the category of commercial banks also includes Scottish banks.

Another group of non-clearer joint-stock banks are the British overseas banks grouped in the British Overseas Banks Association. Some are separately incorporated banking subsidiaries, controlled by one of the Big Five (now Four), such as Barclays Bank (D.C.O.), Lloyds Bank

145. Great Britain, Committee on the Working of the Monetary System, *Report,* Cmnd. 827, London, 1959 [hereinafter cited as (Radcliffe) Committee, *Report, Cmnd. 827*], p. 43, par. 128.

146. Great Britain, Central Office of Information, *United Kingdom Financial Institutions,* London, 1960, p. 8.

147. (France) *Décret* no. 67-757 of September 1, 1967, p. 52, note 101.

148. National Provincial and Westminster Banks merged in 1968 to form National Westminster Bank Ltd. Lloyds Bank Ltd. was prevented by the Monopolies Commission from joining the merger.

149. Until after the end of the specific period under examination these were Coutts & Co. and the District Bank Ltd., (both owned by the National Provincial Bank Ltd.), Glyn, Mills & Co., and Williams Deacon's Bank (both owned by the Royal Bank of Scotland), Martins Bank Ltd., and The National Bank Ltd. In 1968 Martins Bank was purchased by and became part of Lloyds Bank Ltd. In 1970 Glyn, Mills & Co., Williams Deacon's Bank and The National Bank Ltd. merged to form Williams & Glyn's Bank Ltd.

150. Great Britain, Central Office of Information, *United Kingdom Financial Institutions, supra,* p. 8. A subsequent version of this publication states that "these 11 banks account for over 80 per cent of Britain's banking business". *The British Banking System,* London, 1964, p. 31. In May 1967, an official source estimated that the "Big Five" accounted for about 85% of deposits. Great Britain, National Board for Prices and Income, *Bank Charges (Report no. 34),* Cmnd. 3292, London, 1967 [hereinafter cited as National (Jones) Board, *Report,* Cmnd. 3292] p. 12, par. 18.

Europe Ltd., and Westminster Foreign Bank Ltd. Others are Standard and Chartered Bank,[151] Eastern Bank, National and Grindlays Bank,[152] the Bank of London and South America,[153] the Australia and New Zealand Bank, E.D. Sassoon Banking Co.,[154] and the British Bank of the Middle East,[155] some of whose names are indicative of the parts of the world in which they originally directed their activities.

Finally, completing the group of commercial banks, there are the banking subsidiaries and branch banks which foreign banks have established in London. At the end of 1967 there were over one hundred of these institutions, ranging alphabetically from the Afghan National Bank through the Zivnostenska Banka, illustrating the broad appeal which the City of London has for non-British banks. The majority of these foreign-controlled banking establishments are members of the Foreign Banks and Affiliates Association, which has not, however, included the U.S. branch banks in London.[156]

(b) Regulatory Institutions and Bodies

The principal British regulatory institution, and the one with which the U.S. branch banks are in frequent contact, is the central bank itself. Originally established in 1694 under a Royal Charter[157] accompanied

151. Prior to their merger in 1970, Standard Bank shares were held by Chase Manhattan Bank, N.A. (14.8%), National Westminster (10%), and Midland (5%). Barclays Bank held 10% of Chartered Bank's equity.

152. In 1968 First National City Bank acquired a 40% interest in this bank. Lloyds Bank Europe Ltd. has a 41% interest.

153. In 1965 Mellon National Bank and Trust Co. acquired approximately 14% interest in this bank which was raised to 25% in September 1968. In 1970 Lloyds Bank Ltd. moved to acquire approximately 50% of the stock of the bank. The resulting institution, Lloyds & Bolsa International Bank Ltd., would be jointly owned by Lloyds Bank Ltd. (51.24%) and Mellon (12.63%) with the remaining shares held publicly.

154. In the 1960's Continental Illinois National Bank & Trust Co. acquired 25% of this bank.

155. A subsidiary of the Hongkong and Shanghai Banking Corp., which also has a subsidiary in California. The Hongkong and Shanghai Banking Corporation is the bank of issue for the British Crown Colony of Hong Kong.

156. Great Britain, Central Office of Information, *United Kingdom Financial Institutions, supra,* p. 11. The U.S. branch banks in London name a representative to function as "a point of contact with the authorities in matters concerning the American banks as a whole". Bank of England, 1 *Quarterly Bulletin* 18 (1961). Fear of possible U.S. anti-trust law consequences has tended to discourage U.S. branch banks from taking part in such groupings unless it is mandatory under host country law (e.g., in France).

157. Part of which has been retained in force by Article 1 of the present Charter of 1946. See International Monetary Fund, *Central Banking Legislation,* vol. 1, p. 61, note 137, at pp. 193 and 197-98.

by the Bank of England Act, 1694,[158] the Bank of England was national-ized in 1946 by "an Act to bring the capital stock of the Bank of England into public ownership and bring the Bank under public control . . ."[159] It was made subject to directions which can be issued by the Treasury, after consultation with the Governor of the Bank, which the Treasury considers "necessary in the public interest".[160] As a central bank per se, the Bank of England has a note issue function and, as we have seen, also acts as the lender of last resort (at Bank rate) to the discount market and thus indirectly to the clearing and other banks. In addition, it super-vises the weekly tender of Treasury bills and manages the Exchange Equalisation Account for the Treasury.

As for its regulatory role, the central bank has direct authority over banks under the Bank of England Act, 1946, which provides specifically that:

> "The Bank, if they think it necessary in the public interest, may request in-formation from and make recommendations to bankers, and may, if so autho-rized by the Treasury, issue directions to any banker for the purpose of secur-ing that effect is given to any such request or recommendation:

> Provided that:—

> (a) no such request or recommendations shall be made with respect to the affairs of any particular customer of a banker; and
> (b) before authorizing the issue of such directions the Treasury shall give the banker concerned, or such person as appears to them to represent him, an opportunity of making representations with respect thereto."[161]

Despite this broad mandate, it is noteworthy that according to one of-ficial source the Bank of England was not known to have made formal recommendations or to have issued formal directions to the banks at least up to 1963.[162] The Bank has chosen, on the contrary, to make in-

---

158. Great Britain, Bank of England Act, 1694, 5 & 6 Will. & M., chap. 20.
159. Great Britain, Bank of England Act, 1946, 9 & 10 Geo. 6, chap. 27, Pream-ble. The text of this Act is reproduced in International Monetary Fund, *Central Banking Legislation,* vol. 1, note 1, *supra,* and at 32 *Federal Reserve Bulletin* 479-82 (1946).
160. Bank of England Act, 1946, § 4 (1). It was reported officially in 1964 that "this power in fact has never been used". Great Britain, Central Office of Informa-tion, *The British Banking System, supra,* at p. 3.
161. Act, § 4 (3). Here the term "banker" means "any such person carrying on a banking undertaking as may be declared by order of the Treasury to be a banker for the purposes of this section". Act, § 4 (6).
162. Bank for International Settlements, *Eight European Central Banks,* p. 61, note 139, at p. 119. Near the end of the specific period under study it was observed unofficially that the Bank of England had never "issued a legally binding 'directive' as it is empowered to do under the 1946 Bank of England Act. . ." *The Economist,* vol. CCXXV, no. 6482 (November 18, 1967), "International Banking: a Survey" p. 22.

formal suggestions directly or through the different Associations or Committees referred to in the preceding subsection. Individual banks or bankers are invited from time to time to discuss a particular operation or phase of their banking activities with an official of the Bank of England. When the Bank deems it necessary to institute or modify certain practices, this is made known to the particular banks concerned through such informal contacts, or to a group of institutions via the appropriate Association or Committee. For example, in 1960 the clearing banks were "invited" to make Special Deposits with the central bank as a credit control measure.[163]

Since the U.S. branch banks in London are not members of the Foreign Banks and Affiliates Association, the Bank of England's recommendations are either made known to them directly or via the representative referred to previously. This is in keeping with the accepted practice in the City of London, where formal directives are considered neither desirable nor necessary.[164]

French bodies such as the Conseil National de Crédit and Commission de Contrôle des Banques have no British counterparts. There is a Capital Issues Committee, consisting of seven members appointed by the Treasury, whose approval is necessary for the issuance of equity or debt securities under specified conditions. Otherwise, the British regulatory structure is quite unlike that in France. For example, the Association Professionnelle des Banques in France has statutory powers whereas the British Associations and Committees do not. An appreciation of the sharp differences in the styles of regulation in these two countries, both styles being different from that in Switzerland (while all three host countries' styles differ from that in the home country of the U.S. branch banks), is essential in sensing the particularities and nuances of the operations of these institutions.[165]

(2) Establishment of a U.S. Branch Bank in Great Britain

The detailed French statutory requirements with respect to the establishment of a foreign branch bank have no parallel in British law. At

163. See p. 126, note 123.
164. One knowledgeable U.S.-trained banker in London characterizes the Bank of England's regulatory approach as "informal but precise".
165. For a more complete description of the British banking sector, see John Edwin Wadsworth, "United Kingdom of Great Britain and Northern Ireland", in Beckhart (ed.), Banking Systems, p. 52, note 104, at pp. 769-837. A short but illustrative comparison with the American banking sector is H. W. Auburn, "Banking in the U.S.A. and the U.K.", in Auburn (ed.), Comparative Banking, 3d. ed., Dunstable, Waterlow, 1966, pp. 1-17. Useful descriptions of various phases of British banking can be found among the lectures delivered at the sessions of the International Banking Summer Schools, introduced in 1948 by the Institute of Bankers, London.

the outset, it must be noted that entry into the banking sphere—by national and foreign interests alike—is quite free when compared to the situation prevailing in France. Nowhere in the Britisch statutes is there a requirement that a person or institution, indignenous or foreign, register or obtain permission before commencing banking operations. The Bank Charter Act, 1844[166] has limited itself to specifying simply that:

> "...every Banker in *England* and *Wales* who is now carrying on or shall hereafter carry on Business as such shall...make a Return...of his Name, Residence, and Occupation, or in the Case of a Company or Partnership, of the Name, Residence, and Occupation of every Person composing or being a Member of such Company or Partnership, and also the Name of the Firm under which such Banker, Company, or Partnership carry on the Business of Banking, and of every Place where such Business is carried on..."[167]

Subsequently, the Companies Act, 1948 set forth that:

> "No company, association or partnership consisting of more than ten persons shall be formed for the purpose of carrying on the business of banking, unless it is registered as a company under this Act, or is formed in pursuance of some other Act of Parliament, or of letters patent."[168]

The requirement in the 1844 Act that banking companies file a return has been continued by a provision in the Companies Act, 1948, to the effect that:

> "(1) Where a company carrying on the business of bankers has duly forwarded to the registrar of companies the annual return required by section one hundred and twenty-four of this Act and has added thereto a statement of the names of the several places where it carries on business, the company—
>
> (a) shall not be required to furnish to the Commissioners of Inland Revenue any returns under the provisions of...the Bankers (Scotland) Act, 1826 [or] section twenty-one of the Bank Charter Act, 1844..."[169]

---

166. Great Britain, Bank Charter Act, 1844, 7 & 8 Vict., chap. 32. The original text of this Act appears in International Monetary Fund, *Central Banking Legislation,* vol. 1, p. 61, note 137, at pp. 230-46.

167. Sec. XXI (italics in original). In Scotland there are similar requirements, Bankers (Scotland) Act, 1826, as there are in Northern Ireland, Bankers (Ireland) Act, 1825.

168. Great Britain, Companies Act, 1948, 11 & 12 Geo. 6, chap. 38, § 429.

169. Companies Act, 1948, § 432. Section 124 (mentioned in the above-quoted passage) specifies that "every company having a share capital shall, once at least in every year, make a return containing with respect to the registered office of the company, registers of members and debenture holders, shares and debentures, indebtedness, past and present members and directors and secretary" in a form specified by a schedule to the Act. Reports of individuals carrying on the banking business continue to be required by § 21 of the 1844 Act, a recent text of which is found in International Monetary Fund, *Central Banking Legislation,* vol. 1, *supra,* at p. 247. Banks in Great Britain receive special treatment with regard to balance sheets and profit and loss accounts required to be filed under Schedule 8 of the Companies

A limited liability banking company is further required to make a semi-annual statement concerning its share capital, assets, and liabilities, posting a copy of the statement "in a conspicuous place in the registered office of the company, and in every branch office or place where the business of the company is carried on".[170]

A foreign corporation (referred to in the Companies Act, 1948, as an "overseas company") establishing a branch in Great Britain is required to "deliver to the registrar of companies for registration.—

> (a) a certified copy of the charter, statutes or memorandum and articles of the company or other instrument constituting or defining the constitution of the company, and, if the instrument is not written in the English language, a certified translation thereof;
>
> (b) a list of the directors and secretary of the company ... [giving their names, addresses, nationalities, business occupations, and directorships] ... ; [and]
>
> (c) the names and addresses of some one or more persons resident in Great Britain authorised to accept on behalf of the company service of process and any notices required to be served on the company."[171]

Also, the foreign company is required yearly to "make out a balance sheet and profit and loss account ... in such form, and containing such particulars and including such documents", as would be required of a domestic company, delivering copies to the registrar of companies.[172]

Of the above requirements, it is noteworthy that the only ones which arise from the conduct of a banking business in Great Britain are those set forth in the Bank Charter Act, 1844, as carried forward by § 432 of the Companies Act, 1948, and the semi-annual statement posted "in a conspicuous place" as required by § 433. The other rules are applicable

---

Act, 1948. Specifically, Paragraph 23 of that Schedule exempts a "banking or discount company" from certain of those requirements. Under the Companies Act, 1967 (which has replaced parts of the 1948 Act) the Board of Trade acquired, *inter alia,* the power to amend Paragraph 23 so as to "render a banking or discount company subject to a requirement ... [of Schedule 8 of the Companies Act, 1948] ... to which ... it would [otherwise] not be subject..." Companies Act, 1967, 18 & 19 Eliz. 2, chap. 81, part I, § 12 (1) (a). No alteration was made in the definition of a "banking and discount company" found in paragraph 23 of Schedule 8 of the 1948 Act, which states simply that "in this paragraph the expression 'banking or discount company' means any company which satisfies the Board of Trade that it ought to be treated for the purposes of this Schedule as a banking company or as a discount company". See also Companies Act, 1967, part V, § 123 (2).

170. Companies Act, 1948, § 433 (2).

171. Act, 1948, § 407. See Alfred Frank Topham (ed.), *Palmer's Company Law,* 19th ed., London, Stevens & Sons, 1949, p. 448.

172. Act. § 410 (1). Certified English language translations are required where the original documents are in another language. § 410 (2). See also Overseas Companies (Accounts) (Exceptions) Order 1968, dated January 18, 1968, S.I. 1968 no. 69.

to all foreign corporations engaging in business in Great Britain.

Although no prior permission is needed for the establishment of foreign branch banks in Great Britain,[173] the U.S. banks have made a practice of keeping the Bank of England informed as to their intended establishment and contemplated operations, usually by informal consultations at the central bank. Once opened, a foreign branch bank can take and make deposits and advances in sterling without any formal authority. Also it can take deposits in foreign currencies and make advances to qualified borrowers in these currencies up to the amount taken on deposit.

Additional powers are necessary, however, for a bank which seeks to engage in foreign trade financing, and *a fortiori* in the multinational banking operations that large corporate customers ultimately need and expect. Notably, special permission is needed if the U.S. branch bank seeks to exchange one currency into another or to take a position in foreign exchange. This stems from the Exchange Control Act, 1947, which states that:

> "Except with the permission of the Treasury, no person, other than an authorized dealer, shall, in the United Kingdom, and no person resident in the United Kingdom, other than an authorised dealer, shall, outside the United Kingdom, buy or borrow any gold or foreign currency from, or sell or lend any gold or foreign currency to, any person other than an authorised dealer."[174]

An "authorised dealer" is defined in the Act as:

> "... in relation to gold or any foreign currency, a person for the time being authorised by an order of the Treasury to act for the purposes of this Act as an authorised dealer in relation to gold, or as the case may be, that foreign currency..."[175]

The first such order, issued in September 1947,[176] listed 111 "authorised dealers in all foreign currencies". Among these "authorised dealers" were included all the U.S. branch banks then established in London.[177]

173. In Great Britain the terms "foreign branch" and "overseas branch" are used to refer to the domestic office or branch of a British bank which handles that bank's foreign business. Here and elsewhere in this study the term "foreign branch bank" refers to a branch bank established abroad.

174. Great Britain, Exchange Control Act, 1947, 10 § 11 Geo. 6, chap. 14, § 1 (1).

175. Exchange Control Act, 1947, § 42 (1).

176. Great Britain, H. M. Treasury, Exchange Control (Authorised Dealers) Order, 1947, dated September 25, 1947, S.R. & O. 1947, no. 2071.

177. These were Bank of America, N.T. & S.A.; Bankers Trust Co.; Central Hanover Bank and Trust Co.; Chase National Bank of the City of New York; Guaranty Trust Co. of New York; and National City Bank of New York. The order listed six French branch banks: Banque de l'Indochine; British and French Bank (for Commerce and Industry), Ltd.; Comptoir National d'Escompte de Paris; Crédit

Any U.S. branch bank established after this first order receives a letter from the Bank of England allowing operations on a provisional basis for a six month period, during which it is neither an authorized dealer nor bank for exchange control purposes. At the end of this provisional period it can apply for authorization. Upon the recommendation of the Bank of England, the Treasury will notify the branch bank by letter that it has been authorized and will set forth the limits within which it can take a position in foreign exchange. Beyond these limits the branch bank is required to cover its transactions in the forward market.[178]

In addition to designating "authorised dealers" the Treasury also appoints certain banks as agents for purposes of administering the Exchange Control Act, 1947, as well as the Notices and Orders which are issued pursuant thereto. This agency status is formalised periodically by general notices to banks and bankers that include, *inter alia,* a list of "authorised banks" that are expected to exercise the authority set forth in the general Notices. Typically this includes blanket approval or disapproval of certain types of requests from banks' customers for foreign exchange. In the event of other types of requests, the "authorised banks" seek permission from the Bank of England, acting on behalf of their customers. The same U.S. branch banks that have been designated "authorised dealers" have been made "authorised banks" as well.[179]

c. *Switzerland*

(1) Banking Sector

(a) Banks
The principal legislation affecting banking operations in Switzerland is the Federal Banking Law of November 8, 1934, as amended by the

---

Foncier d'Algérie et de Tunisie; Crédit Lyonnais; and Société Générale. One Swiss branch bank was included, namely the Swiss Bank Corporation. In 1968 the list of "authorised dealers in gold and in all foreign currencies and authorised depositaries" included the London branches of all the U.S. commercial banks listed at p. 38. Exchange Control (Authorised Dealers and Depositaries) Order, 1968, dated October 14, 1968, S.I. 1968, no. 1634.

178. Another element important to a U.S. or other foreign branch bank in London is recognition by the Commissioners of Inland Revenue that it is carrying on a "bona fide banking business". This is accorded on the basis of its having demonstrated that it is equipped with the trained personnel and proper facilities for carrying on the banking business in Great Britain. Without this recognition it cannot receive interest gross on loans made to borrowers. Great Britain, Finance Act, 1965, 13 & 14 Eliz. 2, chap. 25, § 52 (3) (b).

179. See, for example, Bank of England, Exchange Control (General) Notice 1 (first issue), dated October 1, 1947, as amended to February 12, 1960.

Federal Law of March 11, 1971, which entered into force on July 1, 1971.[180] The 1934 Law was enacted primarily as a result of the banking crises and general economic deterioration in Europe in the early 1930's, with "its main object not the supervising of the banks' credit activities but the protection of their creditors".[181] In addition to this law there are regulations issued by the Federal Council and ordinances laid down by the Federal Banking Commission.[182]

Neither the Federal Banking Law nor the regulations and ordinances define "bank".[183] Probably the most suitable working definition in the Swiss context is that an institution using the word "bank" in its name or which refers to its "banking" transactions is considered to be a bank and is treated as such.[184]

Unlike the case in France (until 1966), Great Britain, or the United States, banks in Switzerland are not strictly divided into categories determined by the field of activity in which they can legally operate. Although the Federal Banking Law distinguishes sharply between banks which solicit publicly for deposits and those which do not,[185] an aspect to which we shall return, there is no differentiation between commercial or deposit banks on the one hand and merchant or investment banks on the other. A bank is permitted to operate in both fields, and indeed can

180. Switzerland, Bundesgesetz über die Banken und Sparkassen, Loi fédérale sur les banques et les caisses d'épargne, Legge Federale sulle Banche e le Casse di Risparmio (referred to in the text as the Federal Banking Law), p. 23, note 8.

181. Bank for International Settlements, *Eight European Central Banks,* p. 61, note 139, at p. 287.

182. Earlier in the present Chapter when dealing with the French banking sector it seemed preferable in certain instances to use the French language terminology to avoid possible confusion arising from similar expressions which refer to different concepts or institutions. The choice was further motivated by the fact that in many instances there is no generally acknowledged English language equivalent. In the case of Switzerland, however, one encounters concepts, laws, institutions, and practices in German, French, and Italian, the three official Swiss languages. Fortunately there are commonly accepted English language names and terms for many of these, usually coined or adopted by Swiss institutions themselves in publications or reports destined for persons unfamiliar with the Swiss terminology. Accordingly, we shall use these English language terms wherever possible in the text of this study. In footnotes the native names in German, French, and Italian will be given where greater precision might be of possible assistance to researchers or others interested in this field. In the present case, the Swiss Federal Council is the Bundesrat, Conseil Fédéral, and Consiglio Federale. The Federal Banking Commission is the Eidgenössische Bankencommission, Commission Fédérale des Banques, and Commissione Federale per le Banche.

183. See Robert Reimann, *Kommentar zum Bundesgesetz über die Banken und Sparkassen vom 8. November 1934,* Zurich, Polygraphischer Verlag, 1963, p. 17.

184. In Switzerland there are also "bank-type" institutions which are treated in many respects like banks if they perform certain operations.

185. Federal Banking Law of 1934, as amended, art. 1.

carry on many other activities including stock brokerage and investment company operations. In fact, it is in Switzerland that the U.S. branch banks have encountered the nearest equivalent to "universal banking".[186] Accordingly, it is more meaningful to classify the various Swiss banks by a variety of indices, including their size, origin, main interests, and geographical areas of operation.

The principal categories of banks in Switzerland are:

a. *"big banks"*, which are five institutions so-called collectively because of their size and scope of operations. The Swiss "big banks" most nearly resemble the British clearing banks, the large French *banques de dépôts,* and the major U.S. commercial banks. As listed by the central bank they are the Swiss Bank Corporation,[187] the Swiss Popular Bank,[188] the Bank Leu & Co.,[189] the Union Bank of Switzerland,[190] and the Swiss Credit Bank.[191] Their combined deposits on June 30, 1971 totalled SF 56.4 billion (approx. $13.8 billion),[192] accounting for about half of the published deposits in banks in Switzerland.[193] This figure does not include the extremely large (SF 4.3 billion = approx. $1.1 bil-

186. Some commercial banks in the United States, particularly when numerous one-bank holding companies were being formed in the late 1960's, have aimed at a similar concept sometimes popularly referred to as "department store banking". The latter is essentially oriented towards the retail banking sector, however, and does not include investment banking or underwriting activities, which form an important part of many Swiss banks' operations, nor does it include brokerage activities conducted by the Swiss banks.

187. Schweizerischer Bankverein, Société de Banque Suisse, Società di Banca Svizzera.

188. Schweizerische Volksbank, Banque Populaire Suisse, Banca Popolare Svizzera.

189. Bank Leu & Co., A.G., Banque Leu & Cie S.A., Banca Leu e Cia, whose operations are principally concentrated in and around Zurich.

190. Schweizerische Bankgesellschaft, Union de Banques Suisses, Unione di Banche Svizzere.

191. Schweizerische Kreditanstalt, Crédit Suisse, Credito Svizzero.

192. With the dollar equivalent calculated at the rate of exchange then prevailing, i.e., SF 4.08 = $1. As of May 10, 1971 the Swiss National Bank modified the gold content of the franc so as to revalue it with respect to the dollar from the former rate of SF 4.37 = $1. After August 15, 1971 the rate "floated" even further away from the former parity. Accordingly, Swiss franc amounts that are not keyed to a date (for instance, those contained in various statutory and regulatory articles) are approximated to the dollar at an arbitrary rate of SF 4 = $1.

193. Computed from data contained at Swiss National Bank, 46 (9) *Monatsbericht-Bulletin mensuel* 52-53 (Sept. 1971). If *Kassenobligationen/Kassenscheine* or bonds and *bons de caisse* are included (see p. 95, note 29), their "deposits" would have amounted to SF 63.4 billion. Size alone is not a reliable criterion for classifying the banks in Switzerland. Three of the five banks mentioned are much larger than the other two. Thus, it might be more appropriate to speak of the "Big Three" in practice. Nevertheless, the five "big banks" are usually grouped together.

lion) amounts held by the "big banks" in a fiduciary capacity, which were not required to be made public before the end of 1970.

Unlike the cantonal banks and local joint-stock banks, four of the five "big banks" have networks of branches and agencies spread throughout the entire—albeit small—country. In fact, although the single head office of each is quite definitely its headquarters, the principal branches established in the other Swiss financial centers exercise a remarkable degree of autonomy. Partly the explanation for this lies in the historical evolution of these institutions; and to some extent it reflects the different regional identities found in Switzerland, made apparent in the different cultures and the languages spoken there. In a great many instances, though, this quasi-autonomy results from the different emphasis on various types of banking operations in the three financial centers: Basle, Geneva and Zurich.

b. *cantonal banks,* comprising those created by decrees of the various Swiss cantons or states and having their liabilities backed by the cantonal credit, and those not having an official cantonal guarantee but which have the majority of their directors appointed by the canton. There are 28 cantonal banks, which held SF 28.7 billion (approx. $7.0 billion) on deposit at the end of June 1971.[194] In addition to acting as the cantons' financial institutions these banks have come to operate in nearly all the sectors of banking, from small and medium-sized commercial loans through sizeable credits to larger (usually local) firms and the underwriting of bond issues. There exists an association or union of Swiss Cantonal Banks "to preserve the interests of the cantonal banks within the banking system and in particular to undertake the joint underwriting of new issues".[195]

c. *local joint-stock banks,* which are similar to the Swiss "big banks" in their wide range of operations but are much smaller and concentrate their activities in one city or canton, having few if any branches. Although these banks take deposits and lend mainly to local individuals and business firms, in 1964 they formed an association to facilitate borrowing in the new issue market.

d. *private banks,* which are not organized on a limited liability ba-

---

194. *Ibid.* With the *Kassenobligationen/Kassenscheine* or bonds and *bons de caisse* included the cantonal banks' "deposits" would have stood at SF 37.1 billion. One of the Cantonal Banks (of Bern) has joined with the five "big banks" and the Groupement de Banquiers Privés Genevois (see note 196, *infra*) in the Swiss Bank Cartel, which is essentially a permanent syndicate for underwriting securities issues. It is noteworthy that, another Cantonal Bank (of Zurich) is large enough to rank among the "big banks" in Switzerland.

195. Max Oetterli, First Secretary of the Swiss Bankers' Association, "The History, Structure and Function of Banking in Switzerland", (speech delivered at the Volkshochschule, Zurich, April 25, 1968), p. 3.

sis but rather as partnerships or more rarely as individual proprietorships, meaning that the bankers themselves are fully liable to the extent of their own individual fortunes for the liabilities of their banks. Although in the past the private banks tended to engage in a wide range of operations, since the beginning of the postwar period most of them have come to concentrate on managing their Swiss and foreign customers' large securities portfolios. In the late 1960's, however, a few of the more imaginative Swiss private banks began to experiment with new types of activities, including portfolio advisory services for investment companies and searching for Swiss and foreign venture capital placement opportunities not unlike those normally associated with British merchant banks. There is an Association of Swiss Private Bankers, the principal members being situated in Basle, Bern, Geneva,[196] and Zurich.[197]

e. *foreign-controlled banking institutions,* including branches and subsidiaries of banks established abroad as well as banks chartered under Swiss law but controlled by non-Swiss interests. In addition to those in the three main banking centers there are foreign-controlled banking institutions of some importance in Lausanne and Lugano. At the end of 1969 there were 76 foreign-controlled banks and banking subsidiaries and 11 foreign branch banks operating in Switzerland.[198]

In addition to the various categories identified above there are other types of banks in Switzerland. These include the savings banks,[199] which are scattered throughout Switzerland and whose passbook accounts are guaranteed up to the first SF 5,000 (approx. $1,250) in the case of bank

196. In 1931 seven private banks in Geneva formed the Groupement des Banquiers Privés Genevois. They are: Bordier & Cie, Darier & Cie, Ferrier, Lullin & Cie, Hentsch & Cie, Lombard, Odier & Cie, Mirabaud & Cie, and Pictet & Cie. The Groupement acts as a single unit in underwriting securities issues. In addition to the seven original banks it now includes De l'Harpe, Leclerc & Cie.

197. These include Julius Bär & Co., Orelli im Thalhof, Rahn & Bodmer, and J. Vontobel & Co. In 1962 three private banks in Zurich and one in St. Gallen (Wegelin & Co.) formed a group similar to the one in Geneva.

198. Swiss National Bank, Mitteilungen der Volkswirtschaftlichen und Statistischen Abteilung der Schweizerischen Nationalbank, *Das schweizerische Bankwesen im Jahre 1969,* vol. 54, Zurich, Orell Füssli, 1970, pp. 103-105, where it is indicated that the balance sheet figures for these 87 institutions represented over 10% of the total for the 486 institutions included in the annual statistics prepared by the central bank. By the end of 1970 it was reported that there were 88 foreign-controlled banks and banking subsidiaries and 13 foreign branch banks in the country.

199. *Sparkassen, caisses d'épargne, Casse di risparmio.* Only banks publishing their accounts annually can maintain "savings" accounts or use the word "savings" in their name or in reference to their facilities. Federal Banking Law of 1934, a amended, page 72, note 180, art. 15. Special treatment is provided for savings accounts. Switzerland, Federal Council, Regulation of August 30, 1961, *Recueil officiel suisse* 1961, vol. 2, pp. 703-24, arts. 26 and 27.

failure. There are also the Raiffeisen banks, which are very small co-operative credit institutions located throughout the country, operating much like credit unions in the United States. In addition there are important non-bank financial holding companies and the major insurance companies.

Finally, mention must be made of the Swiss postal giro system, which handles a large part of the payments made by individuals for goods and services. Although most Swiss banks provide (and in the past few years have encouraged) checking accounts for their individual depositors, the use of personal checks is still rather uncommon, due partly to the widespread use of banknotes but principally to this efficient postal giro mechanism, the deposits of which totalled SF 5.2 billion (approx. $1.3 billion) at the end of June 1971.[200]

The closest Swiss counterpart to the major U.S. commercial banks are the three largest of the "big banks", the Swiss Bank Corporation, the Swiss Credit Bank, and the Union Bank of Switzerland. Structurally and operationally these are very nearly universal banks, since except for British-style merchant banking they directly carry out nearly every imaginable type of banking transaction. They provide the wide range of services normally offered by U.S. commercial banks, such as checking and savings accounts, consumer credit or hire-purchase loans, realty mortgages, and safety deposit facilities. In addition, these banks hold seats on the Swiss stock exchanges and buy and sell securities for their own accounts as well as for their customers. They engage in stock and bond underwritings (both Swiss and foreign), handle transactions in gold coin and bullion, buy and sell foreign (including forward) exchange, and through subsidiaries conduct open-end investment company operations similar to the mutual funds in the United States and the unit trusts in Great Britain.

Thus, whereas in each of the French and British banking sectors there is a legal category of bank which most closely resembles the major U.S. commercial banks, the Swiss counterpart is not a type of institution as such. More precisely, it is that portion of the three largest banks' operations conducted in the commercial banking sector.

Before turning to the regulatory mechanism in Switzerland, two features of the Federal Banking Law merit particular attention. First, as stated earlier, a sharp distinction is made between those institutions which solicit publicly for deposits[201] and those which do not. The for-

---

200. Swiss National Bank, 46 (9) *Monatsbericht-Bulletin mensuel* 64 (Sept. 1971).
201. Institutions are deemed to solicit publicly for deposits, within the meaning of the Federal Banking Law, when "either in the press, by advertisements circulated to persons other than their customers, or by other methods of publicity they make it known to the public at large, in show windows or anywhere outside their own prem-

mer cannot be established without prior authorization from the Federal Banking Commission, and are required to file their articles of incorporation or the equivalent with that body.[202] They must maintain minimum liquidity ratios and certain reserves,[203] and are obliged to file and publish periodic statements of condition[204] as well as submit to regular audits.[205]

Institutions in Switzerland which do not appeal to the general public for funds are subject to only two provisions of the Federal Banking Law.[206] They are required to file a confidential statement of condition annually with the central bank,[207] and they must give it advance notice when planning certain investment or lending operations abroad amounting to SF 10 million (approx. $2.5 million) or more.[208] Most of the private banks do not solicit publicly for deposits and comprise the principal group of banks directly affected by this aspect of the law.[209]

The other noteworthy feature of the Federal Banking Law is the provision with regard to the banking secret. As the banking systems of most countries provide for greater or lesser degrees of discretion concerning individual customers' transactions, the banking secret is not a peculiarly Swiss device. In fact, the Federal Banking Law does not define the na-

---

ises, that they accept funds for deposit". Federal Council, Regulation of August 30, 1961, art. 3, repeating the Regulation of February 26, 1935, art. 3, which it replaced. (Translation supplied.)

202. Federal Banking Law of 1934, as amended, art. 3.

203. Law, art. 4.

204. Law, art. 6.

205. Law, art. 18. The nature of the auditing procedure is spelled out, as are the responsibilities of the auditing firm and the bank whose books are under examination. Law, arts. 19-21. The auditing firms themselves are subject to the Federal Council Regulation of August 30, 1961 (replacing the Regulation of February 26, 1935) which sets forth the manner in which they are to be constituted (Regulation, arts. 29-36) and conducted, and gives the type of information which must be contained in the audit (Regulation, art. 37).

206. Federal Banking Law of 1934, as amended, art. 1 (a).

207. Law, art. 7.

208. Law, art. 8. This encompasses transactions such as lending to foreign borrowers, floating foreign stocks, or acquiring stock in foreign companies. If the central bank refuses permission, the contemplated foreign operation cannot be undertaken.

209. The private banks normally accept deposits only from customers "known to the bank". That is, a potential customer must be introduced personally by an already existing client or by another bank with which the private bank has a close correspondent relationship. Although some private banks provide checking accounts for their customers' convenience, small accounts are discouraged. It was reliably estimated by a private source in the mid-1960's that one of the larger private banks had about ten thousand customers, with an average current balance of SF 200,000 (approx. $50,000) per customer.

ture of the banking secret as such. In Switzerland it is actually considered to be an aspect of the professional secret generally, similar to that in the case of a lawyer, physician, or clergyman whose activities necessarily involve confidential contact with a client, patient, or parishioner. The precise nature of the particular banker-customer relationship in Switzerland depends upon the agreement or contact between them, within the ambits of Swiss law.

The unusual characteristic of the banking secret in Switzerland is that criminal penalties are set for its infraction. The Federal Banking Law provides that:

> Art. 47. "Whosoever, as an executive or official, employee, agent, liquidator, or auditor of a bank, as an observer on behalf of the Federal Banking Commission, or as a member or employee of an authorized auditing firm, shall divulge any secret confided in him or that he may know by virtue of his position or employment; or whosoever shall incite another to violate the professional secret, shall be punished by not more than six months' imprisonment or by a fine not to exceed SF 50,000. If the individual in question has acted through negligence the penalty shall be a fine not to exceed SF 30,000. The violation of the secret shall continue to be punishable after the position has been discharged or the employment terminated, or after the individual in question no longer practices his profession. *Provided,* that federal and cantonal legislation concerning information to be supplied to the competent authorities and concerning testimony in the judicial process shall not be affected by the foregoing."[210]

The banking secret is not absolutely inviolate, since under certain circumstances a Swiss court order can be obtained requiring that a bank divulge particular types of information. In the ordinary course of affairs, however, the secret remains intact, even with respect to the Swiss fiscal authorities themselves, as a matter of public policy.[211] Needless to say,

210. Federal Banking Law of 1934, as amended, art. 47 (Translation supplied). It should be noted that the Law contains a number of other provisions relating to different aspects of the banking secret.

211. The Swiss banking secret has occasionally attracted considerable attention in the United States and elsewhere, and has led to U.S. efforts to conclude a treaty with Switzerland which would allow access to information relating to the accounts of certain persons including allegedly delinquent U.S. taxpayers and purchasers of U.S. securities on insufficient margin as well as international criminal interests. It was reported in October 1971 that the two parties had arrived at a draft text for an agreement aimed at Swiss accounts of persons engaged in "organized crime" but without any provision for the other U.S. aims. The Swiss banking secret has also lain behind the attempts of some U.S. legislators (notably Representative Wright Patman, Chairman of the House Banking and Currency Committee) to require *inter alia* that American banks and others report all inward and outward foreign financial transfers over a certain minimum amount. See United States, Congress, House of Representatives, Banking and Currency Committee, *Report* no. 91-975, 91st Cong., 2d. Sess., March 28, 1970, on H.R. 15073 (Currency and Foreign Transactions Reporting Act, Pub. Law 91-508), section dealing with Foreign Transactions; and 9 *International Legal Materials* 583 (1970). See also p. 181, note 119.

there does not exist in Switzerland any counterpart to the Service Central des Risques in France; nor as one author has pointed out, is there any "closely-knit" system of credit checks as known in the United States.[212]

An ancillary device sometimes used by Swiss banks is the numbered account, where only a few (usually senior) individuals in a bank know the identity of a particular customer, whose account simply bears a number or other coded designation. This practice is not designed to provide any additional privacy with respect to the authorities, or general public, but rather to reduce exposure to the minimum extent feasible. Of course, handling a great many accounts in this manner would be a cumbersome operation; but numbered accounts are provided where the situation appears to require this special treatment.[213]

(b) Regulatory Institutions and Bodies

Banking activities in Switzerland come under the regulatory authority of three bodies—two official and one unofficial.

The first body is the Swiss National Bank,[214] with its administrative headquarters in the capital city of Bern and its principal operating seat in Zurich. Branches are located in Basle, Geneva, and six other Swiss cities. The National Bank is chartered as a joint-stock bank with over half of the shares held by the cantonal governments or cantonal banks, the remainder being widely held by private shareholders. Although the Swiss federal government does not own any stock of the National Bank, the Federal Council appoints 25 of the 40 members of the Bank's Governing Council, including the two senior officers.

The National Bank has a monopoly of the banknote issue, which by law must be covered by at least 40% in gold which remains inside the country.[215] In return for the note issue monopoly the National Bank pays the cantons a small annual stipend for each inhabitant.

212. H. J. Bär, *The Banking System of Switzerland*, 2d. rev. ed., Zurich, 1957, p. 51.

213. For a clear account of certain legal implications of the Swiss banking secret see two articles by Maurice Aubert, "Secret et responsabilité des banques suisses envers les héritiers", [Swiss] *Semaine Judiciaire*, no. 39, pp. 1-46, (Dec. 1964) and "Portée du secret des banques envers le pouvoir judiciaire", *Id.*, no. 39, pp. 609-52 (Dec. 1967).

214. Schweizerische Nationalbank, Banque Nationale Suisse, Banca Nationale Svizzera. Organized in 1905 and put into operation in 1907. The present legislation in force is the National Bank Law of December 23, 1953, *Recueil officiel suisse 1954*, pp. 613-32. An English language translation of this law is found at International Monetary Fund, *Central Banking Legislation*, 1967, vol. 2, p. 50, note 92, at pp. 705-23.

215. National Bank Law, art. 19 (2). In practice the gold cover has been maintained at a level well above the legal minimum. For instance, at the end of 1969 the gold cover represented 91% of the currency in circulation. Switzerland, Herausge-

Most of the usual central bank regulatory tools are unavailable in Switzerland. Although from time to time the banks voluntarily agree to deposit or otherwise place funds with the National Bank, a subject to which we shall return, there are no legally required minimum reserves. Also, rediscounting with the National Bank is a rare practice in Swit-- zerland although the central bank legally can serve as a lender-of-last-resort on bills with two good signatures and maturing within 3 months.[216] Partly this is because in normal times Swiss banks generally are very liquid, a reflection of the high degree of savings in the country as well as the presence of non-residents' funds on deposit despite the lower rates of interest paid in Switzerland compared with other countries. There is another reason, too, for the relative infrequency of rediscounting. This stems from the banks' preference for borrowing elsewhere—particularly from other banks—when temporarily short of funds rather than borrowing at the central bank. Accordingly a change in the rediscount rate does not have the effect that it does in the other two host countries or in the United States.[217] When they do borrow at the National Bank, Swiss banks normally use so-called "Lombard advances" against collateral security.[218]

Another factor in Switzerland is the absence of short-term government debt, also a reflection of the public orientation towards thrift. This means that there is no basis for a well developed money market, and that central bank open market operations are not feasible.[219] For the most part, the National Bank has resorted to selling gold or foreign exchange to the banks when desirous of absorbing excess liquidity. It has also sold them medium-term bonds and then held the proceeds in operations known as "sterilizing rescriptions".[220]

---

geben vom Eidgenössischen Statistischen Amt, Bureau Fédéral de Statistique, *Statistisches Jahrbuch der Schweiz, Annuaire statistique de la Suisse,* Basle, Birkhäuser, 1970, p. 262.

216. National Bank Law, art. 14 (1). Rediscounting at the central bank would appear to have increased during the late 1960's. See *The Economist,* vol. 232, no. 6578 (September 20, 1969), p. 85. This was a reflection of the profitable rate arbitrage opportunities to be had in connection with the Euro-dollar market.

217. In his interesting work on Swiss monetary policy Tschopp deals with the relative absence of rediscounting in the context of attempts to check inflationary pressures from within and without. See Peter Tschopp, *Inflation et politique monétaire, le cas de la Suisse,* Geneva, Editions Générales S.A., 1967, pp. 176-77.

218. National Bank Law, *supra,* art. 14 (4). There is a "Lombard rate" set by the National Bank.

219. The situation was only slightly affected by a 1953 modification permitting otherwise eligible securities with maturities of two years or less to be included in the note coverage. National Bank Law, art. 19 (1).

220. For example, SF 400 million were so "sterilized" in 1960.

Unable to make full use of these tools—compulsory reserve requirements, changing the rediscount rate, and open market operations—the Swiss National Bank relies on a fourth device which is also utilized extensively by the Bank of England: moral suasion. Before this method can be seen in context, however, two more regulatory bodies, one official and the other unofficial, must be identified.

The official body is the Federal Banking Commission, created by the Federal Banking Law[221] as the administrative agency in this field. The Commission is composed of from seven to nine members who are required to be experts in the field but who must at the same time be free of any ties with individual banks or auditing firms. The body reports to the Federal Council, which is responsible for its operations and for naming its members. The Commission decides whether institutions fall within the ambits of the Federal Banking Law,[222] and issues ordinances covering banking operations in Switzerland. The Commission can require that a bank auditor's report be turned over to it,[223] can impose administrative restrictions on a bank found to be operating irregularly,[224] and can assign an observer to the staff of a bank when serious irregularities threaten creditors' rights.[225] The powers and functions of the Federal Banking Commission were substantially augmented by the 1971 amendment to the (1934) Federal Banking Law.

The third body, an unofficial organ, is the Swiss Bankers Association,[226] which was formed in Basle in 1912 "to preserve and represent the interests and rights of the Swiss banking industry, to protect the interests of its members against unfair competition and to safeguard Swiss savings capital, especially investments in securities".[227]

Its membership comprises both individuals and institutions, and covers all the types of banks named in the preceding section as well as other types of financial institutions including stock brokerages, holding companies, and investment companies. The Swiss Bankers Association is instrumental in acting as the banks' spokesman with regard to legislation under consideration in the Federal Parliament or when voluntary restraints are being arranged with the National Bank.

It is now in order to return to the question of moral suasion, the most

---

221. Federal Banking Law of 1934, as amended, p. 72, note 180, arts. 23-24.
222. Switzerland, Federal Council, Regulation of August 30, 1961, p. 75, note 199, art. 4 (1) (a).
223. Federal Banking Law of 1934, as amended, art. 23bis.
224. Law, art. 23ter.
225. Law, art. 23quater.
226. Schweizerische Bankvereinigung, Association Suisse des Banquiers, Associazione Svizzera dei Banchieri.
227. Oetterli, p. 74, note 195, at p. 6.

effective regulatory device in the Swiss banking sector. In the words of two authorities:

> "Thus the Swiss appear to have found a means of exercising some control over monetary conditions in spite of the weakness of the legal framework. This way of doing things appeals to a country where governmental intervention in economic affairs is generally disliked and, as long as the commercial bankers are satisfied that voluntary co-operation is reasonably consistent with their own long-term interest, no doubt the Swiss will be able to enjoy some of the fruits of intervention while preserving the appearance of non-intervention."[228]

Moral suasion largely takes the form of gentlemen's agreements between the banks, acting through the Association, and the National Bank. The first such agreement dated from 1927 and provided that the banks would notify the National Bank when placing a foreign loan.[229] Other similar agreements followed during the 1930's covering matters such as interest rates, mortgage foreclosures, foreign-held Swiss franc accounts, and steps to thwart banknote hoarding. During World War II dollar and gold transactions were similarly regulated, as were construction credit and foreign-held funds in the postwar years.[230] Of more recent vintage, on June 15, 1955 a gentlemen's agreement between the banks and the Swiss National Bank went into effect, whereby banks with assets over SF 50 million placed $3^1/_2\%$ of their liquid assets ($2^1/_2\%$ in the case of private banks) in blocked accounts at the central bank.[231] There was a similar agreement in March 1961.[232]

Seen out of context these voluntary restraints might appear benign, especially when viewed from abroad. In fact, the gentlemen's agreements can be quite strict.[233] Moreover, they are made between persons living in a small country where, as in the City of London, most of the principals directly know—or know of—one another and share a common sense of responsibility. This is especially striking when strictly commercial considerations are subordinated to something in the nature of a civic obligation.

This is partially due to the fact that unlike the banking industry in most countries, banks in Switzerland comprise more than a service or ancillary sector functioning as an accessory to commerce or industry. In fact, banking in Switzerland is a major industry, contributing appre-

228. Sayers and Linder, *infra*, pp. 195-96.
229. Bank for International Settlements, *Eight European Central Banks,* p. 61, note 139, at p. 297.
230. *Id.,* p. 298.
231. See New York Times, May 30, 1955, p. 17, col. 2 (late city edition).
232. See Richard Sidney Sayers and W. Linder, "Switzerland" in R.S. Sayers (ed.), *Banking in Western Europe,* p. 56, note 119, at p. 196.
233. See for example pp. 212-13 and 249-50. Some question may be raised as to how well these agreements would work if participants' profits were seriously squeezed.

ciably to the country's foreign revenues. Thus, any civic feeling for the commonweal is weighted by the knowledge that the effect of a voluntary restraint will not be slight.

Another important factor, however, is that these gentlemen's agreements are set in a political and social climate where abuse would surely increase demands for more direct controls over the banking industry. Indeed, such sentiments are sometimes aired; and legislative steps were initiated in the mid-1960's to accord greater regulatory powers to the National Bank.[234] The participants in the gentlemen's agreements are not unaware of the need to avoid actions that might unduly upset the *status quo*.[235]

(2) Establishment of a U.S. Branch Bank in Switzerland

The Federal Banking Law is specifically applicable to Swiss branches of foreign banks.[236] Through 1967 an ordinance of the Federal Banking Commission issued in 1936 required that special permission

234. In 1966 a proposal was made for an "Instrumentarium" to give the National Bank additional powers. These included the possibility of open market operations through the sale and repurchase of the Bank's own certificates of deposit (the need for which has given rise to little dispute, although the Swiss banks' liquidity would present a stiff challenge to the central bank if mopping-up operations were used), the requirement of minimum legal reserves (which the banks have been willing to accept if the amount is set on increases in their liabilities from a base period and not on their global balance sheet figures), and the power to set limits on credit expansion (to which the banks are firmly opposed). The issues were debated in the Federal Parliament and discussed in the national press, and were the object of a study by a special commission. This resulted in a decision to shelve the proposed legislation in favor of a new gentlemen's agreement between the banks and the central bank, which became effective on September 1, 1969. This convention deals only with minimum reserves and credit ceilings because it was decided that a broader interpretation of existing law already permits open market operations. The Swiss Bankers Association invited all banks with balance sheets exceeding SF 20 million (approx. $5 million) to join in; and most of them have done so. For an interesting appraisal of this "supergentlemen's agreement", as he calls it, see René Erbe, "Instruments of Monetary Policy in Switzerland", 5 *Journal of World Trade Law* 209-14 (1971).

235. For a more complete description of the Swiss banking sector see "Le franc suisse et la politique monétaire et financière de la Suisse depuis 1960", [French] *Notes et Etudes Documentaires,* September 5, 1966, pp. 1-37 (Paris); and Reimann, p. 72, note 183. Useful English language works are Hans Bär, *The Banking System of Switzerland,* 3d. rev. ed., Zurich, Buchdr. Schulthess, 1964; Eugen Grossmann, "Switzerland" *in* Beckhart (ed.), *Banking Systems,* p. 52, note 104, at pp. 693-732; and Sayers and Linder, *supra,* pp. 174-196. A more recent book, unfortunately encumbered with factual inaccuracies, is T. R. Fehrenbach, *The Swiss Banks,* New York, McGraw-Hill, 1966 (later republished in London under another title and subsequently translated into French), a review of which is found at 53 *American Bar Association Journal* 555-56 (June 1967).

236. Federal Banking Law of 1934, as amended, *supra,* art. 2.

to establish a branch bank be obtained from the Commission, with which the head office bank's by-laws and most recent balance sheet had to be submitted.[237] In January 1968 the Commission replaced this with a new ordinance requiring any foreign bank seeking to establish a Swiss branch to file its request with the Commission, for transmittal (along with the Commission's recommendation) via the Federal Department of Finances and Customs to the Federal Council, for the grant or denial of the requisite permission.[238]

Until the 1971 amendment to the (1934) Federal Banking Law provision was made for the Federal Council to require that the home country of the head office bank, i.e., the United States, reciprocally permit Swiss banks to establish branches there. Under the Law as amended in 1971 this reciprocity must be guaranteed by the government of the foreign country in question or by the foreign interests seeking to establish the Swiss branch.[239] The U.S. branch bank in Switzerland must be enrolled in the Commercial Register maintained by the local cantonal authorities,[240] similar to the case in France. The individual in charge of the branch bank is not required to be a Swiss national, but he must be domiciled in Switzerland and is required to have full authority to represent the head office bank.[241] No special permission is needed to deal in foreign exchange.

As in France and Great Britain, once established the U.S. branch bank is treated in most respects as a Swiss-chartered bank even though for corporate law purposes it is a branch and not a subsidiary. A separate set of books must be kept showing the branch bank's operations and submitted along with the head office bank's global figures to the Federal Banking Commission.[242] Its records are audited like those of any

237. Switzerland, Federal Banking Commission, Ordinance of February 15, 1936, p. 23, note 8, art. 3 (2).
238. Switzerland, Federal Banking Commission, Ordinance of January 18, 1968, p. 23, note 8, arts. 2 (3) and 3 (1). Additional information requirements were added by the new Ordinance.
239. Federal Banking Law of 1934, as amended, art. 3 bis (a).
240. Ordinance of February 15, 1936, art. 3 (2), replaced by Ordinance of January 18, 1968, art. 7. It should be noted that the local cantonal authorities are in a position to influence considerably the establishment of a foreign branch bank (or any institution likely to request permission to employ at least some non-Swiss personnel) by virtue of their power to issue residence and work permits.
241. Ordinance of February 15, 1936, art. 3 (1), replaced by Ordinance of January 18, 1968, art. 8. Cf. United States, Department of Commerce, Bureau of Foreign Commerce, *World Trade Information Service*, "Establishing a Business in Switzerland", Washington, 1959, p. 7.
242. Ordinance of February 15, 1936, art. 6 (1) (a) and (b), replaced by Ordinance of January 18, 1968, art. 10 (1) and (2). The new Ordinance provides that the individual foreign branch bank's figures do not have to be made public unless it provides savings account facilities for its customers. Ordinance, art. 10 (3).

84

bank in Switzerland.[243] The requirements as to capital reserves and liquidity[244] applicable to all banks apply to the branch bank. It must submit its balance sheet annually to the National Bank[245] and notify it in advance of any foreign (i.e., outside Switzerland) credit or loan operations exceeding SF 10 million (approx. $2.5 million) and underwriting or private placement operations exceeding one year.[246]

If the foregoing seems less involved than in Great Britain, and much less so than in France, one must take into account that until mid-1971 the legal requirements for establishing a bank in Switzerland (as opposed to the Swiss branch of a bank chartered abroad) were even less stringent.[247] Nonetheless, to establish a bank in Switzerland, there is still no obligation to show an economic necessity; nor does the management of a proposed bank have to prove that it possesses the necessary skills for conducting a banking operation, although the 1971 amendment to the (1934) Federal Banking Law now provides that the individuals responsible for a bank's management must have a sound reputation and must be able to guarantee their conduct.[248] During the period from mid-1945 until early 1969 foreigners wanting to establish a bank in Switzerland had only to meet the same formal requirements as Swiss nationals.[249]

243. Ordinance of February 15, 1936, art. 10 (1), replaced by Ordinance of January 18, 1968, art. 5 (1).

244. Federal Banking Law of 1934, as amended, arts. 2 and 4. Federal Council Regulation of August 30, 1961, p. 75, note 199, arts. 9-17.

245. Law, art. 7.

246. Law, art. 8.

247. When the Swiss government proposed stricter rules for the supervision of foreign-controlled banks in 1968, one member of the Federal Banking Commission was reported to have said that "up to now, it has been easier to start a bank in Switzerland than a cafe". International Herald Tribune (Paris), November 28, 1968, p. 9, col. 4.

248. Federal Banking Law of 1934, as amended, art. 3 (c).

249. On March 21, 1969, the Federal Council issued a Decree tightening the requirements for establishing foreign-controlled (defined as over 50% foreign participation) banks or banking subsidiaries effective for three years beginning July 1, 1969. *Recueil officiel suisse* 1969, pp. 450-52. *Cf.* I.M.F., *(Twenty-first) Exchange Restrictions*, 1970, p. 464. As a result, applicants were required to obtain permission from the Federal Banking Commission (as was already the case of foreign banks seeking to establish branches in Switzerland). A newly-established foreign-controlled bank or subsidiary had to undertake to abide by Swiss credit and monetary policies, and could not advertise, inside or outside Switzerland, in such a way as to emphasize or exploit its "Swiss" character. These last two requirements were largely the result of a growing uneasiness on the part of many Swiss lawmakers and bankers that the community of interests underlying the gentlemen's agreements might not be shared by many of the newcomers. *Cf.* Max Oetterli, "The New Legislation on Foreign Banks in Switzerland", 120 *The Banker* 78-81 (1970). The 1971 amendment to the (1934) Federal Banking Law incorporated these two provisions of the Federal Council Decree of March 21, 1969, as article 3 bis (b) and (c). Some stricter ele-

Another important factor is the absence of any foreign exchange regulations similar to those in France and Great Britain. As we shall see, this has made operating conditions in Switzerland fundamentally different from those in the other two host countries. In the present context, however, that of establishing the branch bank, it simply means that a horde of formal regulations and a complicated administrative apparatus do not exist.

---

ments proposed in this context were not included in the 1969 Decree or in the 1971 legislation. One of these would have set the foreign participation level at 20%. Another would have obliged all foreign-controlled banks established within the previous ten years, as well as newcomers, to indicate in their name and in printed materials their non-Swiss character. On April 20, 1970 the Federal Banking Commission issued a circular letter interpreting the law as requiring a foreign bank already having a Swiss branch to obtain permission before opening additional branches.

Chapter Three

"HOST CURRENCY DEPOSIT AND LENDING OPERATIONS:
MID-1945 THROUGH 1958"

I. TAKING HOST CURRENCY DEPOSITS

A. *Need for Acquiring Host Currency Deposits*

In this study we are dealing with foreign branches of commercial banks, whose own funds represent only a part of those available for advances to customers. Unlike investment banks or merchant banks, which are in a position to lend relatively large amounts of their own capital or that of their wealthy private or institutional clients, the bulk of commercial banks' supply of lendable funds consists of customers' deposits, of money obtained temporarily from other sources, or from the monetization of credit. Perhaps it is appropriate to review several fundamental technical principles at this point before turning to the operations of the U.S. branch banks in the host countries.

1. *Importance of Primary Deposits Generally*

A commercial bank can lend three types of funds. First, it can lend its own funds to the extent permitted by law or by its own internal statutes, drawing from any capital surplus that may have been earned or contributed by the bank's owners.

Second, a commercial bank can lend the funds arising out of checks and currency brought in for deposit. Such deposits are termed "primary deposits". Here the commercial bank acts as an intermediary between those individuals and institutions having excess funds and those needing credit. The bank's margin of gross profit is represented by the difference between the rate of interest paid, if any, on the depositors' funds and that charged to the borrowers of these funds.

Monetizing credit, the third type of commercial bank lending, consists of crediting to borrowers' current accounts[1] the amounts which they have borrowed, and allowing them to draw upon these accounts. Known

1. Not to their time deposit accounts.

as "derivative deposits" and conceptually quite different from the primary deposits described above,[2] these amounts are not segregated on the bank's balance sheet. The apparent creation of money from the lending operation is not, however, without limits. The necessity to maintain a certain level of reserves against depositors' withdrawals is an initial limitation. More important is the reserve ratio that the bank may be required to maintain by law or by local banking convention.[3]

In addition to augmenting its total supply of lendable funds by one of the three methods described above, a commercial bank may find it necessary upon occasion to increase the liquidity of its assets. In this event it may, if eligible, elect to borrow from the central bank or in the money market, depending upon the facilities available in the particular system. Such borrowing may allow the bank to earn a profit by re-lending the borrowed funds to a customer, but it will not increase its ability to create deposits, for the bank has incurred a debt while acquiring its borrowing customer's equivalent obligation. As an alternative the bank may also choose to rediscount its paper at the central bank or elsewhere when in need of liquid funds.[4] Here again, since it has replaced one asset by another, there will be an increase in its ability to create deposits only to the extent that the newly acquired asset is retained as non-earning reserves.

In banking systems where overdraft lending is practiced the necessity to maintain reserves against customers' potential withdrawals requires that primary deposits be acquired. Repayment of overdrawn funds will not increase reserves so as to allow the creation of additional deposits

2. "The distinction between primary and derivative deposits is of great importance in considering the effect of banking operations on the total money supply. The deposit of checks serves merely to transfer demand deposits from one bank to another or from one account to another and does not alter the total. When deposits are created through the exchange of currency for demand deposits there is an expansion of deposits but this is accompanied by an equivalent reduction in the amount of currency at the disposal of the public. The effect is to exchange one type of circulating medium, currency, for another, demand deposits, but not to increase the total volume of circulating medium. The creation of derivative deposits, on the other hand, constitutes an increase in the total circulating medium." Charles R. Whittlesey, *Principles and Practices of Money & Banking,* New York, The Macmillan Company, 1948, p. 109.

3. "The role of reserves in limiting the expansion of demand liabilities rests on the existence of a particular ratio of reserves to liabilities, and as long as that ratio is maintained it makes no difference whether it is established by law or by custom." *Id.,* p. 130.

4. In France and Great Britain the indigenous counterparts of U.S. commercial banks use different variations on this alternative. In Switzerland they are even more reluctant to follow this path than are commercial banks in the United States. But see page 80, note 216.

unless the repayment is accompanied by a simultaneous reduction of the amount of future overdraft privileges.

For the commercial bank, then, there can be no question as to the ultimate necessity to acquire primary deposits. The possibility of creating derivative deposits may appear to induce a great amount of leverage for the commercial bank; but internal drain[5] and the reserve factors are such that the vast majority of the lending operations in a banking system do not result in a change in the banks' overall total deposits.

2. Types of Host Currency Accounts

The U.S. branch banks, like the other banks in each of the host countries, take host currency funds for deposit into two basic types of account, a distinction being made as to the length of time during which the funds are expected to remain on deposit.

a. Current Account

The first type, sometimes referred to as a sight deposit, corresponds to what is known as a demand deposit in the U.S. federal banking law,[6] and includes the commercial accounts of business firms and institutional depositors generally as well as the checking accounts of individuals. In the host countries it is known variously as a current account, *compte à vue, compte courant, Sichtkonto, Kontokorrent, conto a vista,* or *conto corrente*. This category of account, hereafter referred to in the present study as a current account, is one where the depositor can demand full payment of the amount maintained in the account without giving prior notice to the bank.

Member banks and insured non-member banks in the United States are not permitted to pay interest on such accounts.[7] In the host countries the practice varies. In Switzerland the banks by general consensus pay a small rate of interest on such accounts whereas in France and Great Britain no interest is paid.[8]

---

5. That is, the drawing down of such deposits by checks made payable to payees maintaining accounts in other banks inside the country. External (as opposed to internal) drain occurs when such funds leave the banking system by departing from the country or when they are held in the form of bank notes.

6. See, for example, United States, Board of Governors of the Federal Reserve System, Regulation D, 12 C.F.R. § 204.1 (a).

7. United States, Board of Governors of the Federal Reserve System, Regulation Q, page 93, note 21. See also Federal Deposit Insurance Regulations, 12 C.F.R. § 329.2 (a) and (b).

8. See Great Britain, Central Office of Information, *The British Banking System,* page 64, note 150, at p. 31. Interest was paid in France until mid-1967.

b. *Time Deposit Account*

The second type of account resembles what the U.S. federal banking law refers to as a time deposit.[9] In the host countries it is known variously as a deposit account, *compte à échéance fixe, compte à terme, compte de dépôt, Zeitkonto, Depositenkonto,* or *conto depositato.* Hereinafter this second type of account will be referred to as a time deposit account.

Host currency time deposit accounts can be opened for varying periods in the host countries, with prior notice being required for withdrawal in some cases. For example, in Great Britain the sole type of time deposit account provides for seven days' notice. In France a depositor can arrange to "fix" a portion of the funds in a current account by agreeing not to draw the balance below a certain minimum level, on which amount the bank agrees to pay interest during a specified period. The "fixed" portion is voluntarily blocked, but can be released upon payment of a penalty charge set in accordance with a general instruction from the Conseil National de Crédit.[10] In France and Switzerland there is also an arrangement under which a customer places funds with a bank and is issued a type of cash voucher, which resembles to some extent the certificate of deposit used in the United States.[11]

As in the United States, interest is paid on time deposit accounts in the host countries. Until October 1, 1971 there was in Great Britain the "London Deposit Rate" (LDR) set at two points below Bank rate, which the clearing banks paid on all time deposit accounts by common consent.[12] Although one authority pointed to "the practice of London branches of leading foreign commercial banks to observe the rules of the gentlemen's agreement" with regard to deposit rates,[13] the LDR was "lower than the rate offered on foreign-owned [sterling] deposits by most of the overseas and foreign banks in London and the accepting houses".[14] Presumably a distinction has been made between foreign- and

---

9. See, for example, Regulation D, *supra,* 12 C.F.R. § 204.1 (b). In the United States, as in the host countries, savings deposits fall into this category, with special rules covering use of the word "savings". See for example page 75, note 199.

10. See J. S. G. Wilson, *French Banking Structure and Credit Policy,* page 56, note 119, at p. 56.

11. See page 95, note 29.

12. (Radcliffe) Committee, *Report,* Cmnd. 827, pp. 43-44, pars. 131-32. The LDR was abandoned as a result of the Bank of England's new policy on competition and credit control. See Bank of England, 11 *Quarterly Bulletin* 189-93 (1971).

13. Paul Einzig, "London", *in* Guenther Reimann and Edwin F. Wigglesworth (eds.), *The Challenge of International Finance,* New York, McGraw-Hill, 1966 p. 250.

14. "Inflows and Outflows of Foreign Funds", Bank of England, 2 *Quarterly Bulletin* 97 (1962).

British-owned deposits, for it has been indicated officially that the U.S. branch banks in London have been among those "able to compete for foreign-owned [sterling] deposits by offering generally higher rates than a foreign depositor is likely to get from a domestic bank".[15]

3. Importance of Host Currency Deposits (mid-1945 through 1958)

In a country where there exists no control of foreign exchange, or only a slight regulation thereof, banks as well as their customers can look beyond the national currency when seeking funds, being able to convert into and out of that currency without incurring penalties or expensive exchange charges and commissions. During the first thirteen and one-half years of the period under study no such freedom existed in France and Great Britain, where tightly conceived and administered schemes controlled the ownership, possession, and transfer of foreign exchange. Accordingly, the period from mid-1945 through 1958 was one in which the operations of the U.S. branch banks, like those of the indigenous and other foreign banks in the host countries, were necessarily circumscribed.

In essence, it was either impossible or very complicated for the locally resident company or individual to borrow foreign currency; and loans to non-residents were strictly supervised. A network of U.S. branch banks or other units operating abroad did not provide the advantages which have been present since 1959. There was, of course, during the earlier postwar period a pattern of overall direction, especially in the case of those U.S. banks with branches in several foreign countries. Moreover, each of the U.S. branch banks had—or appeared to have—behind it the resources, financial and otherwise, of the head office bank in the United States. There was not, however, the apparent integration of action that has marked the later operations of these branch banks, the representative offices, and the other elements of the major U.S. commercial banks' overseas networks in the years following the return to external convertibility of the principal Western European currencies.

Taking the foregoing into account, let us now turn to the first phase of the operations of the U.S. branch banks to be brought under study, namely the acquisition of host currency primary deposits during the period from mid-1945 to the end of 1958.

B. Legal Authority to Take Host Currency Deposits

In its operations a U.S. branch bank is subject to at least two sets of na-

---

15. *Id.*, p. 98. But see Bank of England, 6 *Quarterly Bulletin* 112 (1966).

tional laws, viz., those of the United States and those of the particular host country in which it is established.

1. *U.S. Law*

We have already seen that the establishment of the overseas branches of national banks is expressly permitted under Section 25 of the Federal Reserve Act of 1913, and that under Section 9 of that Act state member banks are placed on the same footing as national banks in this respect.[16] It has also been noted that under its power to issue regulations governing the conduct of these U.S. branch banks abroad, the Board of Governors of the Federal Reserve System was content until 1963 to deal only with the suspension of foreign branch operations during disturbed conditions,[17] and that it was not until 1964 that the Comptroller of the Currency issued the International Operations Regulation.[18] As a result, the U.S. branch banks cannot be said to have been hampered by U.S. federal laws or regulations in this respect.

A serious theoretical impediment for the U.S. branch banks would have been a prohibition of their payment of interest on demand deposits or a restriction of the rates of interest which they can pay on time deposit accounts. The Banking Act of 1933 added the following new paragraph to Section 19 of the Federal Reserve Act:

> "No member bank shall, directly or indirectly, by any device whatsoever, pay any interest on any deposit which is payable on demand: *Provided,* ... that this section shall not apply to any deposit of such bank which is payable only at an office thereof located outside of the States of the United States and the District of Columbia. . ."[19]

The Banking Act of 1933 also added a second new paragraph providing that:

> "The Board of Governors of the Federal Reserve System shall from time to time limit by regulation the rate of interest which may be paid by member banks on time and savings deposits, ... *Provided,* that the provisions of this section shall not apply to any deposit which is payable only at an office of a member bank located outside of the States of the United States and the District of Columbia."[20]

The prohibition in the first added paragraph and the instructions con-

16. See pp. 38-39.
17. See p. 41.
18. See pp. 41-42.
19. United States, Federal Reserve Act of December 23, 1913, chap. 6, § 19 (par.) as added June 16, 1933, chap. 89, § 11 (b), 48 Stat. 181, as amended; 12 U.S.C. § 371a.
20. Federal Reserve Act, § 19, 48 Stat. 182, as amended; 12 U.S.C. § 371b.

tained in the second are remedial, and hopefully preventive, measures which were taken in the aftermath of the banking crisis in the United States during the early 1930's. The provisos take into account the fact that such prohibitions or limitations are not usual abroad and that— at least from a domestic viewpoint—they probably are not necessary with regard to deposits in U.S. branch banks overseas.

In both instances, the legislation is reflected in (Federal Reserve) Regulation Q, entitled "Payment of Interest on Deposits," which provides that:

> "... [N]o member bank of the Federal Reserve System shall, directly or indirectly, by any device whatsoever, pay any interest on any demand deposit."[21]

and that:

> "Except in accordance with the provisions of this part, no member bank shall pay interest on any time deposit or savings deposit in any manner, directly or indirectly, or by any method, practice, or device whatsoever. No member bank shall pay interest on any time deposit or savings deposit at a rate in excess of such applicable maximum rate as the Board of Governors of the Federal Reserve System shall prescribe from time to time..."[22]

The provisos added to the Federal Reserve Act in 1933 are retained in Regulation Q, as follows:

> "The provisions of this part do not apply to any deposit which is payable only at an office of a member bank located outside of the States of the United States and the District of Columbia."[23]

The theoretical impediment to the U.S. branch banks' operations has lain in the possibility that the effect of the proviso in Regulation Q and those in the Act itself might be eliminated or altered so as to impose on U.S. branch banks abroad the type of prohibition or limitation embodied in Regulation Q. No such change in the statute has occurred; nor has any interpretation to Regulation Q[24] ever limited the freedom of the overseas branch banks in this respect. From the juridical viewpoint it is significant that the potential tool has been at hand but has not been utilized.

---

21. United States, Board of Governors of the Federal Reserve System, Regulation Q, 12 C.F.R. § 217.2 (a), effective January 1, 1936, as amended at 2 Fed. Reg. 370. It is noteworthy that deposits in member banks with maturities of less than 30 days are considered to be demand deposits. § 217.1 (a).

22. Regulation Q, § 217.3 (a).

23. § 217.0 (c). The essence of this sub-section is repeated in a footnote to § 217.6.

24. Interpretations to Regulation Q appear in the Federal Register and are compiled in the Code of Federal Regulations as 12 C.F.R. §§ 217.101 et seq.

2. Host Country Laws

Having established that the U.S. branch banks are virtually free under U.S. federal laws to take deposits on equal terms with the other banks in the host countries, it is now appropriate to examine the French and British laws in this regard.[25] It is to be noted that it is not our purpose to consider the entire gamut of the French and British laws, but only those which bear on the U.S. branch banks' operations in a manner germane to the subject under study.

a. *France*

In France there exists a statutory designation of deposits[26] that, in the view of one authority, reflects the legislators' adoption of an analytic and descriptive method, taking account of banking practice and terminology, rather than an attempt to synthesize a legal definition as such.[27] The pertinent language is found in the law of June 13, 1941 where it is stated that:

> "Deposits are considered to be all funds, regardless of how characterized, taken by any person or enterprise from any other person, with or without a stipulation as to the payment of interest, whether upon the solicitation by the taker or at the request of the placer, when the former has the right to use the funds for his own activity with the duty nevertheless of keeping the funds safe and of paying them out to third parties or to the placer himself at the latter's order by means of checks, drafts, or otherwise, to the extent that sufficient funds remain with the taker, and the duty to receive and add to such funds any moneys which the taker holds for the placer either by arrangement or by virtue of accepted practices."[28]

This portion of the statute is amplified in the succeeding article which goes on to include as deposits certain types of funds received by banks

25. Separate treatment will not be given to the Swiss laws in this context since during the period 1945-1958 no U.S. commercial bank had yet established a branch bank in that country.

26. For the legal nature of a deposit in French law see Branger, p. 56, note 119, at vol. 1, pp. 47-48 and 55-76. See also Nussbaum, p. 45, note 73.

27. P. Dupont, page 56, note 120, at p. 108.

28. *Loi* no. 2532 of June 13, 1941, p. 50, note 92, art. 4. The French text is: "Sont considérés comme fonds reçus sous forme de dépôts, quelle que soit leur dénomination, tous fonds que toute entreprise ou personne reçoit avec ou sans stipulation d'intérêt de tous tiers, sur sa sollicitation ou à la demande du déposant, avec le droit d'en disposer pour les besoins de son activité propre, sous la charge d'assurer audit déposant un service de caisse et notamment de payer, à concurrence des fonds se trouvant en dépôt, tous ordres de disposition donnés par lui, par chèques, virements ou de toute autre façon, en sa faveur ou en faveur de tiers et de recevoir, pour les joindre au dépôt, toutes sommes que ladite entreprise ou personne dépositaire aura à encaisser pour le déposant soit d'accord avec celui-ci, soit en vertu de l'usage."

that might otherwise be categorized as special contractual arrangements. These are funds placed in a current account even though the account may be overdrawn, amounts placed with the taker for an agreed-upon time period or made subject to a notice requirement prior to withdrawal, funds to be used for specified purposes by the taker in accord with the depositor, and those for which the latter receives a note or similar instrument (particularly a *bon de caisse*)[29] as evidence of the transaction.[30]

As previously noted in Chapter Two, *banques de dépôts* in France were not permitted until 1966 to take deposits for periods exceeding two years.[31] The effect of Articles 4 and 5 of the 1941 law was that banks in this category could obtain funds from third parties in a variety of ways, but that the moneys so received came under the technical heading of "deposits" and thus fell within the two year limitation.

Turning from the banking law to that regulating foreign exchange, an important distinction exists in France between resident and non-resident bank accounts, stemming from a set of 1939 exchange control *décrets*[32] and subsequent modifications, which were later codified in a *décret* issued in July 1947.[33] "Residents" were defined in an accompanying *arrêté* (ministerial order) as individuals habitually dwelling in France, and French or foreign corporations and institutions insofar as they were established in France.[34] French franc accounts of residents were, without specific authorization, restricted to purely internal operations in the sense that they could be freely debited or credited only with respect to payments and transfers inside the French franc zone. They could not, for example, be used to purchase foreign currency or to make payments outside the zone without prior permission of the Office

29. In France, *bons de caisse* or cashier's bonds are obligations of a bank issued with maturities of 6, 12, and 24 months at a fixed rate of interest. Usually negotiable, they resemble in some respects the certificates of deposit issued by commercial banks in the United States except that technically they are an obligation of the issuer rather than evidence of a deposit. In Switzerland banks issue similar instruments *(Kassenobligationen, bons de caisse, buoni di cassa)* on a continuing basis at tellers' windows, for periods up to five years. There is a secondary market in these. See Grossman, "Switzerland", *in* Beckhart (ed.), p. 52, note 104, at pp. 699-70.

30. *Loi* no. 2532 of June 13, 1941, *supra*, art. 5.

31. See p. 51, note 99.

32. France, Ministère des Finances, *Décrets* of December 9, 1939; *Journal officiel*, September 10, 1939, pp. 11271-83.

33. France, Ministère des Finances, *Décret* no. 47-1337 of July 15, 1947; *Journal officiel*, July 20, 1947, pp. 6987-91.

34. The French language text is: "*Résidents:* les personnes physiques ayant leur résidence habituelle en France et les personnes morales françaises ou étrangères pour leurs établissements en France." France, Ministère des Finances, *Arrêté* of July 15, 1947, title I, art. 1 (3); *Journal officiel*, July 20, 1947, pp. 6991-93.

des Changes, normally requested by a *banque agréée* on its customer's behalf.[35]

For non-residents there were several types of franc accounts. First there were accounts which could be held by residents of the "dollar area"[36] and of the French Somali Coast. Operations of such accounts had to receive permission from the Office des Changes;[37] but blanket permission was accorded for certain transactions. For example, these accounts could be freely credited with the proceeds of the cession of foreign exchange to the Office des Changes.[38] Later they could be credited with the equivalent in francs of the sale of foreign exchange on the so-called *marché libre* or free exchange market[39] in Paris (except for banknotes), with the franc equivalent of the hard currency proceeds of French franc sales on the exchange markets in the national countries of the *marché libre* currencies, and with amounts transferred from other accounts in the same category. They could be debited for the reverse operations, as well as for payments made through the French franc zone.[40] In July 1954 these accounts, which were originally designated by the country of residence of the account holder, were merged into the category known as *comptes francs libres* or free franc accounts.[41]

Second, there were non-resident accounts for residents of certain other non-dollar area countries outside the French franc zone, designated according to the country of the account holder's residence. These accounts could be converted without specific authorization into and out of the national currency of the account holder's residence, but not into other

35. Detailed instructions were periodically provided by an *avis* (notice) for the banks' guidance. See, for example, France, Office des Changes, *Avis* no. 202; *Journal officiel*, September 25, 1947, pp. 9641-43.

36. "On January 20, 1952, the following territories were listed as comprising the dollar area for this purpose: Canada, Colombia, Costa Rica, Cuba, Dominican Republic, El Salvador, Guatemala, Haiti, Honduras, Nicaragua, Panama, Philippine Republic, United States and dependencies, and Venezuela." I.M.F., *(Third) Exchange Restrictions*, 1952, p. 96, n. 5.

37. *Arrêté* of July 15, 1947, *supra*, title III (2), art. 20.

38. France, Office des Changes, *Avis*, no. 231; *Journal officiel*, September 25, 1947, pp. 9664-65.

39. The currencies originally traded on the *marché libre* were the Portuguese escudo and the U.S. dollar. Various other currencies, including the Belgian, Djibouti, and Swiss francs, the Canadian dollar, and the Mexican peso were later added at different times; and the Belgian franc was shifted to the "official exchange market" with the formation of the European Payments Union. (See note 42 *infra*). The *marché libre* was so designated even though the French government could control the quantity of francs offered for sale.

40. See, for example, France, Office des Changes, *Avis* no. 647, title II, (I) and (II); *Journal officiel*, March 22, 1958, pp. 2798-2800.

41. France, Office des Changes, *Avis* no. 573; *Journal officiel*, July 11, 1954, pp. 6594-95. See I.M.F., *(Sixth) Exchange Restrictions*, 1955, p. 147.

currencies. Eventually a distinction was made for those non-dollar area currencies which related to European Payments Union (E.P.U.) member countries.[42] Accounts of E.P.U. country residents could be converted without permission into and out of other E.P.U. member currencies, but not into those of the dollar area currencies.

On March 22, 1958 the non-resident accounts thus far described were separated into three broad categories.[43] *Comptes francs libres* were the successors of the previous group so designated, *comptes francs transférables* included certain currencies inside and outside the E.P.U. group, and *comptes francs bilatéraux* were created to contain accounts for residents of those countries with which France had made bilateral payments agreements.

Three other special types of non-resident accounts existed. These were the *comptes tourisme* created in April 1953 for the convenience of temporary visitors to France,[44] the *comptes intérieurs de non-résidents* for French nationals temporarily abroad or foreign nationals temporarily employed or stationed in the French franc zone,[45] and *comptes d'attente* (suspense accounts) which authorized banks could open without permission for persons whose residence status had not yet been determined and for non-residents' transactions in French franc securities.[46]

b. *Great Britain*

In the absence of a banking law *per se*,[47] the two principal sets of rules and regulations affecting the deposit-taking operations of the U.S.

---

42. European Payments Union Treaty, signed September 19, 1950 in Paris. See p. 156, note 2.

43. See Office des Changes, *Avis* no. 647, *supra,* title I, art. 1.

44. France, Office des Changes, *Instruction* no. 536 of April 3, 1953, as amended. These "tourist franc accounts" could only stand in the name of individuals, who themselves could personally draw banknotes or travelers cheques during their sojourn in France, but could not write checks or make payments in favor of third parties. If a tourist franc account had a credit balance upon the individual's departure from France, the sum could not be withdrawn but could only be used (by the individual himself) during a later visit to the country.

45. See France, Office des Changes, *Avis* no. 587; *Journal officiel,* March 20, 1955, pp. 2860-61, which modified *Avis* no. 208; *Id.,* September 25, 1947, p. 9646. French nationals serving abroad in the civil or military services did not qualify for such accounts. International officials stationed in France or in the French franc zone could have them if they were not themselves French nationals.

46. See *Arrêté* of July 15, 1947, *supra,* title II, art. 23. See France, Office des Changes, *Instruction* no. 775 of January 21, 1959; Banque des Règlements Internationaux [Bank for International Settlements], *Réglementation du commerce de l'or et des devises en France,* vol. 2, Basle, 1946 *et seq.,* p. 37-IN-775.

47. From 1963 banks have been subject to the Protection of Depositors Act, 1963, 14 & 15 Eliz. 2, chap. 16. Section 25 (1) (d) of that Act brings foreign branch banks within its scope.

branch banks in Great Britain are those designed to control credit and those dealing with the rationing of foreign exchange.

With regard to the control of credit, the pertinent statute is the Borrowing (Control and Guarantees) Act, 1946.[48] This " ... Act to provide ... [*inter alia*] ... for the regulation of the borrowing and raising of money ..." has been described as an enabling act containing few detailed provisions but giving the Treasury the power to regulate the flow of the country's capital resources as part of the pattern of a controlled economy.[49]

Despite the extremely broad scope of this Act as set forth in its preamble, however, the Act provides that:

> "(2) Any reference in this Act to the borrowing of money—
> (a) ...
> (b) does not include a reference to the acceptance by a person carrying on a banking undertaking of moneys to be placed to the credit of a current or deposit account."[50]

Accordingly, the taking of deposits by banks is expressly placed outside the scope of the Borrowing (Control and Guarantees) Act, 1946.

Of greater importance to this phase of the subject under study is the other area of regulation, i.e., the rationing of foreign exchange, which is embodied in the Exchange Control Act, 1947[51] and the orders issued thereunder. In this connection, the Act provides that:

> "Except with the permission of the Treasury, no person resident in the United Kingdom shall lend any money, Treasury bills or securities to any body corporate resident in the scheduled territories which is by any means controlled (whether directly or indirectly) by persons resident outside the scheduled territories. . ."[52]

Further along the same Act declares that:

> "... any transaction with or by a branch of any business whether carried on by a body corporate or otherwise, shall be treated in all respects as if the branch were a body corporate resident where the branch is situated. . ."[53]

---

48. Great Britain, Borrowing (Control and Guarantees) Act, 1946, 9 & 10 Geo. 6, chap. 58.

49. Sheldon and Drover, p. 62, note 140, at p. 614.

50. Borrowing (Control and Guarantees) Act, 1946, *supra,* art. 4-2 (b).

51. Exchange Control Act, 1947, p. 70, note 174. See F. A. Mann, "The Exchange Control Act, 1947", 10 *Modern Law Review* 411 (1947). This Act was preceded by the Defence (Finance) Regulations, S.R. & O. 1939, no. 1620, which had emanated from the Emergency Powers (Defence) Act, 1939, 2 & 3 Geo. 6, chap. 62. See F. A. Mann, "Exchange Restriction in England", 3 *Modern Law Review* 202 (1940).

52. Exchange Control Act, 1947, § 30 (3). The "scheduled territories" comprise the group of countries and dependencies usually referred to as the "sterling area".

53. Act, Section 39 (1) (a). Identical language appeared in Great Britain, H. M. Treasury, Exchange Control (Branches) Order, 1947, dated September 20, 1947, S.R.

In other words, the foreign branch bank is treated like a banking subsidiary.

Now, the deposit of funds in a bank creates a debtor-creditor relationship wherein the depositing customer lends the funds to the bank.[54] Moreover, if the deposit is in the branch of a banking institution the debt is considered to be payable at that branch.[55] Therefore the deposit of funds in a U.S. branch bank in Great Britain is commensurate with the lending of funds to a foreign-controlled banking corporation.

Without a regulatory provision to the contrary, these two parts of the Exchange Control Act, 1947 would make it necessary for all potential depositors to obtain permission before placing funds with the U.S. branch banks in London. Falling clearly (as borrowers) within the scope of the above provisions, the American and other foreign branch banks in Great Britain have benefitted from a subsequent Order which provides that:

> "There shall be exempted from the provisions of sub-section (3) of section 30 of the Exchange Control Act, 1947 ... the lending of any money, Treasury bills or securities by any person resident in the United Kingdom or the Channel Islands to any office or branch in the United Kingdom or the Channel Islands of a bank which is by any means controlled (whether directly or indirectly) by persons resident outside the scheduled territories. . ."[56]

This exemption is underlined with regard to the U.S. branch banks' access to the local money market by an Exchange Control Notice stating that:

> "1. The permission of the Bank of England must be obtained before any new loans (whether by way of advance or overdraft) are granted or Treasury Bills or Securities are lent on or after the date of this Notice by persons resident in the United Kingdom to bodies corporate (other than banks—see paragraph 2 below) resident in the Scheduled Territories which are by any means controlled (whether directly or indirectly) by persons resident outside the Scheduled Territories... Furthermore, it should be noted that any transaction effected on or after October 1, 1947, which would increase an amount outstanding on loan at any time after that date would require permission as new lending. . ."[57]

& O. 1947, no. 2039, which was revoked in 1951 (by S.I. 1951, no. 974) and was replaced by the Exchange Control (Branches and Residence) Directions, 1951, S.I. 1951, no. 962.

54. Nussbaum, p. 45, note 73. For the British law in particular see *Foley* v. *Hill*, 2 H.L. Cas. 28, 9 Eng. Rep. 1002 (1848).

55. See *Richardson* v. *Richardson*, 96 L.J.P. 125 (1927).

56. Great Britain, H. M. Treasury, Exchange Control (Lending to Banks Exemption) Order, 1947, dated September 20, 1947, paragraph 1 (1), S.R. & O. 1947, no. 2045.

57. Great Britain, Bank of England, Exchange Control (General) Notice 4, dated October 1, 1947, par. 1.

The exception made for lending to other banks, referred to in the above-quoted portion of the Act, is as follows:

"2. Permission is not required to grant accommodation or give facilities to banks in the United Kingdom which are:
(a) . . .
(b) Branches of bodies corporate resident outside the Scheduled Territories."[58]

As the Bank of England acts as the agent of the Treasury with regard to banks' conduct under the Exchange Control Act, a blanket exemption has thus been accorded to the U.S. and other foreign branch banks allowing them to seek funds in the London money market without prior permission for each transaction.

Although "residence" is not defined in the Exchange Control Act, a General Notice issued by the Bank of England has set forth the criteria under which authorized banks determine the residence status of their customers.[59] Broadly speaking, under the British exchange control rules "people (and their assets) are classified according to the country in which they normally live".[60]

Host currency accounts in the U.S. branch banks, like those in all banks operating inside the sterling area, have been classified according to the depositor's residence. "Resident sterling accounts" are similar to the French franc accounts maintained by residents of the French franc zone in that without authorization they can only be used for payments within the sterling area. Non-residents' sterling accounts have been progressively grouped into several categories, the first containing accounts designated with reference to the country of the depositor's per-

58. Notice 4, par. 4.
59. See for example Great Britain, Bank of England, Exchange Control (General) Notice, dated March 6, 1950, revised as of June 10, 1955, par. 4. It is noteworthy that "residential status for Exchange Control purposes . . . may be different from residence for other purposes, e.g., income tax. . ." and that "nationality is not decisive to the determination of residential status". Bank of England, *A Guide to United Kingdom Exchange Control*, London, 1968, p. 6.
60. "The U.K. Exchange Control: a Short History", Bank of England, 7 *Quarterly Bulletin* 245, 246 (1967). A useful working definition is that a resident is "any person, firm or corporation residing permanently in or conducting business in one of the 'Scheduled Territories' or any person who has at any time since 3rd September, 1939, resided in the United Kingdom and has not been accorded non-residential status by H. M. Treasury. . ." (Quoted from District Bank, Ltd., Foreign Department, *Digest of the United Kingdom Exchange Regulations*, 9th ed., London, 1951, p. 2) A Direction from the Treasury has specified that "a person or body of persons (whether corporate or unincorporated) carrying on any business or any activity, whether for the purpose of profit or not, in two or more countries shall as respects such business or activity as is carried on in each country be treated . . . as resident in the country in which the business or activity is carried on". Determination of Residence Direction, dated September 20, 1947, S.R. & O. 1947, no. 2054.

manent residence. For example, originally there were "French accounts" for residents of the French franc zone and "Belgian accounts" for those of the Belgian monetary area. Without prior permission, such accounts could be credited with sterling transferred from other accounts bearing the same geographical designation and could be debited for the same purpose, as well as to make payments to residents of the sterling area.

A second group of non-resident accounts were called "American accounts" and could be maintained by residents of the dollar area.[61] Without special authorization they could be credited with amounts from other "American accounts" (not necessarily those of account holders residing in the same country) and with the sterling equivalent of dollars sold by the account holder through an authorized bank. They could be debited for the opposite transactions as well as for payments to all resident and most non-resident accounts.

In addition to the above categories there existed "transferable accounts" and "accounts other than transferable accounts" relating to a group of countries which were in neither of the first two groups. The former could only be maintained inside the sterling area by banks in the designated countries, and needed specific permission from the Bank of England for their establishment. The latter accounts could be maintained in the sterling area by any resident of those countries.

On March 22, 1954 the Treasury acted to place "American accounts" and "Canadian accounts" in a category that was essentially similar to that earlier containing the "American accounts" described above except that the accounts in the new category could be credited with the proceeds of gold sales executed through an authorized dealer and debited for gold so purchased for the account holder in the London gold market.[62] A new category contained what were known as "transferable accounts" that could be maintained by residents of all countries outside the sterling and dollar areas and Canada, thus clustering the many different geographical designations existing theretofore. Not to be confused with the earlier accounts bearing the same label, the new "transferable accounts" could be maintained by any qualified non-resident, not banks alone. These were the accounts that contained the so-called "transferable

61. For British exchange control purposes, the dollar area (referred to as the "American account area") then comprised the countries listed at p. 96, note 36 with the exclusion of Canada and the addition of Bolivia, Ecuador, Liberia, Mexico, and the "Pacific Islands formerly under Japanese administration but now under United States administration". Great Britain, Bank of England, Exchange Control (General) Notice, dated April 4, 1951 (as amended up to October 15, 1952).

62. The London gold market was re-opened on a restricted basis at the same time, having been closed since 1939.

sterling" with which a large part of world trade was financed during this period.[63]

A third category contained "registered accounts" for gold transactions of persons who otherwise qualified for "transferable accounts".

On December 29, 1958, with the introduction of external convertibility, the different non-resident account designations were terminated (except for Egyptian accounts) in favor of a single group known as "external accounts", the designation which has continued to date.[64]

In addition to special arrangements for visitors and temporary residents, including individuals based in the United Kingdom with foreign armed forces as well as foreign diplomatic and consular personnel, there has existed a special group of accounts which deserve mention. These are the "blocked accounts",[65] which contain the proceeds of sterling securities sold by the banks for non-resident account holders and which can be debited for the purchase of qualifying sterling securities.[66] The funds in these "blocked accounts" can also be sold, usually at a discount, in the "security sterling" or "switch sterling" market to non-residents desiring to invest in sterling securities. Although this type of sterling has neither been printed nor coined, it has regularly been traded abroad (e.g., in New York City) and quoted in foreign exchange tables alongside sterling.

C. Depositors and their Accounts

The potential depositors of host currency fall into four general categories; banks, non-banking firms or institutions, individuals, and the U.S. federal government. Having seen the legal authority under which the U.S. branch banks have been able to take host currency deposits, let us now

63. For an interesting description of the mechanics of "transferable sterling" see Burton Crane, *Invisible Pound Reigns in Trade,* New York Times, March 23, 1958, § 3, p. 1, col. 5 (late city ed.).

64. Except for Rhodesian accounts. I.M.F., *(Twenty-First) Exchange Restrictions,* 1970, pp. 515-16.

65. Blocked accounts have been provided for at Exchange Control Act, 1947, p. 70, note 174, § 32. Originally such accounts contained commercial balances blocked due to hostilities in World War II.

66. Great Britain, H.M. Treasury, Exchange Control (Blocked Accounts) Order, 1947, dated September 20, 1947, S.R. & O. 1947, no. 2038 had allowed the purchase of any securities traded on a recognized stock exchange in the United Kingdom which were irredeemable (i.e., equity issues) or not redeemable within ten years from the date of purchase or acquisition. Under the Exchange Control (Blocked Accounts) Order, 1948, dated July 16, 1948, S.I. 1948, no. 1663, the rules were tightened to include only government-issued or -guaranteed securities maturing in not less than ten years from the date of purchase. The rules were later relaxed but have remained in force.

examine their activities in this field with regard to each of the different types of potential depositor, and with special reference to the period prior to the return to external convertibility near the end of 1958.

1. *Banks*

Banks normally maintain working balances in certain other banks to facilitate the transfer of funds among one another. In like fashion, overseas branch banks normally carry on their books deposits in the name of indigenous and other banks in the host countries, as well as deposits originating from banks in other countries, including their own head offices.

a. *U.S. Head Office Bank*

In addition to the initial capital contribution of the head office bank, which is in the nature of a direct investment, the head office bank normally places at the disposal of an overseas branch bank some of its host currency funds on deposit locally in indigenous correspondent banks. Such funds can be marshalled for the branch bank's own operations, either by transferring them to the credit of the branch bank in the indigenous institutions, or by depositing them in the branch bank itself, in the name of the head office. The exchange control laws have not discouraged this, for in both instances the result is that a formerly non-resident account in a local institution becomes a resident account to the extent of the funds on deposit in indigenous banks which no longer stand in the name of the U.S. head office bank.[67]

b. *Other U.S. Banks*

Turning to other sources of potential deposits for the U.S. branch bank established abroad, the head office bank in the United States is in a position to proffer the branch bank as a correspondent in the host country for those larger inland and financial center banks which do not themselves have an establishment there. Even if it is not likely that the U.S. branch bank would be a suitable replacement for already-existing correspondents, it can nevertheless act as an additional banking correspondent.

67. In Great Britain, for example, this stems from the fact that the branch bank is treated by the exchange control regulations as if it were a resident corporation. See p. 98, material cited to note 53. As for the head office deposit in the branch bank, the depositor is considered a resident by virtue of a further provision of the Exchange Control (Branches and Residence) Directions, 1951—Residence, dated May 31, 1951, S.I. 1951, no. 962, to the effect that: "2. A person or body of persons carrying on in the United Kingdom a branch of any business, shall, as respects such business as is carried on by that branch, be treated for all the purposes of the Act as resident in the United Kingdom."

It appears that for a variety of reasons, including other U.S. banks' desire not to lose actual or potential reciprocity with indigenous banks, U.S. branch banks have not often served in such a capacity, and that instances where they are destined to act directly as correspondents for other U.S. banks are rare.[68] In practice, when this does occur, the U.S. head office bank acts as an intermediary, instructing the branch bank to transact the other U.S. bank's correspondent business through one of the head office's own accounts in the branch bank.[69]

c. *Indigenous and Other Banks in the Host Countries*

A third group of banks that are potential depositors of host currency in the U.S. branch bank consists of indigenous host country banks and other foreign branch banks or banking subsidiaries established there, including branches of other U.S. commercial banks. Here the practice appears to have been uneven. Apart from "courtesy accounts",[70] such deposits can arise when an indigenous host country bank uses the U.S. bank's head office as one of its American correspondents and finds it advantageous to maintain a host currency account locally with the U.S. branch bank. More frequently the deposits of indigenous and foreign banks in the host country represent working balances, their size tending to reflect the amount of business transacted locally between them and the U.S. branch bank.

In certain instances some indigenous banks may have at one time expressed indignation at the arrival of a newcomer by their reluctance to make initial deposits of either type. It appears, however, that the need to remain on even, if not cordial, terms with large—indeed, in relative terms, very large—commercial banks from a developed country such as the United States has dictated that a certain amount of any such resentment be taken in stride. Local indigenous banks apparently have found, too, that after an initial flurry of attention stirred by the arrival of a new U.S. branch bank, the latter has tended to settle down into the local environment with, as will be seen, problems of its own.

In any event, friendly attitudes and relationships built up over many decades are not to be cast aside in an arbitrary manner by individuals whose profession, regardless of the side of the Atlantic on which they

68. This would indicate that the arrival of the second and third waves of U.S. branch banks has not caused the earlier established branch banks to lose many host currency deposits formerly in the names of the head offices of the newer arrivals.

69. It can and does arise, however infrequently, that a non-U.S. controlled bank in a third country requests directly that a U.S. branch bank abroad act as its correspondent.

70. As the term suggests, "courtesy accounts" are those maintained by indigenous and other depositors as a small but tangible token of recognition—or in some cases, of welcome.

have learned it, demands that access remain open to their foreign counterparts. In many instances capital flows which appear to be institutional, and which can be measured or characterized as such, can ultimately be traced to relationships between individuals and groups in different links of the chain. Bankers dealing with foreign customers or handling transactions crossing national boundaries are no less aware of this than are individuals producing or marketing merchandise—or extending credit—in the smallest hamlet. Hostile attitudes toward the foreign branch bank, in the present case the branch of a major U.S. commercial bank, have normally been shelved.

2. Non-Banking Corporations and Companies

a. Local U.S. Corporate Subsidiaries

When the first wave U.S. branch banks recommenced or revived their local activities after the end of World War II it was manifest that U.S. corporations and their local host country subsidiaries would be potential customers. Also, the banking needs of these corporations and their subsidiaries have constituted one of the primary reasons for the later arrival of the second wave U.S. bank branches. It is appropriate to ask, then, how these U.S. corporations and their host country subsidiaries have added to the host currency deposits of the U.S. branch banks.

Generally speaking, few U.S. parent corporations have found it necessary to maintain sizeable offshore foreign currency deposits standing in their own names when their foreign corporate subsidiaries can hold such funds. These subsidiaries either receive the funds directly from a payor or lender, or indirectly through another subsidiary or the parent corporation itself. It is on the local subsidiary, then, that attention must be focused rather than on the U.S. parent corporation, quite aside from the impact of the voluntary U.S. corporate Guidelines which were introduced during the U.S. branch banks' second Euro-dollar operating phase, treated in Chapter Five.

(1) Current Accounts

Although the U.S. branch banks have usually offered and sought to handle the local U.S. corporate subsidiaries' entire range of banking needs, the necessity of being on friendly terms with local indigenous bankers dictates that at least some of these subsidiaries' locally held funds be on deposit in indigenous institutions. To a certain degree courtesy accounts fulfil this need; but such token gestures are invariably recognized as such by depositor and banker alike. Frequently, therefore, the local management of a U.S. corporate subsidiary will find it desirable to maintain several active host currency accounts with indigenous banks, using each account for a specific purpose. Thus any current account held at a local U.S. branch bank is rarely, if ever, the subsidiary's only such account.

On the other hand, the U.S. branch banks capitalize on their ability to "speak American" with the Americans in the management of these subsidiaries.[71] If it is decided, then, that a current account or accounts (except for courtesy accounts) must be maintained in a local U.S. branch bank, what factors influence the choice as to the particular branch bank or banks when there are several present?

To the extent that the local management of the U.S. corporate subsidiary is free to make or influence this choice—and we shall have occasion to return to this qualification—the services offered by the various local U.S. branch banks are major influencing factors. Promptness, efficiency, anticipation of the customer's needs, and responsiveness to the banking and non-banking aspects of its local activities all count strongly. The ability to provide introductions in the local community and to interpret local economic and commercial trends is important. Also present is the element of a U.S. branch bank's ability or inability to provide access to host governmental channels when necessary.[72] By no means of minor importance is the capacity to furnish reliable credit information with regard to local companies or individuals. In effect, the typical U.S. branch bank aims at offering the U.S. subsidiary the best of both worlds by attempting to provide much of what an indigenous bank can offer plus the style of banking service that U.S. corporations expect in the United States.

The U.S. branch bank, therefore, not only strives to "speak American" but also to speak the local language. Such a bilingual banking effort is challenging, to say the least. That the first wave banks in particular have acquired a certain expertise would seem evident, especially in their being very much at home in the host environment.[73] Two important factors tend, however, to counteract any element which a U.S. branch bank has in its favor. First, U.S. corporate subsidiaries established in Western Europe and elsewhere abroad generally tend to be net borrowers rather than

71. In a different setting, a Puerto Rican branch bank in New York City, Banco de Ponce, has advertised widely to the Spanish-speaking potential customers in the metropolitan area as "el banco que habla su idoma" (the bank that speaks your own language).

72. Providing lines of communication with host government agencies and officials is understandably the task which most frequently falls to some of the indigenous personnel of the U.S. and other foreign branch banks.

73. Nevertheless it appears that by employing local nationals later arrivals have often been able to match their more firmly entrenched U.S. competitors' local coloring.

depositors.[74] The main reasons for this can be explained as follows:

(i) *Possibility of host currency devaluation.* By avoiding a long position in the host currency, to the extent compatible with normal operations, U.S. corporate subsidiaries can reduce the potential risk of loss in the event of a host currency devaluation. In both France and Great Britain the possibilities of devaluation cannot be described as having been remote. More than once such preventive measures have proved to have been wise.[75] As much as possible host currency receipts have been reinvested or, to the extent permitted by the French and British exchange control regulations, converted into other currencies or transferred to the parent corporations or other subsidiaries established elsewhere.

(ii) *Possibility of nationalization.* In France and Great Britain certain elements of the local economies have been nationalized; and in both countries there has existed continuous pressure in some sectors of public opinion in favor of further extending the nationalized domain. By being as much as possible a net borrower, a foreign corporate subsidiary can yield to any nationalizing host government a greater proportion of debts than assets.

(iii) *Possibility of restrictive measures by host monetary authorities.* Even in the absence of devaluation or nationalization, no U.S. corporate subsidiary financial officer can overlook the possibility of a tightened control over his company's accounts in local banks. Quite aside from exchange controls, with which American and other enterprises have learned to live in France and Great Britain, administrative regulations, including reporting requirements, can render large local accounts unwieldy.

The above reasons can be characterized as external to the U.S. cor-

---

74. A senior officer in one U.S. branch bank indicated that as late as 1966 90% of the loans from his branch were to U.S. corporate subsidiaries whereas only 30% of the deposits in the branch came from them.

75. When the pound sterling and French franc were devalued on September 18 and 19, 1949 respectively, there were not as many U.S. corporate subsidiaries in the host countries as when the French franc was devalued in 1958. In the following period through the end of 1967, which witnessed an enormous increase in the U.S. direct investment in Western Europe, the French franc's growing strength was contrasted with the progressive deterioration of the pound. There is evidence to indicate that the November 1967 devaluation of the latter found some U.S. corporate subsidiaries outside Great Britain purposely short on sterling. In fact, some were said to have made exchange profits on that occasion. See *Business Week,* November 25, 1967, p. 122. With regard to the Deutsche mark revaluation in 1969 see 55 *Federal Reserve Bulletin* 697-98 (1969). More recently, U.S. corporate transactions in the foreign exchange markets have been labelled as one of the important disruptive elements in the spring 1971 preflotation movements into the Deutsche mark. See The Wall Street Journal, May 7, 1971, p. 1, col. 6 (Eastern edition). See also p. 109, note 81. Of course, the August 15, 1971 change in the U.S. policy on the convertibility of the dollar into gold modified the dollar/host currency devaluation aspect.

poration, since in most industrialized countries these "guest" enterprises have relatively little control over such factors, despite the influence that they might bring to bear in certain instances.[76]

There is an internal factor, too, which encourages these corporate subsidiaries to be net borrowers. Corporate treasurers in the United States would not be expected to leave funds lying idle, either inside or outside the United States, when they might be used profitably elsewhere. It is unlikely, then, that a subsidiary in one of the host countries will maintain local balances in host currencies greater than the amounts actually needed for its current operations. Even when exchange control regulations penalize conversion into other currencies the possibility of converting must be contemplated.

There is a second factor that should be recognized. At p. 106 we have made a qualification regarding the extent to which the local management of a U.S. corporate subsidiary is free to make or influence the choice as to where host currency current accounts will be maintained. In some cases the decision is not made locally, but is taken elsewhere in the corporate hierarchy or in the United States by the parent corporation itself. If a particular host country indigenous bank or U.S. branch bank has helped to arrange and finance the local subsidiary's initial establishment in the host country, this bank or branch bank frequently acquires a priority in handling that subsidiary's most important current accounts once operations get underway. In like fashion, where a local U.S. branch bank's head office is one of the parent corporation's principal banks in the United States, this branch bank usually receives the corporate subsidiary's local banking business as a natural conse-

76. After 1962 an additional external reason arose. Prior to the "grossing-up" amendment of the U.S. Internal Revenue Code of that year there were U.S. federal corporate income tax advantages in accumulating overseas profits earned from non-U.S. sources. The law in effect until the amendment required that the parent U.S. corporation report as income only those amounts of such profits actually received from its overseas subsidiaries in the form of dividends paid to the parent corporation or to its U.S. stockholders. Accordingly the foreign subsidiaries, particularly those in countries referred to as "tax havens", could amass host (or other) currency profits for eventual repatriation to the United States or for future investment in the host country or elsewhere. See United States, Congress, Senate, *Report* No. 1881, 87th Cong., 2d Sess., August 15, 1962; *United States Code Congressional and Administrative News*, St. Paul, West Publishing Co. [hereinafter cited as *U.S. Code Cong. Adm. News*], 1962, vol. 2, pp. 3281-98. Under the provisions of the 1962 amendment the profits of U.S. overseas subsidiaries in countries other than those in which the statute defines as economically "less developed countries" are considered to be included in the U.S. parent corporations' gross income regardless of whether these amounts are actually remitted to the parent corporation. Any accumulation thenceforth has not benefitted from the former U.S. tax "deferral" incentive. See generally, United States, Revenue Act of 1962, October 16, 1962, 76 Stat. 1006; 26 U.S.C. §§ 951-72.

quence. This latter phenomenon is either an advantage or a disadvantage to the management of a local U.S. branch bank, depending upon whether it is thus assured of customers or deprived of them.

In any case the situation can change if a local U.S. corporate subsidiary's management finds that a particular U.S. branch bank cannot offer the services provided by indigenous host country banks or by other U.S. branch banks in the locality. The location of the subsidiary's most important current accounts, or the direction which future accounts may take, can be altered to the disadvantage of a U.S. branch bank which is failing to perform satisfactorily.[77]

(2) Time Deposit Accounts

With regard to time deposit accounts there are several important differences. Generally speaking, a current account presupposes a certain continuing contact between a depositor and a banking institution, especially in the case of the current account maintained by a commercial rather than an individual depositor. A time deposit account, on the other hand, usually involves little continuing contact. Here, the funds are placed on deposit with the understanding:

(a) that for a specified period they will not be withdrawn;[78] or

(b) that they will not be withdrawn without advance notice;[79] or

(c) that, in some case, if they are withdrawn it will be at the sacrifice of otherwise anticipated interest.[80]

The customer is primarily interested in whether the banking institution is likely to be able to repay the deposited funds with interest at the time of the withdrawal. He is less concerned with maintaining a continuing working relationship with the bank. In any event, U.S. corporate subsidiaries do not make a practice of amassing funds in host currencies for deposit locally, as noted earlier.[81]

77. It appears, however, that newly-arriving second wave and third wave U.S. branch banks have had no easy task in attracting already established current accounts from earlier arrivals.

78. If not withdrawn at the end of the specified period such deposits are frequently renewable for successive periods.

79. Although in Great Britain such deposits are repayable on seven days' notice, in practice the clearing banks seldom refuse to allow withdrawals on demand. See (Radcliffe) Committee, *Report,* Cmnd. 827, pp. 33-34, par. 131.

80. This is similar to the "alternative withdrawal" method used in the United States. See interpretations to (Federal Reserve) Regulation Q, 12 C.F.R. § 217.105 and 107. See also pp. 218-19.

81. Funds may, however, be placed in large amounts for other reasons, exchange controls permitting, for instance, to profit from (or at least not to lose because of) an expected upward change in the host country parity.

b. *U.S. Corporations Having no Host Country Subsidiaries*

It sometimes occurs that a U.S. corporation has occasion to receive local currency payments in one of the host countries even though it has no subsidiary established there. Ordinarily such payments are for the sale of goods or services, where the U.S. corporation has two alternatives: (1) It can arrange to receive the payment through the auspices of its own U.S. bank and the latter's overseas correspondents. This procedure normally requires at least three or four days from the time payment is ordered until the U.S. corporation has access to the funds. (2) Or the customer can be requested to pay directly into the U.S. corporation's host country account. Here the bank or branch bank receiving the funds can notify the payee in the United States immediately by cable. Moreover it can carry out at once any standing orders of the U.S. corporation, such as conversion into another currency[82] or immediate transfer to a time deposit account so that interest on the funds can be earned from the same day that they are received.

Although indigenous host country banks are in a position to offer these facilities, head office banks in the United States are more likely to become aware of a U.S. corporate customer's need for such service when it arises. The branch bank abroad will be instructed to open the appropriate types of accounts; and the foreign customers will be advised by the U.S. corporation to make payment at that branch bank.

c. *Indigenous Corporations and Companies*

Although the U.S. banks have not been primarily attracted abroad to serve the banking needs of indigenous corporations in the host countries, these cannot be (and have not been) overlooked as potential depositors of host currency.

The current accounts of locally controlled corporations are generally maintained with the local indigenous banking institutions that have traditionally served as their bankers. Newly established local corporations which have no long-established banking connection with an indigenous bank are somewhat more likely to have an account at a local U.S. branch bank, but then only if the activities of the new company require an institution offering expertise that goes beyond the national boundaries of the host country.

Except for courtesy accounts there is, from the point of view of the indigenous company, little incentive to open a current account in a U.S. branch bank unless the services offered by this institution are markedly superior to those already offered by indigenous local banks. This is not to suggest that the American branch banks have not obtained such ac-

---

82. It would be a non-resident account in France and Great Britain.

counts, for they have; but it is evident that local companies' treasurers in these industrialized host countries are not likely to come flocking into a U.S. branch bank as they have in certain countries where the local banking system is less highly developed or where local conditions appear politically or economically unsettled.[83]

That certain U.S. branch banks have openly encouraged these corporations to make deposits is self-evident; but other U.S. branch banks, at least in the first few years of their operations, have been reluctant to seek out locally owned corporations as customers unless it is evident that they may have international business to transact. Also, Western European corporations do not change or add on bankers as easily or frequently as American corporations. Like family physicians, the "traditional" bankers are not likely to be abandoned without some hesitation.

It appears that the results have varied greatly from U.S. branch bank to branch bank and from host country to country. U.S. branch banks in the first wave, being older and better established, have been in a more favorable position than the later arrivals. Since some of these first wave branch banks, or their predecessors, have been present on the local scene for many years, they have been able to expect host currency deposits from local corporations with whom their banker-customer relationship stretches back into the pre-war era. With new indigenous corporate depositors, too, some U.S. branch banks have had a certain added measure of success, principally for the following reasons:

(1) The U.S. bank's head office or one of its other overseas units has proved helpful in the past in arranging or handling a foreign transaction, and can be expected to be even more helpful in the future with a branch physically located in the company's home territory.

(2) Indigenous individuals already known to the locally owned company's management have become associated, frequently in senior positions, with the management of the U.S. branch bank. These persons may formerly have been associated with indigenous banks or with the central bank. Their presence in the U.S. branch bank makes it apparently, and probably genuinely, less foreign. More specifically, it makes the branch bank less American. Figuratively as well as literally, these individuals "speak the same language" as the management in locally owned companies.

---

83. For instance, indigenous banks in Guatemala are reported to have lost one-third of their deposits to a newly established U.S. branch bank. See *Foreign Government Restraints on United States Bank Operations Abroad,* p. 29, note 20, at p. 12. "The influx of foreign banking institutions into Argentina has recently been much criticized locally, mainly because it is they, and not the Argentine banks, which are attracting the lion's share of deposits from public savings." Financial Times, March 24, 1970, p. 5, col. 2.

(3) From the mid-1950's some locally owned corporations with international business have become aware of the newly emerging foreign networks of some of the U.S. banks and have considered it opportune to establish a relationship that might eventually facilitate future borrowing once the exchange control laws were less restrictive. As will be seen in Chapters Four and Five the activity of the U.S. branch banks in the Euro-dollar market has borne out this line of reasoning.

In relation to the current accounts placed by American corporate subsidiaries it was pointed out above that the decision as to where to maintain a host currency account is frequently made in the United States or elsewhere in the corporate structure. A variation on this phenomenon occasionally occurs in the case of a local indigenous corporation doing business in the United States and using an American commercial bank's services there. The most usual situation is that of a host country corporation having a subsidiary in the United States, the reverse situation from that with which we have been dealing. While that subsidiary is using the services of the head office of a U.S. commercial bank, the host country parent corporation sometimes finds it advantageous to maintain local banking relations with that same U.S. bank's host country branch if there is one.

Although this might appear to be a mere courtesy account situation, it is likely that the indigenous parent corporation benefits from increased contact with the U.S. bank's local establishment in the host country. If nothing more, communications are often made smoother and more rapid, a consideration no less vital in the conduct of international financial relations than in diplomatic relations. Equally important is the personal contact with the U.S. branch bank's local staff in the host country. It is not unlikely that some of these individuals will at various times in the future be stationed in the bank's head office in the United States and then be in a position to deal with the corporation's banking problems, and those of its U.S. subsidiary, with greater familiarity.

d. *Local Subsidiaries of Non-Indigenous, Non-U.S.-Controlled Corporations*

A final type of corporate depositor, falling between the indigenous corporation and the local subsidiary of a U.S. corporation, is the local subsidiary of a corporation that is neither indigenous nor American-controlled. As might be expected, subsidiaries whose own home country banks maintain branches in the host country have a certain tendency to gravitate toward those institutions, just as the U.S. corporate subsidiaries, if and when they look beyond indigenous banks, tend to lean more toward U.S. branch banks than toward those from other countries. As in the case of the U.S. corporate subsidiaries, however, accounts maintained by corporations in this fourth group with any branch banks are usually in addition to those maintained in indigenous banks.

Corporate subsidiaries in this group whose home country banks are not present in the host country are more likely candidates for the U.S. branch banks' services. This is especially so if a U.S. branch bank can offer the facilities of branches and representatives located elsewhere, particularly in the non-U.S. corporate subsidiary's home country, i.e., that of its parent.

In this respect those U.S. banks with widely scattered overseas facilities have a competitive advantage. Moreover, the contact between the U.S. branch bank and the non-indigenous non-American corporate subsidiary benefits to some extent by the fact that both institutions are foreign in the host country. Nevertheless, if access to this fourth group of potential corporate depositors is somewhat easier than to the indigenous corporations, it is more difficult than access to the U.S. corporate subsidiaries. Accordingly, the relations between the U.S. branch banks and this group appear to be a hybrid.

3. Individuals

The third potential source of host currency deposits is comprised of individuals residing in the host country and elsewhere.

a. Individuals Residing Outside the Host Country

This group consists of persons maintaining host currency funds on time deposits in the host country, often because of a higher rate of interest than they can obtain elsewhere,[84] current accounts and time deposit accounts containing blocked funds, or funds which family or personal considerations make necessary in the host country even though the depositors reside elsewhere. Heterogeneous in its composition, this group contains some individuals with sizeable accounts who can take advantage of a banking network extending into several countries. On the other hand there are also in this group depositors who maintain only small accounts, for example emigrants, for many of whom a bank account is more a connection with the past than with the present or future.

84. It is unlikely that the U.S. branch banks have received many funds in this category. French franc balances have presented little attraction to depositors having other alternatives. In Great Britain, where higher rates have prevailed, indigenous institutions, particularly the building societies, have received most of the deposits attracted by interest rates. In any event, few U.S. branch banks appear to have been geared to attract such accounts in the host countries, although there is some evidence to suggest that special efforts have been made by some U.S. branch banks to attract deposits originating in the Middle East.

b. *Individuals Residing Locally*

Locally resident individuals can be broken into two sub-groups for purposes of analysing their potentialities as host currency depositors in the U.S. branch banks. These two sub-groups are the non-indigenous residents, including resident Americans, and native residents in the host country.

(1) American Citizens and Other Resident Foreigners

In the host countries there have been sufficient numbers of U.S. citizens in residence to constitute, if not a large, then at least a relatively affluent corps of potential depositors. This group is composed of individuals attached to U.S. diplomatic and consular missions; officials of international organizations; employees of the local subsidiaries of U.S. corporations or, more rarely, of indigenous or other non-U.S. corporations or firms; military personnel stationed in the host country;[85] students; retired persons; professionals including artists, writers, and persons in the theatre or cinema; and an amorphous collection of individuals otherwise employed or unemployed, some wealthy and others of limited means, who are residing in the host country for varying lengths of time for a multitude of different personal reasons. The size and composition of the entire sub-group varies from city to city and has changed with the passage of time. For example, the number of U.S. military personnel has declined while the number of corporate employees has increased.

Many of these Americans maintain host currency accounts, mainly checking accounts, with a local branch of a U.S. bank. The majority of these are "household accounts" opened by persons accustomed to having checking accounts in the United States or elsewhere and likely to make more host currency payments by check than would the indigenous local resident.[86]

These accounts are not likely in most instances to be large. Indigenous banks offer similar, if initially less familiar, services to these individuals, many of whom also maintain accounts in local institutions. Moreover, the prevalence of cash payment, coupled with postal banking services in France (and especially Switzerland)[87] has meant that host currency balances in the accounts in the U.S. branch banks have faced stiff competition.

---

85. This would not apply to the case of Switzerland. Note that military banking facilities are operated abroad by some U.S. banks under agreements made with the U.S. Treasury Department. In addition to maintaining checking accounts for individuals, exchanging U.S. dollars into local currency where permitted, and performing other minor functions these facilities can also provide accounting services to the military bases where they are located.

86. One U.S. branch bank has provided "student account" facilities primarily for Americans and other foreigners enrolled in the local universities.

87. Great Britain had the Post Office Savings Bank during the period under study; but this is not the equivalent of the *giro* system in France. It is noteworthy that in

Of greater importance is the fact that many of these Americans, especially the employees of U.S. corporate subsidiaries and of the U.S. government,[88] receive significant portions of their salaries in dollars deposited directly into bank accounts in the United States or into local dollar accounts,[89] as opposed to host currency accounts, in a local U.S. branch bank, or—more rarely—in indigenous banks. If host currency is needed, these individuals have dollars transferred from the United States or from a local dollar account and converted into host currency balances, which are then drawn down rather rapidly. Except in unusual instances where larger sums are needed, e.g., for the purchase of an automobile or the acquisition or furnishing of a residence, these host currency balances have seldom been large.

At least one U.S. branch bank has required that minimum balances be maintained in current accounts, a practice that undoubtedly discourages many potential depositors whose current accounts can be kept more cheaply (to them) in indigenous banks. This is one desired effect of minimum balance requirements, which spare a bank from the low profit (or loss) involved in maintaining a swarm of small accounts.

Many of the non-American resident foreigners fit roughly into the general categories of employees, students et al. outlined above in the case of the resident Americans. To the extent that these individuals need host currency accounts and find branch banks or banking subsidiaries from their own native countries present locally, their funds tend to be deposited there. Those non-American residents whose national banks are not present in the host country often select U.S. branch banks for their accounts, especially some of the wealthy non-Americans. Frequently members of this latter group have dollar securities portfolios maintained by U.S. branch banks' head offices and find it convenient to have one of their host currency accounts in those U.S. branch banks. In other cases these individuals have entrusted funds directly to U.S. branch banks offering, directly or indirectly, the service of *gérance de fortunes* (literally, management of wealth), which corresponds to a fiduciary or trust company's activity in the United States. In this event,

---

the latter half of the 1960's there was increasing pressure in Great Britain for such a postal giro system, which finally commenced operations in October 1968. See p. 63, note 142. Of the three host countries Switzerland has by far the most efficient postal giro system (being surpassed only by that operating in The Netherlands); and cash payment is predominant there as well.

88. Including U.S. Armed Forces personnel, a large number of whom have portions of their salaries paid (in dollars) directly by "allotments" to members of their families residing in the United States and elsewhere.

89. By 1947 eligible residents of Great Britain could maintain dollar accounts, and by 1950 a similar situation prevailed in France. See pp. 178 and 173 respectively.

there is no necessary connection with the head office bank in the United States.[90]

(2) Indigenous Local Residents

That the U.S. branch banks have enjoyed some success in attracting indigenous residents' host currency deposits there can be little doubt. This is not, however, to suggest that the typical resident native is likely to keep his funds in a local U.S. branch bank. Indeed, the average Frenchman in particular, conscious of inflation and devaluation, has been understandably reluctant to put his funds in any bank—foreign or indigenous—during parts of the period under study.[91] Moreover, the indigenous banks, with their widespread system of branches, offer a far more convenient alternative.

Nevertheless, U.S. branch banks unquestionably do have an appeal for some atypical indigenous residents.[92] Men and women with members of their families residing in the United States, and sometimes elsewhere, often find remittances to and from these relatives easier to arrange through a local U.S. branch bank. Likewise, certain wealthy individuals frequently maintain accounts in the local American branch banks because they are investing or trading in securities traded on (or off) the U.S. stock exchanges, or because they travel to the United States and desire banking contacts and introductions there. Of course, the major indigenous banks offer similar services through their correspondent relationships with commercial banks in the United States. In fact, such services become almost identical once the traveller finds himself outside the head office bank's city, for a local U.S. correspondent bank would then enter the picture in any event. Only in states with laws like those of California does he find the widely scattered sister-branches of the branch bank in his native country.[93]

90. In the 1960's, in addition to the *gérance de fortunes,* there were U.S. branch banks that made available to individual customers the head office banks' common trust funds. This necessarily involved the transmission of information and funds, but did not involve the local personnel in the host country in terms of making investment decisions. By the end of the decade some U.S. branch banks served as sales points for shares in investment funds available to non-U.S. citizens and residents.

91. It appears that some did, thinking that the branch of a foreign bank would be further removed from the French government (particularly the fiscal authorities) than one of the nationalized *banques de dépôts* would have been. No evidence has been found to substantiate this reasoning.

92. The head of an important banking house in one of the host countries has indicated privately that for many years he himself has continued to maintain a personal checking account with the local branch of one U.S. bank because of the "excellent service and frills" to which he has grown accustomed.

93. The states of Illinois, Massachusetts, New York, and Pennsylvania, *inter alia,* do not permit state-wide branch banking. National as well as state-chartered banks

116

4. U.S. Federal Government

The U.S. federal government, in several ways, constitutes a potential depositor of some consequence. U.S. law provides that national banks[94] and state member banks[95] can serve as depositaries of U.S. federal government owned funds. A branch bank overseas does not become a U.S. depositary automatically, application to the U.S. Treasury Department being necessary. In cities where there are several U.S. branch banks, no single establishment has carried the entire amount on deposit, which is divided among several of those present.

The U.S. government maintains accounts of a reasonably permanent nature. Host currency accounts are used by the diplomatic and consular missions to cover current expenses similar to those of commercial depositors, e.g., salaries, rental, and general overhead expenses. The U.S. Armed Forces likewise maintain accounts to handle the procurement of local commodities and the payment of civilian personnel.

Most important is the fact that the U.S. federal government and its agencies are net depositors rather than borrowers. The balances in these accounts tend to rise or fall without notice, sometimes dropping suddenly as large withdrawals are made; but they do not become negative, unlike the current accounts of corporations exercising their overdraft privileges. This factor alone has made the U.S. governmental accounts highly prized.

II. HOST CURRENCY LENDING OPERATIONS

A. Nature and Composition of the Local Market

Gathering deposits represents part of the cost side of a commercial bank's operations. In lending these funds it expects to make a profit. We have seen in the preceding section that the U.S. branch banks are

---

are subject to this prohibition by virtue of the McFadden Act, which does not allow national banks to establish branches in states where state-chartered banks cannot do likewise. 12 U.S.C. § 36 (c) as amended. New York law will change in 1976.

94. R. S. Section 5153, March 3, 1901, chap. 871, 31 Stat. 1448 as amended; 12 U.S.C. § 90. In addition to serving as a depositary the overseas branches of national banks can act "if required to do so as fiscal agents of the United States". United States, Federal Reserve Act of December 23, 1913. c. 6 Sec. 25, 38 Stat. 273; 12 U.S.C. § 601.

95. Federal Reserve Act of December 23, 1913, chap. 6, § 15, 38 Stat. 265; 12 U.S.C. §§ 391-92. The first of these sections includes an obligation to "act as fiscal agents of the United States" when "required by the Secretary of the Treasury".

not in a position to amass the large amounts of host currency deposits that the indigenous banks can attract. This does not mean, however, that the U.S. branch banks have had no lendable funds at their disposal. First, they have access to the local money markets, in which they try to borrow funds[96] at a rate of interest which will allow them a margin of profit when these funds are re-lent to their customers at a higher rate. Second, there are head office funds that can be called upon in certain cases. Finally, even if the U.S. branch banks do not possess a broad deposit base, they nevertheless do manage to attract some host currency deposits. Let us now turn to the market in which the U.S. branch banks have conducted their host currency lending operations, with special reference to the first wave branch banks' activities during the period from the end of World War II through 1958.

1. *Principal Borrowers*

In following the sequence adopted in the preceding section, we shall examine four principal categories of potential customers for advances from the U.S. branch banks: banks, non-banking corporations or companies, individuals, and governments.

a. *Banks*

With a dearth of host currency deposits, the U.S. branch banks are "always in the money market", but rarely as lenders. Occasions arise, of course, where a U.S. branch bank has a temporary excess of funds, and lends on call in the local money market; but these instances are the exception to the normal course of events. It can safely be stated that although other banks borrow occasionally from the local U.S. branch banks, the former do not constitute a group of borrowers as such.

b. *Non-Banking Corporations and Companies*

The announced purpose for which most of the first wave of U.S. branch banks were established was to help meet the foreign trade financing needs of their U.S. corporate customers, including the host country subsidiaries of these corporations. This is the most important single group of potential borrowers. A local U.S. corporate subsidiary becomes a borrowing customer as a result of contact between it and the branch bank, contact between the parent U.S. corporation and the head office bank in the United States, or both. This contact is natural, for the U.S. corporate executives expect to be in touch with U.S. bankers both at

---

96. That is, to "buy deposits"—a practice that has gathered momentum, particularly in their Euro-dollar operations.

home and abroad. Moreover, the U.S. branch banks are often familiar with the U.S. corporations' overall banking needs and the credit risks involved, which facilitates fitting local host country contact into a corporation's global—in the literal sense of the word in some instances—relationship with a U.S. bank.

A commercial bank in the United States having no branch in a particular host country can steer its customer toward indigenous banks when that customer intends to establish a subsidiary there; but a U.S. branch bank already on the scene has a significant advantage in the natural contact that arises between it and a newly established U.S. corporate subsidiary once the latter commences operations.

If the U.S. corporate subsidiaries are in this sense the "natural" potential customers of the U.S. branch banks generally, local indigenous corporations or companies are not. There is contact between the branch banks and this latter group of potential borrowers, but not in the same atmosphere. Nonetheless, the first wave branch banks can claim, with some justification, that indigenous host country corporations and companies have been nearly as much their "natural" customers as the U.S. corporate subsidiaries. Having been present on the local banking scene as long or longer than some of the potential indigenous borrowers themselves, they have hardly been in a foreign environment. The indigenous corporation and company must therefore be included in the group of potential borrowers, it being noted that the first wave branch banks have had a distinct advantage over more newly-arrived competitors in the later years when the second and third waves were coming onto the scene.

c. *Individuals*

Locally resident individuals, indigenous and foreign, including U.S. nationals, might appear to be potential borrowing customers; but the U.S. branch banks do not deal to any appreciable extent in this retail lending market,[97] even those branch banks whose head offices have been or become[98] active retail banks in the United States.

Except in unusual circumstances a local indigenous individual can-

97. See Bank of England, 5 *Quarterly Bulletin* 308 (1965). One U.S. bank has recently entered the personal loan sector in Great Britain, however, with units called "moneyshops" that are situated close to potential customers rather than in the City or West End of London.

98. For example, the Chase National Bank of the City of New York, a wholesale institution, acquired the city-wide branch network of the Bank of the Manhattan Company, a retail bank, when the two merged in 1955. Six years later there occurred the merger between The Hanover Bank (wholesale) and the Manufacturers Trust Company (retail).

not be expected to turn to a U.S. or other foreign branch bank for an advance.[99] A locally resident U.S. national might, on the other hand, appear to be a more likely borrower. Particularly this would seem likely if he were employed by a U.S. corporate subsidiary which uses a U.S. branch bank for some of its local banking needs, or if a bank which he uses in the United States has a local branch in the host country. It appears that the U.S. branch banks have occasionally accommodated loan requests from these individuals, but that none have been prepared to engage in this field to any appreciable extent. In general, the management of the U.S. branch banks do not consider the personal lending field as within the scope of their *raison d'être* in the host countries.

d. *Governments*

Host governments might appear as potential borrowers from the U.S. banks. In 1949, for example, the French government borrowed from a consortium of New York City banks.[100] Such loans are normally negotiated with the head office banks in the United States, however, where the loans are made.[101] The presence of a U.S. branch bank on the borrower's own territory can facilitate communication between the borrower and the head office bank. Also it is probable that the position of a U.S. branch bank in the view of host monetary authorities does not suffer by virtue of a head office loan to the host government. Essentially, however, such loans lie outside the normal field of operations of a branch bank. Host governments, therefore, cannot logically be included as potential borrowing customers of the branch banks.

The U.S. government is, as we have seen, a depositor of some importance. As previously noted, however, local disbursing officers of U.S. government funds normally do not run negative balances in their accounts. Accordingly, this government, too, is not among the potential borrowers.

---

99. Although such circumstances do arise from time to time, it appears that unless the individual has some established connection with the branch bank or with the head office bank he is usually encouraged to borrow elsewhere. Moreover, the question immediately arises as to why he has been unable to obtain or unwilling to seek credit with an indigenous institution.

100. The consortium included the Chase National Bank of the City of New York, the First National Bank of New York, the French-American Banking Corporation, the Guaranty Trust Company of New York, and J. P. Morgan and Company. This $75 million loan was secured by gold which the Banque de France had deposited at the Federal Reserve Bank of New York, and was made to refinance credits extended the previous year to France by that Bank. See New York Times, Nov. 1, 1949, p. 37, col. 6 (late city edition).

101. The advent of the voluntary U.S. Guidelines for bank lending in 1965 and the measures that followed would now have to be taken into account.

B. *Legal Authority to Lend Host Currencies*

From the foregoing it is evident that the U.S. branch banks are in the host currency wholesale lending markets just as they are in the wholesale borrowing markets. In their lending operations they are subject once again to two types of laws, U.S. laws and those of the host countries.

1. *U.S. Law*

Earlier in the present Chapter we observed that U.S. federal laws and regulations have not hampered the host currency deposit-taking operations of the U.S. branch banks. As to their lending operations, no U.S. laws or regulations provide for the scrutiny of their advances. Federal Deposit Insurance premiums need not be paid by U.S. banks on deposits in their branches abroad since these deposits are not insured.[102] Nor were U.S. banks required to maintain reserves against foreign branch deposits[103] until (Federal Reserve) Regulation M was amended in 1969.[104] The only apparently relevant limitation was their inability until 1963 to guarantee the debts of U.S. corporate subsidiaries or other borrowers,[105] although *stricto sensu* this does not involve a lending operation.

2. *Host Country Laws*

a. *France*

In France the U.S. branch banks are generally subject to the same banking rules and regulations as the indigenous French banks with regard to their lending operations. Principally these have stemmed from the laws applying to all *banques de dépôts* in France, such as the prohibition against participating in more than 10% (now 20%) of the capital of any borrowing enterprise (except in other banks or financial institutions as necessary for their functioning), and against lending more than 75% (now 100%) of a bank's own resources to one borrower.[106] The only two special rules for foreign branch banks are those previously noted

102. Federal Deposit Insurance Corporation Act, p. 37, note 39; 12 U.S.C. § 1813 (1) (5).

103. United States, Board of Governors of the Federal Reserve System, Regulation D, 12 C.F.R. § 204.2 (b), 27 Fed. Reg. 7627, August 2, 1962.

104. 12 C.F.R. § 213.7, 34 Fed. Reg. 13409, August 20, 1969. See 55 *Federal Reserve Bulletin* 657 (1969). A corresponding amendment was made in Regulation D at the same time. See *Id.* 656 and 12 C.F.R. § 204.5 (c). See also page 273.

105. This disability was removed when (Federal Reserve) Regulation M was revised. See 12 C.F.R. § 213.4 (a), 28 Fed. Reg. 8361, August 15, 1963.

106. See p. 51, note 100 and p. 52, note 101.

requiring a separate set of books reflecting their operations on French territory and the obligation to maintain a minimum capital in France equal to that required of indigenous banks as measured by their operations.[107]

Of greater bearing on host currency lending operations have been the credit control measures aimed at checking inflationary pressures in France. The banking sector of the economy has a twofold contact with the government in this respect. First, as previously observed, the major *banques de dépôts* were nationalized and the *banques d'affaires* brought under direct governmental scrutiny. Second, the postwar French Plans[108] have required the participation of the banks in their lending operations. More precisely, controls on lending have been deemed necessary if the economy's progress under the Plans is to be guided by any semblance of order.

Whereas the French credit controls have had little if any direct effect on the deposit collecting activity of the U.S. branch banks they have directly affected their lending operations. Like all French banks, the U.S. branch banks were required by the Conseil National de Crédit from January 1947 onwards to screen all requests for advances exceeding FF 2 million (approx. $1.7 million), while requests for sums exceeding FF 30 million (approx. $24.2 million) had to be referred to the Banque de France for clearance.[109]

The qualitative credit control scheme adopted by the French government was difficult to apply effectively.[110] From the outset the absence of well-defined criteria for the banks to use in screening their customers'

107. See p. 59, note 130.

108. The Plans have been successively designed to further specific goals. The First Plan (1947-1950 and extended to 1953) laid stress on expanding the coal and steel, transportation, farm equipment, electricity, cement, and fuel industries. The Second Plan (1954-1957) was a continuation of the First in many respects, but widened the scope to include agriculture and housing, among other industries. For an informative source with regard to the recently terminated Fifth Plan (1966-1970) see Commissariat Général du Plan d'Equipement et de la Productivité, *Ve Plan, 1966-1970,* Rapport Général de la Commission de l'Economie Générale et du Financement, 2 vols., Paris (Documentation française, M. 494), 1966. The Sixth Plan is now in force.

109. In February 1948 the latter figure was raised to FF 50 million; in April 1950 to FF 100 million; in October 1951 to FF 500 million, at which time commercial bills were first included in this qualitative control, while simultaneously the rediscount rate was raised and reintroduced as a means of affecting credit conditions; and in July 1959, to FF 1 billion (i.e., NF 10 million). See p. 176, note 104. This progression does not indicate a relaxing of control over credit as much as the deteriorating value of the French franc.

110. For a useful analysis of the French post-war credit control scheme during its early phases, see Board of Governors of the Federal Reserve System, "Postwar Credit Controls in France", by Albert O. Hirschman and Robert V. Rosa [sic], 35

requests and the difficulty in relating these requests to the exigencies of the First Plan made the qualitative method basically unworkable. Probably of greater importance was the "loophole" provided for the discounting of commercial bills, which allowed this important financing method to remain outside the quantitative control of the authorities.

In September 1948 the Conseil National de Crédit ordered all banks to maintain their holdings of Treasury obligations, called *bons de Trésor*,[111] at 95% of the amount held on September 30th of that year, and to place at least 20% of any new deposits into this form of investment.[112] Also, each bank was accorded a limit with respect to the rediscount facilities which it might be accorded at the central bank.[113] With the passage of time the French credit control mechanism came to rely increasingly on quantitative measures, coupled with the 1951 revival of the use of the central bank rate which the government's cheap money policy had kept low.[114]

Federal Reserve Bulletin 348-60 (1949). See also Germain-Martin, "France", p. 52, note 104, at pp. 292-301. A later examination of the French controls is found in J. S. G. Wilson, *French Banking Structure and Credit Policy,* p. 56, note 119, at pp. 376-432.

111. That is, Treasury bills, which the banks could purchase at any time directly from the government. The influence of this "open window" policy on liquidity finally led to the institution of a public auction of French Treasury bills in 1963. Today the bills to which the banks in France are obliged to subscribe are called *certificats de trésorerie* (Treasury certificates). Since the period from 1961-1966 during which *banques de dépôts* were required to maintain a Treasury coefficient (see p. 185, note 135 and p. 242, note 158) only those which the banks take above their required limits have been referred to as Treasury bills.

112. This is the so-called *plancher* (floor) requirement, designed to stop the banks' practice of acquiring lendable funds by selling off their government obligations. The use of 1948 as a base year lasted until July 19, 1956 when a flat 25% requirement was instituted. See also p. 185, note 135.

113. This is the so-called *plafond* (ceiling) requirement. If a bank sought to rediscount at the Banque de France in excess of its plafond, it was obliged to pay a 1% penalty surcharge on the first ten per cent over the limit, the practice being called *"enfer"* ("hell"). A bank forced to seek rediscounts above the ten per cent penalty zone at the central bank paid a $2^{1}/2\%$ surcharge, termed *"super-enfer"*. The banks were not permitted to charge their customers in turn for these penalties. In December 1967 the *"super-enfer"* category was ended when the *"enfer"* surcharge was raised to its present level of $2^{1}/2\%$.

114. The central bank rate in France for rediscounting Treasury bills and self-liquidating commercial paper was raised $^{1}/8\%$ in January 1947, to $1\frac{3}{4}\%$. Subsequently it was changed to $2^{1}/2\%$ in October 1947; to $3^{1}/2\%$ in September 1948 and to 3% later in the same month; to $2^{1}/2\%$ in June 1950; to 3% in October 1951; to 4% in November of the same year; to $3^{1}/2\%$ in September 1953; to $3\frac{1}{4}\%$ in February 1954; and to 3% in December of that year, where it remained until it was raised to 4% and then to 5% in April and August 1957 respectively. See Federal Reserve Bank of New York, *Foreign Central Banking: the Instruments of Monetary Policy,* by Peter G. Fousek, New York, 1957, pp. 27-30.

For the present study the factor of primary interest is that the U.S. branch banks have been treated by the credit control mechanism like any other banks in France. No special regime has been instituted to supervise their activities; and no special requirements have been imposed on them. The U.S. branch banks and their customers have had no special advantages or handicaps stemming from the French government's efforts to control inflation.

French exchange control laws and regulations apply to bank lending operations differently than do the credit control measures. At the present stage of our examination we are primarily interested in the French franc lending operations of the U.S. branch banks prior to the return to external convertibility near the end of 1958. It was shown in the preceding section that the exchange control laws have made a distinction between French franc accounts maintained by residents and non-residents of the French franc zone. In like fashion they have differentiated between various loan transactions depending upon the residence of the borrower and lender.

The 1947 *décret*, which codified then existing laws dealing with exchange control, laid down the general rule that all settlements between French residents and non-residents need prior authorization from the Office des Changes.[115] French residents could neither borrow from nor lend money to non-residents without permission. Generally speaking, blanket permission was given to the *intermédiaires agréés* to satisfy most of the short-term credit needs of French exporters, with specific instructions issued periodically to provide for the discounting of their drafts drawn on foreign importers.[116] Also, smaller transactions were accorded general permission, with the limits modified as conditions warranted.

For the U.S. branch banks in France the exchange controls have been relatively more important than for banks in France generally. This is due to the fact that as foreign institutions they are bound to be more heavily oriented toward non-domestic transactions than indigenous banks. Indeed, to be so oriented has been the primary intent of the U.S. branch banks. As a result of the French exchange control mechanism, its theoretical aspects as well as the manner in which it has been applied, the U.S. branch banks have suffered no discrimination with regard to their host currency lending operations. Nevertheless, it is clear that their special reason for being in the host country has produced the inevitable

115. Ministère des Finances, *Décret* no. 47-1337 of July 15, 1947, p. 95, note 33, title III. The Office des Changes shortly thereafter issued a set of notices dealing with a wide range of operations in foreign exchange. *Avis* nos. 202-277, *Journal officiel*, September 25, 1947, pp. 9641-9706.
116. See, for example, Office des Changes, *Instruction* no. 603 of February 3, 1955.

result of their being more sharply affected by the system than the indigenous banks.

b. *Great Britain*

The U.S. branch banks in postwar Great Britain have conducted their host currency lending activities in an atmosphere that is legally quite different from that in France. We have already seen that the establishment of a branch bank in Great Britain can be accomplished with much less formality than in France. In terms of operating rules, too, the British formula does not attempt to segregate the branches of foreign banks. For example, the French and Swiss banking law requirements that a special set of books be maintained has no precise British legal counterpart although in practice the branch bank in Great Britain keeps similar records. Indeed, in a system where no separate banking law exists it is perhaps normal to expect that foreign banks' branches would be assimilated with relative ease into the banking community as far as their lending operations are concerned.

It is interesting, therefore, to note that in a sense the U.S. and other foreign branch banks have been slightly removed from the clearing banks, which they most closely resemble. For example, until September 16, 1971 banks operating in Great Britain had no minimum legal reserve requirement.[117] Nonetheless, from December 1946 the clearing banks in London maintained (first by mutual accord with the Bank of England, and subsequently "reinforced by official prescription")[118] a cash ratio[119] of 8% and a liquidity ratio[120] of 30% (later 28%). The U.S. and other foreign branch banks, like the merchant banking houses, remained out-

---

117. Bank of England, 2 *Quarterly Bulletin* 250-51 (1962). See generally Bank for International Settlements, *Eight European Central Banks*, p. 61, note 139, at pp. 108-09. All banks in Great Britain have been subject to minimum reserve requirements since September 16, 1971 as a result of the move taken by the Bank of England following its paper on Competition and Credit Control that was circulated in the spring of that year. See Bank of England, 11 *Quarterly Bulletin* 189-93 (1971). The reserve ratio was set initially at $12^1/2\%$.

118. Bank of England, 9 *Quarterly Bulletin* 177 (1969).

119. That is, cash as a percent of gross deposits. "Cash" consists of till money (vault cash) plus non-interest-bearing deposits with the Bank of England. See (Radcliffe) Committee, *Report*, Cmnd. 827, p. 52, par. 147.

120. That is, the percentage of a bank's liquid assets compared with its gross deposits. The numerator of this ratio consists of "cash" (as defined in the preceding footnote) plus call money and bills discounted, including Treasury bills. *Id.*, p. 47, par. 139. The 30% figure was reduced in September 1963 to 28%. National (Jones) Board, *Report*, Cmnd. 3292, p. 15, par. 20. See Speech by the Governor of the Bank of England, October 16, 1963, Bank of England, 3 *Quarterly Bulletin* 295 (1963). See also, *Id.* 257.

side the scope of this convention[121] although they were always free to maintain similar ratios voluntarily.[122]

In addition to the cash and liquidity ratios, the clearing banks have also been subject to so-called "Special Deposit" requirements from July 1958 when they, the Scottish banks, and the Bank of England made an agreement under which the latter could call for special interest-bearing deposits amounting to 1% of the banks' total deposits (½% in the case of the Scottish banks).[123] Another privilege enjoyed by the U.S. branch banks along with other foreign and overseas banks and the merchant banks is that unlike the clearers, they were not until 1971 required to furnish monthly financial statements. This was the case notwithstanding a statement by the Radcliffe Committee that it saw "no reason why other banks should not provide and publish regular statements of assets and liabilities on a comparable basis with those of the clearing banks".[124]

If in some respects the U.S. branch banks are on the periphery of the British banking sector it is nevertheless clear that they are expected to comply with the credit control measures administered by the Bank of England. The principal legislative measure behind the program is the Borrowing (Control and Guarantees) Act, 1946 which contains a provision for bank lending similar to the exemption for the receipt of moneys on deposit.[125] The Act provides that references to the borrowing of money, as defined in the Act:

> "shall not apply to the borrowing of money by any person (other than a local authority) in the ordinary course of his business from a person carrying on a banking undertaking."[126]

Moreover, the subsequent Control of Borrowing Order, 1947 exempts from the Act:

---

121. (Radcliffe) Committee, *Report, supra,* p. 63, part. 177.

122. "For the other [i.e., non-clearing] banks, in particular the overseas and foreign banks in London, there can be no single definition of liquid assets or standard of liquidity because their requirements and operating conditions vary so widely. Moreover, their U.K. operations form only a part of their total business and many of these banks can, if necessary, look to their head offices for assistance". Bank of England, 2 *Quarterly Bulletin* 253 (1962). But see p. 241.

123. The agreement did not go into effect until April 28, 1960. See Great Britain, Central Office of Information, *United Kingdom Financial Institutions,* p. 64, note 146, at p. 8. See also p. 189, note 156, and p. 246. The Special Deposits did not qualify for inclusion in the numerator of the cash or liquidity ratios described above. Bank for International Settlements, *Eight European Central Banks, supra,* at p. 118.

124. (Radcliffe) Committee, *Report,* p. 287, par. 814.

125. See page 98, material cited to note 50.

126. Borrowing (Control and Guarantees) Act, page 98, note 48, par 1—(1) (d). Similar language is included in Great Britain, H. M. Treasury, Control of Borrowing Order, 1958. S.I. 1958, no. 1208.

"... borrowing by any person, other than a local authority, where the money borrowed is repayable on demand or not more than six months after demand and the loan is wholly unsecured or is secured only by a bill of exchange payable on demand or at a fixed period not exceeding six months after the date of the borrowing or after sight or by a promissory note payable not more than six months after the date of borrowing..."[127]

Thus it would appear that as in the case of taking deposits, the banks' normal commercial lending operations lie outside the ambit of the Borrowing (Control and Guarantees) Act, 1946. In practice, however, this has not been the case. The principles of the Act have been "deemed by the Treasury to apply also to bank lending and money".[128]

The initial statement of these principles (formally addressed to capital issues but, as will be seen, applicable to short-term bank lending) was contained in the document entitled Capital Issues Control—Memorandum of Guidance to the Capital Issues Committee, presented to Parliament by the Chancellor of the Exchequer on May 31, 1945.[129] This Memorandum stated that:

"The objects of the control are to ensure (a) that subject to the possibilities of the capital market and the circumstances, the order of priority of capital issues is determined according to their relative importance in the general national interest, having regard, particularly, to current Government policy in respect of physical investment; and (b) that in all cases where consent is to be given, the time of raising the capital is settled with a view to preserving orderliness and avoiding congestion in the capital market."[130]

Another pertinent provision of this Memorandum of general principles was the statement that:

"The Committee is asked to restrict the amounts of permissible issues where the amounts proposed appear to involve obvious over-capitalisation or excessive working capital."[131]

A subsequent statement of guiding principles was contained in the document entitled Capital Issues Control—Special Memorandum to the Capital Issues Committee, which the Chancellor presented to Parliament on December 2, 1947.[132] This Special Memorandum stated that the 1945 Memorandum (Cmd. 6645) had been "re-examined in the light of current conditions", adding that "the serious changes in the balance of

127. Great Britain, H. M. Treasury, Control of Borrowing Order, 1947, dated May 21, 1947, S.R. & O. 1947, no. 945. Identical language is contained in the Control of Borrowing Order, 1958, supra.
128. International Monetary Fund, Central Banking Legislation, 1961, vol. 1, p. 61, note 137, at p. 206.
129. Cmd. 6645.
130. Id., § 1.
131. Id., § 10.
132. Cmd. 7281.

payments position and the consequent need for internal economic adjustments call for a considerable revision of emphasis in the instructions upon which the Commitee work".[133] After referring to a 1948 White Paper on Capital Investment,[134] the December 1947 Special Memorandum stated that it had been decided that:

> ". . . substantial modifications must be made.
> The main objectives are:
> (a) to reduce the total demands of capital projects upon manpower and upon steel, coal, and other materials in order that the requirements of the export industries and other vital purposes may be met;
> (b) to ensure that there is a concentration of effort on completing as rapidly as possible the most important schemes."[135]

The Special Memorandum went on to state that:

> "The general rule must be postponement of capital outlay, wheter on building or on plant and machinery, except where the project gives a considerable return, directly or indirectly, in increasing exports or saving imports from difficult sources, or is of importance to such basic industries as agriculture, coal and steel production."[136]

It must be stressed that although both the 1945 Memorandum and the 1947 Special Memorandum were expressed in terms of controlling capital issues, their objectives have been applied to short-term bank lending that falls technically outside their scope. Banks have been expected to prevent nominally short-term credits from being stretched-out in a way that would circumvent official policy. Borrowers' genuine short-term credit needs are to be distinguished from the building up of excess cash reserves or the financing of unnecessary inventory or raw material stockpiling.

The second area of regulation governing bank lending is found in the Exchange Control Act, 1947[137] and the Notices and Orders issued thereunder. The British exchange control rules do not affect the extension of sterling credits to residents of the sterling area (with an important exception to be noted below) because these are considered to be internal transactions. The rules have, however, prohibited advances to non-residents without permission from the Bank of England.[138] Blanket per-

---

133. *Ibid.*
134. Cmd. 7268. This White Paper had been presented by the Chancellor of the Exchequer to Parliament in December 1947.
135. Cmd. 7281.
136. *Ibid.*
137. Exchange Control Act, 1947, p. 70, note 174.
138. See F. E. Notice 224 dated July 20, 1945. See also Great Britain, Bank of England, Exchange Control (General) Notice 67, dated July 2, 1957, par. 22. For the rules in force before the return to external convertibility see generally District

mission has been accorded for short-term financing of most export trans-actions,[139] it having been specified originally that repayment of such credits was to be made in sterling from accounts "appropriate to the country or account area of the borrower", unless otherwise authorized by the Bank of England.[140]

The exchange control rules have also applied to another important part of the business of the U.S. branch banks in London (as well as the British overseas banks and the accepting houses), namely the extension of sterling credits to non-residents of the sterling area for purchases from other non-residents. This business was seriously interrupted when the financial repercussions of the 1956 Suez Canal crisis led the Bank of England on September 20, 1957 to withdraw permission for these ad-vances.[141] This meant that the U.S. branch banks in London and the others mentioned above were cut off from an important part of their clientele, as were the latter from a primary source of credit. By Feb-ruary 1959 the restriction had been lifted;[142] but by then, as will be seen in Chapter Four, a new financing medium had begun to be developed by some of these banks.

The important exception to the freedom from British exchange con-trol rules with regard to internal advances, alluded to above, is that the rules apply to the extension of credit to resident corporations which are controlled by non-residents of the sterling area. This is directly pertinent to the U.S. branch banks' operations because it affects their advances to the British subsidiaries of U.S. corporations. The same portion of the Exchange Control Act, 1947 that would cut off the U.S. branch banks themselves from borrowing in the London money market also applies to these corporate borrowers, since they, too, are "con-trolled . . . by persons outside the scheduled territories".[143] Taken alone, the 1947 Act would make it necessary to obtain permission before the U.S. branch banks (or other lending institutions) could extend credit to this important group of potential borrowers.

The Exchange Control Notice that opens the money market to the U.S. branch banks contains a subsequent provision, however, permitting U.S. corporate subsidiaries to borrow locally, as follows:

Bank Limited, *Digest of the United Kingdom Exchange Restrictions,* p. 100, note 60, at p. 27.

139. Exchange Control (General) Notice 67, *supra,* par. 24.

140. Notice, par. 26.

141. I.M.F., *(Ninth) Exchange Restrictions,* 1958, p. 209. A similar restriction, still in force, was imposed in October 1968. See p. 247, note 186.

142. Bank of England, 7 *Quarterly Bulletin* 152 (1967).

143. Exchange Control Act, 1947, *supra,* § 30 (3). See p. 98.

"Permission as required under the terms of this Notice is hereby given to banks to grant loans (whether by way of advance or overdraft), to continue existing loans and to lend Treasury Bills or Securities to bodies corporate resident in the Scheduled Territories and controlled by persons resident outside the Scheduled Territories."[144]

This blanket permission has varied as the exchange control rules have been tightened or relaxed. For example, as of August 30, 1954 U.S. corporate subsidiaries (and other non-resident controlled borrowers) could borrow only up to £ 50,000 (approx. $ 140,000) without permission;[145] but by February 1, 1955 this limit was removed, and the authorized banks were to use their own discretion as to the size of such advances.[146]

Broadly speaking, then, overall permission was thus granted to the U.S. branch banks to lend to this important group of customers. It must be emphasized, however, that this freedom arises not from the Exchange Control Act itself but from specific exemptions and permission embodied in Orders and Notices issued by the Treasury and the Bank of England. From a juridical point of view the position of the U.S. branch banks has thus been less strong than if the statute itself opened the field. The exemptions and permission could have been removed or modified, to the detriment of the U.S. branch banks, by means of succeeding Orders or Notices, or by the withdrawal of the 1947 Notice itself, a simpler process than a parliamentary modification of the Exchange Control Act.

C. *Types of Advances*

Having seen the authority under which the U.S. branch banks can make host currency advances, it is now appropriate to turn to an examination of the types of advances that have been utilized.

1. *Short-term Lending*

In their short-term host currency lending activities the U.S. branch banks are in a position to employ some techniques normally used in the host countries as well as to adapt methods used in the United States. The principal categories available for short-term credit operations have been fixed advances, advances in current account or overdrafts, discounting, and acceptance financing.

---

144. Bank of England, Exchange Control (General) Notice 4, dated October 1, 1947, par. 4.

145. I.M.F., *(Sixth) Exchange Restrictions*, 1955, p. 309.

146. Bank of England, Exchange Control (General) Notice 4, *supra*, as amended February 1, 1955.

a. *Fixed Advances*

Commercial banks in the United States normally meet a customer's needs for short-term credit by making fixed advances under which the full or discounted amount of the advance is credited to a current account, usually a newly-opened current account, to be drawn upon as needed. The deposit thus created is a derivative deposit.[147] Interest is calculated on the entire amount during the life of the loan, regardless of how rapidly or to what extent the balance is drawn down. As a rule commercial banks in the United States require that a borrower leave a minimum amount (from 10% to 20% of the amount of the loan) on deposit in the account, constituting a "compensating balance" or "supporting balance" as it is sometimes called. This sum is included in the base against which interest is calculated, which means that the real cost to the borrower is increased accordingly.[148]

Rarely used in France, fixed advances are not unknown in Great Britain,[149] where they normally are payable on demand[150] or six months thereafter,[151] and they are occasionally used in Switzerland for periods as short as six months. Fixed loans are not, however, the usual method of granting short-term credits in any of the host countries. Although the U.S. branch banks have made an effort to include the American-style fixed advance among their lending techniques, they have done so with only limited success. Local European customers do not readily accept the requirement of a compensating balance and generally prefer to borrow, whenever possible, under arrangements with which they are more familiar and which they consider less costly. Some U.S. corporate subsidiaries may be less reluctant to borrow in this fashion; but they, too, have frequently preferred other methods. Let us turn, therefore, to the more commonly used forms of short-term lending in the host countries.

147. See pp. 87-88.

148. *Cf.* Major B. Foster and Raymond Rodgers (eds.), *Money and Banking*, 3d. ed., New York, Prentice-Hall, 1947, p. 149. See also John A. Cochran, *Money, Banking and the Economy*, New York, Macmillan and London, Collier-Macmillan, 1967, p. 163 where the author notes that a bank is "usually willing to relate this requirement to the average deposit over the entire year, though sometimes a bank insists that this minimum deposit must be maintained at all times".

149. Especially in London. Elsewhere in Great Britain lending is more often by overdraft.

150. Advances are rarely, however, called on demand. See National (Jones) Board, *Report*, Cmnd. 3292, p. 27, par. 51. See also "Bank Liquidity in the United Kingdom", Bank of England, 2 *Quarterly Bulletin* 248, 254 (1962).

151. Allowing them to qualify for the exemption provided by the Control of Borrowing Order, 1947 (see page 127). For the same reason fixed advances in Great Britain are usually unsecured or secured by sight bills or by paper maturing within six months after sight or after the date of the borrowing.

b. *Advances in Current Account — Overdrafts*

Whereas commercial banks in the United States have not customarily lent via previously arranged overdrafts, or advances in current account,[152] this method is normally used for short-term financing of domestic business in Great Britain and Switzerland and is also utilized to some extent in Great Britain for foreign trade financing. In France, overdraft facilities are usually provided only on an informal basis; i.e., the bank will agree informally to allow overdrafts to help a customer with a temporary need for funds, but normally will not enter into a written agreement to that effect. In the host countries a bank granting an overdraft facility will customarily allow the borrower to have a net debit balance in his current account[153] not to exceed a certain agreed-upon maximum amount. The customer's checks and orders for payment are honored up to this amount; and deposits to the account are treated as repayments, reducing the outstanding advance accordingly.

Overdrafts in Great Britain and Switzerland are either secured or unsecured, depending upon the identity of the customer and the size of the advance, i.e., upon normal banking-risk factors. In Great Britain they are nominally payable on demand. In France, secured advances in current account are less common, occuring only in those infrequent cases where a bank is committed formally to allowing overdraft privileges to a customer.[154]

Interest charges may be calculated on three bases:

(1) the maximum debit balance to be allowed, whether utilized or not, on which a small interest charge may be made;

(2) the largest debit balances occuring during the interest period; and

(3) the movement in the account, i.e., the frequency with which funds are drawn down or deposited.[155]

The rates charged are generally related to the central bank rate; and secured overdrafts usually incur reduced charges.

Although in some respects similar to the "line of credit" arranged by a U.S. commercial bank for a domestic customer in the United States, the pre-arranged overdraft or advance in current account is not to be

---

152. A commercial bank in the United States is not prohibited from honoring a customer's check that exceeds the amount on deposit in his current account, and—in effect—advances funds to the customer in so doing. The practice was long discouraged, however; but see pp. 146-47.

153. In arranging advances in current account it is not usually the practice to create a separate account for the purpose.

154. This is the so-called *crédit mobilisable,* whereby with prior permission from the Banque de France a bank can grant overdraft facilities secured by a bill rediscounted at the central bank.

155. This is in the nature of a service charge or commission.

132

confused with that practice. By extending its customer a line of credit the commercial bank in the United States is committed to honor the potential borrower's future loan requests up to a certain amount as long as there is no relevant change in the underlying conditions upon which the line has been accorded.

Rather than being an agreement under which the customer can draw funds immediately, the line of credit is an "agreement to agree" in the future under a set of prescribed conditions. Many of the preliminary inquiries will already have been made, the customer's balance sheet will have been examined, and the actual advance, when—and if— made, can be handled quickly. To this extent it is advantageous to the potential borrower, for he knows the conditions under which his loan request will be granted and can organize his affairs accordingly. It is not, however, an advance.

The overdraft lending method has definite advantages to the borrower compared to the fixed advance method described in the preceding section. Except for the relatively small charge on the maximum debit balance to be allowed, the borrower pays interest only on the amounts actually drawn down and for the exact periods during which the bank's funds are being used. There is, of course, no required compensating balance.

Of equal, if not greater, importance, the borrower is not penalized, so to speak, for operating within a more comfortable upper limitation on the credit immediately available. In the case of fixed advances the borrower must always consider whether to round up to a higher figure when estimating future credit needs in order to allow for unforeseen contingencies. In overdraft lending, too, the borrower must estimate these same needs with an equivalent extra margin for error. He does not, however, pay interest on the unused margin. Understandably, from the borrower's point of view the greater flexibility of the overdraft arrangement is an advantage.[156]

The locally established U.S. corporate subsidiaries have been aware of these advantages and have usually sought overdraft facilities from the host country banks and the U.S. branch banks. As a result, even if there has existed a group of customers familiar with fixed advances, this does not mean that the method itself has found favor.

---

156. There is an interesting inflationary aspect in the fixed advance not found in the overdraft lending technique. Since with the former the borrower pays interest on the funds comprising the extra margin for error, whether or not drawn down, there exists a certain encouragement to go ahead and draw them for the purchase of goods or for short-term investment. In this context see Anand G. Chandavarkar, "Unused Bank Overdrafts: Their Implications for Monetary Analysis and Policy", International Monetary Fund, 15 *Staff Papers* 491-530 (1968), especially p. 496.

c. *Discounting Drafts or Bills*

By far the most common method in France, trade bills are also discounted in Switzerland, and both trade and bank bills are used in Great Britain. With a maximum maturity of 90 days in France[157] and Switzerland and of 180 days in Great Britain, the maturities are generally less in France and Great Britain, running normally from 30 to 60 days in the former and up to 90 days in the latter. Self-liquidating in nature, trade bills are rediscountable at the Banque de France, the Swiss National Bank,[158] and in the London discount market[159] respectively. In all three countries the interest rates on these bills are indirectly related to the central bank rate. Both France and Great Britain have well organized money markets for discounted bills; and in both countries these instruments comprise a significant part of the assets of financial institutions. There is no such formal market in Switzerland.

d. *Discounting Notes*

In France there is a form of commercial short-term borrowing whereby a firm executes negotiable promissory notes payable to the order of a bank, which then discounts them. These notes differ from so-called "commercial paper" in the United States[160] in that the French instruments are required to bear three signatures (that of the borrower, the discounting bank, and a second bank whose signature is arranged by the discounting bank) and needs the approval of the Banque de France in order to be eligible for rediscount. The maturities of such notes do not exceed 90 days; but they can be renewed up to nine months, or to twice that period under certain circumstances. By this method commercial borrowers have been able to obtain working capital. More importantly, by having the notes accompanied by a lien on material purchased with the borrowed funds, they can be renewed up to eighteen months.

157. In order to be eligible for rediscount at the Banque de France.

158. Trade bills are rarely rediscounted in Switzerland despite this technical facility.

159. As acceptances. The Bank of England does not rediscount bills directly.

160. "Commercial paper" in the United States consists of unsecured, non-interest-bearing promissory notes executed by large firms whose high credit standing justifies their being taken without collateral and allows them to be traded freely in the open market. These notes normally run from three to six months in maturity and are traded on a discount basis in denominations ranging from $2,500 to $50,000. See generally Herbert Spero, *Money and Banking*, 2d ed., New York, Barnes & Noble, 1953, pp. 79-81. U.S. commercial paper is not to be confused with the French *papier commercial*, which term embraces both bills and notes arising out of and linked with a sale of merchandise, as opposed to *papier financier*, which describes instruments used to raise working capital. Thus, commercial paper, as the term is used in the United States, would more closely resemble *papier financier* than its apparent French language cognate.

e. *Acceptance Financing*

An alternative to discounting customers' bills or notes lies in the possibility of accepting drafts or bills of exchange drawn on the bank itself, payable at a future date. Here the accepting bank does not part with its own funds, but "lends" its name to the drawer of the bill, who can then obtain a more favorable rate of interest in the acceptance market.[161] For the use of its name and superior credit standing the accepting bank charges a commission to the drawer of the bill, who is obliged to supply the bank with the necessary funds for payment of the instrument at maturity.[162] In both France and Great Britain there are active markets for bankers' acceptances, the maturities of which are within the limits required for discounting as noted in the foregoing section in the discounting of bills of exchange.

Prior to passage of the Federal Reserve Act of 1913 national banks in the United States were not allowed to deal in or create bankers' acceptances.[163] Section 13 of that Act provides as follows:

"Any member bank may accept drafts or bills of exchange drawn upon it having not more than six months sight to run, exclusive of days of grace, which grow out of transactions involving the importation or exportation of goods; or which grow out of transactions involving the domestic shipment of goods provided shipping documents conveying or securing title are attached at the time of acceptance; or which are secured at the time of acceptance by a warehouse receipt or other such document conveying or securing title covering readily marketable staples."[164]

A member bank is not required to maintain reserves against its acceptances outstanding, but it is prohibited from accepting for any one borrower an amount exceeding 10% of the bank's paid-up and unimpaired capital stock and surplus without being provided with security in the form of "attached documents or by some other actual security growing out of the same transaction as the acceptance".[165] The total amount of acceptances outstanding for all customers cannot exceed one-half of such capital and surplus unless under (Federal Reserve) Regulation C the

---

161. For example, in Great Britain trade bills are normally discounted at 1% to 2 1/2 % over Bank rate. Bankers' acceptances are discounted at a rate that is near 1/4 % below Bank rate. In all cases, the identity of the parties and their credit standing determine the exact rates.

162. In Great Britain the commission usually ranges from 1% to 2%. This raises the real rate paid by the borrower. Nevertheless, this form of credit is usually less expensive than the trade bill or trade acceptance.

163. See generally Max J. Wasserman, Charles W. Hultman, and Laszlo Zsoldos, *International Finance,* New York, Simmons-Boardman, 1963, pp. 160-62.

164. United States, Federal Reserve Act of December 23, 1913, chap. 6, § 13; 38 Stat. 263, as amended; 12 U.S.C. § 372.

165. *Ibid.*

bank has been authorized to accept bills up to 100%,[166] in which case acceptances growing out of domestic transactions in the United States cannot exceed 50% of the total.[167]

f. *Special Arrangements for Financing Exports*

Generally speaking, merchants dealing with local suppliers and customers over the years obtain and extend credit in an atmosphere where the parties are familair with one another. On the contrary, trading with persons in foreign countries or in distant provinces of the same country involves added risks, which have led to the use of trade and bankers' acceptances for supplying short-term funds.

Not only were colonial transactions financed in London and Paris by this inexpensive, self-liquidating, and relatively low-risk method; a large part of the world's commerce benefited from the efficient and flexible facilities in these financial centers. For example, transactions between U.S. and Latin American merchants often were financed by sterling acceptances through London banking institutions in the period before direct access to U.S. bank financing became available. Indeed, this was one of the primary reasons behind legislation allowing U.S. member banks to deal in and create acceptances under the 1913 reforms mentioned earlier.

The desire of the postwar U.S. branch banks to finance the foreign trade of U.S. corporate subsidiaries, and in some instances of indigenous borrowers, naturally has brought them fully into the export sector of the host banking communities. It is a sector that has been vital to the postwar economies of the host countries, and one that has undergone change. In France and Great Britain, however, it is dominated by official agencies created to render short-term foreign trade financing much less expensive.[168] This has not kept the U.S. branch banks out of

166. Board of Governors of the Federal Reserve System, Regulation C, 12 C.F.R. § 203.1 (e), 11 Fed. Reg. 8901, August 17, 1946. Such authority can be rescinded on not less than 90 days' notice in writing to the bank.

167. Federal Reserve Act, *supra,* as amended by Act of June 21, 1917, chap. 32, § 5, 40 Stat. 235; 12 U.S.C. § 372; and Regulation C, *supra.*

168. In France the Compagnie Française d'Assurance pour le Commerce Extérieur (COFACE) and the Banque Française du Commerce Extérieur (BFCE) operate in harmony to provide a method whereby export risks are insured by the former and a signature (for rediscounting at the Banque de France) furnished by the latter. See Pierre Jasinski, "Export Financing in France", 4 *Journal of World Trade Law* 426-46 (1970). In Great Britain the Export Credits Guarantee Department (ECGD) of the Department of Trade and Industry (formerly the Board of Trade) insures loans against the greater part of normal commercial risks as well as against certain economic and political risks. Eligible export paper, backed by a ECGD guarantee, also benefits from a preferential borrowing rate (about 1% above Bank rate). In Switzerland the banks provide short-term credit for exporters, which occupy a proportion-

the field, but it has offered an unlikely terrain for innovation in those two host countries.

2. Medium- and Longer-Term Lending

a. Host Country Methods

Facilities for medium-term financing of domestic transactions are similar in the host countries to the extent that there are no established markets for medium-term acceptances, bills of exchange, or promissory notes. As a result, borrowers' needs are usually handled either through overdrafts or fixed loans. Here, however, the similarity ends.

In Great Britain (credit controls permitting) and in Switzerland it has been possible for an established customer to obtain overdraft facilities on a quasi-permanent basis under which he can be nearly certain that he will not be required suddenly to repay the debit balance in his account.[169]

In France such arrangements are uncommon; but a method exists for obtaining a similar extension of credit. Here the borrower's promissory notes are made automatically renewable every three months for up to five years, the notes being deemed eligible for rediscount by the Banque de France if they bear three signatures in addition to that of the borrower,[170] and if they come to the central bank via a public financial institution. The lending bank or discounter does not have direct access to the Banque de France on these instruments.

In both Great Britain and France medium-term fixed loans are available, but under quite different circumstances and conditions. In Great Britain the banks themselves make fixed loans up to five years at interest rates that are allowed to vary within a range of maximum and minimum figures to take account of possible variations in Bank rate during the life of the loan. Usually such advances have been slightly more expensive to the borrower than overdraft facilities; but their attraction to the borrower is the assurance that the loan will not be called during a pre-determined period. Principal is amortized on a basis which takes account of the expected profitability of the borrower's project.

Medium-term loans in France are almost invariably handled through the official machinery provided for this purpose. Essentially this means

---

ately larger share of productive industry than in the other two host countries. This is largely because so much of Swiss industry is essentially export-oriented.

169. See National (Jones) Board, *Report,* Cmnd. 3292, p. 27, par. 51.

170. See Marchal, p. 56, note 119 at p. 263. An illuminating description of the various paths through which these instruments may ultimately reach the Banque de France is found in Branger, p. 56, note 119, at vol. 2, p. 368-71.

that the Crédit National has discounted eligible loans.[171] That body determines whether a loan request qualifies for discount based upon the degree to which the proposed advance appears to fit within the needs of the current Plan, the applicant's resources for raising medium-term capital by other means (e.g., by issuing securities or by self-financing), and the degree of risk involved. The lending bank can rediscount eligible loans at the Crédit National, which itself has access to the Caisse des Dépôts et Consignations if additional liquidity is needed. This latter establishment can in turn rediscount the borrower's obligations at the Banque de France, the credit instrument by this stage having acquired the borrower's plus three additional signatures, viz., those of the lending bank, the Crédit National, and the Caisse des Dépôts et Consignations.

In France,[172] Great Britain,[173] and Switzerland[174] there are special arrangements for financing medium-term foreign trade operations.

Longer-term credit needs in the host countries are usually met by non-bank lending. New issues of stocks and bonds as well as rights offerings to existing equity holders are commonly employed, permission being necessary for significant amounts. In France this is sought from the Ministère des Finances, and in Great Britain from the Capital Issues Committee of the Treasury.

b. *U.S. Method*

In the domains of medium- and longer-term lending the U.S. branch banks are equipped with a particularly useful tool. This is the "term loan" which was developed in the 1930's in the United States when medium- and longer-term credit was extremely difficult to obtain. Airlines, railroads, petroleum and chemical companies, metals producers, extractive industries, public utilities, and other borrowers of large amounts for fixed capital assets constitute the market for these usually unsecured advances, which can extend up to fifteen years,[175] interest and amortization of principal being repaid in installments over the life of the loan. These installments are designed to correspond with the earnings generated by

171. See Fernand Baudhuin, *Crédit et banque,* 2d ed., Paris, Librairie Générale de Droit et de Jurisprudence, 1949, p. 203.

172. Available under the BFCE/COFACE.

173. Available under the ECGD.

174. Available under the Export Credit Guarantee Scheme, by which certain longer-term risks are covered by the state while the lending banks provide commercial credit.

175. Different authors give varying typical lengths for term loans, as follows: two to ten years, Foster and Rodgers, p. 131, note 148, at p. 219; five to eight years, Cochran, p. 131, note 148, at p. 155; and five to fifteen years, Whittlesey, p. 88, note 2, at p. 53.

the project to be undertaken or the assets to be acquired with the proceeds of the term loan.

For larger commercial borrowers use of the term loan avoids the formalities involved in issuing securities. Smaller corporations in the United States have also benefited from the development of this type of advance, since it obviates equity financing in many instances where potential dilution of existing shareholders' equity is unacceptable to the borrowers. Large term loans are usually undertaken by a group of banks and insurance companies, pension funds, and other non-bank lending institutions. The commercial banks take the earlier-maturing portions of the loan and the other lenders in the group hold the later-maturing portions.

An important advantage of the term loan lies in the opportunity it provides borrowers and lenders alike to design a vehicle which fits as nearly as possible the exact circumstances surrounding the borrower's need for credit and its capacity to repay the loan. Moreover, during the life of the loan, it is not uncommon for the parties to adjust amounts or payment periods to reflect modifications in the originally planned schedule. This flexibility holds a special attraction in tight and easy money conditions alike, encouraging large corporate borrowers to turn to commercial banks for advances which are considered by many bankers and economists as lying fundamentally outside the operational scope of these institutions, the greater part of whose assets are payable to depositors on demand.[176]

Although in Great Britain the medium-term fixed loans described above at page 137 are similar in some respects to the U.S.-style term loans, the latter involve much greater bank participation in the borrowing corporation's cash management. The U.S.-style term loans were virtually unknown in France or in Switzerland.[177] The management of U.S. corporate subsidiaries in the host countries have not been unaware of the advantages which term loans hold for their operations, however, nor have they been reluctant to explore with U.S.-trained bankers the possibilities of tailoring term loans to fit their medium- and longer-term credit needs. Thus the U.S. branch banks have possessed a non-

---

176. Before the introduction of the large denomination certificate of time deposit in 1961 (see p. 219), the bulk of U.S. commercial banks' time deposit accounts were maintained for individual savers. Although the banks have the right to require a prior notice before allowing amounts to be withdrawn from these accounts, in practice they have permitted depositors to withdraw funds on demand.

177. The higher degree of self-financing in Switzerland reduces somewhat the demand for term loans there. Nevertheless, the efforts of U.S. branch banks in Switzerland to provide term loans has been partly reflected in a growing awareness of this technique among Swiss bankers and corporations.

local technique with which they are thoroughly familiar and which they have been in a position to develop in their operating areas.[178]

III. ROLE OF THE U.S. BRANCH BANKS

Having examined the host currency activities of the U.S. branch banks with particular reference to the period of restricted convertibility, let us now attempt to define certain emerging patterns which will become clearer in the succeeding Chapters but which must at this stage be isolated and identified.

A. *Absence of Changes in the Laws*

We have seen that both from the point of view of the U.S. laws as well as from that of the host country legal systems the U.S. branch banks have operated under no significant handicaps in seeking to acquire deposits or make advances of host currencies. From the point of view of the United States, the host currency operations of these branch banks have represented a minor activity financially and one that has doubtlessly benefitted the U.S. firms engaged in business in these countries or trading with companies there. As for the host country laws, there evidently has been felt no need to protect the indigenous banking institutions by restrictive legislation.

Seen in restrospect the French and British legislation most certainly facilitated the host currency operations of these branch banks during the period through the end of 1958 and thereafter, for they have operated on legally equivalent terms with the indigenous banks. The written laws alone, however, do not tell the entire story, especially in Great Britain, where specific exemptions could have been limited in scope or withdrawn altogether and where non-legal sanctions could have been brought to bear informally.

Here again, however, it appears that the U.S. branch banks' potential capacity to attract host currency deposits or to make advances has presented no real concern to the indigenous banking authorities. In fact, during the period from mid-1945 through 1958 in which our examination is concentrated at this point, Western Europe as a whole was attempting to regain its postwar posture. The presence of these healthy U.S. financial institutions with dollar imports which represented lendable funds could

178. For discussions of term loans during the 1950's and 1960's in the United States, see Federal Reserve Bank of New York, "Term Lending by New York City Banks", 43 *Monthly Review* 27 (1961); and "Term Lending by New York City Banks in the 1960's", 49 *Id.* 199 (1967).

hardly have been undesirable. It is not surprising, then, that the home and host countries' laws and rules surrounding these operations remained intact and favorable during this period.

B. *Wholesale Banking Market*

1. *Taking Deposits*

On their home territory in the United States a few of the major commercial banks until rather recently concentrated in the wholesale market, their customers being comprised mainly of large corporations and other financial institutions.[179] These banks form a minority among the banks whose branches' operations are under study, however, since most of the major U.S. commercial banks have operated more in the retail than in the wholesale market in the United States, their deposits coming from individual customers and small firms more than from larger ones.

Regardless of their activities in the United States it cannot be said that the U.S. branch banks in the host countries have been strenuously engaged in drawing deposits from the retail banking markets there. Locally resident individuals may be depositors in these branch banks, but by no means on the scale that the indigenous banks in the host countries enjoy, or that would constitute active participation in the United States retail market. The U.S. branch bank's individual depositor in the host country is not typical of the great mass of residents and salary/wage earners making deposits in current and time deposit accounts. Either he is a foreigner in that country or, if a native, has some unusual reason for having a current account in a U.S. branch bank. As for time deposit accounts, there are fiscal advantages for the individual depositor at a state operated or backed institution.

Of far greater importance to the U.S. branch bank is the corporate depositor. The local U.S. corporate subsidiary is avowedly the customer whose presence has encouraged the U.S. banks in question to maintain branches abroad. Other corporations, notably locally-controlled companies, have also constituted to some extent a source from which potential deposits can be drawn. It is not difficult to appreciate, therefore, that the phenomenon of maintaining fewer accounts—but larger ones— is a natural pattern into which the U.S. branch banks have fitted. The exceptions to this rule are, as we have seen, those first wave branches which have acquired a certain patina over the years. Even in their case, however, the retail has never held the lure of the wholesale market.

179. In the United States they are sometimes referred to as "bankers' banks". Today, Morgan Guaranty Trust Co. is the only major commercial bank that still falls in this category.

In the wholesale host currency markets the U.S. branch banks have been faced with a problem common to all commercial banks, to wit, how to increase their individual shares of the total deposits available in the banking system. In the absence of a mass of individual local depositors this problem becomes particularly acute. It is understandable, then, that U.S.-trained bankers have been led to seek the deposits of companies already served by indigenous banks. Simply stated, the U.S. corporations' and their local subsidiaries' deposits alone can never suffice.

The indigenous corporations are not impervious to the advantages in having some competition in the sector of their traditional bankers. It appears, however, that the accounts of indigenous corporate depositors are more likely to be attracted by the fact or hope that a U.S. branch bank might ultimately offer non-local services. The attraction of the U.S. branch bank lies more in what it represents in larger terms, i.e., an integral part of an established and reputable U.S. financial institution. Better relations in the long run with the U.S. head office bank can be of no harm to locally-controlled corporations, especially those engaged in or contemplating foreign transactions.

Consequently one is forced to conclude that active or even, by host country standards, aggressive conduct in attempting to garner the deposits of indigenous corporations probably is unnecessary for the U.S. branch bank. That contact must be made is unquestionable. The task of the U.S. branch bank is, however, not to convince the potential depositor that it can surpass the local indigenous banks at their own practices. Rather it is to show that in utilizing the local U.S. branch bank the customer gains direct access to banking expertise and facilities located outside the host country.

The locally controlled company whose activities do not go beyond the host country's frontiers are understandably less interested in such advantages than are those with interests abroad. The entire local wholesale market does not, accordingly, constitute a potential source of deposits.

2. Making Advances

The U.S. branch banks are also in the wholesale rather than the retail host currency lending markets. Their infrequent advances to individuals constitute the exception to a general practice of concentrating their activities among locally established corporations and companies, as well as to local public borrowers.[180] The principal bank-customer contact

---

180. In London, for example, the overseas and foreign banks generally as well as the accepting houses have been noted as "employing a greater proportion of their sterling resources in loans to local authorities than the domestic banks. . ." Bank of

is, therefore, with the management of these business enterprises, including but not exclusively the U.S. corporate subsidiaries established there, a group more interested in borrowing than in depositing.

Of course, the management of the locally established U.S. corporate subsidiaries are simultaneously making contact with other banks, both indigenous and other (i.e., non-U.S.) foreign branches; but it has been inevitable in the normal course of events that U.S. bankers and U.S. corporate management personnel would come into contact with one another.

An analysis of the attitude shown by the indigenous members of the host country banking sectors toward this contact shows that whereas most, if not all of these indigenous bankers might well prefer to have the U.S. corporate subsidiaries as their own clients, four factors mitigate their feelings:

First, most of these U.S. corporate subsidiaries are already their clients to some extent. The American corporate management has reasoned, correctly it seems, that regardless of the relationship that already exists or might arise between a U.S. corporate subsidiary and the local branches of U.S. banks it is always a sound policy to have local banking connections. This means directing at least part of their business to indigenous institutions. Whereas a U.S. branch bank might be established locally, who can guarantee that it will still be there two decades hence? On the other hand it seems unlikely that a reputable indigenous institution will disappear from the scene. It might fail. It might eventually be merged into another local institution. It might even be nationalized. It will probably not, however, move elsewhere, disappearing entirely from the local community.

Second, as seen from the viewpoint of the indigenous banker, the American corporate subsidiaries may not themselves be long-standing clients for local banks in any event. As shopping around among banks it not a practice shunned by the management of these subsidiaries, what guarantee can there be that today's client will develop the sense of loyalty to "his banker" that an indigenous company can be expected to acquire? Indeed, as the counterpart of the element raised in the preceding paragraph, what certainty is there that the U.S. corporate subsidiary itself will remain in the host country? It may one day be whisked away by the parent corporation or be swallowed up as a result of a merger.

Third, the indigenous bankers realize that frequently the issue as to which bank or banks to use in the host country is not decided locally

England, 2 *Quarterly Bulletin* 93, 98 (1962). For local authority loans and their relationships to the U.S. branch banks' later operations in the Euro-dollar market, see p. 247.

143

but is resolved across the Atlantic or elsewhere. It must be added in this connection, however, that some of the indigenous banks are in a position, through their own overseas establishments and particularly those in the United States, to influence these decisions in their favor.

Fourth and finally, most of the indigenous bankers recognize that the local U.S. corporate subsidiaries are natural clients for the U.S. branch banks. They can understand a tendency for American businessmen to feel at ease when dealing with American bankers. In like fashion these indigenous banks with establishments in the United States, or contemplating such, naturally expect to handle much of the banking requirements of the U.S. subsidiaries of their own nationally owned and controlled corporations.

What about the U.S. branch bank's contact with indigenous corporations and companies? There is no gainsaying that the U.S. branch banks, in varying degrees, have contemplated serving the needs of indigenous commercial borrowers. More importantly, those U.S. banks which have been increasing the number of their branches and representative offices abroad have been ready to take greater advantage of their augmented networks. This was hardly feasible to any great extent, however, when the French franc and pound sterling were not even externally convertible into U.S. dollars or other hard currencies, i.e., during the period when the first wave branch banks alone occupied the field. Later this would change.

If the indigenous bankers' have reacted generously to the U.S. branch banks' contact with U.S. corporate subsidiaries, the same cannot always be said for the contact with indigenous corporations. In certain instances where the indigenous bankers have considered that the U.S. branch banks were making efforts to invade a "reserved" territory by soliciting or accepting business from locally owned institutions, the reaction has been anything but calm.[181] Occasionally this feeling has been aggravated by a report that in certain cases an indigenous customer has decided independently to try the services of a U.S. branch bank for a particular transaction, perhaps almost as an experiment, rather than as a result of a direct solicitation. In communities where most of the senior indigenous banking management know, or are themselves, the members of local corporate management, even a temporary switch to a foreign branch bank can hardly be cordially received.

---

181. It sometimes has ranged from cool resentment to outright indignation. One indigenous banker likens the phenomenon to a dinner guest trying to lure away the butler (who has been with the host's family for as long as anyone can remember). A similar reaction has been observed when a U.S. branch bank is considered to be "raiding" indigenous institutions in a search for locally qualified staff.

C. *Degree of Success in Host Currency Operations*

If the U.S. branch banks have not been hindered locally in seeking to attract host currency deposits, and if their "foreignness" is not a disadvantage without certain qualified advantages, how well have they succeeded in drawing in deposits? In fact, their performance has not been outstanding when compared to that of the indigenous institutions, or indeed to that of the U.S. head office banks themselves in their own native territories. Effectively removed from the major part of the retail deposit market by the force of circumstances, and finding themselves with U.S. corporate subsidiary customers which prefer to borrow rather than to deposit funds, these branch banks are unquestionably at a disadvantage.

The situation has certainly not been a hopeless one by any means. Were it so, the first wave branch banks would hardly have opened or re-opened their doors and the later second wave would merely have been a ripple. In fact these branch banks have managed with varying degrees of success to acquire host currency deposits. Moreover, there are the local money markets and, ultimately, the head office bank itself if and when the need for lendable funds justifies resorting to this source. This latter factor, too, would change eventually.

As for the degree of their success in host currency lending operations during the period from mid-1945 through 1958, measurement of the amount of profit or loss is difficult; but two points seem indisputably clear:

(1) The success or failure of these operations must be measured as a part of the emerging pattern of overseas banking operations of each particular U.S. bank involved. If a given branch did no more than break even, it could still justify its existence as an outpost, as an added service facility to actual and future customers, and as an announcement to the world's banking and trading communities that a particular bank was actively committed to functioning in the international circuit. Even if a branch bank lost money for longer than the head office might reasonably have expected, intangible benefits—in addition to the need to save face—made it wise to keep the branch in operation. New techniques were being observed at close hand. New tools were being mastered. The banks and their stockholders could feel, with some justification, that they were keeping abreast of the demands of a shrinking postwar world.

(2) The net profits that were made, and the net losses that occurred, were probably not large. Had the former been enormous, there is no doubt but that a herd of U.S. commercial banks would have stampeded to join in the activity, and that host banking authorities would have severely modified the entry requirements. In fact, there was nothing of the kind. Had the losses been too difficult to absorb, the head office

145

banks in the United States would have had to close the branches or reduce their staffs. No such cutback took place.[182]

To the extent that the operations of these branch banks have been profitable in the narrow sense, i.e., locally, their success appears to have been based largely on three factors: (1) the better costing of operations; (2) the restriction of the major part of their activities to the wholesale market, where economies of scale are possible to achieve; and (3) the willingness to operate on narrower profit margins, with the knowledge that a single branch alone is not the entire apparatus but only one part in a larger machine, the entire future of which will not be put into jeopardy by thin margins locally.

If on the deposit side of their activities the first wave U.S. branch banks were operating at a disadvantage, they had greater scope in their host currency lending. Here at least they could participate in local commercial banking activities, learning those local techniques which were new to them while simultaneously demonstrating some American techniques locally.

Unquestionably the most important local procedure which the U.S.-trained bankers have encountered is overdraft lending. Although the word "overdraft" itself has tended to evoke a host of unfavorable images in their home country, the U.S. branch banks have been in daily contact with this flexible—and profitable—lending device. Indigenous employees of the U.S. branch banks and of local U.S. corporate subsidiaries, familiar with overdrafts, undoubtedly have contributed here to the knowledge of the U.S.-trained bankers.

The future potential impact of this new skill on the United States domestic banking community is not without interest. In the mid-1950's several U.S. banks instituted overdraft lending schemes (under names such as advance credit, plus check, and instant credit) for individual customers in the United States. By the latter 1960's more banks had started in this field; and it was reported that by June 1968 over eight hundred U.S. banks had overdraft lending schemes for their customers, with $646 million in credit extended in this manner.[183]

In commercial lending, too, it is likely that individuals in U.S. corporate management with overseas experience in overdraft credit facili-

---

182. Note that during the interwar period a number of U.S. branch banks abroad were closed. See Tamagna and Willis, p. 40, note 56, at p. 1289. The greater relative size of the major U.S. commercial banks during the postwar period has helped them absorb the costs of establishing branches, which in some instances (especially in London) are considerable.

183. Federal Reserve Bank of New York, 51 *Monthly Review* 13-14 (1969). See also 99 (3) *Forbes* 24 (1967), and Norris Willatt, "The Overdraft Comes to America," 117 *The Banker* 428-33 (1967).

ties will be increasingly ready to seek similar arrangements for parent corporations and subsidiaries in the United States. In addition, any foreign bank established in the United States and prepared to offer such facilities will find a favorable response among those U.S. corporate treasurers who have utilized the method abroad.

The U.S.-trained bankers have been learning new skills, but in a climate where their relative inexperience probably has proved as much a help as a hindrance. For them the concept of the "good old days" in past generations simply has had no real impact. They have not been as inhibited by conservative attitudes because—literally speaking—there has not been as much for them to conserve. They have been present in the host countries to build a new edifice, not to preserve an ancient one.

If they have acquired new skills, the U.S.-trained bankers also have contributed some as well. In this context the most important phenomenon has been the introduction of the American style term loan to the European banking communities. This has involved not only the willingness of the U.S. branch banks to engage their resources for periods longer than those normally considered short-term in Western Europe, but also the capacity to measure, assess, and advise upon the customer's future needs in light of the potential revenue-generating capacities of the activities to be financed by these term loans. Moreover, although the U.S.-trained bankers have not ignored the borrower's balance sheet assets, they have developed the practice of basing advances on cash flow[184] as well. Doubtless the indigenous banks have possessed the skills required to undertake such loans; but with no dearth of lending possibilities on short-term bases, they have not been forced (nor until recently in France, able) to innovate to the same extent as the U.S. branch banks.

U.S. corporate subsidiaries have made full use of this device whenever possible to finance their medium-term credit needs. Two factors weigh in favor of the U.S. branch banks' capacity to make term loans to these customers. First, the U.S.-trained bankers are familiar with the operating techniques—and tempos—of the U.S. corporate borrowers and can assess the term loan projects realistically. They have already acquired the necessary "know-how" in the United States. Second, the local term loans can frequently be tied into a U.S. corporation's overall borrowing needs and specifically into the general line of credit it enjoys from a particular U.S. bank as a whole, both in the United States and abroad. The task of tailoring the loan is thus made easier, since the

184. For the concept of cash flow from the investor's standpoint, which is pertinent in the present context, see Benjamin Graham, David L. Dodd, and Sidney Cottle, *Security Analysis, Principles and Technique,* 4th edition, New York, Mc-Graw-Hill, 1962, pp. 172-83.

U.S. branch bank normally has access to information furnished by the head office bank (or by another unit in the bank's network) which eliminates many steps in the evaluation and preparation of the loan. As the multinational banking operations of the U.S. branch banks began to take shape this global-lending experience proved invaluable.

Indigenous host country corporate treasures might be excused for having paused to wonder initially whether the U.S. term loan technique could be of help to them. They have not, however, been slow to grasp its advantages; and indigenous commercial borrowers have been increasingly willing to try it. Although the locally-controlled corporations in France have been less likely to be swayed from their bankers' traditional techniques than were their British counterparts,[185] in both host countries the term loan has aroused the interest of the indigenous banking institutions.

Another area in which the U.S. branch banks can claim to have made a contribution lies in the costing of their operations. There is no question but that these institutions have a better notion of how much the various steps of their operations actually cost than do many of the indigenous banks. Likewise the U.S. branch banks charge their customers so as to keep these costs from unduly reducing their profit margins.[186]

It must be said in defense of the indigenous banks that they frequently feel called upon to handle certain types of low income producing tasks, almost in the nature of public service, that foreign branch banks often do not feel obliged or inclined to undertake.[187] Thus, the U.S. branch banks have been able to discourage small accounts with frequent transactions by making them subject to minimum balance requirements or bank service charges that either render them profitable or induce their holders to place them elsewhere. Other time-consuming assignments which cannot justify themselves on the earnings statement are avoided. To do so has not been difficult for the U.S. or other foreign branch banks, for they have not been invited to enter a host country to cater to the banking needs of the general public. Even in the wholesale markets, though, the U.S. branch banks have proved themselves able to allocate income and cost items efficiently, a practice that has not been lost upon their indigenous competitors.

---

185. This is primarily due to the official French mechanism for handling medium- and longer-term transactions. Individual banks and bankers have had less room for innovation.

186. See National (Jones) Board, *Report,* Cmnd. 3292, especially p. 45, par. 125.

187. There is nothing particularly European in this phenomenon. In the United States the head office banks are subject to the same notion of public service to the communities in which they operate.

D. *Acclimatization—a First Step toward Multinational Banking*

There is a second tier of skills, which could almost be termed habits, that the U.S.-trained bankers have acquired. Less technical or precise than banking techniques, these constitute an appreciation of the medium in which individual bankers are living and operating. For example, they have learned that the typical European firm does not switch bankers or "shop around" as frequently as its American counterpart. They have learned also that the European businessman is normally reluctant to state in writing his firm's probable needs for credit because, if refused, he does not relish having permanent evidence of the fact residing in anyone's files, including his banker's.

The U.S.-trained bankers have been observing, too, along with some of the U.S.-trained management employees of locally established American corporate subsidiaries, that many agreements which would be reduced to writing in the United States are handled quite effectively on the simple spoken word. The tendency of U.S.-trained businessmen—and even more so, that of their U.S. attorneys—to put all agreements into writing proves in many instances to be superfluous.[188] In addition, it is obviously annoying to their indigenous colleagues, who see little need for it. As in a small town where a man's word is considered to be as good as his signature, these U.S.-trained bankers have been dealing in a small community whenever they entered the domain of the local business sector.

Between the level of new primary banking skills and that of the appreciation of a no-longer-foreign environment lies an intermediate zone containing elements of both, and of great importance to the U.S. branch banks as institutions. In France and Great Britain during the period through 1958 they were acquiring direct exposure to banking under stringent credit and exchange controls. In fact, in both countries the U.S. branch banks still actually operate as agents of the host governments by virtue of their being accorded the *agréée* or authorized status necessary for engaging in foreign exchange transactions.

Of course, this has involved learning the local rules and regulations, and how to comply with them. More important, though, has been the need for the U.S.-trained bankers to grasp the differences in regulatory "style" in the two host countries.

In France the government is officially and manifestly present in all

---

188. Of course, binding unwritten agreements are not unknown in the United States. For example, floor traders on the principal securities and commodities exchanges are bound by their word (or hand signals) alone. This is the case as well in the foreign exchange markets in New York City and other world financial centers.

transactions of more than minor importance. Although the 1945 nationalization of the major *banques de dépôts* does not appear to have altered their operations drastically, these nevertheless became state-owned and state-operated institutions. In addition, all banks in France are subject to a host of *lois, décrets, ordonnances, arrêtés,* and *avis* that fill the French *Journal officiel.* Reports are required, forms have to be completed and filed, official directives must be followed. U.S.-trained bankers experiencing the French "style" of regulation are generally in agreement that the application of federal and state laws and regulations in the United States, even at its most stringent degree, falls far short of what banks in France have come to accept as normal governmental presence.

In analysing the French credit and exchange control regulations, in a country where monetary policy has predominated over fiscal policy, it is striking to note that constant attempts have been made to maintain a complicated apparatus in operating trim by means of frequent adjustments and occasional overhauls.[189] Not since the years of World War II have U.S. banks operated domestically in this medium, even after the 1968 U.S. capital movements controls, although there are some similarities with the Federal Reserve open market policies and the changes in the discount and margin rates as well as in the U.S. banks' reserve requirements.

In Great Britain, on the other hand, where greater emphasis has been placed on fiscal policy, the situation is vastly different, even though the regulatory authorities there have been coping with economic problems no less serious than those in France. Having at its disposal three tools for implementing its policy, viz., the Bank rate, open market operations, and moral suasion, the Bank of England unquestionably relies most heavily on the last of these. For example, the Borrowing (Control and Guarantees) Act, 1946 refers to exempted bank lending to a customer as that which is "in the ordinary course of his business".[190] Although that Act contains a section interpreting certain words and terms used in the text of the statute,[191] no mention is made as to what constitutes lending in the ordinary course of the borrower's business. Here, under the aegis of the Bank of England Act, 1946[192] the central banking authorities might have been justified in issuing an implementing notice to help bankers and borrowers alike in distinguishing exempted from prohibited transactions. In fact, the banks have been given no such guideline, but,

189. For example, France, Office des Changes, *Avis* nos. 202-277, p. 124, note 115.
190. See p. 126, material cited to note 126.
191. Act, § 4.
192. 9 & 10 Geo. 6, chap. 27. See page 66.

150

according to two authorities, have been requested to interpret the term strictly[193] and are "expected to comply with the spirit rather than the letter of this provision", ensuring that the exemption is not used "to permit long-term capital borrowing without Treasury consent".[194]

Letters from the Chancellor of the Exchequer addressed to the banks have appeared from time to time, in which the bankers' attention has been invited to the official Memoranda in determining their lending policies. One such letter is reported to have appeared in October 1949, in which the banks were requested to help keep in check inflationary tendencies in the economy; and another in 1951, when the Korean War was in progress, which noted that priority should be given to borrowing related to rearmament projects.[195] With the return of a Conservative government in 1951 and the re-adoption of Bank rate as an instrument of monetary policy[196] in November of that year, the basic style of regulation did not change. The banks themselves have been the judges of whether their individual lending policies conform with the official program, and have themselves decided which borrowers' applications were required to be submitted for Treasury approval.

In an atmosphere where no need is felt for more formalized regulatory measures, the banks are, in effect, morally bound to cooperate with the monetary authorities. Of course there is always the possibility that legal sanctions can be adopted in the event that a bank or group of banks refuses to follow the lead of the Bank of England. The existence of this ultimate weapon does not alone, however, explain the spirit of cooperation which the responsible governmental authorities find among the banks. The essential element lies in the fact that the banking community in the City of London is a small one. Most of the individuals concerned know—or know of—one another. Moreover, there appears to be a mutual reliance on their collective effort to maintain the integrity of the banking system, on whose preservation and strengthening they all have depended.

It is important to see the host currency operations of the first wave U.S. branch banks as lying inside the framework described above, because the same structural elements have strongly influenced the U.S. branch banks' Euro-dollar operations, as will be seen in the following Chapters.

---

193. Wadsworth, p. 67, note 165, at p. 798.
194. Sheldon and Drover, p. 62, note 140, at. p. 615.
195. Wadsworth, *supra*, pp. 798-800. The Bank of England *Quarterly Bulletin*, issued from 1960, now reproduces certain letters of this nature.
196. Since 1934 Bank Rate had been held down to 2%. For changes subsequent to the November 1951 change to $2^{1}/_{2}$%, see Fousek, p. 123, note 114, at pp. 27-30.

E. *Significance of the Presence of the U.S. Branch Banks*

In their skewed stance of being more active as lenders than as takers of deposited host currency funds, the first wave U.S. branch banks were unquestionably growing into a role within the inherent limitations and advantages of the host country banking sectors. It is interesting to observe what one host country's banking authorities considered contemporaneously to be the role of foreign banks generally and of U.S. branch banks in particular. The Radcliffe Committee Report issued in Great Britain in 1959 contained a section on "overseas and foreign banks"[197] which characterized "the principal business of these banks, whether they are head offices or only branches of banks domiciled elsewhere" as arising from "overseas trade".[198] The Report divided this principal business into three aspects as follows:

> "(1) the banks operate as exchange dealers;
> (2) they grant credits to finance the movement of goods between the United Kingdom and the other countries in which they operate (and, exceptionally, trade which does not touch the United Kingdom at all); these credits include acceptance credits giving rise to bills of exchange which can be negotiated in the discount market; and
> (3) they employ in London funds arising from their general business."[199]

With particular regard to their lending activities, this same Report set off the American banks. The Report stated:

> "There are some advances to customers who are resident in the United Kingdom, apart from those connected with the financing of overseas trade, and some deposits from such customers, but for the most part the overseas banks accept such domestic business only incidentally to their main business. The American banks, however, do not limit their banking business in the United Kingdom in this way, and have ventured rather further and more actively into such business than the other overseas banks. In conducting domestic banking business the overseas banks generally conform to rules governing the clearing banks, whether these rules come from the monetary authorities or arise from the banks, [sic] own agreements. This domestic business is negligible in comparison with the activity of the clearing banks."[200]

It is fair to say that the above description, with some necessary modifications, can be applied to the French banking sector as well. In essence, the indigenous and other foreign banking institutions took the presence of

---

197. (Radcliffe) Committee, *Report,* Cmnd. 827, pp. 70-72, pars. 197-201.
198. *Id.,* p. 71, par. 199.
199. *Ibid.* Here the Committee added the following explanation: "Some of them are heavily engaged, in their London offices, in providing economic information; this arises from and is mainly incidental to their international banking business... [I]n the present chapter we are concerned with their activities only insofar as they affect lending and borrowing within this country." *Ibid.*
200. *Id.* p. 72, par. 201.

the U.S. branch banks in their stride. Even a group of active, industrious, well-established U.S. branch banks seems to have presented no real threat to other members of the banking community. Even though certain of their advances outstanding might have represented operations that could otherwise have been undertaken by indigenous French or British banks, the total amount was small in comparison to the overall flow through these banking centers.

In fact, the presence of foreign banks was desirable from several points of view. The Radcliffe Report pointed out that the bulk of the quick assets of the overseas and foreign banks was comprised of gilt-edged securities, and that accordingly the United Kingdom government could borrow from non-residents through these banks.[201] On the other hand, the fact that the foreign branch banks were normally in the money market seeking funds meant that they constituted an additional outlet for any excess deposits of indigenous banks.

Seen from a broader point of view, theoretically as well as temporally, the presence of foreign branch banks means that indigenous institutions and monetary authorities can acquire links with the head offices of these banks and with the other units abroad of those banks having them. Such links are valuable. Moreover, the fact that major banks from abroad would choose to maintain establishments in a particular host country endorses the importance of its financial center.

That the first wave U.S. branch banks presented no real threat to the local host communities or to the U.S. banking system is evident from the absence of legislation that would have hindered their operations. As we have seen, both the credit control and the exchange control laws and rules in the host countries were occasionally modified from mid-1945 through 1958; but at no point did these laws or rules discriminate against U.S. branch banks or those from other countries.[202] In Chapter Two we have seen how their establishment was facilitated by both U.S. and host country laws, and in the present Chapter how their host currency deposit taking and lending ability was not hampered by legal barriers. The primary reason behind this can best be summarized by referring to a statement made by the Radcliffe Committee with regard to the treatment of the overseas and foreign banks in the 1959 Report referred to above:

201. *Id.*, pp. 71-72, par. 200. The Committee also stated that "it is as holders of Government bonds and as operators in the discount market that the overseas banks have their main relevance to the liquidity structure of the economy". *Id.*, p. 72, par. 201.

202. It is noteworthy that pressure was building up in these and other host countries to bring about a modification of the New York State law allowing foreign agencies but prohibiting the establishment of foreign branch banks. Restrictive legislation or conventions in the host countries would have hindered seriously the reciprocity principle on which this pressure was largely based. See p. 32.

"We must emphasize that the overseas and foreign banks are diverse in their interests and their experience; only their relative unimportance in the domestic financial scene can excuse our summary treatment of them as a single group in this chapter."[203]

Times were changing, however, and with them the medium in which the U.S. branch banks were going to operate in the succeeding decade. It is to this new medium that we now turn.

203. (Radcliffe) Committee, *Report, supra,* p. 70, par. 197.

Chapter Four

"SHORT-TERM EURO-DOLLAR BORROWING AND LENDING: 1959 TO MID-1963"

I. BACKGROUND

During the thirteen and one-half years to which particular attention was given in Chapter Three, the first wave U.S. branch banks in Western Europe were operating in a medium that was undergoing gradual but nearly constant change. By the end of 1958 the first regular transatlantic jet air service had been inaugurated, bringing these branch banks into much closer physical contact with their head offices than theretofore, just as it was bringing widely scattered European subsidiaries of American corporations closer to their parent companies and to one another. By this time, too, the teleprinter links between various units in some U.S. banks' overseas networks were becoming vital to their day-to-day operations. Personal or telegraphic consultation among foreign branch banks or with the head office bank in the United States was no longer being reserved for only the most important decisions.

Along with these transportation and communication developments more fundamental changes were taking place. Economical and political instability in Western Europe were fading; the French Republic was on the verge of reorienting many of its external and internal polices; international trade was on the upswing, stimulated by the first four rounds of tariff negotiations under the auspices of the General Agreement on Tariffs and Trade (GATT); and the Treaty of Rome, calling for a European Economic Community leading hopefully to a common market in Europe, was about to go into effect.

Directly related to the subject at hand were two fundamental changes which were to have a profound impact on the operations of the U.S. branch banks in France and Great Britain as well as in Switzerland and elsewhere outside the United States.

The first of these was the return to external convertibility among the countries which had signed the European Monetary Agreement,[1] the suc-

1. Signed August 5, 1955 in Paris. As provided by the Protocol of Provisional Application to the Agreement, signed the same day, the Agreement provisionally entered into force with the return to external convertibility. English language trans-

cessor to the European Payments Union.[2] The new Agreement was designed to lower many of the legal barriers which had impeded the flow of capital from one financial center to another and which had made it difficult to utilize a network of overseas branch banks to its fullest capabilities.

The second of these changes was the transition from a period in which there was a shortage of U.S. dollars outside the United States to one in which they began to be held by certain non-U.S. individuals and institutions as an earning reserve in much the same way as some foreign central banks were eventually going to hold them as an international monetary reserve currency.

When certain non-U.S. residents began to accumulate sizeable holdings of dollars the potential conditions for a market in this currency started to take shape, one that the modified exchange control barriers would allow to extend beyond the confines of any single host country. Under these altered conditions a metamorphosis was to occur in the operations of the U.S. branch banks. Before analysing certain legal aspects of these operations it is necessary to examine briefly these two modifications, namely (1) the structural changes in Western European political and economic institutions, and (2) the new market in U.S. dollars on deposit outside the United States, that we now know as Euro-dollars.

A. *Structural Changes*

The French franc and pound sterling became externally convertible[3] on December 27, 1958 under the terms of the European Monetary Agreement. The Swiss and Belgian francs and the Deutsche mark were fully convertible. The establishment of external convertibility meant, and still means, in the sterling area for example, that a non-resident (regardless of his or its nationality) legally possessing pounds sterling could freely convert this "external sterling" into any other currency. Inside Great Britain, on the other hand, pounds sterling possessed by local residents, again regardless of their nationality, were not and are not so convertible except in special cases. Similar conditions applied and apply, *mutatis mutandis,* to French francs.

---

lations of the texts of the Agreement and the Protocol are found in Council of Europe, III *European Yearbook* 213-51 and 251-55 (1957).

2. The predecessor European Payments Union (E.P.U.), created by the Treaty signed in Paris on September 19, 1950, was terminated with the provisional entry into force of the European Monetary Agreement, as provided by Article 36 (c) of the former and Article 27 (c) (i) of the latter. An English language translation of the E.P.U. Treaty is found in II *Id.,* 363-413 (1956).

3. Other currencies similarly affected were the Italian lire, the Dutch florin or guilder, and the Danish, Norwegian and Swedish crowns.

The external sterling or francs possessed by the hypothetical non-resident can be in the form of banknotes or, as is more often the case, in the form of a bank account denominated in sterling or francs. With the advent of external convertibility the distinctions between "transferable" and "official" sterling or francs were no longer necessary.

External convertibility was not produced by the waving of a magic wand, and could not have been instituted without a gradual return to greater confidence in the currencies involved. As a simultaneous operation the French franc was devalued to a new rate of FF $493.7 = \$1$, a level at which it appeared unlikely that frequent official intervention would be necessary. The fact that there was no massive conversion into dollars or other (hard) currencies, as there had been in 1947 during the ill-fated British attempt to re-establish the pound sterling as an international currency with the help of the U.S. loan of that year,[4] was a significant and favorable indication of the growing strength of these currencies. Indeed, this had been the goal of the European Payments Union, toward which gradual progress had been made during the period through the end of 1958.[5]

On January 1, 1959, during the same week in which external convertibility was re-established, the European Economic Community (E.E.C.) was brought into being as provided by the Treaty of Rome.[6] This Treaty, which envisages the ultimate establishment of a common market and eventual political unity in Western Europe, contains provisions dealing with most aspects of the economies of the member states. One such provision is of potential importance to the banking sectors in both member and non-member states. This calls for "the abolition, as between member states, of the obstacles to the free movement of persons, services and capital . . ."[7]

Banking services connected with movements of capital are to be "effected in harmony with the progressive liberalisation of the movement of

4. On August 20, 1947 the British government had halted the conversion of sterling which in a few weeks had nearly depleted the $3.7 billion available from the U.S. loan.

5. The then U.S. Marshall Plan Ambassador for Europe, Milton Katz, was quoted as saying that the European Payments Union had been "designed to liberate intra-European trade by assuring convertibility of European currencies, including the pound sterling, in current accounts. . ." N.Y. Times, September 20, 1950, p. 15, col. 3 (late city edition).

6. 294 *United Nations Treaty Series* 17-136, signed on March 25, 1957 by the same six Western European states that simultaneously signed the Treaty creating Euratom and that had previously created the European Coal and Steel Community, viz. Belgium, France, Italy, Luxembourg, The Netherlands, and the Federal Republic of Germany. An English language translation of the Treaty is found in Council of Europe, IV *European Yearbook* 413-537 (1958).

7. Treaty of Rome, art. 3 (c). The quoted passages cited to this and the following notes are taken from IV *European Yearbook, supra.*

capital"[8] which is covered by Articles 67-73 of the Treaty. Under these latter provisions, restrictions on the movement of capital "belonging to persons resident in member states" are to be abolished progressively.[9] The member states are also to "endeavour to avoid introducing within the Community any new exchange restrictions which affect the movement of capital and current payments connected with such movement, and making existing rules more restrictive".[10]

As yet there has not been great progress towards the formal evolution of a common banking sector in the member states of the European Communities through the unification of the applicable laws.[11] Whereas anti-trust and fiscal laws—and philosophies—have undergone considerable examination, and in some instances modification, banking laws and regulations have not.[12] It would seem that from the legal viewpoint[13] this is due principally to two factors: (1) the other issues, such as anti-trust and taxation, appear to have been of greater immediate importance, and (2) the banking sector is one in which laws and regulations are relatively less numerous, greater emphasis being laid on informal suggestions or advice.

If the establishment of the E.E.C. has not had a direct legal influence

8. Treaty, art. 61 (2).
9. Art. 67 (1).
10. Art. 71. But see p. 209, text cited to note 32.
11. *Cf.* Charles Campet, "Le Marché commun bancaire", *Revue du Marché Commun,* no. 137, pp. 441-46 (1970). An earlier appraisal of some interest in retrospect is J. B. de la Giroday, "The Effects of the European Economic Community on the Banking Business within It," 18 *The Business Lawyer* 1025-54 (1963).
12. An especially revealing account of the underlying difficulties in harmonizing the laws governing banking establishments in the E.E.C. is found in Fédération Bancaire de la Communauté Economique Européenne, *Rapport, 1968-1970,* Brussels, 1971, pp. 10-12. The relative lack of progress in the banking sector is striking when compared to the field of anti-trust regulation. With regard to the latter, one expert aptly notes that "there is already a European set of rules on cartels—which albeit by fits and starts—has come into effect and which now, as far as interstate commerce within the Community is concerned, has pushed the application of national law into the background and according to some has even excluded it". L. J. Brinkhorst, "European Law as a Legal Reality", *in European Law and Institutions,* Edinburgh, University Press, 1969, p. 17. Here we must take account of a fundamental difference between anti-trust law and doctrine and that in the banking sector and others. See Pierre A. Lalive, "Harmonisation et rapprochement des législations européennes", *in L'intégration européenne,* Geneva, Georg, 1964, pp. 45-77, where Professor Lalive draws attention to the Communities' emerging anti-trust law being a *création directe* and thus an atypical body of law in this sense. *Id.,* pp. 50 and 66.
13. From a non-legal point of view there has understandably been some hesitation in organizing a banking system which excluded London, New York City, and Zurich, in particular during the late 1960's and early 1970's when enlargement of the E.E.C. was holding many other important matters at a standstill, including attempts at reducing non-tariff barriers to international trade.

158

on the operations of the U.S. branch banks in Western Europe,[14] there has most certainly been an indirect influence of considerable magnitude. The Treaty of Rome and the spirit behind it have unquestionably encouraged U.S. corporations in the drive to expand their operations and to increase their direct investments in a more stable Western Europe. It has also aroused the imaginations of some European corporate managers, who have themselves been stimulated to look beyond their own national frontiers. Most of the largest industrial and commercial corporations in Western Europe already had this frame of reference; and some of the medium-sized corporations and companies had already begun to adopt it before 1959. The main impact, and in this sense the real influence, of the E.E.C. has fallen on those firms (regardless of their size) who for the first time have become aware of the advantages which they might obtain, as well as those which their competitors locally and in other member states would likewise receive.[15]

While the Treaty of Rome contains specific provisions concerning banking activities related to capital movements, the treaty creating the European Free Trade Association (E.F.T.A.) is less precise. Article 29 of the Treaty of Stockholm[16] deals with "invisible transactions and transfers" but states that "the obligations with regard to the freedom of such transactions and transfers undertaken by them [i.e., by the signatory states] in other international organizations are sufficient at present".[17] Article 30 treats "economic and financial policies" but provides only that the states will "periodically exchange views on all aspects of those policies".[18]

Although the Treaty of Rome has had an indirect influence on the operations of the U.S. branch banks, this cannot be said of the Treaty of Stockholm. Much less has it had any direct influence. If anything, the

14. It is to be noted that in the future an enlarged E.E.C. could have greater direct influence, for example with the inclusion of Great Britain and/or one or more of the Scandinavian countries.

15. *Cf.* Henri Schwamm, "Swiss Industrial Penetration in the Common Market", International Credit Bank, 8 (3) *Quarterly Review* 9-17 (1970), especially p. 15. One French banker in Paris thinks that the major Western European banks have always been "internationally minded". According to him the existence of the E.E.C. has prompted local corporate customers to ask their bankers how the E.E.C. might affect their operations. Formerly, he adds, the bankers usually took the initiative in raising such topics.

16. 370 *United Nations Treaty Series* 3-28. Signed on January 4, 1960 and entered into force on May 3, 1960. In addition to Great Britain and Switzerland, other original signatory states were Austria, Denmark, Norway, Portugal, and Sweden. Iceland has since joined and Finland has become associated with the E.F.T.A.

17. Treaty of Stockholm, art. 29. The quoted passages cited to this and the following notes are taken from the official English language text of the Treaty, found in the *United Nations Treaty Series.*

18. Treaty, art. 30.

hesitation to take steps toward greater economic and political unity is reflected in an absence of interest in modifying local legislation or practices. Paradoxically the indirect influence of the Treaty of Rome has spilled over into the member countries of the E.F.T.A., since most bankers and their corporate customers in these countries appear to have taken the agreement behind the E.E.C. more seriously than the Treaty of Stockholm as far as potential long-run effects on their own international operations are concerned.[19]

B. *Emergence of the Euro-dollar Market*

From the end of 1958 there began to develop an increasing awareness of what is now known as the Euro-dollar. Ill-defined and often misunderstood by those not closely following its development, the Euro-dollar has become a significant factor in the operations of both the U.S. branch banks and the indigenous banks in Western Europe and elsewhere.

During the early postwar years there was a serious shortage of U.S. dollars outside the United States. Stripped of their earning power, entire sectors of industry in Western Europe were forced to rely heavily on the funds made available under the European Recovery Program ("Marshall Plan") for their purchases of capital goods. With their gradual return to production, however, these industrial sectors were increasingly capable of acquiring dollars in sufficient quantities to finance purchases in the dollar area and elsewhere, occasionally having temporary excesses.

These dollars came from several sources. Current payments made in dollars for goods or services constitute the first category. The U.S. government disbursed dollars for many of the local needs of U.S. and other military personnel stationed in France[20] and Great Britain. American companies purchased in Western Europe with dollars, as did American tourists, who were beginning to appear in greater numbers with the improvement of travel and lodging facilities. In essence, the U.S. trade balance, although not in deficit, nonetheless was not as overwhelmingly positive as in the earlier period.

Along with these public and private expenditures of U.S. origin, dollars were also used by non-U.S., non-Western European purchasers of goods and services in Western Europe. These purchasers were themselves receiving dollars, for example as royalty payments on films, patented processes, and mineral rights or production. In addition to these current expenditures in dollars, the direct investments of many U.S. corporations

19. See generally Schwamm, *supra.*
20. These dollars eventually qualified for treatment in France under the E.F.AC. rules. See pp. 174-76.

abroad, and principally in Western Europe, were giving rise to increasingly large dollar amounts available in the host countries.[21] These capital exports were contributing to the balance of payments deficits of the United States, a phenomenon which eventually came to cause consternation, as will be seen in the following Chapter. At this stage in our examination, however, the important fact is that U.S. dollars were accumulating outside the United States.[22]

These "external dollars" could be held in the form of U.S. banknotes; but more usually they, like external sterling or francs, were placed on deposit in banks. The growing supply of external dollars was the basis for a market in them. Had the volume of these offshore dollars not increased to create a surfeit where formerly there had existed a shortage, the Euro-dollar market could never have taken on the dimensions to which we shall have occasion to refer later in the present and following Chapters.

No attempt has been made in the present study to write a treatise on Euro-dollars. Several authors have dealt with the subject;[23] and some

21. Exchange control in France and Great Britain prevented investors residing in "hard currency" countries from financing their investments with host currency acquired abroad. The necessary host currency either had to be drawn from external accounts, or hard currencies had to be exchanged into host currency at the official rate on the local market. See, for example, France, Office des Changes, *Avis* no. 669, *Journal officiel*, January 21, 1959, pp. 1130-32.

22. "Foreigners have acquired most of their dollar deposits because the United States has had a balance of payments deficit; and they will continue to acquire dollar funds if the deficit continues." Altman, "Recent Developments in Foreign Markets for Dollars and Other Currencies", note 23, *infra*, at p. 83. Altman qualifies this observation in a note as follows: "Unless, as is unlikely, all the dollars paid out to finance the deficit are converted into gold and/or paid over to the International Monetary Fund in connection with a U.S. drawing of foreign currencies." *Id.*, p. 83, n. 67.

23. See, for example, Paul Einzig, *The Euro-Dollar System: Practice and Theory of International Interest Rates,* 4th edition, London and New York, Macmillan, 1970; Norris O. Johnson, *Eurodollars in the New International Money Market,* New York, First National City Bank, 1964; Oscar L. Altman, "What Does it Really Mean? Euro-Dollars", International Monetary Fund/International Bank for Reconstruction and Development, 4 *Finance and Development* 9 (1967); Alexander K. Swoboda, *The Euro-Dollar Market: an Interpretation,* Princeton, Princeton University Press (Essays in International Finance, no. 64), 1968; and Fritz Machlup, "Euro-Dollar Creation: A Mystery Story", Banca Nazionale del Lavoro, 94 *Quarterly Review* 219-60 (1970), and Princeton, Princeton University Press (Reprints in International Finance, no. 16), 1970. For an important series of articles on the subject see Oscar L. Altman, "Foreign Markets for Dollars, Sterling, and other Currencies", International Monetary Fund, 8 *Staff Papers* 313-52 (1960-61); "Canadian Markets for U.S. Dollars", 9 *Id.* 297-316 (1962); "Recent Developments in Foreign Markets for Dollars and Other Currencies", 10 *Id.* 48-96 (1963); and "Euro-dollars: Some Further Comments", 12 *Id.* 1-15 (1965). See also the articles reproduced in Eric B. Chalmers (ed.), *Readings in the Euro-dollar,* London, W. P. Griffith, 1969.

recent textbooks on monetary economics or money and banking have devoted chapters or sections to it.[24] The importance of the Euro-dollar to this study[25] is such, however, that it seems appropriate to emphasize certain basic notions and relevant facts before analysing further the operations of the U.S. branch banks.

In the nature of a *caveat* it must be noted that Euro-dollar operations have not constituted the sole activity of the U.S. branch banks since 1959. Although they have become increasingly important and have eventually percolated into many of the other operations of the U.S. branch banks, they represent only one aspect of the overall activities undertaken by these institutions. By virtue of their nature, however, and eventually of their dimensions, operations in the Euro-dollar market have constituted the most important single element in their activities, and certainly the most significant.

1. *Definition*

Although various authors had differing definitions for the Euro-dollar in the earlier phases of its development, it has generally come to be accepted in the three host countries and in the United States that a Euro-dollar represents a debt denominated in U.S. currency owed by a banking institution located outside the United States as a result of a dollar on deposit in that institution.[26] Some observers have restricted their definitions to include only those dollars deposited outside the United States by non-U.S. citizens who reside outside the United States.[27] With the passage of time, however, it has become clear that a dollar debt owed by a U.S. branch bank in France, Great Britain, or Switzerland to a depositor residing in Denver or Minneapolis or San Francisco is treated like an equivalent

24. See, for example, Fred Hirsch, *Money International,* London, A. Lane (Penguin), 1967, pp. 168-73; and Marchal, p. 56, note 119, at pp. 335-48.

25. Professor Swoboda concludes that Euro-dollar operations are significant for multinational banking because "they provide a crucial link between national money markets". Alexander K. Swoboda, "Multinational Banking, the Euro-Dollar Market and Economic Policy", 5 *Journal of World Trade Law* 121-30, 125 (1971).

26. See H. Christie, "Eurodollars and the Balance of Payments", 117 *The Banker* 34-45 (1967); Robert C. Effros. "The Whys and Wherefores of Eurodollars", 23 *The Business Lawyer* 629-644, 629 (1968); and Milton Friedman, "The Euro-Dollar Market: Some First Principles", *The Morgan Guaranty Survey,* October 1969, pp. 4-14, p. 5. In light of the last of these see Fred H. Klopstock, "Money Creation in the Euro-Dollar Market—A Note on Professor Friedman's Views", Federal Reserve Bank of New York, 52 *Monthly Review* 12-15 (1970).

27. Cf. *The Wall Street Journal,* August 24, 1967, page 6, col. 2 (Eastern edition), where Euro-dollars were said to be "so called because title to them is owned by interests outside the United States. . ."

debt owed to a resident of any foreign country. Moreover, this is the case regardless of the depositor's nationality.

There are Euro-currency units other than the Euro-dollar. French francs on deposit in a bank outside France have come to be called Euro-French francs, as British pounds on deposit in a bank outside the sterling area are referred to as Euro-sterling. There exist Euro-Swiss francs, Euro-guilders, and Euro-D. marks as well as other Euro-currencies. Markets for Euro-sterling exist in Paris and in the Swiss financial centers; and Euro-French francs are traded in Switzerland and in London. Many of the major U.S. banks have operated in all these markets, especially those having branches in two or more foreign countries. By far the most important Euro-currency in terms of the absolute amounts on deposit, however, is the Euro-dollar. Because of this and the fact that the dollar is the national currency of the U.S. head office banks we have concentrated on the Euro-dollar operations of the U.S. branch banks.

The term "Euro" is misleading in that it implies that the dollar debt is owed by or to a person or institution in Europe or of European nationality or origin. In fact, a U.S. dollar denominated deposit in a bank or branch bank in Tokyo represents Euro-dollars, as does a similar deposit in a banking institution anywhere else in the world, except in the United States.[28] Indeed, U.S. dollars on deposit in Canadian banks have constituted a significant portion of the Euro-dollar total, especially in the earlier years of the market.

The prefix "Euro" is not the only one that has been attached to this unit. As early as 1959 references were made to "continental dollars", which were defined as "dollars kept on time deposit at London banks by continental holders".[29] That definition would have been too restrictive for what later came to be called Euro-dollars, since the latter need not be in London banks nor are they necessarily placed on time deposit. Nonetheless the reference to these dollar deposits indicates that their existence was not going unnoticed. One authority on the subject would prefer the term "guest currencies" when referring to Euro-currencies generally, thereby avoiding the "Euro" label, and another expert the term "vehicle currencies".[30]

---

28. In the late 1960's attention was drawn to Euro-dollar deposits in the U.S. Virgin Islands, which are considered "foreign" territory for this and some other (notably customs) purposes.

29. N.Y. Times, November 8, 1959, § 3, p. 1, col. 2 (late city edition). This article cited an unidentified source as estimating the total amount of "continental dollars" as approximately $500 million.

30. Joseph Dach, "Legal Nature of the Euro-dollar", 13 *American Journal of Comparative Law*, 30-43, 30 (1964); and Swoboda, *The Euro-Dollar Market: An Interpretation, supra*, p. 3 and pp. 5-11.

In any event, the use of the term "currency" is hardly less confusing. As one observer has pointed out,[31] it is significant that the financial press has included Euro-dollars in the sections covering short-term interest rates rather than among the foreign exchange quotations. Even this practice fails to take account of Euro-dollars in those current accounts on which no interest is paid.[32] Essentially, the Euro-dollar is not a unit of currency, but rather a unit of private debt denominated in U.S. dollars between a banking institution and a depositor.

2. Underlying Factors

With the gradual easing of the dollar shortage there could have been progressively larger dollar accounts at U.S. banks in the name of non-U.S. residents. In fact, dollars held by many public entities and private persons and institutions outside the United States are placed on deposit with banks in the United States. Two factors have worked against such a build-up, however.

a. Political Aspects

First, several authors record the fact that since the early postwar years there have been dollar deposits of Eastern European governments placed in Western European banks rather than in banks in the United States. This has been held to be due to a fear on the part of these depositors that dollar accounts in U.S. banks might be blocked in times of political uncertainty or crisis.[33] Indeed, it has been claimed that the telegraphic address ("Eurobank") of the Soviet-controlled Banque Commerciale pour l'Europe du Nord in Paris was the original reason for the dollars on deposit at that bank being referred to as "Euro"-dollars.[34]

Not all such accounts have been in Western European banks (e.g., many have been in Canada), nor have they been channelled solely for reasons of political uncertainty. As early as 1946 the Bank of Finland was reported to have opened a dollar account for a Soviet bank into which the latter was to pay amounts designated by a U.S.S.R.-Finland trade treaty.[35] The placing of most dollar deposits of Eastern European states has, however, been heavily influenced by political considerations. Dollar holders in other areas of the world often prefer dollar deposits outside

31. Johnson, *supra,* p. 4.
32. Cf. Klopstock, *supra,* p. 14.
33. "... Communist-controlled banks adopted the habit of camouflaging their ownership of some dollar deposits by redepositing them with European banks." Paul Einzig, *supra,* p. 3.
34. Cf. Arturo Lando, *Eurodollar,* Naples, 1964, p. 3.
35. See New York Times, May 4, 1946, p. 4, col. 6 (late city edition).

the United States for a quasi-political reason, namely, their reluctance to expose their deposit so directly to the U.S. fiscal mechanism.

b. *Lower Yields on U.S. Securities and Bank Deposits*

A second and fundamentally more important element working toward a build-up of dollar deposits in banks outside the United States has lain in the lower net yields available on U.S. federal government obligations and on bank deposits. Holders of dollars not wishing to switch into other currencies[36] have several alternatives if they wish to place their funds in short-term dollar-denominated federal government obligations in the United States, the most liquid of which are the 90-day U.S. Treasury Bills. Although the yields[37] on these are generally lower than the interest rates paid on other types of securities in the United States, they attract dollar holders who are willing to forego a somewhat higher return in favor of a broader market in which large holdings can be disposed of rapidly. Equity issues, of course, do not lend themselves to the same portfolio functions as that performed by such debt securities.

During the specific period under study U.S. tax considerations did not render U.S. Treasury Bills and other highly liquid fixed interest federal government securities any more or less attractive than deposits in U.S. banks for U.S. taxpayers, including U.S. citizens wherever resident,[38] U.S. corporations,[39] resident aliens,[40] non-resident aliens engaged in trade or business inside the United States,[41] and resident foreign corporations.[42] This arose from the fact that these taxpayers paid U.S. income tax on the interest received on fixed interest securities as well as on time deposit accounts.[43]

On the other hand, for non-resident aliens and foreign corporations, in both cases not engaged in trade or business within the United States, "interest on deposits with persons carrying on the banking business" was

---

36. Dollar holders can, of course, "swap" (see p. 190, note 159) rather than "switch" into another currency. In either case the new temporary holder of the dollars faces the same decision described below as to where and how to place the short-term dollars. If he in turn decides to switch or swap, the decision is passed down along the line of transactions.

37. "Yields" here taken to comprise the interest rate on instruments held to maturity as well as the return available on sale prior to maturity.

38. United States, Internal Revenue Code of 1954, as amended; 26 U.S.C. § 1.

39. Code; 26 U.S.C. § 11.

40. Code; 26 U.S.C. § 1. See *Commissioner of Internal Revenue* v. *Patino*. 186 F. 2d 962 (4th Cir. 1950).

41. Code; 26 U.S.C. § 871 (c).

42. Code; 26 U.S.C. § 882.

43. "... Gross income means all income from whatever source derived...", Code; 26 U.S.C. § 61.

exempt from U.S. income tax,[44] whereas interest earned on securities was treated as U.S. source income[45] and was subject to a 30 per cent tax[46] withheld at the source by the payer.[47] Bilateral tax treaties served to reduce the rate in certain instances.[48] Nevertheless, bank accounts unquestionably had an advantage to this group of potential depositors by virtue of the tax exemption.

Two elements reduced this advantage, however. First, a great many of the large potential depositors were in fact engaged in trade and business in the United States and hence could not benefit from the exemption. Second, (Federal Reserve) Regulation Q has placed limitations on the rates of interest which member banks can pay on time deposit accounts in the United States. As previously noted, Regulation Q forbids the payment of interest on demand deposits,[49] and from 1956 limited the interest rate payable on time deposit accounts to 3 per cent for terms of six months or more, 2½ per cent on deposits for periods less than six months and not less than 90 days, and 1 per cent on deposits for periods of less than 90 days.[50] It is to be recalled that deposits for periods of less than 30 days are treated as demand deposits[51] and thus can receive no interest whatsoever.

In December 1961 Regulation Q was amended to raise the maximum interest rates to 4 per cent on deposits having maturities of 12 months or more, 3½ per cent on maturities of less than 12 months and not less than 6 months, 2½ per cent on maturities of less than 6 months and not less

44. Code; 26 U.S.C. § 861 (a) (1) (A).
45. Code; 26 U.S.C. § 861 (a) (1).
46. Code; 26 U.S.C. §§ 871 and 881.
47. Code; 26 U.S.C. §§ 1441 and 1442.
48. For example, it was reduced to 15 per cent by the France-United States Convention for the avoidance of Double Taxation, July 25, 1939, 59 Stat. 893, T.S. No. 988, 125 U.N.T.S. 259 (effective December 30, 1944), art. 6(a) added by Convention, June 22, 1956, 8 U.S.T. 843, T.I.A.S. No. 3844, 291 U.N.T.S. 101 (effective June 31, 1957); to 5 per cent by Switzerland-United States Convention, May 24, 1951, 2 U.S.T. 1751, T.I.A.S. No. 2316, 127 U.N.T.S. 227, art. VII (1) (effective September 27, 1951); and eliminated entirely, i.e. reduced to 0 per cent by United Kingdom-United States Convention, June 6, 1946, 60 Stat. 1377, T.I.A.S. No. 1546, 6 U.N.T.S. 189, art. VII (effective July 25, 1946). Article VII of the bilateral treaty with the United Kingdom was subsequently amended by the Supplementary Protocol, March 17, 1966, 17 U.S.T. 1254, T.I.A.S. No. 6089, 590 U.N.T.S. 216 (effective September 9, 1966).
49. (Federal Reserve) Regulation Q, § 217.2, p. 93, note 21.
50. 12 C.F.R. § 217.6 (1959); 21 Fed. Reg. 9691, December 7, 1956. Theretofore the respective rates had been fixed since January 1, 1936 at 2½ per cent, 2 per cent, and 1 per cent respectively. 12 C.F.R. § 217.3 (1949); Supplement to Regulation Q, 1936.
51. Regulation Q, § 217.1, page 93, note 21.

than 90 days, and 1 per cent on maturities of less than 90 days.[52] This upward revision appears to have increased temporarily the attractiveness of time deposit accounts in U.S. banks. Of greater significance was the amendment of the Federal Reserve Act in October of the following year,[53] exempting for three years "time deposits of foreign governments, monetary and financial authorities of foreign governments when acting as such, or international financial institutions of which the United States is a member" from the ceilings imposed by Regulation Q, which was later modified accordingly.[54]

Notwithstanding these official attempts to encourage dollar deposits in U.S. banks, many banks abroad, where lending rates were generally higher than those in the United States (with the notable exception of Switzerland), were usually willing to pay higher rates on dollar deposits than those permitted by Regulation Q (Switzerland again excepted). Funds searching higher rates of return were consequently placed with these banks outside the United States and made up the bulk of the deposits on which the Euro-dollar market was based.

II. TAKING EURO-DOLLAR DEPOSITS—FIRST PHASE (1959 TO MID-1963)

A. *Legal Authority to Take Euro-dollar Deposits*

1. *U.S. Law*

As noted above, the tax exemption that deposits in U.S. banks offered to non-resident aliens and foreign corporations, in both instances not engaged in trade or business in the United States, did not extend to an important group of potential depositors because the latter were so engaged. They were taxed on the theory that interest on their U.S. bank deposits

52. 12 C.F.R. § 217.6 (Supp. 1962); 26 Fed. Reg. 11798, December 8, 1961.

53. United States, Federal Reserve Act, December 23, 1913, chap. 6, § 19 (j), as added June 16, 1933, chap. 89, § 11 (b), 48 Stat. 182, and as amended October 15, 1962, Pub. Law 87-827, 76 Stat. 953; 12 U.S.C. § 371 (b). For the legislative history see *U.S. Code Cong. Adm. News,* 1962, vol. 2, p. 3271.

54. 12 C.F.R. § 217.3 (a) (Supp. 1963); 27 Fed. Reg. 10251, October 19, 1962. In 1965 the exemption was extended for three additional years to October 15, 1968: Pub. Law 89-79, July 21, 1965, 79 Stat. 244; 12 U.S.C. § 371 (b). Regulation Q was again modified: 12 C.F.R. § 217.3 (a) (Supp. 1966); 30 Fed. Reg. 9978, August 11, 1965. For the legislative history of Pub. Law 89-79 see *U.S. Code Cong. Adm. News,* 1965, vol. 1, p. 1917. A subsequent amendment in 1968 removed the need for a terminal limit on time deposits of foreign monetary authorities and international organizations, reflected in 12 C.F.R. 217.3 (g); 33 Fed. Reg. 15408, October 17, 1968; 34 Fed. Reg. 9702, June 21, 1969, and 34 Fed. Reg. 18157, November 13, 1969.

constituted "income from sources within the United States".[55] By extension, interest on deposits in U.S. branch banks abroad, whether received in dollars or in host (or other) currency, was also considered as U.S.-source income to these recipients and thus was subject to U.S. federal income tax.[56] U.S. branch banks abroad were thus placed at a disadvantage with regard to indigenous banks and other foreign branch banks in the host countries. According to the U.S. Senate Finance Committee:

> "As a result of the rule described above non-resident aliens and foreign corporations often are reluctant to deposit funds with foreign branch banks of U.S. corporations since, if (for other reasons) they are considered to be engaged in a trade or business in the United States, the interest paid on their deposits in these foreign branches is subject to U.S. tax. Their reluctance is increased by the fact that foreign persons engaged in business in the United States can avoid U.S. tax on the interest their bank deposits earn by keeping their funds in a bank chartered in their own country or any other country other than the United States, rather than in the foreign branch bank of a U.S. corporation. As a result, foreign branch banks of U.S. corporations are at a serious competitive disadvantage with the banks chartered in the country where they are doing business."[57]

Even though this disadvantage was the rationale for a subsequent change in the U.S. federal tax laws with regard to interest earned on bank deposits by non-resident aliens and foreign corporations,[58] it is suggested that the disadvantage was less serious than might have appeared. The U.S. branch banks abroad are exempt from the Regulation Q limitations on the rates of interest which they pay on time deposit accounts and demand deposits.[59] Accordingly they could often nullify the tax law disadvantage by quoting competitive rates to the depositors when the credit markets allowed.

Furthermore, the U.S. branch banks are relieved of paying U.S. Federal

55. Internal Revenue Code of 1954, as amended; § 861 (a) (1).

56. United States, Congress, Senate, Finance Committee, *Report* No. 1707, 89th Cong., 2d Sess., October 11, 1966, on H.R. 13103 (Foreign Investors Tax Act, Pub. Law 89-809), § IV (b). See *U.S. Code Cong. Adm. News,* 1966, vol. 3, p. 4457.

57. *Ibid.* Non-resident aliens and foreign corporations definitely considered to be engaged in a trade or business in the United States "for other reasons" were not alone in their reluctance. In another part of its Report the Committee noted that "foreign persons often have been uncertain as to whether they would be held to be 'engaged in business in the United States' and that as a result they have been reluctant to deposit their funds in foreign branch banks of U.S. corporations for fear this might subject their estate to U.S. tax. As a result they are likely to place their deposits in competing foreign banks. Thus the present treatment clearly discriminates against the U.S. branches and adversely affects their ability to compete in foreign countries". *Id.,* p. 4498.

58. See pp. 205-207.

59. (Federal Reserve) Regulation Q, page 93, note 21.

168

Deposit Insurance premiums on their deposits;[60] and until 1969 U.S. banks had no reserve requirement imposed on their foreign branch deposits.[61] We shall have occasion to return to these offsetting advantages in a different context in Chapter Five.[62] For present purposes it is sufficient to bring into focus the fact that the U.S. branch banks were thus until 1969 relieved of certain costs which branches and head offices in the United States are required to cover. Smaller depositors might be deterred by the lack of U.S. Federal Deposit Insurance protection. This could not, however, seriously affect the decisions of professional and institutional depositors placing sums far greater than the F.D.I.C. limits in the Euro-dollar market, where other inherent risks outweigh that of the possible failure of the major U.S. commercial banks in question. Indeed, valuable reputations and assets were placed directly behind the debts (represented by these deposits) owed by their branches, i.e., by the U.S. banks themselves. We shall, however, have occasion to scrutinize this question again in a different legal context after mid-1963.

Finally, yield and risk aspects aside, some potential depositors are unwilling to expose their financial operations too directly to the U.S. federal government. Accordingly, an examination must be made of the U.S. federal laws affecting the separate status of records held and deposits taken by the U.S. branch banks, concentrating at this stage on the first phase of their Euro-dollar operations.

As for the records, it will be recalled that the Federal Reserve Act requires that a bank "conduct the accounts of each foreign branch independently of the accounts of other foreign branches established by it and of its home office".[63] In 1959 a federal Court of Appeals referred to this as "nothing more than a 'bookkeeping' statute, designed to make examination into the financial condition of national banks, particularly the foreign operations of such banks, as simple as possible".[64]

In that case, a U.S. bank had argued successfully in the lower federal court,[65] *inter alia,* that certain records located at its branch bank in Panama were not in the head office bank's possession, custody, or control. This argument was rejected by the Court of Appeals, which ordered the

60. Federal Deposit Insurance Corporation Act, § 2 (3), p. 121, note 102.
61. (Federal Reserve) Regulation M, § 213.7, p. 121, note 104. See p. 273.
62. See p. 255.
63. Federal Reserve Act, § 25, p. 39, note 49.
64. *First National City Bank of New York* v. *Internal Revenue Service* 271 F. 2d 616, 619 (2d Cir. 1959); cert. denied, 361 U.S. 948 (1960). The court went on to say that "reduced to its simplest terms, it is an instruction to the national banks operating foreign branches to keep separate *accounts* for each such branch, and not to lump the *accounts* together or to include them in the accounts of the home office". (italics in original).
65. 166 F. Supp. 21 (So. Dist. N.Y. 1959).

bank to produce the records at the New York City office of the U.S. Internal Revenue Service, which was investigating the U.S. federal tax liability of a Panamanian corporation with offices in New York City and in Panama City, Panama.[66] To many depositors this decision may not have weakened the attractiveness of U.S. branch banks as depositaries for Euro-dollars. For others, however, it was doubtlessly a hindrance.

As for the separate status of branch bank deposits, as opposed to records, the Federal Reserve Act stipulation that accounts at a foreign branch be conducted "independently" is in harmony with the previously noted principle that deposits are considered to be situated and payable only at the branch unless payment there has been wrongfully refused upon demand.[67]

In 1963 this issue was brought under scrutiny when the same federal Court of Appeals reversed part of a lower federal District Court order which had enjoined two U.S. banks from "selling, transferring, pledging, encumbering, disposing of or distributing any property or rights to property" of a foreign corporation.[68] The case involved a U.S. federal tax lien on the assets of a foreign corporate depositor with an alleged income tax liability of over $19 million. In the lower court, the U.S. government had sought the injunction to prevent the allegedly delinquent taxpayer's bank accounts, including those in one of the defendant bank's overseas branches, from being paid out pending an adjudication of the case on its merits. In

66. The federal Court of Appeals agreed that production of the Panama records should not be ordered if that "would require action by personnel in Panama in violation of the constitution and laws of Panama". 271 F.2d 619. This element was of importance in subsequent cases decided in the same court. The following year it dealt with the issue whether the New York City agencies of Canadian banks were required to produce records located outside the United States. *Clement J. Ings et al.* v. *Murray Ferguson, Trustee,* 282 F.2d 149 (2d Cir. 1960). Here the Court decided that the records could best be obtained via letters rogatory, which would permit a Canadian court to decide upon the contested issue of whether Quebec law prohibited "banks and their employees from sending outside the Province any of the documents..." *Id.,* 151. In 1968 the same federal Court of Appeals affirmed a lower federal District Court order that a U.S. bank has to comply with a federal grand jury subpoena requiring that records at an overseas branch be produced in connection with an alleged violation of the U.S. federal anti-trust laws even though compliance with the subpoena would subject the U.S. bank to possible civil liability under the host country law. In so doing, the Court noted that the country in which the branch bank was located (Federal Republic of Germany) had a public policy in favor of bank secrecy but no specific laws on the subject. *United States* v. *First National City Bank of New York,* 396 F.2d 897 (2d Cir. 1968). Cf. American Law Institute, *Restatement* (2d), *Foreign Relations Law of the United States,* § 40 (1965). See 47 *Texas Law Review* 703-707 (1969).

67. See p. 45.

68. *United States* v. *First National City Bank,* 210 F. Supp. 773 (So. Dist. N.Y. 1962).

reversing the District Court order insofar as it applied to any deposits held abroad, the federal Court of Appeals said:

> "Although the result here is in large part dictated by a [New York] state rule having its genesis in policy considerations having little to do with the collection of the revenue, application of that rule to the facts here comports with sound reason and public policy. Unfortunate as it may be that Omar [the foreign corporation] will be able to escape, at least partially, from a possible tax liability involving substantial sums, in the long run it is unlikely that a different rule here would provide much consolation to the Internal Revenue Service. The artful tax dodger would not have to be too sophisticated to realize that all he need do to escape liability is to place his deposits in a bank of local origin that is beyond the power of our courts. This would lead only to harmful consequences for our banking system abroad without any concomitant benefits here at home."[69]

Thus, the accessibility of books and records maintained by U.S. branch banks abroad was not held to jeopardize the separate status of their depositor's accounts.[70]

2. Host Country Laws

a. France

In order to examine the laws governing the U.S. branch banks' taking of dollar deposits in France during the period following the return to external convertibility at the end of 1958, it is necessary to take into account the evolution of the French exchange control rules up to that point, particularly with regard to non-French franc accounts.

In late December 1945 the French government had acquired the authority[71] to requisition all gold and foreign currency and securities, including holdings located abroad, belonging to French nationals residing in France or to institutions recognized as *personnes morales*[72] to the extent that they were established on French territory.[73] Less than two months later there

---

69. *United States* v. *First National City Bank,* 321 F.2d 14, 24 § (2d Cir. 1963).

70. Less than two years later, however, this decision was reversed by the U.S. Supreme Court. See pp. 202-204.

71. France, *Loi* no. 45-0140 of December 26, 1945, title III, arts. 3-5; *Journal officiel,* December 27, 1945, p. 8609.

72. Roughly equivalent to the notion "legal entity" in Anglo-American jurisprudence, the term *personne morale* in French law includes the *société anonyme* (S.A.) and *société à responsabilité limitée* (S.à R.L.). See p. 30.

73. During World War II the provisional government had imposed similar requirements. See *Ordonnance* of October 7, 1944; *Journal officiel,* October 9, 1944, pp. 897-98; and *Ordonnance* of May 1, 1944 (signed at Algiers); *Journal officiel,* May 6, 1944, p. 366.

had appeared a *décret* which required that such property be turned over to the Exchange Stabilization Fund.[74]

For banking institutions this decree covered all their accounts in foreign currency, whether those of the banks themselves or those which represented the counterpart of foreign currency accounts maintained for customers. As for these latter accounts, the banks were authorized to convert them automatically into French francs when transferring the foreign currency to the Office des Changes, which administered the Fund.[75]

By mid-1947 the various regulations concerning foreign currency holdings had been codified in a *décret*[76] which applied to all residents of the French monetary area, regardless of their nationality, who had been required to deposit with an authorized bank all foreign banknotes, checks, letters of credit, notes, bills of exchange, or other sight or short-term credit instruments in their possession unless permission to do otherwise had been obtained from the Ministre des Finances.[77] These authorized banks were in turn required to declare to the Office des Changes the existence of such foreign currency instruments held on deposit for their customers.[78]

The resident depositors were required to turn over[79] to the Exchange Stabilization Fund all foreign currency receipts arising out of the export of goods or services as well as all income from capital situated abroad.[80] In addition, the Office des Changes had the authority to require that foreign currency from other sources be turned over.[81] The resident account holders were automatically credited with the French franc equivalent (at the official rate) of the foreign currency so transferred.[82]

In addition, French monetary area residents were required to make known their holdings abroad,[83] an exemption being made for amounts less than FF 20,000 (approx. $1,700).[84] For banks and other financial institutions this meant not only those in their own names but also those held for their customers.

74. France, Ministère des Finances, *Décret* no. 46-177 of February 13, 1946; *Journal officiel,* February 14, 1946, p. 1302.
75. *Décret* no. 46-177, art. 2.
76. Ministère des Finances, *Décret* no. 47-1337 of July 15, 1947, p. 95, note 33.
77. *Décret* no. 47-1337, title II, chap. II, § 1, art. 15.
78. Art. 20.
79. Delays were allowed for turning over foreign currency, e.g., one month (and eventually three months) in the case of export receipts. See Ministère des Finances, *Arrêté* of July 15, 1947, p. 95, note 34, *supra,* art. 12. During the delays, therefore, residents could legally maintain accounts in dollars, if only for brief periods and under special circumstances.
80. *Décret* no. 47-1337 *supra,* art. 32.
81. *Décret,* art. 35.
82. Art. 38.
83. Art. 52.
84. Art. 55.

172

In September 1950 the rules had been relaxed to allow bona fide resident holders of dollars to maintain dollar accounts in French banks.[85] Although exporters' dollar receipts generated abroad (except for the "E.F.AC." exempted portions, as noted further along) still had to be turned over in accordance with Article 32 of the *Décret* no 47-1337, a resident of France possessing dollars from other sources could deposit them with a bank in the United States to the credit of an *intermédiaire agréé* or authorized bank in France, which in turn would carry an account in dollars for him. Thus, the eligible French resident could not maintain an account in dollars abroad in his own name, but could have a dollar account in a local bank.[86]

In November 1951 the Office des Changes published an *Instruction* with regard to foreign currency accounts held by *intermédiaires agréés*.[87] The Office expressed concern at the increasing balances in these accounts, calling attention to the European Payments Union agreement under which France along with the other signatory states had agreed to:

> "... use its best endeavours to ensure that abnormal balances in the currencies of other Contracting Parties are not held by banks other than central banks or otherwise placed so that they are excluded from the calculation of bilateral surpluses or deficits."[88]

Although dollars were not directly implicated, since the United States was not a member of the E.P.U., the action taken by the French Office des Changes is of interest. The Office announced that thenceforth the *intermédiaires agréés* would be allowed to maintain two types of foreign currency accounts: (1) those in their correspondent banks abroad, and (2) those maintained on the books of the Exchange Stabilization Fund. They were to establish the latter type of account by transferring to foreign central banks, for the account of the Banque de France, the excess balances in their accounts held with foreign correspondent banks, receiving in re-

85. France, Office des Changes, *Avis* no. 471; *Journal officiel,* September 21, 1950, p. 9931.
86. Similar treatment was allowed for Canadian dollar accounts. France, Office des Changes, *Avis* no. 469; *Journal officiel,* September 5, 1950, p. 9594. An earlier *Avis* no. 451 had covered accounts in pounds sterling and in Swiss francs. *Journal officiel,* March 21, 1950, p. 3152. Authorized residents' dollar holdings were not, however, free from the vicissitudes of the French economy during the years to follow. In fact, French banks were ordered in December 1957 to lend to the French government 30% of their dollars on deposit abroad. This was carried out by having an equivalent percentage of their dollar accounts transferred to the account which the Banque de France maintained in the Federal Reserve Bank of New York. See N. Y. Times, December 7, 1957, p. 1, col. 2 (late city edition).
87. France, Office des Changes, *Instruction* no. 477, November 17, 1951.
88. Agreement for a European Payments Union, page 156, note 2, part I, art. 4 (f).

turn a credit in the Fund's books. It was provided that as need arose the first type of account would be replenished by transfers from the Fund.

As indicated earlier there was an "E.F.AC." exemption from the requirement that export receipts be turned over to the Exchange Equalization Fund. Exporters could retain a portion of these receipts to cover expenses abroad connected with their export activities, such as sales representation and advertising costs. This was known as the "E.F.AC." or *exportations-frais accessoires* (i.e., exports—related expenses) exemption.[89] An eligible exporter in France could maintain an account in French francs (*compte E.F.AC. en francs*) or in a foreign currency (*compte E.F.AC. en devises*) depending upon the currency in which he was paid for goods and services sold abroad. It was common for exporters to have both types of E.F.AC. accounts, and in the second category to maintain a separate E.F.AC. foreign currency account for each type of foreign currency received, e.g., an *E.F.AC. compte dollars U.S.A.* for deposits of U.S. currency and an *E.F.AC. compte francs belges* for deposits of Belgian currency.[90]

The portion retained by the exporter and deposited in an E.F.AC. account for such expenses was originally set at 10%.[91] Later the portion depended upon the type of currency received by the exporter, e.g., 15% for dollars or French francs paid out of *comptes francs libres*[92] and 10% for other currencies.[93] Part of the E.F.AC. foreign currency accounts (12% of the export receipts in the case of dollars or French *francs libres*) could be debited by the bank in which they were maintained, without authorization from the Office des Changes, for payment of commissions to foreign sales agents, advertising costs abroad, business trip expenses, insurance, freight, and other specified charges. Other types of payments needed special permission.[94] For several years an exporter was allowed to use, with relative freedom from restriction, the remaining 3% of his dollar or *franc libre* export receipts for any purpose whatsoever.[95] This limited freedom was terminated, however, as of November 1, 1953 at which time the entire 15% (in the case of the dollar and *franc libre* re-

89. France, Office des Changes, *Avis* no. 318; *Journal officiel,* April 21, 1948, p. 3914. See *Arrêté* of July 15, 1947, *supra,* art. 12. See also Office des Changes, *Avis* no. 483, Title IV (III) (1); *Journal officiel,* Janary 5, 1951, pp. 180-212.

90. France, Office des Changes, *Avis* no. 501, title I (I) (A) (5); *Journal officiel,* June 17, 1951, pp. 6382-88.

91. *Avis* no. 318, *supra,* par. 1.

92. See p. 96.

93. *Avis* no. 501, *supra,* title I (III) (2) and (3).

94. *Avis* no. 501, *supra,* title II.

95. This relative freedom was not, however, without surveillance. For example, the bank in which the account was maintained was obliged to verify that the exporter did not use the 3% to build up hidden reserves abroad. *Avis* no. 501, *supra,* title II (III) (5).

174

cepts) was made subject to the E.F.AC. rules.[96] Simultaneously there was added the requirement that 10% of any unused E.F.AC. account balances at the end of each quarter be converted into French francs.[97]

Also, the E.F.AC. foreign currency account holder could use these funds to engage in certain foreign exchange arbitrage transactions. Operations of this nature could be made without specific authorization if they conformed to the rules set forth in pertinent notices issued by the Office des Changes.

Residents owning securities denominated in dollars or other foreign currencies could deposit them with *intermédiaires agréés,* who could maintain foreign currency accounts into which dividends or sales proceeds in foreign currency could be deposited. The account holder was required to convert these funds into French francs within one month after receipt.[98]

Thus, the French requirements with regard to residents' foreign currency bank accounts were rather complex and were very detailed. As might be expected, those concerning non-residents' accounts were much less so. In Chapter Three it was seen that non-residents were allowed to maintain special types of accounts in French francs which allowed conversion into and out of various foreign currencies depending upon the country of residence of the account holder.[99] The July 15, 1947 *Arrêté* had accorded specific authorization for foreign currency accounts in the names of non-residents, called *comptes en devises ouverts au nom de non-résidents.* Such accounts could be opened only with the prior permission of the Office des Changes;[100] and all credit and debit operations had to receive similar prior authorization.[101]

Blanket permission, however, was accorded for certain entries in a French bank's books with regard to the maintenance of foreign currency accounts in banks abroad either for the bank itself or for its eligible customers. Thus, a French bank or U.S. branch bank in France could maintain dollar accounts in New York City or elsewhere. In addition, automatic permission was granted to debit a non-resident holder's account, other than the account of a correspondent, with funds transferred to the Exchange Equalization Fund or to credit the account with payments made by another non-resident to the account holder.[102]

After the return to external convertibility at the end of 1958, residents

96. France, Office des Changes, *Avis* no. 563, § I; *Journal officiel,* September 25, 1953, pp. 8447-48.

97. *Avis* no. 563, § III.

98. See France, Office des Changes, *Instruction* no. 674 of September 18, 1956, title II, § II (I) (2).

99. See pp. 96-97.

100. *Arrêté* of July 15, 1947, *supra,* art. 27.

101. Art. 28.

102. Art. 30.

of the French franc zone continued to be eligible to maintain dollar accounts under special conditions. There was no immediate easing of the requirements for such accounts; but by 1962 a partial relaxation of the exchange control system became apparent. This was reflected, for instance, in a modification of the E.F.AC. account requirements. An *avis* issued by the Ministère des Finances in March of that year directed that thenceforth the entire E.F.AC. account (i.e., 15% of the export receipts) could be used freely once the exporter had received a general or special authorization from the Ministère.[103] The *avis* also eased the requirement as to the forced conversion (into French francs) of unused E.F.AC. account balances by providing that this would thereafter occur every six months instead of every quarter, the minimum balance being set at NF 1,000 (approx. $200)[104] regardless of the foreign currency in question.[105] Later the same year the forced conversion requirement was abolished altogether.[106]

Whereas the relaxation of the exchange control rules was only partial for the dollar deposits of residents, and came slowly, an *instruction* issued early in 1959 made freely available to non-residents the foreign currency in the accounts maintained for them abroad by French banks.[107] The same *instruction* permitted similar treatment for foreign nationals resident in France. Accordingly, French or foreign nationals with bona fide residence abroad and foreign nationals residing for limited periods in France could thenceforth have their dollar accounts in French banks freely at their disposal, both inside and outside the French monetary area.

103. France, Ministère des Finances et des Affaires Economiques, *Avis* no. 739; *Journal officiel,* March 20, 1962, p. 3065. Under *Décret* no. 59-1438 of December 21, 1959 the Office des Changes had been dissolved as of January 1, 1960, its functions thenceforth being divided between the Banque de France (essentially the financial aspects) and the Ministère (export-import and foreign investment). *Journal officiel,* December 22, 1959, pp. 12195-96.

104. The intention to institute a *"nouveau franc"* (NF) or new franc worth 100 existing francs was announced by *Ordonnance* no. 58-1341 of December 27, 1958; *Journal officiel,* December 28, 1958, p. 11935. It replaced the *"franc"* as of January 1, 1960. See Ministère des Finances et Affaires Economiques, *Décret* no. 59-1450 of December 22, 1959; *Journal officiel,* December 23, 1959, pp. 12253-54.

105. *Avis* no. 739, *supra.*

106. France, Ministère des Finances et des Affaires Economiques, *Avis* no. 755; *Journal officiel,* December 21, 1962, p. 12440.

107. France, Office des Changes, *Instruction* no. 772 of January 21, 1959, title I (2). Several months later there was a change made in the regime for non-residents' accounts in French francs as well. In July 1959 the *comptes francs libres* and *comptes franc transférables* (see p. 97) were fused into a single category known as *comptes étrangers en francs convertibles.* The *comptes francs bilatéraux* became *comptes étrangers en francs bilatéraux.* Office des Changes. *Avis* no. 682; *Journal officiel,* July 26, 1959, pp. 7441-43. See also I.M.F., *(Eleventh) Exchange Restrictions,* 1960, p. 136.

Here was one-half of the key to starting Euro-dollar operations in earnest, for banks in France could take dollars with relatively few restrictions from at least one group of potential depositors, i.e., non-residents. Still, even with these accounts there were rules to be observed and checks to be made. For instance, *intermédiaires agréés* still had to satisfy themselves that a bona fide non-resident status existed. Official forms still had to be filled out and records maintained.

For purposes of comparative analysis, then, it is to be kept in mind that there was a relaxation of the French exchange control strictures on the taking of dollar deposits during the first phase of the U.S. branch banks' Euro-dollar operations, particularly with regard to non-residents' accounts. Despite this, the complicated machinery that had been developed during the years prior to the end of 1958 continued to exert an inhibitive force. The complex rules and regulations under which banks in France had operated in the period from mid-1945 through 1958 had left their pattern on the fashion in which they operated in the years to follow. Particularly in comparison with the British system this is relevant; and it is that body of laws to which we now proceed.

b. *Great Britain*

As with the case of the French law on the taking of dollar deposits, it is necessary initially to take into account the British laws and regulations prior to the return to external convertibility at the end of 1958. Before World War II banks in London took deposits in dollars and other foreign currencies from both resident and non-resident customers. With the outbreak of hostilities in 1939 these accounts came under the British wartime exchange controls. Residents of the sterling area, or sterling bloc as it then was known, were obliged to exchange into pounds, at the official rate of exchange, any dollars and certain other "specified"[108] currencies which they held. Also, most privately owned securities denominated in these currencies had to be turned over to the British government in exchange for sterling at the official rate. The effect of these measures was to transfer out of private hands dollars that would otherwise have been available for deposit in British banking institutions.

The exchange control system instituted in 1947 modified the wartime measures by providing *inter alia* that authorized banks in Great Britain could take dollars and other foreign currencies on deposit from eligible depositors. The latter were divided into two groups: residents and non-

---

108. So called because they were specified in lists accompanying the rules. The Exchange Control Act, 1947 specified particular foreign currencies in an annex. See also, for example, H. M. Treasury, the Exchange Control (Specified Currency) Order, 1951, S.I. 1951, no. 1730.

residents. In essence the system has changed only slightly over the intervening years. Certain categories of residents have been granted permission to hold and deposit foreign currency for specific purposes. To date, however, the vast majority of the residents of the Scheduled Territories, as the sterling area has come to be called officially, cannot legally possess dollars except in limited amounts.

As for residents, the Exchange Control Act, 1947 calls for the surrender of any foreign currency (and gold) held by them without Treasury permission to retain or otherwise dispose of it.[109] For the purposes of our analysis the provision for certain authorized holders of dollars is of primary importance. Although there has been no British counterpart to the complex E.F.AC. system in France, certain exporters have been eligible to have "retained currency accounts" to which their dollar receipts could be credited.[110] Also, resident holders of dollar-denominated securities have been permitted to sell these for dollars, which they can reinvest in similar securities or sell to other residents who wish to do so. These funds usually bring a premium when converted into sterling, which has led to their being called "premium dollars". They have also been known variously as "investment dollars" or "security dollars" and sometimes as "switch dollars", being bought and sold in a pool, the premium rising or falling as American securities have appeared more or less attractive as investments.

As for the non-residents, once an authorized bank has established the bona fide non-resident character of the firm's or individual's residence, it has been able either to maintain a dollar account in its own books or to maintain one in the depositor's name in a bank outside the sterling area.[111]

Dollars owned by non-residents and by residents falling into the categories described above have constituted the sources from which banks in Great Britain have been able to take deposits in that currency, i.e., original Euro-dollar deposits. It is noteworthy that dollars coming from outside the sterling area are free from the regulation that applies to resident-held funds. This factor has allowed a freedom for expansion in the one sector that has not existed in the other. In comprehending the Euro-dollar operations of the U.S. branch banks, then, a salient fact is that this legal structure has favored a preponderance of non-resident owned dollars

109. Exchange Control Act, 1947, p. 70, note 174, part. I.

110. See, for example, Great Britain, Bank of England, Exchange Control (General) Notice 45, dated March 12, 1959 (third issue), paragraph 7. (Earlier issues were dated March 1, 1951 and October 31, 1957).

111. See, for example, Great Britain, Bank of England, Exchange Control (General) Notice 29, dated June 10, 1955 (second issue), paragraph 7 (b). (Earlier issue was dated March 6, 1950).

available for deposit in London. As will be seen, this has greatly affected the nature of the U.S. branch banks' operations.

A word must be added as to the interest rates paid on Euro-dollar deposits in London. Although the LDR was not a legal limitation on the percentage paid by the clearing banks on sterling deposits,[112] it nevertheless had the same effect as if enforced by the government. The LDR did not, on the other hand, apply to foreign currency time deposit accounts. The clearing banks and other banks in London have been free to compete for dollar accounts by adjusting their interest rates. Moreover, unlike sterling time deposit accounts, which are always at seven days' notice, dollar accounts can be taken for varying maturities.[113]

For two reasons this is significant. First, it means that the U.S. branch banks' principal indigenous counterparts, the clearers, have not been impeded from entering the competition for dollar deposits, along with some of the accepting houses and British overseas banks. If the clearing banks failed to do so until relatively recently, as they did, it has not been due to any legal or quasi-legal restriction. Second, the flexibility offered by varying maturities in their dollar deposits has allowed banks to adjust their intake of funds with their advances. Without the seven day limit on the very short end, a taker can balance its Euro-dollar book to accommodate call or overnight money and 48 hour fixes, or other arrangements sought by potential depositors.

B. *Status of the Deposits*

Let us assume that a corporate depositor presents for deposit at an indigenous bank or a U.S. branch bank in London a check in dollars drawn on a Boston bank. If the London bank or branch bank has an account in that Boston bank, the latter credits the account with the amount involved and reduces the drawer's account balance by the same amount. If the London bank or branch bank has no account in that particular Boston bank and does not choose to establish one, it will direct that an account in one of its correspondent banks in the United States be credited, the amount passing through the U.S. clearing channels like any other instrument transmitted for collection. The debt between the depositing corporation and the London bank or branch bank is "located" in London; but the ultimate dollar debt which underlies the London debt is "located" in Boston or New York City or wherever in the United States the London bank or branch bank has the correspondent account.[114]

---

112. See p. 90.
113. *Cf.* Bank of England, 1 *Quarterly Bulletin* 20 (1961).
114. An indigenous bank in London with a branch or subsidiary in the United

In the rare instance where a depositor presents dollar banknotes for deposit in London, the bank or branch bank may retain them if its foreign exchange department is temporarily in short supply. In this case there would be no similar debt in the United States behind the London debt. Banks do not, however, make a practice of keeping excess amounts of banknotes in their vaults or tills. Unless they expect corporate or other Euro-dollar depositors to request payment in the form or U.S. banknotes, which normally they will not, the excess banknotes are exchanged for other currency or transferred for deposit in a dollar account in the United States or, more rarely, elsewhere.

If the corporation presents the check for deposit in a dollar account in a bank or branch bank in Paris the situation is similar to that described in London if the bank or branch bank maintains an account in the United States. Frequently, though, in this case there is a further link in the chain, since some of the banks and branch banks on the European continent maintain dollar deposits in London banks or branch banks,[115] which in turn has accounts in the United States. A U.S. branch bank in Paris can "maintain its own book" in the Euro-dollar market,[116] or it can forward the funds for deposit in London.

The Euro-dollar debt owed to a depositor by a bank or branch bank outside the United States differs in its legal nature from a dollar-denominated debt stemming from a deposit in a bank or branch bank inside the United States. In the latter case both the *lex debitoris* and the *lex monetae* are the same, viz., U.S. law. In the former case, however, a Euro-dollar deposit results in the introduction of a second set of laws, those of the host country.[117] Accordingly the depositor runs any potential risk inherent therein, as well as in U.S. law.

Risks in the host country law include, for instance, that local exchange control rules may alter, delay, or prohibit altogether, the payment of the debt—i.e., the withdrawal of the deposit—at maturity. Through 1967 the risk of detrimental U.S. exchange control measures was not appreciable, although there was the possibility that individual foreign banks' accounts in their U.S. correspondent banks might be blocked for particular rea-

---

States will normally maintain its correspondent account there. In like fashion, the London branch of a U.S. bank will maintain an account in its head office bank.

115. If the U.S. branch bank on the Continent has a sister branch in London, the deposit will normally go into an account there.

116. I.e., it can borrow and lend Euro-dollar deposits in the inter-bank market as well as lend to eligible end-users of Euro-dollars. An officer in one U.S. branch bank in Paris has stated that the first Euro-dollar transaction at that branch bank took place in 1958.

117. *Cf.* Lalive, p. 45, note 74.

sons.[118] Since 1968 the likelihood of U.S. exchange control restrictions has become less remote. Indeed, the capital movements controls put into effect in January of that year may prove to have been the harbinger of more stringent U.S. measures in the 1970's.[119]

In addition to the question as to the law governing foreign currency debts as such,[120] a Euro-dollar deposit also raises the issue of distinguishing between the money of account and the money of payment,[121] since the bank or branch bank taking the Euro-dollar deposit may have the option of satisfying the debt in host currency. As Dach points out, French, British, and Swiss laws *inter alia,* each in its own fashion, provide in effect that French francs, pounds sterling, or Swiss francs respectively can be used to retire a Euro-dollar debt unless the contract between the depositor and the bank stipulates otherwise.[122]

The existence of more than one set of legal rules is an added reason for the Euro-dollar depositor's need for confidence in the bank taking his funds. In this respect the branches of the *major* U.S. commercial banks have had a standing equivalent to that of their host country counterparts, and an advantage over less well known institutions there or elsewhere.

118. The accounts of some non-U.S. banks have been blocked temporarily in connection with alleged securities law or stock exchange violations in the United States.

119. For instance, in October 1970 the Currency and Foreign Transactions Reporting Act (Pub. Law 91-508) was passed, which now requires *inter alia* that individual capital movements in excess of $5,000 be reported as the U.S. Secretary of the Treasury may prescribe (§ 231), as he has, as from August 1, 1971, and directs him to require "any resident or citizen of the United States, or person in the United States and doing business therein, who engages in any transaction or maintains any relationship, directly or indirectly, on behalf of himself or another, with a foreign financial agency to maintain records or to file reports, or both", setting forth information which includes the identities of the parties and the types of transactions and amounts involved (§ 241). The latter provision is the authority for the U.S. Internal Revenue Service requirement that taxpayers indicate the existence of any bank, securities, or other financial account in a foreign country on their returns for 1970 and thereafter. See 56 *Federal Reserve Bulletin* 933-34 (1970). See also p. 78, note 211.

120. See generally Nussbaum, p. 45, note 73, at pp. 340-59.

121. See F. A. Mann, *The Legal Aspect of Money,* 2d. ed., Oxford, Clarendon Press, 1953, pp. 158-59.

122. Dach, p. 163, note 30, at pp. 35-37. See also Nussbaum, *supra,* pp. 360-64. Dach concludes that "... it can be said that while the laws ... permit the repayment of foreign money deposits in local currency, the general terms of the banks sometimes enforce, sometimes abrogate the rule, and sometimes they are silent on the subject. The only conclusion one can reach, therefore, is that before forming an opinion whether the money of payment will be that of the money of account, the agreement between bank and customer has to be scrutinized". Dach, p. 37.

III. LENDING IN THE EURO-DOLLAR MARKET—FIRST PHASE (1959 TO MID-1963)

A. *Legal Authority to Lend in the Euro-dollar Market*

1. *U.S. Law*

It was during the first phase of their Euro-dollar market operations that the U.S. Congress passed a law designed "to improve the usefulness of national bank branches in foreign countries".[123] Enacted in 1962, this law added the following new paragraph to Section 25 of the Federal Reserve Act:

> § 604 (a). "Regulations authorizing exercise by foreign branches of usual powers of local banks; restrictions
>
> . . . .
>
> Regulations issued by the Board of Governors of the Federal Reserve System under ... [Section 25 of the Federal Reserve Act] ..., in addition to regulating powers which a foreign branch may exercise under other provisions of law, may authorize such a foreign branch, subject to such conditions and requirements as such regulations may prescribe, to exercise such further powers as may be usual in connection with the transaction of the business of banking in the places where such foreign branch shall transact business. Such regulations shall not authorize a foreign branch to engage in the general business of producing, distributing, buying or selling goods, wares or merchandise; nor, except to such limited extent as the Board may deem to be necessary with respect to securities issued by any 'foreign state' ..., shall such regulations authorize a foreign branch to engage or participate, directly or indirectly, in the business of underwriting, selling, or distributing securities."[124]

The Report of the U.S. House of Representatives Committee on Banking and Currency, commenting favorably on this legislation prior to its passage, had examined the need for the amendment in light of competitive conditions abroad. The Report referred to an opinion expressed to the Committee by the Board of Governors of the Federal Reserve System to the effect that:

> "... legislation ... similar to this bill would reduce the obstacles to effective competition by national banks abroad by permitting the powers of foreign branches to be adjusted more realistically to the conditions existing in places where they are located, while at the same time providing suitable safeguards to assure that such foreign branches would not engage in such business as investment banking or manufacturing."[125]

---

123. Pub. Law 87-588, 76 Stat. 388. By extension, state member bank branches abroad are also beneficiaries of this law. Federal Reserve Act, § 9, p. 39, note 50.

124. Federal Reserve Act, § 25, p. 39, note 49; paragraph added August 15, 1962 by Pub. Law 87-588, 76 Stat. 388; 12 U.S.C. § 604 (a).

125. United States, Congress, House of Representatives, Committee on Banking and Currency, *Report* no. 2047, 87th Cong., 2d Sess., July 27, 1962, on S. 1771. See *U.S. Code Cong. Adm. News*, 1962, vol. 1, pp. 2141-43.

The House Committee Report added that the Board of Governors had:

> ". . . also expressed the opinion that through the regulatory authorization of certain limited kinds of guaranties, repurchase agreements, acceptance financing, real estate loans, and other practices usual to the banking business abroad but restricted under existing laws relating to national banks, the activities of foreign branches of national banks abroad may be greatly facilitated, under appropriate regulations, without jeopardizing the integrity of American banking."[126]

Three letters supporting the amendment were addressed to the House Committee by the Board of Governors of the Federal Reserve System, the Treasury Department, and the Federal Deposit Insurance Corporation.

In its letter dated September 11, 1961 the Board of Governors noted that the bill was "virtually identical" to proposed legislation that had passed the Senate in 1957. The letter stated that:

> ". . . in recommending such an amendment in 1956, the Board of Governors expressed the opinion that it would reduce the obstacles to effective competition by national banks abroad. . .
>
> The Board of Governors continues of the opinion that such legislation is desirable 'for the furtherance of the foreign commerce of the United States,' the express purpose for which national banks were originally authorized to establish branches abroad. . ."[127]

A letter dated September 14, 1961 from the General Counsel of the Treasury Department stated that the proposed legislation was:

> ". . . necessary because in some places foreign branches of national banks cannot exercise powers normally incident to banking in these places and, therefore, cannot serve to the fullest extent possible the banking needs of their customers."[128]

A similar letter dated September 11, 1961 from the Chairman of the Federal Deposit Insurance Corporation supported the bill, referring to specific competitive disadvantages suffered by U.S. branch banks abroad, noting especially that

> ". . . foreign branches of national banks, unlike the banks in some foreign countries, may not give guarantees for the payment of customs duties, or for the payment of funds when specified deliveries are made or other transactions performed and may not accept drafts for shipments within the foreign country, in which it is located, even though they may accept drafts for shipments within the United States. Such disparities would seem to impair the usefulness and competitive strength of foreign branches of national banks."[129]

---

126. *Ibid.*
127. The text of this letter is reproduced at *Id.,* p. 2143.
128. *Id.,* pp. 2143-44.
129. *Id.,* pp. 2144-45.

The 1962 amendment to Section 25 of the Federal Reserve Act was reflected the following year when the Board of Governors revised and greatly expanded Federal Reserve Regulation M. Whereas this Regulation had theretofore dealt only with the suspension of U.S. branch banks' operations during "disturbed conditions", it since has covered a wide range of issues dealing with their establishment[130] and operations. The revised Regulation M contains the following new section:

§ 213.4 "Further powers of foreign branches

. . . .

In addition to its other powers, a foreign branch may, subject to . . . [restrictions covering commercial and manufacturing as well as most investment banking operations] . . . and so far as usual in connection with the transaction of the business of banking in the places where it shall transact business:

(a) Guarantee customers' debts or otherwise agree for their benefit to make payments on the occurrence of readily ascertainable events . . . [subject to limitations as to the total amounts of customers' obligations generally or those of any particular customer]. . .;

(b) Accept drafts or bills of exchange drawn upon it, which shall be treated as 'commercial drafts or bills' . . .;

(c) Acquire and hold securities (including certificates or other evidences of ownership or participation) of the central bank, clearing house, governmental entities, and development banks of the country in which it is located . . . [up to a specified amount in relation to its deposits] . . .;

(d) Underwrite, distribute, buy, and sell obligations of the national government of the [host] country . . .; but no bank may hold, or be under commitment with respect to, obligations of such a government as a result of underwriting, dealing in, or purchasing for its own account in an aggregate amount exceeding 10 per cent of its capital and surplus;

(e) Take liens or other encumbrances on foreign real estate in connection with its extensions of credit. . ."[131]

The broad scope of Regulation M as revised has been extremely favorable to the U.S. branch banks' multinational operations. It has contributed significantly to providing a wide U.S. legal framework in which to manoeuver, with virtually no fear of violating the U.S. federal banking laws in emulating host country banks and other foreign branch banks or banking subsidiaries there. In effect, the revised legislation and the resulting regulatory measures treat the U.S. branch banks abroad more like foreign banks established and operating abroad than like branch extensions of U.S. firms engaged in the commercial banking business.

Conceptually this has widened the gap between U.S. banks in the United States and their branch banks operating abroad. This might seem

130. See p. 41.
131. (Federal Reserve) Regulation M, 12 C.F.R. § 213.4, as added by 28 Fed. Reg. 8361, August 15, 1963 (1966 Supplement). With the issuance of Regulation M, Revised, 32 Fed. Reg. 4399, March 23, 1967 these provisions have, with a slight modification of (e), become § 213.3 (b) (1)-(5).

to reflect a step toward avoiding any extraterritorial extension of the legislative or administrative competence of the United States. Such a hypothesis does not stand up under examination, however, because elsewhere in the revised Regulation M the U.S. head office banks were clearly charged (until March 1967)[132] with causing their branch banks to comply with notices that the Board of Governors might issue.[133]

In fact, the legislators and administrators have treated the U.S. branch banks abroad as different from U.S. banks and domestic branches because in fact they are different. The resulting law and regulation, however, heighten the paradox of branches that are partially treated as separate entities. For instance, the limits on the underwriting, distribution, purchase, and sale of host government obligations are set in relation to the U.S. banks' own capital and surplus,[134] because the foreign branches technically do not have such. This particular part of Regulation M could have been drafted so as to refer to the amounts of the U.S. banks' capital and surplus allocated to the operations of their branch banks abroad without having lost its significance. By attributing only certain aspects of autonomy to the branch banks, however, the Board of Governors in this case appears to have dealt realistically with a new phenomenon.

2. Host Country Laws

a. France

In Chapter Three it was necessary to take account of the French credit control measures when analysing the effect of host country laws on the U.S. branch banks' lending operations. In that instance, the operations were conducted in the host currency. Whereas these credit control measures have continued to be applied as an anti-inflationary policy instrument in France,[135] they have been aimed primarily at the banks' franc lending and not at their advances in foreign currencies to eligible borrowers, covered by exchange rather than credit controls.

In keeping with the liberalisation of exchange controls after the return to external convertibility, the *intermédiaires agréés* were allowed in early 1959 to lend foreign currency balances held with correspondent banks abroad to residents of the French franc zone to finance import and export transactions. For other purposes, residents needed specific per-

132. See p. 48.
133. Regulation M, 12 C.F.R. § 213.5 (b). See p. 48.
134. 12 C.F.R. § 213.4 (d), *supra,* now § 213.3 (b) (4).
135. For instance, the *plancher* requirement (see p. 123, note 112) was lowered to 20% in January 1961 at which time a Treasury coefficient was introduced. In June 1961 and again in March 1962 the *plancher* requirement was further reduced to 17.5% and 15% respectively.

mission[136] to borrow if the amount exceeded the equivalent of FF 100 million (approx. $200,000) with interest being limited to 6% for a term of five years.[137] In July 1959 the maximum permissible interest rate was reduced to 5%.[138] In February 1962 the amount was raised to NF 2 million[139] (approx. $400,000), the maximum interest rate and term remaining at 5% and five years respectively;[140] and in August 1963 these limits were lowered to FF 1 million[141] (approx. $200,000) at 4% for two years,[142] where they remained until the French exchange controls ended as of January 31, 1967.[143] At each instance the provision as to the limits specified that it applied not only to individual transactions but also to the total borrowings outstanding at any time for any resident borrower. A corollary to these rules has lain in the requirement that non-residents obtain permission to borrow dollars or other foreign exchange from banks in France.

In effect, the above provisions have meant that Euro-dollar financing has not been normally available for business needs in France other than for the direct financing of imports and exports. The U.S. branch banks and others in France have not been cut off from the Euro-dollar market; but loans to resident borrowers, large enough to be on a profitable basis, have needed specific authority. For example, a $200,000 Euro-dollar loan for 90 days at $3/4$% p.a. margin would have yielded only $375 in gross earnings to the lending bank. Economies of scale, so to speak, have not been made possible.

Although the U.S. branch banks in Paris have made some Euro-dollar

136. From the Office des Changes, except under certain conditions, when the permission had to be obtained from the Ministère des Finances. These conditions included cases where the amount exceeded the equivalent of FF 50 million (approx. $100,000), meaning that for purposes of normal Euro-dollar transactions the latter had to be consulted.

137. France, Office des Changes, *Avis* no. 669, title I (I) (A) (5) (b); *Journal officiel,* January 21, 1959, pp. 1130-32.

138. France, Office des Changes, *Avis* no. 680; *Journal officiel,* July 21, 1959, p. 7204.

139. For the *"nouveau franc"* (NF) see p. 176, note 104.

140. France, Ministère des Finances et des Affaires Economiques, *Avis* no. 735; *Journal officiel,* February 24, 1962, p. 1891.

141. Use of the *nouveau franc* was discontinued on January 1, 1963 as provided in *Décret* no. 62-1320 of November 9, 1962, and the French monetary unit was thereafter again to be called the "franc" (FF) which is the unit now in use. Pre-January 1, 1960 currency units are designated *"anciens francs"* or "old francs"—one hundred of these equalling one franc. See International Monetary Fund, *Schedule of Par Values,* (50th issue), Washington, 1970, p. 17.

142. France, Ministère des Finances et des Affaires Economiques, *Avis* no. 762; *Journal officiel,* August 7, 1963, p. 7340.

143. See pp. 209-10 and 243-44. Exchange controls were reintroduced in 1968. See p. 210, note 36.

loans to end-users, and although Euro-dollar activities have become more important to some banks in that city, the U.S. branch banks have been understandably inclined to channel their excess Euro-dollar deposits to the London branches of their banks, where the latter have been able to marshall the funds and make larger and more profitable loans. As the exchange control laws have made it more difficult to attract dollars in Paris, they have also made it more difficult to lend dollars. The utility of a rapidly moving market, such as that in which Euro-dollar deposits are transferred from bank to bank across national frontiers, has been reduced by the French restrictions.

b. *Great Britain*

The Euro-dollar lending operations of the U.S. branch banks in Great Britain can be separated into four general categories: (1) lending dollars directly to residents, (2) converting dollars into sterling for lending to residents, (3) lending dollars directly to non-residents, and (4) converting dollars into sterling for lending to non-residents. In the absence of any "banking laws" governing their lending operations, our analysis must concentrate on the British credit and exchange control laws and regulations.

Taking the first of the four lending situations above, dollar loans to sterling area residents come under exchange control restrictions. In the first Euro-dollar operating phase, with which we are primarily concerned at this point, approval was granted for credits not exceeding 180 days in length when sought for legitimate foreign trade transactions; beyond that, permission was necessary.[144] Accordingly, borrowing for fixed capital expenditures or direct investment abroad had to be approved. In July 1961 balance of payments difficulties forced the British government to withhold permission for such investments unless they were capable of providing immediately favorable effects on the balance of payments.[145] The Bank of England modified its position in May 1962 to allow British firms to draw upon the investment dollar pool[146] for direct investments abroad that did not qualify for official exchange under the July 1961 standards.[147] In October 1962 the Bank withdrew these restraints and notified the various banking associations accordingly.[148]

As for the second category of lending, a bank in London can convert

144. Bank of England, 3 *Quarterly Bulletin* 32 (1963).
145. 7 *Id.* 258 (1967). Also *Cf.* 4 *Id.* 8 (1964).
146. See p. 178.
147. 3 *Id.* 1 (1963).
148. 2 *Id.* 237 (1962).

dollars into pounds and lend these to residents.[149] This comes within the credit controls imposed by the monetary authorities. Moreover, although the borrower does not need to obtain exchange control permission, the lending bank has its own foreign currency position to maintain. This means that as an "authorised bank" it can allow its dollar liabilities (i.e., deposits) to be out of balance with its dollar claims (i.e., advances) by only a certain amount. Otherwise, it will exceed the open position[150] which the Bank of England allows it to maintain.[151] In order to cover its foreign exchange position beyond that limit the bank therefore must swap rather than switch into sterling, which it is willing to do only so long as the cost of forward dollar cover does not wipe out the margin of profit it expects to earn on the sterling advance.

Passing over the third category (lending dollars directly to non-residents) for the moment to examine the fourth, banks in Great Britain cannot lend pounds to non-residents without exchange control permission.[152] It is true that when the sterling is sought to purchase British exports permission is forthcoming. Also, during the U.S. branch banks' first Euro-dollar operating phase from 1959 to mid-1963 it was usually possible for non-residents to obtain pounds for part of their direct investments in the sterling area. This meant, however, that operations in this quadrant were not free from regulation. Moreover, the bank had to watch its open position in foreign exchange as was the case with sterling loans to residents.

Indeed, the only sector unhampered by exchange or credit control rules is the third category, i.e., foreign currency loans made to non-residents with other non-residents' deposits. Thus, banks in London have been able to "marry" non-residents' dollar deposits with other non-residents' needs for dollar credits. It will be recalled that in September 1957

149. 2 *Id.* 93 (1962). For the U.S. branch banks in London this has frequently meant lending to local authorities. See p. 247. For an appraisal of the broader significance of this type of lending, and the growth of what have been called the "parallel money markets" in London, see Jack Revell, *Changes in British Banking; the Growth of a Secondary Banking System,* London, Hill, Samuel & Co., 1968, particularly pp. 31-33.

150. The Bank of England has allowed authorized banks to maintain open positions in foreign exchange, both spot and forward, since December 1951. 7 *Id.* 256 (1967). See also, I.M.F., *(Third) Exchange Restrictions,* 1952, p. 164.

151. A bank that is not an authorized bank for exchange control purposes in Great Britain can take deposits in, for example, Deutsche Marks and can lend these immediately, but it must avoid taking a position in that currency. Authorized status allows a bank to build up a base of foreign currency deposits from which advances can be made. It also makes it permissible for a bank to convert one currency into another, i.e., to engage in the swap or switch operations needed for going out of dollars and into sterling to lend the latter currency, as described above.

152. See pp. 128-29.

the Bank of England withdrew authorized banks' permission to provide sterling credits for non-residents' purchases from other non-residents of the sterling area.[153] In the words of one observer:

> "The curtailment of these sterling credits created a gap in the credit facilities available for financing foreign trade. Continental and other overseas borrowers, deprived of their normal credit facilities, were willing to pay high rates for alternative facilities. London banks were thus able to offer high rates for dollar deposits and to outbid New York banks, ... [and] ... were thus able to continue to meet a large part of the credit needs of their overseas clients—but by lending dollars instead of sterling."[154]

The indifference of the British exchange control laws in this lending sector has allowed—indeed, encouraged—banks in London to utilize it. It is not surprising, then, to note that by far the major part of the Euro-dollar lending from London has been to non-resident borrowers.[155]

Earlier in the present Chapter it was observed that the British regulatory structure has left free the taking of non-residents' dollar deposits. The counterpart to that is the phenomenon seen above, namely, that the lending sector left untouched is that of foreign currency advances to non-residents. It has been inside this unregulated area that all banks in Great Britain could have expanded. In light of the restrictions placed on the host currency lending operations of the clearing banks[156] they might have been expected to push into this field as did the merchant banks, the British overseas banks, and especially the U.S. branch banks in London. The absence of the clearers[157] has meant that the most powerful potential competitors have not until fairly recently begun to engage im-

---

153. See p. 129.

154. Paul Einzig, "Dollar Deposits in London," 110 *The Banker* 23, 24 (1960).

155. For example, see the tables at Bank of England, 4 *Quarterly Bulletin* 100 (1964).

156. The system of Special Deposits, under which the clearing and Scottish banks had agreed in July 1958 to place funds with the Bank of England, went into effect in April 1960. See page 126. During more than half of the first Euro-dollar operating phase this regime was in force. The percentage rate varied, being raised twice, in June 1960 and September 1961 to three times the original levels (i.e., to 3% for the clearing banks and $1\frac{1}{2}\%$ for the Scottish banks); and then lowered in three stages (May, October, and December 1962) to terminate. The Bank of England has later had occasion to use this instrument again. See p. 246. Note that this Special Deposit scheme did not apply to U.S. branch banks, *inter alia*. In September 1971 all banks in Great Britain were made subject to a new Special Deposit requirement under the present Bank of England policy on competition and credit control.

157. "... at least one-third of all dollar financing arranged through London is arranged by the London branches of American banks. The Eurodollar market is just one of the many major fields of expansion that British clearing banks have so far shunned except sometimes in the peripheral sense of 'melting' some dollar balances into sterling for domestic lending." *The Economist*, vol. 220, Supplement p. x, September 18, 1966.

portantly in these operations, even though no legal constraints have pre-vented them from doing so.

B. *Lending Techniques in the First Euro-dollar Operating Phase*

If the Euro-dollar itself does not constitute a new phenomenon,[158] the Euro-dollar market must be recognized as an innovation of significant importance. *Stricto sensu* this is a wholesale market (hereinafter referred to as the "inter-bank market") comprised of banks and a few larger financial institutions of other types, including insurance companies, which buy and sell among themselves unsecured short-term deposits of Euro-dollars.

A bank or branch bank may have no immediate need for dollars on deposit, on which it is paying, e.g., $6^3/_4\%$ interest p.a. It can lend this deposit to another bank at a rate of $6\ ^{13}/_{16}\%$ p.a. for a brief period, sometimes at call. Each institution has a limit on the amount of Euro-dollar deposits which it will advance to any other single institution. Early Euro-dollar loans were made only in round units of $1 million, although with the passage of time loans of half that size or less have come to be made between certain banks. The lending and borrowing institutions usually deal through brokers when placing and taking Euro-dollar deposits locally. When they look beyond national frontiers, on the other hand, they usually deal directly with one another although there are efficient brokers on the Continent through whom business can be channeled.

More broadly speaking, the Euro-dollar market contains original non-bank depositors and ultimate non-bank borrowers, i.e., the initial suppliers and the end-users of funds. A bank borrowing a Euro-dollar deposit in the inter-bank market may do so in order to lend dollars to an eligible (under the applicable exchange control rules) customer seeking a credit in that currency. Frequently, however, the customer does not want dollars but needs host or some other currency. In this case the bank borrowing the Euro-dollar deposit can swap[159] into the particular currency sought by its customer and make the loan in that other currency.

---

158. "There is nothing new about banks taking deposits in foreign currencies. Banks on the Continent and in the United States took sterling deposits before World War I for investment in the London market. A similar business in U.S. dollars developed between the two great wars, particularly among Canadian and Swiss banks with a competitive advantage *vis-à-vis* U.S. banks of freedom from Federal Reserve rules and regulations... The something new that got added... was the innovation of lending or investing dollar deposits in Europe." Johnson, p. 161, note 23, at pp. 6-7.

159. Einzig defines "swap" in this context as the "purchase of spot exchanges against sale of forward exchanges or sale of spot exchanges against purchase of forward exchanges". Paul Einzig, *A Textbook on Foreign Exchange*, London, Macmillan, 1966, (appendix I), p. 244.

In the alternative the customer can itself take Euro-dollars and perform the swap operation independently.

Thus a customer seeking pounds sterling can borrow them in London at the prevailing rate[160] or, if eligible to borrow dollars, will borrow these if the Euro-dollar rate[161] plus the cost of the swap do not equal the prevailing rate for sterling. The swap cost is affected directly by the forward rate (for the period in question) between dollars and the desired currency. The borrowing end-user customer can, if not otherwise prohibited by pertinent laws or its own internal by-laws or charter, also elect to assume an uncovered forward position—i.e., forego the swap.

Earlier in the present Chapter it was stated that the "ultimate debt" which underlies the Euro-dollar deposit is located at the bank in the United States in which the Euro-dollar deposit taking bank maintains its correspondent account. When an advance is made to another institution in the inter-bank market the borrowing bank will direct the lending bank to instruct the latter's correspondent bank in the United States to transfer the appropriate sum to the borrowing bank's own correspondent bank (or account, in case both use the same U.S. bank for this purpose) in the United States.

When a Euro-dollar deposit leaves the inter-bank market, i.e., when a bank or other institution in that market advances a dollar deposit to an end-user, the latter directs that the sum on deposit in the United States be transferred to its own account in a bank in the United States or to an account in another bank outside the United States, in which case the sum is shifted to the U.S. correspondent bank of the non-U.S. bank in which the end-user maintains the account. In this latter case another Euro-dollar deposit is created. Only if the end-user borrower seeks U.S. dollar banknotes does the sum standing behind the Euro-dollar deposit actually leave the U.S. banking system.

The U.S. branch banks, of course, maintain their own correspondent accounts in their respective head office banks in the United States. To the extent that they are able to convince end-user Euro-dollar deposit borrowers to deposit the funds in the lending U.S. branch banks themselves (or in their head offices), the sum on deposit in the United States does not shift to another bank. The portion of the borrowed funds representing a compensating balance would remain in this fashion. U.S.

160. Clearing banks' lending rates have ranged from Bank rate to Bank rate plus 2% depending upon the borrower and the type of advance. See National (Jones) Board, *Report*, Cmnd. 3292, p. 36, par. 83.

161. For Euro-dollar rates in London from March 1959 through July 1969 see Einzig, p. 161, note 23, at pp. 193-97 (Appendix II). Euro-dollar rates are compared with others (e.g., bankers' acceptances, Treasury Bills) in *Altman*, "Euro-Dollars: Some Further Comments", *Id.* at p. 9.

branch banks which form part of a multinational network of banking facilities sometimes allow an end-user customer to maintain its compensating balance in another branch bank in the network when it particularly suits the customer to do so. As far as the head office is concerned, the sum would simply figure in an account in the name of another of its branch banks rather than that of the lending branch.

A word of caution is necessary with regard to the term "end-user" in that it implies the "consumption" or spending of the borrowed funds, or more correctly, the borrowed deposits. It frequently arises that this non-bank entity does not spend them, but uses them for interest rate arbitrage or window dressing purposes. It is noteworthy, too, that even when a genuine end-user obtains a Euro-dollar advance destined for spending there often will be a delay during which it leaves the sum on deposit in one bank or another.

IV. ROLE OF THE U.S. BRANCH BANKS

A. *Nature of the Market*

1. *Short-term*

In the U.S. branch banks' first Euro-dollar operating phase the market provided what was essentially a method for handling short-term credits. It was one in which deposits could be withdrawn on demand or were fixed for relatively short periods, and in which borrowers sought trade financing or working capital more often than investment capital. From the depositors' viewpoint, placing dollars on deposit in a bank outside the United States was seen as an alternative to purchasing dollar trade or bank bills, U.S. Treasury bills, or commercial paper. Depositors rarely tied up their funds for more than 90 days, even though borrowers frequently desired longer-term accommodation for specific purposes. Since the latter were often allowed by their banks to roll-over their short-term Euro-dollar borrowings, both sides of the market could usually be accommodated.

2. *Wholesale*

Although exchange control regulations in France and Great Britain prevented many companies and institutions from placing dollars on deposit or from borrowing foreign currency, sufficient deposits were placed and taken to constitute a real market in Euro-dollars. On the other hand, individuals' deposits of U.S. dollars outside the United States contributed only slightly to the total mass of Euro-dollars. Nor did private individuals normally borrow in the market, where the inter-bank sector dealt in round lots of $1 million and where end-users sought large sums for commercial, industrial, and financial purposes. Already the Euro-dollar market was essentially wholesale.

In the case of the indigenous deposit banks the market was thus of primary interest only to one part of their clientele, the retail sector being largely excluded. For the U.S. branch banks, however, which were concentrating their operations largely in the wholesale markets in any event, the Euro-dollar market constituted a device which could be made available to a relatively larger proportion of their clientele. It was to be expected that the newly emerging medium would have potentially greater impact on the operations of the U.S. branch banks, then, than on those of the indigenous banks.

3. *Competitive*

As noted previously the rates paid on Euro-dollar deposits were higher than those paid on corresponding deposits placed with banks in the United States. At the same time, loans in Euro-dollars had to be made below the rates prevailing in New York City in order to attract those borrowers who had access to that source of funds. Margins were therefore thinner in the Euro-dollar market than in New York City.

Moreover, since local deposit rate conventions did not apply, there was room for competitive bidding for Euro-dollar deposits. Deposit rate competition was nothing new to bankers trained in the United States; and thin margins were a normal part of branch bank operations, especially those more recently established and not possessing a group of clients of long-standing.

With relation to their indigenous competitors, then, the U.S. branch banks found themselves under no handicap in adapting to these operating conditions in the Euro-dollar market.[162]

B. *Implications for the Operations of the U.S. Branch Banks*

In the same sense that U.S. corporate subsidiaries in the host countries could be said to have constituted "natural" customers for the U.S. branch banks, the Euro-dollar has been a "natural" commodity in which they could deal. They have also dealt in the other Euro-currencies;[163] and many

---

162. By the end of the U.S. branch banks' first Euro-dollar operating phase in mid-1963 the Euro-dollar market had grown to about $5 billion. *Cf.* Bank for International Settlements, *Thirty-fourth Annual Report,* Basle, 1964, p. 130.

163. Their operations in the other Euro-currencies have not been as extensive as in dollars. If, for example, Dutch florins or guilders are taken on deposit by a U.S.

non-U.S. banks and branch banks have dealt in Euro-dollars. There has been, however, a tendency to associate U.S. financial institutions with U.S. dollars, and by extension, with Euro-dollars. From the outset U.S. branch banks have appeared logically to be among the lenders of and depositaries for U.S. currency, or more precisely, for dollar-denominated deposits and loans.[164]

In a sense this tended to modify the "stance" of the U.S. branch banks in their deposit-taking and lending operations during the first Euro-dollar phase to mid-1963. In Chapter Three it was shown that in their host currency operations the U.S. branch banks are less often takers than lenders vis-à-vis original depositors and end-users of funds. That is, their stance is skewed in this sector. Moreover, it will be recalled that they are able to lend to host currency end-users (without swapping out of dollars) primarily by borrowing in the inter-bank money markets in the host countries. In the inter-bank host currency sector, too, their stance is skewed, but in the opposite sense.

With the advent of the Euro-dollar market the U.S. branch banks still had a dearth of host currency deposits, but they were frequently able to satisfy end-user borrowers' host currency needs by swapping out of Euro-dollars into host currency and lending the latter. This reduced dependence on the local money markets tended to reduce the one-sidedness of their stance there.

With regard to original depositors and end-users of funds the U.S. branch banks' stance was no less skewed than if host currency alone is considered. To the extent, however, that original depositors and end-users could be taken collectively without division on the basis of the currency in which their transactions were denominated, it is evident that funds of original depositors were now more nearly able to accommodate end-users' credit needs. This favored an equilibration of the U.S. branch banks' stance in this sector, too.

With this taken into consideration, it is necessary to examine three as-

---

branch bank in Paris, it usually redeposits them at once in a sister branch bank or correspondent bank in The Netherlands unless the Paris branch has a customer seeking an immediate Euro-guilder loan. The theory behind this practice lies in the assumption that a bank in the country where the funds are host currency normally has more frequent demands for them. By mid-1963 Euro-currencies other than the Euro-dollar amounted to $2 billion. *Bank for International Settlements, supra.*

164. This has led to a number of related service activities that are not strictly speaking deposits or loans, but which are profitable in a broader context. Some U.S. branch banks, for example, encourage smaller local banks to maintain dollar accounts for clearing checks drawn on banks in the United States. No minimum balances are required and no service fees charged; but the U.S. branch bank has the use of the "float" which is, in some instances, considerable.

pects of the Euro-dollar market's impact on the operations of the U.S. branch banks in the host countries, particularly during the first phase.

1. *Importance of Network Operations*

The Euro-dollar market ignores the political frontiers lying within its bounds. Host country laws determine who is eligible to participate in the market locally and the extent to which it can be used for borrowing or placing dollar deposits. Once a borrower or lender is in the market, however, it matters little whether he is in one or another European financial center. Rapid teleprinter and telephone communication make the inter-bank market rates immediately available, not only to banks seeking to attract depositors' funds or to satisfy the needs of end-user customers, but also to the arbitrageurs, whose operations narrow the interest rate spreads between different centers and between deposit or loan maturities. Foreign exchange dealers or traders have been able to use their already existing communication links and techniques for operating with these deposits, and can gauge the forward and spot rates so as to make realistic quotations for swap operations.

It has been noted that the interest rates are highly competitive in this market. Significantly this element of competition carries out beyond the bounds of any particular financial center, making it possible for a bank to bid not only in its own locale but also anywhere in the market. Extremely large deposits or borrowings can and do affect the Euro-dollar market rates. It is noteworthy, however, that a single participant in the market can rarely raise or lower the price appreciably by offering to take or place deposits. The Euro-dollar market has thus tended toward a condition of perfect competition.[165]

Prior to the return to external convertibility of the principal Western European currencies the U.S. branch banks had operated primarily in their local host markets. As the Euro-dollar market has taken form, those U.S. banks with branches in several financial centers have been able to contribute to the competitiveness of the market in the sense referred to in the preceding paragraph. Time delays are kept to an absolute minimum; and offers to take or place deposits are made nearly simultaneously at the branches in several cities. These intra-bank channels help to put market participants in even faster and more direct contact than they would otherwise be. Also, to the extent that communication costs can be absorb-

---

165. Even the very large banks or other institutions have been "price *takers*" in this respect, to use Samuelson's sobriquet. See Paul A. Samuelson, *Economics,* 6th ed., New York, McGraw-Hill, 1964, p. 451. Of course, the public institutions which have come to utilize the market (e.g., some central banks) have not played the same role, although even they have found the market vast.

ed into fixed overhead expenses, borrowers' and lenders' bids are less affected by geographical separation.

In a narrower sense those banks with branches in several financial centers have been able to compete more effectively in the Euro-dollar market. Deposits can be transferred more easily and more cheaply[166] from one branch to another; and by means of swaps eligible borrowers' short-term credit needs are freed from the availability of any particular host currency in a local market. In a sense, during the first Euro-dollar operating phase there began to develop the intra-bank money markets or networks in which participants have an advantage over other banks and branch banks which are not included. Of course, banks without direct branch links have recourse to their correspondent banks in other cities. They cannot, however, rely on receiving preferential treatment similar to that given to another branch in the same bank's network. A telephone call or teleprinter message to another branch in the same bank's network can often accomplish in several minutes what the best of correspondent relationships might not be capable of producing in a day.

Here a bank's representative offices can in some cases steer potential borrowing or lending customers to a branch in London or elsewhere. Here, too, an affiliated bank can take deposits in dollars and place them at the disposal of the entire network as an alternative to arranging short-term redeposit facilities at a favorable rate in the inter-bank market.

Whereas the U.S. branch banks as a group did not offer serious competition in the host currency markets during the period mid-1945 through 1958, those U.S. branch banks which have been able to offer their customers rapid communications facilities and well-integrated multinational banking networks have had a decided advantage over their competitors since 1959.[167]

2. Necessity for a London Branch Bank

The tightly-knit web of banking houses clustered around the Bank of England has proved to be a highly efficient Euro-dollar market place. When the British credit restrictions of September 1957[168] caused some borrowers to look for new sources of funds, the Euro-dollar in a short time proved to be a welcome—if novel—mechanism for them and lenders

---

166. Since intermediaries' commissions are not incurred.

167. Two additional points worthy of consideration are: (a) their contribution towards the reversal of corporate hoarding tendencies and the placing of corporate deposits with near-banking institutions, and (b) their effect on reducing the indigenous banks' monopsonistic influence over deposit rates and their monopolistic influence over lending rates in the host countries.

168. See p. 129, text cited to note 141.

alike. The established links between different institutions in the City of London and abroad were quickly adapted to the passage of Euro-dollar deposits. The grooves along which sterling credits flowed in the past attracted and carried Euro-dollars with little apparent difficulty.

The importance of the City of London as the emerging center of the new international money market has influenced the operations of branch banks from countries other than the United States. For the latter, however, London has had a second attraction in that Great Britain was becoming host to a greater concentration of U.S. corporate subsidiaries than any other single country in Western Europe or elsewhere.[169] A London branch has permitted a U.S. bank to maintain direct contact abroad with many of its important U.S. corporate clients' overseas operations. In other Western European host cities many factors, including the density of U.S. corporate subsidiaries directly accessible, have affected the choice of whether to rely on a local correspondent bank, to locate a representative office, to purchase a participating interest in an indigenous banking institution, or to establish a branch bank. In London, however, effective operation during the first Euro-dollar operating phase was becoming increasingly difficult without a full-fledged branch bank. Multinational banking would have been impossible without one.

3. *Arrival of the Second Wave Branch Banks*

The evolution of a truly international money market, from its embrionic stage at the outset to a workable, vigorous operating medium coincided with the establishment of new U.S. corporate subsidiaries in the host countries.[170] The corollary to this phenomenon was the growing awareness on the part of some of the major U.S. banks not already established abroad that they ran the risk of losing actual as well as potential customers if they failed to expand their operations sufficiently.

The Euro-dollar market per se was not the primary reason to establish branch banks in the host countries, although it did represent a significant

169. "Last year [1969], for example, I estimate that U.S. subsidiaries in Britain accounted for about 14 percent of the output and nearly a fifth of the fixed capital formation in manufacturing industry and sold about a quarter of Britain's manufacturing exports... [O]n current trends something like a fifth to a quarter of Britain's manufacturing output will be in the hands of American-controlled enterprises by the end of this decade." United States, Congress, *Hearings* before the Subcommittee on Foreign Economic Policy of the Joint Economic Committee, 91st Cong., 2d Sess., part 4 (The Multinational Corporation and International Investment). (1970), Statement of Prof. John H. Dunning, University of Reading, England, July 28, 1970, p. 796.

170. The direct investments of U.S. corporations in Western Europe contributed indirectly to the Euro-dollar pool from which they and their subsidiaries sought to borrow.

element in an evolution which these institutions could not ignore. The principal reason for the establishment of the second wave branch banks was to serve directly their customers located in or near the host countries in order to compete effectively with the first wave branch banks already established. In effect, this was an attempt to bridge the widening gap in various banks' direct overseas experience. Those major U.S. commercial banks not already established in the host countries were forced to decide whether they were ready to follow their clients and competitors onto the Western European stage of operations.

It is not surprising that the period from 1959 to mid-1963 witnessed the establishment of two new U.S. branch banks in London. These were the branches of the Chemical Bank New York Trust Co. (1960), and the Continental Illinois National Bank and Trust Co. of Chicago (1962). Thus by the end of the first Euro-dollar operating phase the number of major U.S. commercial banks with branches in the host countries had grown from six[171] to eight.[172]

These moves must be viewed against the larger background of the major U.S. commercial banks' operations in other Western European countries and elsewhere. Moreover, the new second wave arrivals in London could not be described as unskilled in the intricacies of providing many of their U.S. and foreign corporate customers' needs even though they were as yet lacking the direct, firsthand experience in the Euro-dollar market that the banks with first wave branches had been acquiring.

It is significant that whereas a California bank had been the sole non-New York City institution among those with first wave branches, by the end of the first Euro-dollar operating phase non-New York City banks comprised two of the eight. The second wave branch established by a bank in Chicago reflected the rising multinational aspirations of some bankers there due to the prospect of the St. Lawrence Seaway. This was a qualitative change in the structure of the U.S. banking sub-community that was emerging in the host countries.

With such qualitative as well as quantitative modifications taking place, the U.S. branch banks as a group began to attract more attention locally. The arrival of the second wave branch banks endorsed the notion that the major U.S. commercial banks had found sufficient reason to extend their activities directly into the host countries.

---

171. The U.S. banks with first wave branch banks already present at the start of this phase were: Bank of America, N.T. & S.A.; Bankers Trust Co.; Chase Manhattan Bank; First National City Bank of New York; Manufacturers Hanover Trust Co. of New York; and Morgan Guaranty Trust Co. of New York.

172. No additional branch banks were established in France during this period. In Switzerland, First National City Bank of New York was preparing to open a branch bank in Geneva later in 1963.

Chapter Five

"LONGER-TERM EURO-DOLLAR OPERATIONS IN A CHANGING MARKET AFTER MID-1963"

I. CHANGING INFLUENCES IN THE EURO-DOLLAR MARKET

It has been noted previously that the U.S. balance of payments deficit has reflected a flow of dollars into the hands of non-residents of the United States, many of whom have deposited these funds in dollar accounts outside the United States. During the period which we shall characterize as the second phase of the U.S. branch banks' Euro-dollar operations in the three host countries, i.e., from mid-1963 through the end of 1967, the United States continued to show a persistent payments deficit. Accordingly, one of the essential conditions which led to the breadth and depth of the Euro-dollar market during the first phase remained dynamically the same during the second.

Two additional influences, however, came to bear on the operations of the U.S. branch banks, each of which was partially caused by and partially resulted from the other. These were the steadily rising interest rates in the world money markets and the growing need for longer-term Euro-dollar credits. Before analysing the legal and financial aspects of the second phase of the U.S. branch banks' Euro-dollar operations, it is necessary that these two new influences be appraised.

A. *Higher Interest Rates*

From mid-1963 onwards it became increasingly expensive to borrow money in the United States, where higher interest rates reflected growing investment in the private sector as well as continuing efforts in spatial research and greatly increased military expenditures, particularly those related to a growing military commitment in Southeast Asia. In Western Europe, too, interest rates were generally rising, faster (than in the United States) in some countries (e.g., Great Britain)[1] and slower in others (e.g.,

---

1. In addition to anti-inflationary policies in Great Britain, high interest rates also reflected official efforts to bolster sterling against outward flows of hot money.

France and Switzerland) but nonetheless rising in response to the increasing demands of larger corporate borrowers seeking greater amounts of funds to satisfy their growing fixed and working capital needs.

In fact, Western European money and capital markets were barely able to satisfy the swelling demands placed on their facilities. These were further strained in early 1965 when the U.S. balance of payments Guidelines, coupled with a simultaneous modification in the Interest Equalization Tax law with regard to commercial bank lending to "non-U.S. persons", effectively shunted many potential borrowers away from New York City, where qualified corporations and individuals had theretofore been able to obtain short- and medium-term funds more cheaply than in either London or Paris. This must be taken into account in analysing these U.S. measures (to which we shall return) as well as the pertinent host country laws in the period through the end of 1967.

B. *Need for Larger and Longer-Term Credits*

There arose a need for larger and longer-term credits during the second phase of the U.S. branch banks' Euro-dollar operations, due in part to two direct causes that were increasingly felt in Western Europe.

First, advanced technology in many industrial sectors was making it necessary for manufacturers to acquire ever costlier plant and equipment. Automation in certain factories, larger rail and highway vehicles for hauling bigger payloads, increasingly expensive aircraft for both long- and short-range transportation, more refined cargo ships with costly installations of refrigeration or freight-handling equipment—all these were appearing in greater numbers together with advanced electronic data processing equipment that found buyers both in manufacturing and service industries. Since most of the needed equipment could not yet be leased, the Western European company that could not self-finance such purchases turned first to its bankers for the necessary credit.

Western European companies faced with the necessity for acquiring larger, more costly equipment naturally desired that it be suitable for or adaptable to their contemplated operations over a period of several years to obviate replacing the new machinery too soon in the future. Hence, in addition to seeking larger amounts of credit, these borrowers sought credit for terms longer than the short-term periods normally handled by commercial bankers.

Second, as progress continued in the direction of economic harmonization in Western Europe, especially in the six countries of the European Economic Community, companies were expanding the scope of their operations to adapt to larger markets. Although proposed international corporate mergers (i.e., across national boundaries)[2] encountered serious obstacles,[3] even within the so-called Common Market,[4] corporate mergers were taking place inside the different countries of Western Europe.[5] This was not only to satisfy the demands in broader markets but also to generate economic units of comparable size to foreign, especially American, companies that were appearing in greater numbers in these same markets.[6]

The evolution of larger borrowers meant that the bargaining positions of individual commercial banks would change in Western Europe. On the one hand, the negotiating advantage of the borrower was improved, for it became increasingly important to the lending institution to attempt to satisfy the credit requirements of a company that had been a reliable customer in the past, and which now was seeking much larger sums. On the other hand, the merging of some borrowing firms meant that instead of one "traditional" banker there might now be two or more, faced either with competing with one another or with joining together to arrange advances for customers that had changed in nature as well as in size. For

2. See Günther Beitzke, "Les conflicts de lois en matière de fusion de sociétés (droit communautaire et droit international privé)", 56 *Revue Critique de Droit International Privé* 1-22 (1967), and Hans-Rudolf Bener, *La fusion des sociétés anonymes en droit privé*, Geneva, Société Générale d'Imprimerie, 1967, especially pp. 59 et seq.

3. So much so that in 1969 one authority on the subject was prompted to conclude that "when it comes to international concentration it is fair to say that practically nothing at all has been done yet". Henri Schwamm, "Banks and Industrial Concentration", International Credit Bank Geneva, 7 (2) *Quarterly Review* 16-28, 27 (1969). In his careful appraisal of the role of banks in arranging and financing corporate mergers Professor Schwamm indicates different ways in which investment banks, merchant banks, and *banques d'affaires* might be able to pave the way for increased international mergers in the future. In this context it is noteworthy that *banques universelles* or the Swiss "big banks" would have a distinct advantage, as would the U.S. branch banks in Switzerland and perhaps eventually in France if (Federal Reserve) Regulation M were again modified (see page 184) to broaden further their powers so as to permit additional transactions which are "usual in connection with the transaction of the business of banking" in the host country. It is unlikely, however, that any further modification will allow U.S. commercial banks' foreign branches to engage in foreign investment banking operations much beyond those already permitted in Regulation M.

4. For a discerning view of the legal obstacles in the context of an attempt to draft a statute for a European company see Dennis Thompson, *The Proposal for a European Company*, London, Chatham House, 1969, pp. 15-16.

5. *Cf.* Jean Meynaud and Dusan Sidjanski, *L'Europe des Affaires*, Paris, Payot, 1967, pp. 35-39.

6. For a readable if not wholly convincing portrayal that captures some of the flavor accompanying this phenomenon, see generally, Jean-Jacques Servan-Schreiber, *Le défi américain*, Paris, Denoël, 1967, which later appeared in English translation under the title *The American Challenge*, New York, Atheneum, 1969.

some lending institutions this meant the loss of clients; for others, it meant larger clients or sharing with other banks their "traditional" customers.

U.S. corporate subsidiaries located in the host countries and borrowing there were subject to the same forces, although the element of "tradition" was greatly reduced or nonexistent. As will be seen later in the present Chapter, they, too, were important participants in the operations of the U.S. branch banks' operations during this period.

II. TAKING EURO-DOLLAR DEPOSITS—SECOND PHASE (MID-1963 THROUGH 1967)

A. *Legal Authority to Take Euro-dollar Deposits*

1. *U.S. Law*

During the second phase of the U.S. branch banks' Euro-dollar operations there were important changes in the U.S. federal law.

a. *Banking Law*

In Chapter Four it was observed that the Board of Governors of the Federal Reserve System greatly enlarged the scope of Regulation M in 1963.[7] It is to be noted that these new rules came into effect on August 15, 1963, just after the second Euro-dollar operating phase had begun in the summer of 1963, but that they did not impinge directly upon the deposit-taking activities of the U.S. branch banks. Neither were these activities affected by a modification in the maximum interest rates allowable under Regulation Q, for the U.S. branch banks remained exempt from its provisions.[8]

If the U.S. federal banking laws were not modified adversely with regard to the deposit-taking operations, there nevertheless did occur an important change in the interpretation of one of these laws. It will be recalled that in 1963 a U.S. federal Court of Appeals had refused to uphold a lower federal court injunction preventing amounts from being paid out of an allegedly deficient taxpayer's account in a U.S. branch bank abroad pending determination of any possible tax liability.[9]

In early 1965, having agreed to take the case on a writ of *certiorari*

7. See p. 184.
8. (Federal Reserve) Regulation Q, 12 C.F.R. § 217.6 (n. 8), 31 Fed. Reg. 12676, September 28, 1966. As noted earlier, the Regulation Q exemption for foreign official deposits was extended for three additional years in 1965, through October 15, 1968 and later extended without limit. See p. 167, note 54.
9. *United States* v. *First National City Bank,* 321 F. 2d 14 (2d Cir. 1963), pp. 170-71.

during which the injunction remained intact,[10] the U.S. Supreme Court considered the "narrow issue" of "whether the creditor (the United States) may by injunction *pendente lite* protect whatever rights the debtor (Omar) may have against respondent", the latter being the U.S. bank.[11] Reversing the 1963 decision of the federal Court of Appeals, the U.S. Supreme Court concluded that the federal District Court injunction would lie. In so doing, it stated that:

> "If such relief were beyond the authority of the District Court, foreign taxpayers facing jeopardy assessments might either transfer assets abroad or dissipate those in foreign accounts under control of American institutions before personal service on the foreign taxpayer could be made."[12]

Two judges dissented from this decision on grounds that the Court had neither *in personam* jurisdiction over the allegedly deficient taxpayer, even under the so-called "long arm" statute of the State of New York,[13] nor *quasi in rem* jurisdiction by virtue of the funds on deposit in the foreign branch bank, because these were not payable in New York City unless the depositor's demand for payment at the branch bank had been wrongfully refused.[14]

It is clear from the language of the majority opinion quoted above that in rendering judgment the Court was of the opinion that U.S. head office banks maintained control over the operations of their branch banks abroad, and that this control was sufficient to permit funds deposited in these branch banks to be blocked by injunctions issued against the U.S. banks themselves.[15] This view was amplified by the Court's discussion *obiter dictum* of the status of a U.S. branch bank abroad. It stated:

> "Whether the Montevideo branch is a 'separate entity', as the Court of Appeals thought, is not germane to the present narrow issue. It is not a separate entity in the sense that it is insulated from respondent's managerial prerogatives. Respondent has actual, practical control over its branches; it is organized under a federal statute, 12 U.S.C. § 24, which authorizes it 'To sue and be sued, complain and defend, in any court of law and equity, as fully as natural persons'—as one entity, not branch by branch. The branch bank's affairs are, therefore,

---

10. 325 F. 2d 1020 (2d Cir. 1963).

11. 379 U.S. 378 (1964).

12. *Id.* at 385.

13. New York Civil Practice Law and Rules, § 302 (a).

14. *Cf. Sokoloff* v. *National City Bank,* 250 N.Y. 69, 164 N.E. 745 (1928).

15. Presumably the case would be different for funds deposited in a foreign banking subsidiary of a U.S. bank. There the deposits would be in a separate entity incorporated or chartered under foreign law, with a separate management albeit under control of the parent U.S. bank. A federal order transmitted to that foreign management via the U.S. bank itself could give rise to suits in the foreign host country preventing the subsidiary's management from acting upon the instructions. *Cf. Fruehauf,* p. 29, note 18.

as much within the reach of the *in personam* order entered by the District Court as are those of the home office...

That is not to say that a federal court in this country should treat all the affairs of a branch bank the same as it would those of the home office. For overseas transactions are often caught in a web of extraterritorial activities and foreign law beyond the ken of our federal courts or their competence. We have, however, no such involvement here, for there is no showing that the mere 'freezing' of the Montevideo accounts, pending service on Omar, would violate foreign law,...or place respondent under any risk of double liability... And if, as is argued in dissent, the litigation might in time be embarrassing to United States diplomacy, the District Court remains open to the Executive Branch, which, it must be remembered, is the moving party in the present proceeding."[16]

Although the Court limited itself to what it termed a "narrow issue", the *obiter dictum* hardly encourages individuals and firms with doubts as to their immunity from suit in the United States to place their funds on deposit in U.S. branch banks abroad. Particularly this is so in light of the Court's having embraced the notion that such funds can be blocked *pendente lite* even though a court may not have jurisdiction at the outset and may never acquire it. Thus, a non-resident non-citizen of the United States can be deprived of the use of funds on deposit in a U.S. branch bank abroad during the period in which it is being decided whether jurisdiction exists and, if so, whether the funds should be ordered paid over to a third party. The potential depositor would be exposed to this risk in suits brought by private as well as public claimants. Moreover, he would not necessarily be an active party to the action while the existence or absence of jurisdiction is determined. In this context it is noteworthy that the foreign depositor (Omar) was not served personally in the cited proceedings.

The *Omar* decision might not be an appreciable deterrent for depositors intending to place their funds in accounts for only very short periods. Longer-term depositors, however, cannot view it with equanimity; and it was precisely this group of depositors that was becoming increasingly important as the second Euro-dollar operating phase evolved. In fact, the potential risk to the depositor increases in direct proportion to the length of the maturity of the deposit, and thus operates as a serious hindrance to the U.S. branch banks' ability to compete with other institutions taking longer-term Euro-dollar deposits.

The conflicting aims underlying the U.S. federal revenue laws and the federal banking laws could not have been more apparent. In the *Omar* case, the Court resolved them not so much as to favor one over the other, but so that a presumably public interest in enforcing the revenue laws will prevail over an apparently private interest in maintaining a smoothly functioning multinational banking apparatus. It is suggested, however, that the issues were not as clear-cut as the majority opinion of the Court

16. *United States* v. *First National City Bank, supra,* at 384-85.

would imply, for there is also a public interest element in the maintenance of the multinational banking apparatus. U.S. banks have repeatedly stressed this in expanding their operations,[17] as have the legislators in widening the U.S. legal structure that has allowed these activities to take place.

b. *Tax Law*

During the second phase of the U.S. branch banks' Euro-dollar deposit-taking there was a modification in the U.S. federal tax treatment of non-resident aliens' and foreign corporations' bank account interest earned from deposits in banks in the United States and in U.S. branch banks abroad. In Chapter Four it was shown that non-resident aliens and foreign corporations engaged in business in the United States were taxed on the interest earned on funds deposited in banks in the United States and in U.S. branch banks abroad.[18]

Seeking "to place foreign branch banks of U.S. corporations in a

---

17. In its brief filed with the U.S. Supreme Court, the U.S. stakeholder bank urged the Court to affirm the decision of the U.S. Court of Appeals, stating *inter alia:* "The fact is that to indulge petitioner [the United States] in its demand for extra-territorial powers would cause irreparable damage to the national interest. The area of damage extends beyond the immediate interest of the banks. A declaration that United States courts will cause the 'freezing' of deposits in the foreign branches of American banks would unmistakably seriously impair, if not destroy, the ability of United States banks to compete abroad; to the extent the 'freezing' program was implemented, American banks would be subjected to loss consequent upon the breach of their contractual obligations in foreign countries; it would result in a withdrawal of foreign currency deposits which inescapably would cripple the ability of American banks to finance the foreign commerce of the United States; it would thus immediately and adversely affect the United States balance of payments; it would necessarily open the door to invasion of the sovereignty of the United States through the assertion of corresponding rights by foreign governments; and, perhaps worst of all, it would degrade the reputation of the United States as a nation operating under law rather than expediency." (pp. 31-32). The bank's arguments would equally apply to Euro-dollar deposits. Further along, the brief contained the statement that: "So long as the United States asserts the right to sequester property in the foreign branches of American banks whenever an official in Washington believes it is appropriate to do so, the competitive disadvantage to the American banks, the starvation of the financial arteries which nourish American foreign trade, and the pressures on the United States balance of payments will continue." (pp. 35-36). This brief is set forth in American Society of International Law, 3 *International Legal Materials* 1004-29 (1964). The opinion of the two dissenting Supreme Court Justices noted that "Citybank alleges that its foreign banking business will be hurt because foreign depositors will be discouraged from using United States banks for fear that their funds can be reached by United States courts. There is no sure way to gauge the seriousness of this possibility, but since Citybank is an innocent stakeholder here, doubt should be resolved in its favor", *United States* v. *First National City Bank, supra,* at 402.
18. See pp. 167-68.

competitive position with the other banks in the foreign countries where they are doing business",[19] the U.S. Congress included in the Foreign Investors Tax Act of 1966 amendments to the Internal Revenue Code of 1954 which provide *inter alia* that:

> § 861 *"Income from sources within the United States*
> (a) *Gross income from sources within the United States.*—The following items of gross income shall be treated as income from sources within the United States:
> (1) *Interest.*—Interest ... on ... interest bearing obligations of residents ... not including—
> ...
> (F) interest on deposits with a foreign branch of a domestic corporation or a domestic partnership, if such branch is engaged in the commercial banking business."[20]

By virtue of this amendment, non-resident aliens and foreign corporations are not obliged to pay U.S. federal income tax on interest earned from deposits in U.S. branch banks abroad regardless of whether they are engaged in business in the United States. A companion amendment to the estate tax portion of the U.S. Internal Revenue Code provides that such deposits will not be included in an individual non-resident alien's taxable estate.[21] No longer is it necessary for individuals or corporations to determine whether they are likely to be considered as engaged in business in the United States before deciding whether to deposit funds in a U.S. branch bank abroad.

An unquestionable burden was thus lifted from the U.S. branch banks in their quest for deposits abroad. For U.S. commercial banks generally the effect has been muted to some extent by the simultaneous amendment of another portion of the U.S. Internal Revenue Code. Theretofore "interest on deposits with persons carrying on the banking business" in the United States had not been considered U.S.-source income for purposes of taxing non-resident aliens and foreign corporations as long as they were not engaged in business there.[22]

Recognizing "that it is questionable whether interest income of this type which is so clearly derived from U.S. sources should be treated as though derived from sources without the United States and thereby escape U.S. taxation",[23] the Congress repealed the special privilege which

19. United States, Senate, Finance Committee, *Report* no. 1707, p. 168, note 56.

20. United States, Internal Revenue Code of 1954, chap. 736, 68 A Stat. 275, as amended by Pub. Law 89-809, Title I, § 102 (a) (2), 80 Stat. 1541; 26 U.S.C. § 861 (a) (1) (F).

21. Code, 68 A Stat. 397 as amended by Pub. Law 89-809, Title I, § 108 (d), 80 Stat. 1572; 26 U.S.C. § 2105 (b) (2).

22. See pp. 165-66 and 167-68.

23. United States, Senate, Finance Committee, *Report, supra,* p. 4456.

had been accorded to banks. The law as changed in 1966 now provides that interest received by a non-resident alien individual or foreign corporation from U.S. banks, savings institutions, and insurance companies will not be treated as U.S.-source income "if such interest is not effectively connected with the conduct of a trade or business within the United States".[24]

Oddly enough, the limitation placed on interest rates by Regulation Q plus the revised tax status of foreign branch bank account interest earnings has theoretically placed U.S. banks having no branch banks abroad at some competitive disadvantage with respect to those that have. This is because the interest earned on deposit in U.S. branch banks by non-resident alien individuals and foreign corporations need not be effectively disconnected with the conduct of a trade or business in the United States for the tax-exempt status.

2. Host Country Laws

a. France

Whereas during the first phase of the U.S. branch banks' Euro-dollar operations there had occurred no pertinent major modification in the French banking laws,[25] the second phase witnessed important changes which have affected the deposit-taking activity of all banks in France. These changes came about partly as a result of a Report made by a special Commission appointed by the Ministre des Finances to study certain aspects of the Fifth Plan.[26] The first modification took place with a law redefining *"banques de dépôts"*, which the *Loi* of December 2, 1945 had defined as those banks which took from the public sight deposits or time deposits with maturities not exceeding two years.[27]

In January 1966 the relevant section of the 1945 statute was altered to define *banques de dépôts* more broadly as those banks whose prin-

---

24. Internal Revenue Code of 1954, as amended; 12 U.S.C. § 861 (a) (1) (A). Compare 12 U.S.C. §§ 871 (a) (1) (A) and 881 (a) (1). See also 12 U.S.C. § 871 (a) (1) and 881 (a) (1) prior to the 1966 amendment.

25. The only change during the first phase was a *décret* modifying the banking law so that banks operating primarily in the money market could not take deposits from the public except in amounts fixed by the Conseil National de Crédit in relation with their capital. Ministère des Finances et des Affaires Economiques, *Décret* no. 60-139; *Journal officiel*, February 18, 1960, p. 1588.

26. France, Commissariat Général du Plan d'Equipement et de la Productivité, *Ve Plan, 1966-1970*, Rapport général de la Commission de l'économie générale et du financement, La Documentation française (M. 494), Paris, 1965.

27. *Loi* no. 45-015 of December 2, 1945, p. 50, note 95, art. 5, as amended by *Loi* no. 46-1071 of May 17, 1946, art. 2; *Journal officiel*, May 18, 1946, p. 4271.

cipal activity consists of credit operations and of taking sight and time deposits from the public.[28] The present law thus narrows greatly the distinction in France between *banques de dépôts* and *banques d'affaires* since both can now take longer-term deposits, an operation formerly restricted to the *banques d'affaires*.

This change might not appear at first glance to be important in a country where the possibility of currency devaluation has made depositors reluctant to deposit funds for any length of time. It has meant, however, that *banques de dépôts* and ipso facto the U.S. branch banks in France have gained greater maneuvering room in which to take longer-term deposits. It also has great potential significance for operations with full convertibility restored.

During the second Euro-dollar operating phase the French exchange control system also underwent major revision. It will be recalled that during the first phase there had been a gradual easing of the rules with regard to the utilization of funds on deposit in E.F.AC. accounts. In January 1966 the Ministère des Finances announced that the E.F.AC. system had become subject to so many exceptions that it no longer served any useful purpose and that accordingly it was to be terminated.[29]

A further revision in May 1966 gave authorized banks permission to open non-French franc accounts "for any person, irrespective of nationality and country of residence",[30] the procedures for handling the accounts depending upon the residence of the depositor and whether he was a French national. In November of the same year the compulsory

28. "Les banques de dépôt sont celles dont l'activité principale consiste à effectuer des opérations de crédit et à recevoir du public des dépôts de fonds à vue et à terme." Ministère de l'Economie et des Finances, *Décret* no. 66-81, Art. 6; *Journal officiel,* February 1, 1966, p. 913. The earlier law had provided that: "Les banques de dépôts sont celles qui reçoivent du public des dépôts à vue ou à terme qui ne peut être supérieur à deux ans." *Loi* no. 45-015 of December 2, 1945, *supra.*

29. "De nombreux assouplissements ont été apportés au cours de ces dernières années à la réglementation des changes et du commerce extérieur. Dans le domaine des paiements courants avec l'étranger, ces assouplissements sont si importants qu'ils enlèvent tout intérêt aux règles particulières prévues, pour le paiement des frais accessoires aux exportations de marchandises, par le régime des comptes 'Exportations-Frais accessoires' (comptes E.F.AC.). Par ailleurs, l'extension à trois mois du délai dans lequel doivent être apportées sur le marché des changes les devises étrangères soumises à l'obligation de cession,... permet aux exportateurs de conserver un fonds de roulement en monnaies étrangères susceptible d'être utilisé pour tous paiements à l'étranger autorisés à titre général ou particulier... Il a été décidé, dans ces conditions, de mettre fin au régime des comptes E.F.AC." Ministère des Finances et des Affaires Economiques, *Avis* no. 788, paragraph I; *Journal officiel,* January 8, 1966, p. 244.

30. See I.M.F., *(Eighteenth) Exchange Restrictions,* 1967, p. 227.

deposit of foreign currency and securities owned by residents and non-resident French nationals was terminated.[31]

By far the most far reaching exchange control revision occurred, however, when a law was passed in December 1966 which provided for the termination of all then-existing rules and regulations as of January 31, 1967 and established the framework for a new policy with regard to foreign financial transactions engaged in by French residents and nationals. The new policy, stated in the law, was that such transactions would thenceforth be free except as limited by certain provisions in the new law itself, taking into account international conventions to which France was a party.[32]

The first implementing *décret,* issued on January 27, 1967 in conjunction with the new law, raised no impediments for the placing of French and foreign currency accounts in France or abroad by residents or non-residents alike.[33] This meant that banks in France could continue to take dollar deposits from anyone, as they had been permitted to do since May of the previous year. Importantly, it meant further that all dollar accounts could be treated in the same fashion regardless of the depositors' nationality or residence.

The January 1967 *décret* also gave banks in France a privileged status with regard to borrowing abroad. The *décret* set forth the requirement that prior authorization be obtained from the Ministère for all funds borrowed abroad by residents except where the funds were linked with direct overseas investment as defined by the *décret* or with current foreign trade transactions, were for amounts not in excess of FF 2 million[34] (approx. $400,000), or where they were made by authorized banks.[35] This privilege allowed banks in France freely to take Euro-dollar de-

31. Ministère des Finances et des Affaires Economiques, *Avis* no. 794; *Journal officiel,* November 18, 1966, p. 10061.

32. "Les relations financières entre la France et l'étranger sont libres. Cette liberté s'exerce selon les modalités prévues par la présente loi, dans le respect des engagements internationaux souscrits par la France." *Loi* no. 66-1008 of December 28, 1966; *Journal officiel,* December 29, 1966, pp. 11621-22. This new policy of "free" transactions ironically allowed less liberty in lending operations. See pp. 243-44.

33. Ministère de l'Economie et des Finances, *Décret* no. 67-78 of January 27, 1967; *Journal officiel,* January 29, 1967, pp. 1073-74. This *Décret* was accompanied by an *Arrêté* of the same date, setting forth the manner in which the *Décret* would be put into effect. *Id.,* pp. 1074-75.

34. That is, the former limits of two years and 4% on the maturity and interest rate were dropped. See p. 186.

35. *Décret* no. 67-78, *supra,* Title III. Art. 6 (3). Elsewhere (Title II, Art. 2) the *Décret* ended the French franc zone, reserving nonetheless special treatment for countries whose banks of issue and currencies were related to the Banque de France and the French franc.

posits from banks in other countries and thus, to borrow in the international money market for the first time without obtaining permission.[36]

b. *Great Britain*

During the second Euro-dollar operating phase there occurred a modification of the British exchange control rules affecting the inflow to the pool of investment dollars. In April 1965 the Chancellor of the Exchequer announced that thenceforth the recipients of hard currency legacies would have to convert the entire amount of their newly acquired holdings into sterling at the official rate.[37] Prior to this, they had enjoyed access to the investment dollar pool, which usually had allowed the conversion of their holdings into sterling at attractive premiums.

The Chancellor also announced that whenever residents sold any securities denominated in these foreign currencies they had to surrender one-fourth of the sale proceeds for sterling at the official rate, being able to convert only the remaining three-fourths at the investment dollar rate.[38] A further change affected individual residents who were

36. This remained so until civil disorders in May 1968 led to the reintroduction of exchange control. As a result *Décret* no. 67-78 was largely suspended by Ministère de l'Economie et des Finances *Décret* no. 68-481 of May 29, 1968; *Journal officiel,* May 31, 1968, p. 5308 reinstating *inter alia* non-resident accounts and a surrender requirement for foreign currency. *Décret* no. 68-788 of September 4, 1968; *Journal officiel,* September 5, 1968, pp. 8513-14 canceled *Décret* no. 68-481 and its implementing regulations, thus abolishing the temporary return to exchange control. Later in 1968, however, exchange control again became necessary and resulted in *Décret* no. 68-1021 of November 24, 1968; *Journal officiel,* November 25, 1968, pp. 11081-82. A companion decree specifically brought under control all claims and liabilities (both in French francs and in foreign currencies) that banks in France maintained with regard to non-residents. *Décret* no. 68-1022 of November 24, 1968; *Id.* p. 11082. *Décret* no. 67-78 was again modified by *Décret* no. 69-264 of March 21, 1969; *Journal officiel,* March 27, 1969, pp. 3066-67. A circular bearing the same date provided an exemption for authorized banks' borrowing from non-residents. See *Id.,* pp. 3068-70 and I.M.F., *(Twentieth) Exchange Restrictions,* 1970, p. 177. On August 10, 1969 the French franc was devalued from FF 4.94 = $1. to FF 5.55 = $1. In May 1971 a new (to postwar France) type of control was introduced to prevent an overabundance of hot money from flowing into the country. The reserve requirement on foreign-owned French franc deposits was raised to 100% and a limitation was placed on the interest paid on them. Later, a two-tier exchange rate was inaugurated after the August 15, 1971 change in the U.S. policy on the convertibility of the dollar into gold.

37. Bank of England, 6 *Quarterly Bulletin* 14 (1966), and 7 *Id.* 258 (1967).

38. Under the new regulations, from April 1965 onwards "even a switch from one dollar security to another involves the surrender of 25% of the sale proceeds through the official exchange market—and therefore requires the purchase of further investment dollars if the level of investment is to be maintained". 6 *Id.* 15 (1966). In December 1970 the Bank of England changed the rules covering the purchase

not nationals of sterling area countries. Whereas they had theretofore been able to convert dollars or other hard currency advantageously into pounds via the investment dollar pool, these individuals could now continue that practice only if they agreed to receive their salaries in sterling at the official rate.[39]

These measures, which pinched off a part of the flow of dollars into the investment dollar pool, have been of twofold importance to the U.S. branch banks in London. First, they have further reduced the amount of privately held resident dollars that might find their way into deposits, meaning that the U.S. branch banks and the other institutions seeking dollar deposits have continued to rely most heavily on dollars from non-resident sources, a sector that has remained untouched by regulation.

Second, the new measures have put pressures on the investment dollar premium (which at the time were already building up for other reasons, notably fears of sterling devaluation).[40] The premium, which represents the amount over the official exchange rate that a sterling area resident must pay in pounds in order to obtain dollars eligible for investment in hard currency securities, reached new heights in October 1967 when it stood at $33^1/_8\%$.[41] This movement has paralleled that of increasingly higher interest rates prevailing in the international money market for Euro-dollars, reinforcing the tightness of margins within which operations have had to be conducted.[42]

---

of foreign securities with borrowed investment currency to allow greater freedom for professional portfolio managers, who can borrow for indefinite periods and can sell customers' securities without paying the 25% penalty unless the proceeds are converted into sterling. This means that amounts realized on the sale of dollar securities can be held in dollar accounts as working reserves. See *Financial Times*, December 24, 1970, p. 1, col. 7.

39. See N.Y. Times, April 9, 1965, p. 41, col. 2 (late city edition).

40. On November 18, 1967 the pound was devalued from £ 1 = $2.80 to £ 1 = $2.40.

41. Bank of England, 7 *Quarterly Bulletin* 340 (1967). By mid-April 1968 the premium rose to $49^1/_2\%$, when it was reported that the pool had become so small that $50,000 was the largest transaction that could be made. 227 (6504) *The Economist* 72 (April 20, 1968). In 1969 and 1970 the investment dollar premium was even higher—reaching 56%—but was reduced when the market for property currency (i.e., for the purchase of foreign real estate) was merged into the investment currency market. See 236 *Id.* 70 (August 22, 1970).

42. As of August 31, 1971 the Bank of England acted to curb the amounts of foreign-owned sterling that banks could take on deposit, and limited the interest that could be paid. As in France, this resulted in the paradox of restrictions on exchange flows in both directions.

c. *Switzerland*

When introducing the French and British laws and practices affecting the taking of dollars on deposit it was necessary in Chapter Four to retrace briefly the exchange control laws and regulations leading up to the period in question. In the case of Switzerland, an entirely different analytical approach must be employed.

It is sometimes stated that Switzerland has been free of postwar exchange controls. This is incorrect, although as pointed out by the Bank for International Settlements, "Switzerland has never had to introduce foreign exchange restrictions because of inadequate monetary reserves".[43] The Swiss authorities have in fact resorted to two types of control, direct and indirect, affecting foreign exchange operations.

The direct controls have taken the form of bilateral clearing agreements or unilateral regulations governing payments with certain countries whose exchange restrictions threatened the Swiss currency. At the end of 1952, for instance, twenty-two such agreements were in force, covering a sector of controlled payments which included the French monetary area and the sterling area.[44] Payments to residents of the controlled sector had to be made through the Swiss Clearing Office; and of direct relevance to the present study, there were controls on Swiss bank accounts of residents of the controlled sector. By the end of 1956 funds in such accounts could be transferred freely to accounts of other residents of the controlled sector.[45] On December 30, 1958 the Swiss regulations were modified to remove from the sector those countries or monetary areas which had agreed to restore external convertibility. Thereafter no direct exchange controls applied to Swiss bank deposits made by residents of these countries.

Unlike the direct controls, the indirect controls have not been designed as a defense against other countries' measures but rather to stanch the inward flow of foreign depositors' funds, including hot money, from all sources. At some times these indirect controls have taken the form of agreements between the banks and the central bank. For instance, on August 18, 1960 a gentlemen's agreement made Swiss francs deposited by non-residents since July 1st of that year subject to three months' notice for withdrawals, provided that no interest could be paid on them,

---

43. Bank for International Settlements, *Eight European Central Banks*, p. 61, note 139 at p. 286.

44. I.M.F., *(Fourth) Exchange Restrictions*, 1953, p. 340.

45. As of January 1, 1957 the Federal Decree of September 28, 1956 on measures of economic defense in relation to other countries, and the Federal Council Decree of December 17, 1956 on controlled payments with other countries, came into effect. These revised and recodified theretofore existing rules. See I.M.F., *(Ninth) Exchange Restrictions*, 1958, p. 385.

and even extracted a negative deposit interest in the form of a penalty commission of 1% p.a. to be paid by the non-resident depositor on amounts left on deposit for less than six months.[46] Exceptions were made for accounts of less than SF 50,000 (approx. $11,650) and for correspondent banks' normal working balances.[47] These restrictions were considered necessary to keep non-residents' funds from adding to inflationary pressures already being felt in the economy of the small country.[48] Moreover, the absence of a formal money market structure made it particularly difficult for the Swiss monetary system to cope with any large or sudden influxes of funds.

The August 1960 gentlemen's agreement was renewed periodically,[49] the last extension being projected to carry it through August 17, 1964. Before that date had been reached, however, the agreement was terminated (on March 31, 1964) and replaced by a new convention which forbade the payment of interest on non-residents' Swiss franc accounts on deposit from January 1st of that year, and removed the three months' withdrawal notice requirement. Savings accounts of SF 20,000 (approx. $4,650) or less, central banks' balances, and "unused portions of proceeds of issues of securities in Switzerland, and of credits obtained from Swiss banks" were exempted.[50]

Running parallel with this new agreement was the formulation (on March 16, 1964) of direct anti-inflationary measures calling for the Federal Council to prohibit banks in Switzerland from paying interest on non-residents' deposits received after January 1st, 1964, directing them to give non-resident depositors of such funds notice of cancellation, and directing them to deposit the Swiss franc equivalent of all non-residents' deposits in a special account of the Swiss National Bank to the extent that these funds were not re-invested abroad in foreign currency. The prohibition on non-residents' purchase of Swiss real estate and securities out of such deposits was also included. On April 24, 1964 the above arrangement was given the effect of law, which ended

46. Bank for International Settlements, *supra,* p. 299. A somewhat similar agreement had been in effect from 1955 to early 1958. *Ibid.* The banks were also obliged to prevent non-residents from purchasing Swiss real estate or securities with funds deposited or borrowed in Switzerland.

47. This particular gentlemen's agreement was said to have been at least partially necessitated by events in the Congo which caused a sudden inward flow of Belgian-owned funds. *Cf.* 110 *The Banker* 626 (1960).

48. See Hans J. Mast, "International Issues in Europe", *Opera Mundi EUROPE* nos. 368 and 369 (August 4 and 11, 1966).

49. On August 14, 1963 the 1% p.a. penalty charge on non-residents' funds on deposit for less than six months was abandoned. I.M.F., *(Fifteenth) Exchange Restrictions,* 1964, p. 441.

50. I.M.F., *(Sixteenth) Exchange Restrictions,* 1965, p. 490.

the need for the gentlemen's agreement between the banks and the central bank.[51] The purpose of these measures was to isolate as completely as possible the internal Swiss economy from the inflationary effects of inward flows of non-resident funds.[52] They were terminated on March 17, 1967.[53]

At this stage in our examination the important point to note is that although a distinction has been made between residents' and non-residents' funds none has been drawn between fully convertible and externally convertible currencies. As far as Swiss law is concerned residents of Switzerland could (and can) possess dollars or any other currency. Only the deposit or use of non-residents' funds has been covered by the measures outlined above.

Since the Swiss franc has been fully convertible, it has made no intrinsic difference whether a non-resident has sought to shelter host currency or dollars (or any other fully or externally convertible currency) in Switzerland, except insofar as the depositor has wished to stay in one currency or another so as to hedge against unfavorable (to him) changes in parity between currencies. Indeed, whereas until mid-1971 the dollar was consistently more attractive in this respect than either the French franc or the pound sterling, the Swiss host currency has been at least as attractive as—and sometimes moreso than—the dollar, except for those depositors who have contemplated spending their dollars within a reasonably short period after placing the deposit.

There is and has been, however, a sharp difference in the yield available on dollar and Swiss franc deposits. Compared with the rates on dollar deposits in London or in the United States, for example, the non-resident placing Swiss francs on deposit in Switzerland has received a lower yield on his placement, and at times has even paid a penalty for the privilege, as seen above. The lower yield aspect has also applied, of course, to residents of Switzerland who, in the late 1960's for instance, could choose between depositing Swiss francs in Switzerland at,

51. Switzerland, Federal Council, Order of April 24, 1964, *Recueil officiel suisse* 1964, p. 413. See *Id.* pp. 414-21.

52. I.M.F. *(Nineteenth) Exchange Restrictions,* 1968, p. 398.

53. For a perceptive appraisal of these Swiss measures see Tschopp, p. 80, note 217 at pp. 186-191. In order to prevent the internal economy from being swamped by large amounts of foreign-held funds that were flowing into Switzerland in the summer of 1971, the Swiss National Bank imposed a 100% reserve requirement on additions to foreign-owned deposits after July 31, 1971 unless the counterpart was invested outside Switzerland by the bank in question. From August 16, 1971 interest was no longer paid on foreign-owned Swiss franc deposits held for less than six months. See I.M.F., 23 *International Financial News Survey* 265 (August 25, 1971). The six month criterion then was dropped, so that no interest was paid regardless of the deposit term.

say 3¹/₄% or switching or swapping into dollars for deposit in London at, say 8½%.[54]

The accumulation of non-resident deposits in Switzerland generally has been discouraged by a further factor, namely the federal withholding tax levied on interest paid on bank deposits. This has resulted from a 1943 law imposing a 27% tax at the source on dividends paid by Swiss companies as well as on interest from bonds, from loans in excess of SF 30,000 (approx. $7,500) extending for more than two years, and from bank deposits.[55] Swiss residents paying local income taxes can obtain a tax credit for the amount withheld when filing their returns, or a refund to the extent that the amount withheld exceeds the tax due. Non-residents, however, cannot offset or recover the withheld tax except under tax treaty arrangements.[56] On October 13, 1965 the withholding tax provision was modified so as to set the rate at 30% from January 1, 1967.[57] The 3% coupon tax was terminated when the new withholding tax rate went into effect.[58] For non-residents the rate increase from 27% to 30% further reduced the net yield on Swiss bank deposits unless assisted by a tax treaty.[59]

With no yield advantage for residents or non-residents maintaining dollars on deposit in banks in Switzerland, the question arises whether there have been such deposits. There have. In fact, Swiss banks have for

54. $25,000 has been the minimum amount for such Euro-dollar deposits in London. Swiss residents not possessing the required minimum amount have still been able to take advantage of the higher interest rates in London for dollar deposits by pooling their holdings with those of other potential depositors. (See note 61, *infra*.) Another alternative for the Swiss resident not possessing the required minimum for depositing dollars in London has been the alternative of placing them on deposit in savings banks or in savings and loan associations in the United States. In both cases this is largely theoretical in that the vast majority of Swiss residents either have not been aware of these other alternatives or have not considered the marginal benefits worthwhile, tending to trust local currency and institutions in any event. The nationality of the resident (14.2% of the local population was non-Swiss as of the 1960 census according to the Federal Statistical Bureau) would make little difference in most cases. Of course there have been some better informed or more sophisticated residents of Switzerland who have taken advantage of the higher yields. As for borrowing locally at the lower Swiss rate for placement abroad at the higher rate, see page 250.

55. Switzerland, Federal Council, Federal Anticipatory Tax Order of September 1, 1943, Art. 4, *Recueil officiel suisse* 1943, pp. 709-18.

56. See Federation of British Industries, *Taxation in Western Europe, 1963,* (5th revised edition), London, 1963, p. 253. The tax does not apply to accounts maintained by other banks.

57. I.M.F., *(Eighteenth) Exchange Restrictions,* 1967, p. 576.

58. I.M.F., *(Nineteenth) Exchange Restrictions,* 1968, p. 397.

59. *Cf.* "Changes in the Anticipatory Tax and Abolition of the Coupon Tax", International Bureau of Fiscal Documentation, 6 (2) *European Taxation* 34-38 (February 1966).

many years provided current account facilities in dollars for those Swiss residents, particularly firms, desiring working balances in this currency to settle current payments denominated in dollars.[60] Another group of dollar account holders is comprised of the banks themselves, which have maintained dollar balances with one another in Switzerland and by book entries clear all but the very largest dollar transactions without recourse to correspondent banks in the United States. The total amount on deposit in these working balances has not been large, however, when compared with Swiss franc deposits or with the dollars on deposit in London. With regard to the latter, moreover, it is necessary to examine a special phenomenon which has indirectly linked some banks, including U.S. branch banks, in Switzerland with the London market for Euro-dollar deposits.

This indirect linkage has been provided through so-called "fiduciary placement accounts" for customers seeking a dollar-denominated account with a Swiss bank but yielding more than the local Swiss deposit rates. The customer can confide dollars to the bank in Switzerland, which in turn places the funds in a Euro-dollar time deposit account, in the bank's name but at the customer's risk, in a bank in London or in a London branch of the same bank. The bank in Switzerland is not the taker of the deposited funds, but is merely a "fiduciary" which acts on the customer's behalf and collects a minimal commission for its services. For the customer, this means that the funds yield the seven-day Euro-dollar rate in London less the commission. For the bank in Switzerland it means that dollars can be marshalled for use in London.[61]

The interest generated by the deposit in London is paid over to the customer in Switzerland, but is not subject to the formerly 27%, now 30% withholding tax.

The cumbersome nature of this procedure has not lent itself to depositors seeking quick entry or exit from the Euro-dollar market. Banks in Switzerland have many customers, however, for whom rapid turnover is neither necessary nor desirable. By means of these "fiduciary" ac-

60. See Hans J. Bär, *The Banking System of Switzerland*, 2d. revised edition, Zurich, 1957, p. 77.
61. The minimum amount for such fiduciary placement accounts has been set at $25,000. So-called "special" fiduciary placement accounts are available for amounts of $5,000 or more in round $1,000 lots, with an additional service charge and a requirement that withdrawal notice be given several days prior to the next regular seven-day call for the Euro-Dollar trading date. This has amounted to a pooling of smaller depositors' funds by the bank in Switzerland, which has then made a deposit in the regular $25,000 round lot in London. Even with the additional service charge and the more awkward notice requirement these special accounts have been competitive with other dollar placement possibilities such as commercial paper, acceptances, U.S. bank c.d.'s and U.S. Treasury Bills.

counts banks in Switzerland can place a portion of their customers' funds on deposit on a large scale and earn a 1% margin on a no-risk basis. As the Euro-dollar market took on substantial proportions banks in Switzerland have controlled a sizeable share of the funds on deposit in London, either deposited for their own account or for their customers.[62]

In conclusion it must be stressed that the laws and gentlemen's agreements have tended to isolate the internal Swiss market for dollar deposits. Only the sophisticated resident has placed his funds abroad,[63] and then only when meeting the minimum amount requirements. These legal and quasi-legal measures have helped maintain a markedly lower interest rate in Switzerland,[64] a question to which we shall return. They also reflect the Swiss authorities' desire to prevent the Swiss franc from becoming a *de facto* reserve currency for certain types of transactions.[65]

B. *Techniques for Acquiring Longer-Term Euro-dollar Deposits*

1. *Quoting Competitive Rates*

Essentially any method for attracting longer-term Euro-dollar deposits has involved providing facilities for customers who have desired, or could be encouraged, to place their holdings beyond the periods which earlier represented the usual deposit lengths.

This has involved being able to quote competitive longer-term rates to potential non-bank depositors as well as to bid against other takers in the inter-bank market. In this respect, the U.S. branch banks have had two important advantages. First, a branch bank can deal with some leeway since, at least in theory, its existence depends more upon contributing to the head office bank's overall operations than on individual performance alone. A branch bank can shave its profit margin to an extremely thin return, or even to a temporary loss, and still survive.

62. "... Swiss banks control an estimated 20 to 25 percent of the deposits in the Eurodollar market..." Union Bank of Switzerland, 'The Importance of the Swiss Banks' Foreign Business", Address by A. Schaefer, President of the Union Bank of Switzerland, March 10, 1967, Zurich, 1967, p. 4.

63. In evaluating this phenomenon one must take account of the opportunity of placing funds in the Euro-Swiss franc market. Some banks in Switzerland handle such transactions (in a manner similar to that in the case of the special placement accounts in Euro-dollars) in minimum round lots of SF 250,000 (approx. $58,000).

64. In the late 1960's this situation began to change when some banks in Switzerland started to abandon their cautious approach toward the Euro-dollar market and placed some of their funds there instead of lending them locally. This drain on the supply of money for advances was reflected in a narrowing of the spread between the Swiss and Euro-dollar market rates.

65. For example, diplomatic action was taken to prevent the issuance outside Switzerland of bonds denominated in Swiss francs.

Second, a U.S. branch bank has little reason for apprehension in taking in more longer-term Euro-dollar deposits than might immediately appear relendable. This is due to the existence of the head office bank in the United States as a borrower of last resort which can presumably employ any excess deposits held by its branch bank or banks abroad. As we shall see later in this Chapter the U.S. head office bank eventually became a constant taker; but even during the period before interest rates temporarily peaked out, the head office was always dealing in U.S. dollars with the bulk of its domestic customers in the United States and could thus fit additional funds into its operations without taking foreign exchange rates, including forward coverage, into consideration.

2. Taking Deposits with Alternative Maturities

In a period of rising interest rates, one of the obstacles to be overcome in attracting longer-term Euro-dollar deposits is the potential depositor's reluctance to tie up funds for a period longer than the immediately foreseeable future. This reluctance is due to the desire to have funds readily available so as to obviate more costly borrowing from other sources in the event of an unexpected need, or in the alternative, to be able to place the funds more advantageously elsewhere if rates continue to rise.

A successful method for coping with this problem has been to offer deposits with alternative maturities at the depositor's option. For example, under an alternative maturity deposit arrangement a depositor can expect to receive an agreed-upon rate of interest, say 6% p.a., on funds left on deposit for six months. If needed before that period has expired, all or part of the funds can be withdrawn; but the interest rate is lowered by a penalty rate, frequently 1/4 of one percent. Some of the U.S. branch banks have provided more elaborate arrangements with progressively changing rates stipulated at the time of the deposit. For example, if the funds are withdrawn in 5 months, only 5½% p.a. will be paid, 5% p.a. if they are left for four months, and so on with the rate diminishing progressively to a level at or near that prevailing for short-term deposits.

U.S.-trained bankers are familiar with alternative maturity deposits, which are used in the United States with domestic corporate depositors. On several occasions the Federal Reserve has been called upon to decide upon questions involving the use of this technique in the United States.[66] The U.S. branch banks have been able to fit it into their Euro-

66. See, for example, 12 C.F.R. § 217. 107, 18 Fed. Reg., 6206, September 29, 1953; 12 C.F.R. § 217.112, 21 Fed. Reg. 6269, August 21, 1956; 12 C.F.R. § 217.136,

dollar operations without difficulty. Moreover, treasurers of U.S. corporate subsidiaries abroad have found in this method a device which not only suits their own operations but which also has the advantage of being readily acceptable to their parent corporations, which are likely to consider temporarily excess dollars held by foreign subsidiaries as available for use elsewhere if needed. The U.S. branch banks have had greater success in attracting U.S. corporate subsidiaries to alternative maturity dollar time deposit accounts than to corresponding host currency accounts.

3. *London Dollar Negotiable Certificates of Deposit*

a. *Use of Negotiable Certificates of Deposit in the United States*
Until the latter part of the 1950's the major commercial banks in the United States held sizeable interest-free balances in the current accounts of large commercial depositors. Partly these reflected compensating balances, but mainly they were normal working balances employed by the depositing corporations to meet payroll and other current expenses. Short-term interest rates were such that there was no real incentive for corporations to draw down part of these balances for placement in interest bearing investments.

In the early 1960's, however, higher interest rates began to attract some funds away from these demand deposits, particularly into U.S. Treasury Bills and commercial paper of other corporations. It was becoming apparent that the major U.S. commercial banks, which were accustomed to operating with these "sluggish" corporate funds on which they paid no interest, would have to develop a method to check the outward flow. The large denomination negotiable certificate of deposit, or "c.d." as it is called, has been the most successful of the techniques then adopted.

The first of these negotiable c.d.'s was issued in 1961,[67] at which time U.S. commercial banks' time deposits totaled approximately $80 billion.[68] By the end of 1965 it was reported that member banks had issued nearly $16 billion in negotiable c.d.'s, the bulk of which "by large money market banks to national corporations and other large investors in marketable denominations (generally $100,000 and over)".[69]

---

29 Fed. Reg. 8003, June 24, 1964; and 12 C.F.R. § 217.141, 31 Fed. Reg. 10315, July 30, 1966.

67. 49 *Federal Reserve Bulletin* 458 (1963).

68. 49 *Id.*, 346 (1963). This was exclusive of inter-bank deposits.

69. 52 *Id.*, 468 (1966). This amounted to about 15% of the total time and savings deposits held by individuals, partnerships, and corporations in member banks. *Id.* 467.

b. *Introduction of the London Dollar Negotiable Certificates of Deposit*

The problem which faced the banks and branch banks as interest rates rose in the Euro-dollar market was not the drawing down of corporations' demand deposits but rather that deposits would not be forthcoming as needed. Nevertheless, at the core of both phenomena lay the necessity for obtaining a larger, less volatile deposit base by attracting temporarily unneeded funds.

In late May 1966 one of the U.S. branch banks in London started offering to non-residents of the United States negotiable certificates representing deposits of U.S. dollars placed at that branch. The certificates were issued either as bearer or order instruments[70] in round $1,000 denominations with a minimum face amount of $25,000, maturities being set at 30, 60, 90, 120, 150 and 180 days to coincide with standard Euro-dollar market maturities.[71] Simultaneously it was announced that a U.S. securities firm would maintain a secondary market in these "London dollar negotiable c.d.'s", as they came to be called.

The negotiability of the new instrument has meant that depositors can convert it into cash at market value if needed prior to maturity. The existence of a secondary market permits such conversion to be accomplished rapidly. It was also contemplated from the outset that London dollar negotiable c.d.'s for longer terms and with other than standard maturities could be accommodated by such a secondary market. Moreover, market quotations are immediately available for the purposes of evaluating portfolios and for following the trends in the Euro-dollar market as a whole.

Although the cartel on uniform deposit rates prevented the British clearing banks from immediately using the new instrument to their advantage, within six weeks after the first of these instruments had appeared eight other U.S. branch banks[72] in London and one indigenous non-clearer[73] were also offering London dollar negotiable c.d.'s. The instrument was usually issued to pay $1/8\%$ under the prevailing rate on standard Euro-dol-

---

70. Predominantly as bearer instruments, which has facilitated transfers in the secondary market. For the same reason, purchasers of the certificates have been encouraged to leave them in the custody of nominee banks in London, for which there is no charge.

71. See Einzig, p. 161, note 23 at p. 173 and Appendix I (pp. 169-84) generally.

72. Joining First National City Bank, which had issued the first London dollar negotiable c.d.'s, were Bankers Trust Company, Chemical Bank New York Trust Company, Continental Illinois National Bank and Trust Company of Chicago, The First National Bank of Boston, The First National Bank of Chicago, Irving Trust Company, Manufacturers Hanover Trust Company, and Morgan Guaranty Trust Company of New York. Of the U.S. branch banks then in London only Bank of America, N.T. & S.A. did not promptly enter the field.

73. Bank of London and South America.

lar deposits, some at par and some on a discount basis, with interest calculated on the actual number of days on a 360 day annual basis.

c. *Evolution of the New Instrument*

By November 1966 the market in the new instrument had been in existence long enough to take on a definite structure. Although rising interest rates were a negative force for the expansion of such a market,[74] the issuing banks had been joined by additional newcomers, both indigenous and foreign in origin, including a newly-formed bank jointly owned by a clearing bank and a merchant bank,[75] the European affiliate[76] of another clearing bank, and—ironically—the London branch of the Soviet state-owned Moscow Narodny Bank.[77]

The secondary market, too, was broadening. By mid-summer 1966 an additional U.S. securities firm and a Canadian firm had joined the field,[78] and by autumn several indigenous bill brokers or discount houses were also present, directly or indirectly. In the former case, Bank of England permission to borrow foreign exchange was obtained, authority which had not theretofore been accorded to a discount house.[79] In the latter case, indirect participation in the secondary c.d. market was possible by partial or entire acquisition of London foreign exchange brokers.[80]

In addition to the structural evolution in the market the London dollar negotiable c.d. itself underwent a gradual change in nature. It soon became apparent that the new instrument had an attraction not only for corporate holders of U.S. dollars but also for banks on the Continent, for their own accounts as well as for their customers. As the interest rate on the c.d.'s stayed above that of U.S. Treasury bills, the new instrument offered an alternative to short-term placement in U.S. Treasury obligations.

In an effort to broaden the appeal of the c.d.'s the issuing banks were willing to issue them for amounts as low as $25,000. For the U.S. branch banks, which had come to the host countries' wholesale rather than retail banking markets, this represented a movement away from the trend which had been manifest theretofore. It demonstrated, in any event, their realiza-

---

74. Depositors faced the risk of having to negotiate their certificates at sizeable discounts if interest rates rose markedly.

75. National Provincial and Rothschild (London).

76. Midland International.

77. This may seem paradoxical. Nevertheless, it is worth recalling that Eastern European official dollar-holders were among the first Euro-dollar depositors.

78. Along with White, Weld and Company, who had initiated the secondary market in the c.d.'s, there now were The First Boston Corporation and Nesbitt, Thomson and Company, Limited.

79. The discount house in question was Allen, Harvey & Ross, Limited.

80. Gerrard and Reid, Limited acquired a minority holding in Long, Till & Colvin. Cater, Ryder & Company Limited took over M. W. Marshall.

tion that deposits in the wholesale sector were not the only ones that could be tapped with the new instrument.

As the denomination of the c.d.'s underwent modifications, so did the terms for which they were issued. In July 1967 the U.S. branch bank which had issued the first London dollar negotiable c.d.'s began offering them with maturities up to three years. Theretofore the maximum maturity had been one year, although there had been evidence of attempts to issue them for longer periods.[81] In November 1967 c.d.'s with a maturity of four years were in existence.[82] By this time, too, the British banks were seriously considering the issuance of sterling c.d.'s, although the idea had been contemplated for several years.[83]

d. *Nature of the New Instrument*

Although the London dollar negotiable certificates of deposit do not bear the engraved portraits of famous Americans, in many respects the bearer c.d.'s resemble very large denomination U.S. banknotes.[84] Except for the 2 d British stamp tax levied on the issuance of a certificate, regardless of its face amount, no British taxes have been levied on transfers in the secondary market or elsewhere, or on the presentation of matured c.d.'s for redemption. They pass from bearer to bearer without apparent restriction, their value fluctuating with the quotations in the secondary market if they pass through that medium, or with private bidders' appraisals of the discounted future values of c.d.'s with particular maturities.[85]

Thus, the London dollar negotiable c.d.'s do not circulate at par, and in this respect are not unlike currencies circulating in a foreign exchange market. Moreover, the fact that the new instruments represent private

81. The London branch of the Moscow Narodny Bank, when announcing its entry into the c.d. field in November 1966 had stated its intention to issue certificates with maturities of up to three years beginning in January 1967.

82. For example, in November 1967 it was announced that $15 million in c.d.'s of The First National Bank of Boston were placed through White, Weld & Co., to mature in four years.

83. The difficulty in launching sterling instruments of this kind lay in the possibilities which bearer certificates provide for evading exchange control regulations. Nevertheless on October 1, 1969 permission was given to authorized banks to issue and deal in short-term sterling c.d.'s. The market for them began operations later that month, I.M.F., *(Twentieth) Exchange Restrictions*, 1969, pp. 493-94; and by mid-1970 there were nearly £ 800 million of these outstanding. See *Financial Times*, July 24, 1970, p. 20, col. 6.

84. The introduction of the London dollar negotiable c.d.'s gave rise to the comment that "these look uncommonly like a new, internationally acceptable bank note that could create fresh privately usable international money...", 219 (6405) *The Economist*, May 28, 1966, p. 1000.

85. These appraisals and the values in the secondary market have reflected the assumption that the issuing branch banks would make every effort to keep these instruments from falling too far below par.

rather than public promises to pay does not gainsay their currency-like nature. In many countries, including the three host countries as well as the United States, privately owned banks or companies have in the past been authorized to issue banknotes.[86] Indeed, both the British and French colonial systems placed banknote issuance monopolies with privately owned institutions.[87]

Perhaps the principal difference between the London dollar negotiable certificate of deposit and a banknote is that the c.d. is not payable by the issuer prior to a fixed maturity date,[88] whereas a banknote is normally redeemable at any time after issuance. This line of reasoning does not, however, eliminate entirely the banknote-like quality of the London dollar negotiable c.d. Although privately, and for that matter publicly, issued banknotes can theoretically be presented at any time for redemption by the issuing institution, they normally continue to circulate and are presented only when physically worn, when the bearer deposits them at the issuing bank in the normal course of his affairs, or when he fears that there will be insufficient assets to cover the notes in circulation and presents his notes in an effort to be repaid while assets remain. The redeemable-on-presentation characteristic of the banknote does not ipso facto cause it to be put out of circulation.

Indeed, although c.d.'s are normally presented for redemption promptly upon maturity to avoid loss of interest, there are doubtless occasions where it is not feasible for a certificate to be presented to the issuing bank and where it is negotiated after maturity to a subsequent bearer. Theoretically a c.d., particularly one with a low face value, can remain outstanding and serve as a medium of payment between any two parties who can arrive at a mutually acceptable value. Like travelers cheques issued by privately owned banks or companies, some of which actually remain in circulation for considerable periods after their issuance,[89] the London dollar negotiable c.d.'s are free to circulate as a form of privately issued currency among holders willing to accept them, the values fluctuating in ac-

86. The Bank of Scotland still maintains its own note issue privilege.

87. As noted in Chapter 2 the Banque de l'Indochine was the bank of issue in the former French colony of French Indo-China, and the Hongkong and Shanghai Banking Corporation continues as the issuing institution in the British Crown Colony of Hong Kong.

88. Although the issuing institutions might be willing to honor them at a discount prior to maturity.

89. In some countries with local currency of fluctuating value in terms of more stable foreign moneys, it is not unusual to see sterling and especially U.S. dollar travelers cheques passing from hand to hand in local commercial transactions, these cheques having been endorsed in blank by the original purchaser. Frequently the local currency equivalent is marked on the face of the instrument by hand, in pencilled characters when exchange rates are moving sharply.

cordance with factors like those which influence banknotes not legally tied to a par value.

Ironically the U.S. monetary authorities exercise no direct control over an instrument which most nearly resembles the currency for which they have primary responsibility. Banks and branch banks issuing negotiable certificates representing U.S. dollars placed on deposit in London do so without seeking or obtaining permission from either the U.S. Federal Reserve System or the U.S. Treasury Department. Any direct control that may be applied would be exercised by an alien government.

III. LENDING IN THE EURO-DOLLAR MARKET—SECOND PHASE (MID-1963 THROUGH 1967)

Having determined the legal authority under which the U.S. branch banks took Euro-dollar deposits in the second phase of their operations in this field, and the techniques used for acquiring longer-term deposits, we now turn to the lending side of their operations during this period.

A. *Legal Authority to Lend in the Euro-dollar Market*

1. *U.S. Law*

a. *Banking Law*

During the second phase of their Euro-dollar operations the U.S. branch banks benefitted from a 1966 amendment to the Federal Reserve Act of 1913. This amendment resulted from an Act designed "to eliminate two major open-end exemptions" from the Bank Holding Company Act of 1956[90] and to "bring up to date the regulatory and administrative provisions" of that and related statues.[91] Section 12 (b) of the 1966 Act added a new paragraph to Section 25 of the Federal Reserve Act of 1913, which authorizes national banks with capital and surplus of at least $ 1 million to apply to the Board of Governors of the Federal Reserve System for permission:

> "To acquire and hold, directly or indirectly, stock or other evidences of ownership in one or more banks organized under the law of a foreign country or a dependency or insular possession of the United States and not engaged, directly or indirectly, in any activity in the United States except as, in the judg-

---

90. United States, Bank Holding Company Act of May 9, 1956, chap. 240, 70 Stat. 133-38; 12 U.S.C. §§ 1841-49.

91. United States, Congress, Senate, Banking and Currency Committee, *Report* no. 1179, 89th Cong., 2d Sess., May 19, 1966, on H.R. 7371 (Pub. Law 89-485). *U.S. Code Cong. Adm. News,* 1966, vol. 2, pp. 2385-97.

ment of the Board of Governors of the Federal Reserve System, shall be incidental to the international or foreign business of such foreign bank; and, notwithstanding the provisions of section 23A of this Act, to make loans or extensions of credit to or for the account of such bank in the manner and within the limits prescribed by the Board by general or specific regulation or ruling."[92]

This authority resulted in a new provision in (Federal Reserve) Regulation M the following year, as follows:

§ 213.5 "Loans or extensions of credit to foreign banks
. . . .
A national bank which holds directly or indirectly* stock or other evidences of ownership in a foreign bank may make loans or extensions of credit to or for the account of such foreign bank without regard to the provisions of section 23A of the [Federal Reserve] Act (12 U.S.C. 317c).
* Whether through a corporation operating under section 25 of the Act or organized under section 25 (a) of the Act, or otherwise."[93]

Since the U.S. banks have thus not only been allowed to acquire the stock of foreign banks directly (in addition to doing so through the intermediary of an Edge Act or agreement company) but also to make advances directly to them, they have had a broad U.S. legal framework in which to operate. For example, if it becomes necessary to make short-term advances to an affiliated member of a Euro-dollar loan consortium, to an affiliated bank which is taking a longer-term portion of a Euro-dollar term loan, or to one which needs short-term credits to nourish an underwriting that is not being taken up by non-syndicate purchasers rapidly enough, the U.S. branch bank or the head office bank can operate independently of the limits aimed at supervising such transactions inside the United States.

A U.S. bank with no affiliated banks abroad has not benefitted from this revision; but one which has considered its branch banks and affiliated banks abroad as part of an overall multinational banking structure has been able to engage in a tremendous variety of operations. A statutory alteration of this nature is illustrative of the way in which the U.S. banking laws were being modified from time to time so as to reflect new situations. It is to be noted, too, that the changes were more rather than less permissive.

Of even greater interest analytically, however, are two new measures which were designed to deal with elements both inside and outside the banking sphere, bearing directly on the multinational banking operations of the U.S. banks. It is in examining the fabrication and evolution of these

92. Federal Reserve Act of December 23, 1913, p. 39, note 49; paragraph added July 1, 1966 by Pub. Law 89-485, § 12 (b), 80 Stat. 241; 12 U.S.C. § 601.
93. (Federal Reserve) Regulation M, 12 C.F.R. § 213.5, 32 Fed. Reg. 4399, March 23, 1967. Section 23A of the Federal Reserve Act deals with advances to affiliated banks.

wholly new measures that the interrelationship between the laws and the multinational banking operations becomes even more apparent. It is the first of these, the Interest Equalization Tax, to which we now turn.

b. *Interest Equalization Tax Act*

In Chapter Four it was indicated that the negative international payments balance of the United States reflected the growing supply of Eurodollars available in the market. By 1963 it had become apparent that this negative balance was no longer a temporary phenomenon. Some economists and government officials alike began openly to regard the situation as chronic. On July 18, 1963 President Kennedy asked Congress to institute a law under which U.S. citizens and residents would pay a tax on the purchase of foreign securities, lowering the net yields to bring them into line with those prevailing on comparable securities issued in the United States. This tax, aimed at equalizing temporarily[94] the interest rate between U.S. and non-U.S. credit instruments as far as the U.S. citizen or resident purchaser is concerned, is known as an "interest equalization tax". Not intended primarily as a measure to increase tax revenues,[95] the tax has been designed to remove the attraction of usually higher yielding foreign, especially Western European, debt and equity securities, thereby reducing the export of capital from the United States.[96]

Although the Interest Equalization Tax Act[97] did not become law until September of the following year its proposed retroactive character[98] immediately brought its effect to bear, obliging U.S. persons[99] to pay a tax

94. *Cf. U.S. Code Cong. Adm. News,* 1964, vol. 2, p. 3486. This "temporary" measure was still in force in 1972.

95. It was estimated, however, that the Interest Equalization Tax would "result in a revenue gain of up to $30 million in a full year of operation". United States, Congress, Senate, Finance Committee, *Report* no. 1267, 88th Cong., 2d Sess., July 30, 1964, on H.R. 8000, paragraph III (f) (Pub. Law 88-563), *Id.,* 1964, vol. 2, p. 3508.

96. The Senate Finance Committee described the tax as "designed to bring the cost of capital raised in the U.S. market by foreign persons more closely into alinement [sic] with the costs prevailing in markets in other industrial countries. The tax is designed to aid our balance-of-payments position by restraining the heavy and accelerated demand on our capital market from other industrialized [sic] countries". *Id.,* p. 3478.

97. Interest Equalization Tax Act, Pub. Law 88-563, September 2, 1964; 78 Stat. 809; 26 U.S.C. §§ 4911-31.

98. In his speech, President Kennedy asked that the law be made retroactively effective as of July 19, 1963.

99. The term "United States person" is defined to include, *inter alia,* both citizens and residents of the United States, as well as domestic partnerships and domestic corporations (except for certain corporations registered under the Investment Company Act of 1940 and which elect to be treated as a foreign issuer or obligor). Interest Equalization Tax Act, *supra;* 26 U.S.C. § 4920 (a) (4).

of 15%[100] on the purchase of equity shares from non-U.S. persons. On the purchase of debt obligations the amount of tax was based on a percentage of the actual value, ranging from 2.75% in the case of obligations whose maturity was at least three years to 15% on those maturing in 28½ years or more.[101] These charges have been designed to "reduce the net rate of return on the foreign securities by about 1 per cent per annum".[102]

(1) Commercial Bank Loans

(a) Generally

From the outset commercial banks in the United States, both U.S. banks and the U.S. branches and subsidiaries of foreign banks, have received special treatment under the Equalization Tax Act. Under its provisions as originally enacted the tax did not apply to the acquisition of "debt obligations by a commercial bank in making loans in the ordinary course of its commercial banking business".[103] In recommending this exemption[104] the Report of the Senate Finance Committee had explained that:

> "In part, this is attributable to the fact that the great bulk of commercial bank loans fall within the less than 3-year maturity range and therefore would in any event not be subject to tax. However, this exclusion also recognizes the special role played by banks in support of normal, recurring financing of the international business of American firms."[105]

The legislators were not unaware, however, of the possibility that this exemption might be used to provide bank loans as substitutes for transactions otherwise subject to the Interest Equalization Tax. The Senate Finance Committee Report stated that:

> "Your committee is aware that a generalized exclusion of this type could be abused. Although that is not expected, your committee does consider it necessary to provide specific authority in the bill for the collection of detailed and timely information on the nature of, and trends in, bank lending to foreign persons. The information collected under these reporting requirements will provide

---

100. Act; 26 U.S.C. § 4911 (b) (1).

101. Act; 26 U.S.C. § 4911 (b) (2). The lower limit has since been set at one year. *Cf.* p. 231, note 122.

102. Senate Finance Committee, *Report, supra*, p. 3479.

103. Interest Equalization Tax Act, *supra;* 26 U.S.C. § 4914 (b) (2).

104. Other exemptions recommended by the Senate Finance Committee included issues originating in "less developed countries" (as designated by the President), direct overseas investments, U.S. export financing, and transactions where application of the tax might imperil the stability of the international monetary system. The last of these (26 U.S.C. § 4917) led to the issuance of Executive Order no. 11175 of September 2, 1965, 29 Fed. Reg. 12605, according special treatment to Canadian issues.

105. Senate Finance Committee, *Report, supra*, p. 3493.

a basis both for determining whether a general exclusion of this character should be continued and, if not, for indicating the specific ways in which the general exclusion should then be modified.

The possible need for and practicability of amending this legislation with respect to loans of commercial banks will be reviewed by your committee should this evidence suggest that bank lending to industrialized countries abroad, whose borrowing will otherwise be subject to tax, is rising in amounts out of proportion to a general expansion in the banking business or amounts related to the normal recurring needs of international trade. A sizeable increase in bank lending that appeared to be related to a diversion of credit demands from channels subject to the tax would be a source of particular concern to your committee."[106]

The Senate-House Conference Committee Report which appeared the following month was less willing to adopt a "wait-and-see" attitude. It said:

"Since the third quarter of 1963 (the latest data available on bank credits to foreigners when the House considered this bill), both long- and short-term bank loans have increased. While much of the expansion in bank credits may well be attributable to necessary financing of exports, and be beneficial to the balance of payments, rather than a substitute for taxable obligations, nevertheless, the increase in bank credit since the third quarter of 1963 has convinced the conferees on the part of the House of the desirability of accepting ... the Senate amendment giving the President standby authority to impose the tax with respect to commercial bank loans. The conferees understand that the President will follow closely the volume of commercial bank loans and should he become convinced that they are being used to an appreciable extent as a substitute (directly or indirectly) for obligations taxed by the bill, he will exercise the authority granted to him..."[107]

The result was the inclusion of a separate subchapter in the Act giving the President of the United States such stand-by authority. By Executive Order there could be imposed:

"...on each acquisition by a United States person... which is a commercial bank of a debt obligation of a foreign obligor (if such obligation has a period remaining to maturity of 1 year or more and less than three years), a tax ... [calculated to lower the yield by approximately 1%, as with longer-term obligations not exempt from the tax]..."[108]

This tax should be imposed if—but only if—the President of the United States:

"(1) determines that the acquisition of debt obligations of foreign obligors by commercial banks in making loans in the ordinary course of the commercial banking business has materially impaired the effectiveness of the tax

106. *Id.,* pp. 3493-04.
107. United States, Congress, Senate-House of Representatives Conference Committee, *Report* no. 1816, 88th Cong. 2d Sess., August 15, 1964, to accompany H.R. 8000 (Pub. Law 88-563), (Statement of the Managers on the part of the House of Representatives), *U.S. Code Cong. Adm. News,* 1964, vol. 2, p. 3555.
108. Interest Equalization Tax Act; 26 U.S.C. § 4931 (c).

imposed by section 4911, because such acquisitions have, directly or indirectly, replaced acquisitions by United States persons, other than commercial banks, of debt obligations of foreign obligors which are subject to the tax imposed by such section, and

(2) specifies by Executive order that the provisions of this section shall apply to acquisitions by commercial banks of debt obligations of foreign obligors, to the extent specified in such order."[109]

(b) Loans by U.S. Branch Banks

The Senate Finance Committee, when stating that the exclusion for commercial banks in the United States recognized "the special role played by banks in support of normal, recurring financing of the international business of American firms",[110] went on to state:

"Also, it permits the banks to continue freely their role in financing U.S. exports and their conduct of banking operations in foreign countries through branches. In this latter case, their activities normally consist of receiving deposits in foreign currencies and making loans in such currencies. These transactions, of course, have no effect on the U.S. balance-of-payments position."[111]

Later in the same Report the Committee affirmed that it did not intend that "the interest equalization tax apply to loans or investments in foreign currencies made by foreign branches of U.S. banks to the extent of foreign currency deposits acquired in the ordinary course of their business".[112]

As a result, whereas the Interest Equalization Tax Act gave stand-by authority to the President to terminate if necessary the exemption given to U.S. commercial bank loans, foreign currency loans by foreign branches of qualifying U.S. banks were to remain outside the scope of that authority. A U.S. bank would qualify in this respect by having established and maintained for each of its foreign branches "a fund of assets with respect to deposits payable in foreign currency to customers (other than banks)" of such branches, and by designating the foreign currency loans as part of the "fund of assets" as provided by the Act and by pertinent regulations.[113]

109. Act; 26 U.S.C. § 4931 (a).
110. See material cited to note 105, *supra*.
111. Senate Finance Committee, *Report, supra*, p. 3493. This emphasis on the non-dollar (implicitly host currency) operations of the U.S. branch banks hardly seems justified.
112. *Id.*, pp. 3501-02. Loans and investments of the U.S. branch banks were to be considered as made in the ordinary course of their commercial banking business if they "would be considered to be in the ordinary course of commercial banking business either in the United States or in the foreign countries in which the U.S. bank has foreign branches. . ." *Id.*, p. 3502. Compare with the British "style" examined at p. 150.
113. Interest Equalization Tax Act; 26 U.S.C. § 4931 (c) (2). This section of the Act also specifies that a debt obligation can be designated as part of a "fund of as-

(2) Changes in the Interest Equalization Tax Act

Leaving aside for the moment the rationale behind the special treatment thus accorded to the lending activities of the U.S. branch banks abroad, it is important to follow the developments of the Interest Equalization Tax Act with respect to those activities. On February 10, 1965 President Johnson delivered a balance of payments message to Congress[114] in which he asked that the Interest Equalization Tax Act be extended for two additional years beyond December 31, 1965.[115]

With regard to U.S. commercial bank loans to foreigners the President stated as follows:

> "Bank loans abroad with maturities over one year—not now covered by the tax—increased by more than one-third, or nearly $1 billion, in 1964. The bulk of this money went to other industrialized countries. Of this, only 15 per cent served to finance United States exports.
>
> In my judgment this outflow has reflected substitution for new security issues in an amount sufficient materially to impair the effectiveness of the interest equalization tax."[116]

The President announced that accordingly he had invoked his stand-by authority and by Executive Order[117] was bringing commercial bank loans within the scope of the Interest Equalization Tax, while simultaneously expanding its coverage to include U.S. commercial bank loans to foreign obligors having a term of from one to three years.[118]

In his message the President asked Congress to amend the law so as to include non-bank lending (to foreign borrowers) of one to three years maturity, stating that otherwise the tax would now "discriminate against

---

sets ... only to the extent that, immediately after such designation, the adjusted basis of all the assets held in such fund does not exceed 110 per cent of the deposits payable in foreign currency to customers (other than banks) of the branch with respect to which such fund is maintained". *Ibid.*

114. 111 *Congressional Record* 2468 (1965) (House of Representatives Document no. 83). The text of this speech is set out verbatim at N.Y. Times, February 11, 1965, p. 56 (late city edition).

115. This message outlined a broad program for attempting to rectify the continuing U.S. balance of payments deficit, including the reduction of U.S. tourist expenditures abroad, the stimulation of U.S. exports and of foreign investment in the United States, and voluntary guidelines for U.S. corporate direct investment and bank lending abroad. We shall return to the last of these measures later in the present Chapter.

116. *Congressional Record, supra.*

117. Executive Order no. 11198 of February 11, 1965; 30 Fed. Reg. 1929.

118. In its annual economic survey of the United States in November 1964 the O.E.C.D. dealt with the U.S. balance of payments deficit, and stated that "the application of the IET to bank credits of more than one year's duration could also help to restrain further outflows..." Organisation for Economic Co-operation and Development, *Economic Survey: United States,* Paris, 1964, p. 30.

banks and invite an outflow of funds through non-banking channels".[119]

Nonetheless the Executive Order continued the exemption[120] for the "acquisition of a debt obligation of a foreign obligor repayable exclusively in one or more currencies other than United States currency" which was made "by a commercial bank at its branch outside the United States".[121]

Later that year Congress enacted the Interest Equalization Tax Extension Act of 1965[122] which extended the Act to July 31, 1967 and brought one to three year non-bank lending to foreigners under its scope. The legislators took this occasion to modify the existing exemption with regard to the foreign currency lending activities of the U.S. branch banks abroad. The Senate Finance Committee, when reporting on the Extension Act prior to its passage, had noted that:

> "Although the President has exercised his authority and extended the interest equalization tax to commercial bank loans, acquisitions by commercial banks at branches located outside of the United States of foreign debt obligations repayable in foreign currencies still are exempt (Executive Order 11198). However, the President has the authority at some future time to subject foreign branch acquisitions to the interest equalization tax although the act provides a minimum exemption in the event he takes this action. Under the minimum foreign branch exemption, a foreign branch of a commercial bank is not to be taxable on the acquisition of debt obligations of foreigners, made in the ordinary course of the commercial banking business, to the extent that such loans do not exceed 110 per cent of the branches' foreign currency deposits of other than banks.
> The deposits of foreign banks may constitute a substantial proportion of a branch's foreign currency deposits with the result that the amount of the foreign currency which the branch could lend free of the interest equalization tax could be substantially reduced. Your committee agrees with the House that there is no reason for excluding the deposits of foreign banks from such a branch's permissible loan base since these also represent foreign currency deposits and are no more likely to have an adverse effect on our balance of payments than the branch's other foreign currency deposits."[123]

The Extension Act of 1965 modified the law accordingly and provided that if the President were to make U.S. branch bank foreign currency loans subject to the Interest Equalization Tax, U.S. branch banks would be able to include in their tax free loan base "deposits payable in foreign currency to customers (other than United States persons engaged in the commercial banking business and members of an affiliated group ...)"

119. *Congressional Record, supra.*
120. Interest Equalization Tax Act; 26 U.S.C. § 4914 (b) (2) (A).
121. Executive Order no. 11198 *supra,* section 2 (c) (2).
122. Interest Equalization Tax Extension Act of 1965, Pub. Law 89-243, October 9, 1965; 79 Stat. 954.
123. United States, Congress, Senate, Finance Committee, *Report* no. 621, 89th Cong., 1st Sess., August 17, 1965, on H.R. 4750, paragraph III-18 (Pub. Law 89-243). *U.S. Code Cong. Adm. News,* 1965, vol. 2, pp. 3478-79.

provided that they were designated as part of the "fund of assets" as theretofore.[124]

In 1966 there was a further modification—more potential than actual—of the Interest Equalization Tax Act provisions with regard to loans made by U.S. branch banks overseas. By this time they were able to lend foreign currency to foreign borrowers, regardless of the term of the loan, exempt of the tax as long as the "fund of assets" limits were observed. Their U.S. dollar loans to foreigners with terms under one year were also exempt (as were such loans to foreigners by U.S. banks and other lenders in the United States generally). The exemption did not, however, extend to the U.S. branch banks' dollar loans for periods of one year or more when the borrowers were not "U.S. persons".

The 1966 change occurred in a Senate Finance Committee amendment to the bill which became the Foreign Investors Tax Act of 1966.[125] This amendment[126] modified the Interest Equalization Tax Act so as to allow the President "to exempt from the interest equalization tax U.S. dollar loans made by the foreign branches of U.S. banks (regardless of the maturities involved)"[127] and subsequently to "withdraw or modify the exemption in the event he determines such withdrawal or modification is necessary to preserve the effectiveness of the interest equalization tax".[128] Thus, the U.S. branch banks' Euro-dollar loans for one year or more (to foreign borrowers) still came under the Interest Equalization Tax provisions, but could be made exempt by an order from the President.

On February 22, 1967 President Johnson issued such an order,[129] freeing all the lending activities of the U.S. branch banks—foreign currencies and Euro-dollars alike—from the inhibitive aspects of the Interest Equalization Tax Act regardless of the lengths of the loans and whether or not the borrower is a "U.S. person". Later in 1967 the Interest Equalization Tax Act was again extended for an additional two years, at which time the President was given the authority to vary the rates of tax within a

124. Interest Equalization Tax Act (of 1964), as amended by the Interest Equalization Tax Extension Act of 1965, *supra;* 26 U.S.C. § 4931 (c). Formerly this section had been designated § 4391 (d).

125. Foreign Investors Tax Act of 1966, Pub. Law 89-809, November 13, 1966; 80 Stat. 1539, which was referred to as a "Christmas Tree Bill" while in Congress because of the variety and quantity of unrelated measures that were "hung" upon it prior to final passage.

126. To section 215 of that Act. See United States, Congress, Senate, Finance Committee, *Report* no. 1707, 89th Cong., 2d Sess., October 11, 1966, on H.R. 13103, paragraph I-B (16) (Pub. Law 89-809). *U.S. Code Cong. Adm. News,* 1966, vol. 3, p. 4453.

127. *Id.,* paragraph IV-B (16), p. 4519.

128. *Ibid.*

129. Executive Order no. 11328 of February 22, 1967; 32 Fed. Reg. 3137.

range up to twice the amount previously set forth. The existing exemptions were not, however, changed.[130]

(3) Effect of the Interest Equalization Tax Act on the Operations of the U.S. Branch Banks

It will be recalled that when the Interest Equalization Tax Act formally went into effect in 1964, the overseas U.S. branch banks' lending operations were singled out, it being noted that "their activities normally consist of receiving deposits in foreign currencies and making loans in such currencies".[131] The correctness of this rationale is open to question.

In Chapter Three we have seen why the host currency lending operations of the U.S. branch banks are based more on funds obtained in the local money markets than on local deposits. In Chapter Four we have examined why the Euro-dollar market has held greater attraction for the U.S. branch banks than the host currency markets, and we have noted that when eligible borrowers need host or other non-U.S. currency advances they often obtain them from the U.S. branch banks (or other banks) by means of swap operations tied into Euro-dollar facilities.

As an alternative rationale the proponents of the Interest Equalization Tax provisions facilitating the lending operations of U.S. branch banks abroad might have used a different—equally erroneous—argument, to wit, that the lending operations of these institutions are not of such importance that they merit particular concern. That is, they might have followed a line of reasoning similar to that of the Radcliffe Committee when describing the activities of the U.S. and other foreign banks in London.[132] Here it is to be noted that the Radcliffe Committee itself should probably have taken cognizance of the Euro-dollar market operations which were already emerging, albeit in an early stage of development.[133] Nonetheless, had such a line of reasoning been followed by the U.S. legislators, i.e., that the U.S. branch bank lending activity was irrelevant or insignificant, they would have been justified in ignoring it altogether.

In fact it was definitely not ignored. Not only were the U.S. branch

130. Interest Equalization Tax Extension Act of 1967, Pub. Law 90-59, July 31, 1967; 81 Stat. 145. Subsequently the Act was extended to August 31 and then September 30, 1969 by Pub. Laws 91-50 and 91-65 respectively, and then to March 31, 1971 by the Interest Equalization Tax Extension Act of 1969, Pub. Law 91-128, § 2; 83 Stat. 261. The most recent extension prolongs the measure to March 31, 1973.
131. See p. 229, material cited to note 111.
132. See p. 154.
133. *Cf.* Paul Einzig, "Dollar Deposits in London", 110 *The Banker* 23, (1960). Of course, the argument could be made that the Committee did not have the kind of statistical and other information that is becoming increasingly available in Great Britain.

banks given separate treatment in the original law, their lending operations have continually been reconsidered in the subsequent changes thereto. Nor were the U.S. branch banks hampered by the Executive Order of 1965[134] which extended the Interest Equalization Tax Act provisions to U.S. commercial banks' loans to non-U.S. borrowers. In that instance, their foreign currency loans were exempt, and the bulk of their Euro-dollar loans were at that time short-term, well under the one year limit. When foreign borrowers needed Euro-dollar credits for longer periods, 360-day loans could be "rolled over" without too much difficulty.[135] On the Euro-dollar deposit-taking side of their operations, the law had no bearing.

Eventually, as the Euro-dollar market began to accommodate longer-term operations, the amendment contained in the Foreign Investors Tax Act of 1966[136] followed by the Executive Order of 1967[137] made it unnecessary to continue "rolling over" nominally short-term advances. It is evident that throughout the evolution of the Interest Equalization Tax Act and its accompanying executive measures the U.S. Congress and President have not lost sight of the lending operations of the U.S. branch banks abroad. At no point, however, have they aimed at restricting their Euro-dollar operations. As the need for relaxation of controls has become apparent, is has been forthcoming. Any legal hindrance on the U.S. branch banks' Euro-dollar operations due to the U.S. balance of payments program has had to come, therefore, from another quarter, to which we now turn.

c. *U.S. Voluntary Foreign Credit Restraint Program ("Guidelines")*

In the February 10, 1965 balance of payments message referred to earlier, President Johnson said that he was "asking the chairman of the Board of Governors of the Federal Reserve System in cooperation with the Secretary of the Treasury to enroll the banking community in a major effort to limit their lending abroad".[138] Referred to officially as the "President's program for the voluntary curtailment of foreign credit by banks", this resulted in a simultaneous request by the Board of Governors that U.S. commercial banks keep their credits to foreign borrowers in 1965 at no more than 5% above the level of such credits as of December 31, 1964.[139]

134. See pp. 230-31.
135. *Cf.* 222 (6444) *The Economist* 743 (February 25, 1967).
136. See p. 232.
137. *Ibid.*
138. See p. 230, note 114.
139. 51 *Federal Reserve Bulletin* 257 (1965). Parallel to this program was another for limiting overseas investment by U.S. corporations, administered by the Department of Commerce. For an excellent study of the latter program, see Lawrence C. McQuade, "Corporate Voluntary Balance of Payments Program and the Lawyer",

(1) Guidelines for Banks

The following month the Federal Reserve System issued a set of four-teen "Guidelines for Banks" designed to set out voluntary[140] restrictions on commercial bank loans to foreign borrowers.[141] Guideline 1 specified how a bank was to calculate its base amount as of the end of the fourth quarter in 1965, and set the ceiling for the year 1965 at 105% of that base amount. Other Guidelines exempted loans involving the U.S. Export-Import Bank (Guideline 2), and set "absolute priority" for export credits, informing banks that they "should give the highest priority to loans to less developed countries and should avoid restrictive policies that would place an undue burden on Canada, Japan, and the United Kingdom". (Guideline 4). The banks were also advised to refrain from loan substitu-tion, i.e., from lending to domestic borrowers who might themselves use the funds to invest abroad or who might on-lend to foreign borrowers in a manner that was detrimental to the balance of payments program. (Guideline 13).

Of particular interest to the present study were Guidelines 10 and 14, which were as follows:

10. *Foreign branches*
It is assumed, of course, that U.S. banks having branches, as well as subsid-iaries and affiliates, in foreign countries will not utilize them to avoid the foreign credit restraint program for U.S. banks.

Foreign branches have independent sources of funds in the countries in which they are located and from third countries, in many cases through the attrac-tion of Euro-dollar deposits. The balance of payments program is not designed to hamper the lending activities of the foreign branches insofar as the funds utilized are derived from foreign sources and do not add to the dollar outflow. Concern arises only in those cases where the resources are derived (directly or indirectly) from the United States.

Total claims of the head office on overseas branches, including permanent

---

in Southwestern Legal Foundation, *Private Investors Abroad, Structures and Safe-guards*, Albany, Matthew Bender & Co., 1966, pp. 205-26.

140. The voluntary nature of the Guidelines was frequently alluded to in official U.S. Government statements and publications. See for example Board of Governors of the Federal Reserve System, *Press Release* dated December 3, 1965 (for release on December 6, 1965), 5 *International Legal Materials* 45-47 (1966). In that Press Release there is reference made to the "suggested ceiling" for foreign loans, and to the belief "that banks will continue to cooperate with the spirit as well as the letter of the program ..." Private observers placed less stress on the voluntary nature of the Guidelines. It was generally agreed that the federal government was relying on bankers' and businessmen's voluntary action to do whatever was necessary to help reduce the balance of payments deficit. It seemed clear, however, that if per-suasion failed there would probably be compulsion. Nevertheless, this attempt to use moral suasion is significant.

141. "Guidelines for Banks", 51 *Federal Reserve Bulletin* 371-75 (1965). Guide-lines for non-bank financial institutions were also issued by the Federal Reserve.

capital invested in, as well as balances due from, branches, represent bank credit to nonresidents for purposes of the program".

14. *"Management of a bank's liquid funds"*

Banks that have placed their own funds abroad for short-term investment purposes, including U.S. dollar deposits outside the United States or the acquisition of non-U.S. money market paper, should refrain from increasing such deposits and investments and should, in a reasonable and orderly manner, seek to reduce them. Since such funds are ordinarily placed outside the United States solely to provide a slightly higher rate of return, they are strong candidates for reduction under the program.

This guideline applies equally to deposits and investments payable in foreign currencies and to those payable in U.S. dollars.

This guideline does not call for a reduction in necessary working balances held with foreign correspondents, although such balances are considered claims on nonresidents for the purposes of the program".[142]

From the first part of Guideline no. 10 it is evident that the offshore activities of the U.S. branch banks per se were not to be hampered by the voluntary program. The second part of that Guideline, however, buttressed by the indications in Guideline no. 14, made it clear that the U.S. branch banks in the three host countries and elsewhere abroad could no longer rely on funds from their head office banks to augment freely the supply side of their lending activities. We shall have occasion to return to this aspect of the Guidelines.

(2) Changes in the Guidelines for Banks

In December 1965 the Board of Governors of the Federal Reserve System made known the revised Guidelines for 1966. Noting that as a group the U.S. commercial banks had "stayed well under the suggested ceiling for 1965",[143] the Board indicated that the limit for outstanding foreign loans was to be raised to 109% of the December 31, 1964 base amount, i.e., by an additional 4%. The banks were requested in Guideline 1 (b) to spread this increase evenly over the year, keeping it at 1% per quarter.[144]

With regard to loan priorities, "absolute priority" was again to be given to bona fide export credits (Guideline 4). As for non-export loans, the Board of Governors repeated the instructions of the previous year's Guidelines giving "highest priority" to loans to less developed countries and repeating that banks should avoid restrictive policies with regard to loans destined for borrowers from Canada, Japan, and the United

142. 51 *Id*. 374-75 (1965).

143. Board of Governors of the Federal Reserve System, *Press Release* dated December 3, 1965, *supra.*

144. (Revised) "Guidelines for Banks" (for 1966), 51 *Federal Reserve Bulletin* 1694-98, 1695 (1965). The Revised Guidelines for 1966 are reproduced at 5 *International Legal Materials* 52-61, 53 (1966).

Kingdom. The pertinent Guideline, after reiterating the above, went on to state that:

> "It is expected that the outstanding amount of nonexport credits to developed countries in Continental Western Europe would not be increased during 1966 but rather would be reduced to the extent needed to meet *bona fide* requests for priority credits within the overall ceiling".[145]

Thus, if additional slack were needed in the lending program of any particular U.S. bank, it was to be provided by cutting back on credits extended to borrowers in two of the three host countries (France and Switzerland) as well in other industrialized countries in Western Europe.

When the Guidelines for Banks were again revised, effective October 1, 1966, U.S. commercial banks were given the same 109% limit to their foreign lending for the remainder of 1966 and for 1967.[146] Here, however, the concept of "leeway" was introduced. "Leeway" was defined as "the difference between the ceiling for 1967 ... and the amount of foreign credits outstanding on September 30, 1966" (revised Guideline 1(A)(2)(d)). A commercial bank which had not already expanded its outstanding foreign loans to the 109% total, and thus had "leeway" in which to increase such credits, was requested to limit its operations so as to utilize no more than 40% of its "leeway" through the end of the first quarter of 1967 and then no more than 20% per quarter for the remainder of that year (revised Guideline 1(B)(1)). Moreover, the banks were requested to allocate only 10% of their "leeway" to augmenting non-export credits to borrowers from industrialized countries (revised Guideline 1(B)(3)).

Loan priorities for 1967 were similar to those in the earlier versions with respect to bona fide export credits, and to non-export credits to less developed countries as well as to borrowers from Canada, Japan, and the United Kingdom. This time the pertinent Guideline stated that:

> "It is expected that the outstanding amount of nonexport credits to developed countries in continental Western Europe will not be increased during 1967 unless a bank is in a position to meet all bona fide requests for priority credits within the overall ceiling."[147]

Thus, unlike the previous year, there was to be no cut-back in credits to these countries to meet requests for priority credits. Nonetheless, credits could be extended to borrowers from France and Switzerland and other industrialized countries in Continental Western Europe only if

145. Revised Guideline 4, *Id.* at 1696 and 57 respectively.
146. (Revised) "Guidelines for Banks" (for 1967), 52 *Federal Reserve Bulletin* 1754-57 (1966). The revised Guidelines for 1967 are reproduced at 6 *International Legal Materials* 107-15 (1967).
147. Revised Guideline 4, *Id.*, at 1756 and 112 respectively.

and to the extent that a bank had no outstanding but unsatisfied bona fide requests for priority credits.

On November 16, 1967 the Guidelines were again revised.[148] The 109% limit of the December 31, 1964 base figure was retained, and banks were again requested to use up any existing "leeway"[149] at no more than 20% per quarter for the last quarter of 1967 and for 1968.

The November 1967 version of the Guidelines was destined to be short-lived. On January 1, 1968 President Johnson issued an Executive Order giving the Board of Governors of the Federal Reserve System the authority to:

"... investigate, regulate or prohibit any transaction by any bank or other financial institution subject to the jurisdiction of the United States involving a direct or indirect transfer of capital to or within any foreign country or to any national thereof outside the United States; ... [and to] ... require that any bank or financial institution subject to the jurisdiction of the United States shall cause to be repatriated to the United States such part as the Board may specify of the bank deposits and other short term financial assets which are held in foreign countries by or for the account of such bank or financial institution."[150]

---

148. (Revised) "Guidelines for Banks" (for 1968), 53 *Federal Reserve Bulletin* 1871-73 (1967).

149. "The leeway available on September 30, 1967, together with the increase in the 1968 ceiling related to the alternative method of calculating that ceiling, provides a potential leeway for an outflow of bank credit in 1968 of about $ 1.4 billion." *Id.* at p. 1869.

150. Executive Order no. 11387 of January 1, 1968; 33 Fed. Reg. 47, January 3, 1968. The following day there appeared a new set of Revised "Guidelines for Banks" (for 1968), 54 *Federal Reserve Bulletin* 64-68 (1968). The new set of revised Guidelines for 1968 are reproduced at 7 *International Legal Materials* 72-80 (1968). Rather than control the outflow of funds from the United States, which the Guidelines had theretofore been aimed at accomplishing, the new set of revised Guidelines for 1968 were designed to cause a net inflow of at least $500 million during 1968. As stated in the Preface to this new set of revised Guidelines, "the major effects of the revisions are focused on the developed countries of continental Western Europe". All banks were requested "to reduce the amount of term loans (loans with original maturities of more than one year) to residents of developed countries of continental Western Europe by not renewing such loans at maturity, and by not relending the repayments of such loans to other residents of those countries."

Thus, although the wording of the Guidelines dealing with "foreign branches" and with "management of a bank's liquid funds" was unchanged from that in all the previous versions, there was a considerable difference in the way in which the new set of Guidelines would bear upon the operations of the U.S. branch banks in Western Europe after January 1, 1968. Moreover, the fact that the Federal Reserve now had power to apply direct controls meant that it was hardly appropriate to continue referring to the "President's program for the voluntary curtailment of foreign credit".

When the new measures covering banks' operations went into effect there was

Thus ended the era of the voluntary program, with the institution of a new legal mechanism designed to induce a net inflow of funds towards the United States.

(3) Effect of the U.S. Voluntary Foreign Credit Restraint Program ("Guidelines") on the Operations of the U.S. Branch Banks

In order to analyse the effect of the Guidelines during the second phase of the U.S. branch banks' Euro-dollar operations in the three host countries, the measure should not be considered separately but together with the Interest Equalization Tax as the second element of a program designed generally to improve the balance of payments of the United States. In this context, the (March 1967) views of one member of the Ways and Means Committee of the House of Representatives are pertinent:

> "It is important to emphasize that the administration's investment control programs are threefold. First, there are controls on U.S. investment in foreign equity issues, or U.S. portfolio investment. This program is implemented by the interest equalization tax.
>
> Second is the program to control 'voluntarily' the direct foreign private investments of U.S. businesses in overseas facilities. This program is administered by means of guidelines set by the Commerce Department under which 722 firms agree to restrain foreign capital expenditures and report quarterly the effects of their operations on the balance of payments.
>
> Third is the program to control foreign lending by U.S. banks. This program is implemented by the Federal Reserve Board under a series of guidelines.
>
> . . . .
>
> But the fundamental point I wish to make here is that the Congress itself is unable to assess and decide the total effects of these programs. There are several reasons. First, the 'voluntary' investment and banking programs are not imposed through legislation and therefore there is no ready forum or lever for Congress to use in evaluating them. Congress has not itself taken the initiative that is required to review the program. Second, there is a distinct unwillingness on the part of the administration to present, even in the Ways and Means Committee, a comprehensive picture of the investment control program."[151]

---

an analogous move to modify the corporate guidelines. These were placed under the authority of the Office of Foreign Direct Investments, which is part of the Department of Commerce.

In March 1968 the January 1968 version of the new Guidelines for banks was amended so as to remove Canada from their effect. 54 *Federal Reserve Bulletin* 258-62 (1968). The amendments are reproduced at 7 *International Legal Materials* 444-45 (1968). For more recent versions of the Guidelines see 55 *Federal Reserve Bulletin* 317-20 (1969) and 8 *International Legal Materials* 609-26 (1969), and 56 *Federal Reserve Bulletin* 11-17 (1970) as revised by *Id.* 311, 481-82, and 739.

151. United States, Congress, House of Representatives, Ways and Means Committee, *Supplemental Views* of Thomas B. Curtis, member of the Committee, accompanying *Report*, no. 68, 90th Cong., 1st Sess., March 6, 1967, on H.R. 6098 (Pub. Law 90-59). *U.S. Code Cong. Adm. News*, 1967, vol. 1, pp. 1446-47.

Notwithstanding the indistinct nature of the "voluntary" Guidelines, and the unwillingness attributed to the U.S. administration in the passage quoted above, it is clear that the program influenced the operations of the U.S. branch banks by modifying the structure in which they dealt prior to the imposition of mandatory capital movements controls in 1968.

First, the pre-1968 Guidelines for Banks were accompanied by similar guidelines for U.S. corporations, as previously noted, which called, *inter alia,* for the repatriation of Euro-dollars (and other foreign liquid assets) owned by U.S. corporations.[152] This had the effect of siphoning off a portion of the U.S.-owned dollar deposits available for relending in the Euro-dollar market. For instance, the Bank of England, reporting on a £68 million withdrawal of foreign currency from balances maintained in British commercial banks in the second quarter (May-July) of 1965, commented that "most of this probably reflected the repatriation of funds by U.S. corporations in response to the U.S. measures announced in February to curb the net outflow of private capital".[153] It is probable that the measure also caused or at least greatly influenced the action of a few very large U.S. corporations which put accumulated overseas capital and earnings into banking operations of their own.[154]

Along with the siphoning off of some of the U.S. corporate-owned Euro-dollars as a result of the corporate guidelines, the Guidelines for Banks had a corollary effect in pinching off greatly the flow of new U.S.-source funds into the market. This was because banks in the United States were not supposed to raise their level of outstanding advances to foreign borrowers by more than a small, fixed amount, and eventually in a measured cadence. Of course, a portion of the dollars which had been borrowed by foreigners theretofore had been spent immediately in the United States to cover purchases there; and another portion had been deposited temporarily in banks inside the United States (in addition to required compensating balances) awaiting disbursal. Neither portion entered the Euro-dollar market directly. A third portion, however, had been available for deposit in banks outside the United States to take advantage of the prevailing interest rates, i.e., for "conversion" into Euro-dollars. It was this third portion that was considerably affected by the Guidelines for Banks.

152. See the letter from the U.S. Secretary of Commerce addressed to major U.S. corporations in December 1965 describing the program, reproduced at 5 *International Legal Materials* 30-34 (1966).

153. Bank of England, 5 *Quarterly Bulletin* 224 (1965).

154. For instance in May 1965 The Dow Chemical Co. established the Dow Bank A.G. in Zurich. By 1971 this bank had nearly SF one billion (approx. $230 million) in assets and an office in London. In 1971 the Swiss Federal Banking Commission authorized the establishment of the Bank Firestone A.G.

240

Second, since banks in the United States could no longer lend freely to borrowers abroad, representative offices could not as effectively channel prospective foreign borrowers to their head office banks. On the contrary, these now became *de facto* representatives of the banks' overseas branches and particularly of the branch bank in London, where borrowers benefitted from the special status accorded as well to those from Canada and Japan.

Third, the Guidelines for Banks caused another paradox in undercutting one of the accepted reasons for banks' using overseas branches as opposed to subsidiaries. It had generally been supposed that a depositor, including the smaller one, in a host country would rely upon the foreign (here U.S.) bank's entire asset structure as standing behind his and other deposits in a local branch bank. If funds at that branch were not adequate to meet depositors' withdrawals, then head office funds and those of other branch banks could presumably be marshalled and "pipe-lined" to the branch bank in question.

Since the Guidelines for Banks were only "voluntary" the depositor might have reasoned that they would not have prevented funds in the United States from being included in such a marshalling operation. In fact, however, the small depositor would rarely have known of the foreign banking regulations or Guidelines in any event. It would be more accurate to say that the larger institutional depositor, who knew of the Guidelines for Banks, would have questioned the viscosity of the head office funds. In other words, there was reason to believe that the Guidelines might have sufficiently slowed down the flow of funds from the head office to make them less readily available at the branch bank in the host country. The skeptical depositor of large amounts of host currencies, but more likely dollars, would have had reason to wonder whether a general credit squeeze in the United States might not reduce the head office banks' willingness to make funds available at the branch abroad, using the Guidelines as an excuse.

Another effect of the Guidelines for Banks as an impediment to marshalling of head office funds was that possibly profitable lending transactions at the branch banks could no longer be freely entered into if head office funds were necessary in excess of the permitted level. In effect, the U.S. head office banks' funds were thus broken into two categories, those eligible and those ineligible for lending to foreigners. For the first time since World War II, when these U.S. banks had operated under exchange controls, the fungibility of their dollar deposits was reduced.

If the Interest Equalization Tax had no directly restrictive effect on the operations of the U.S. branch banks, the Guidelines definitely did. Taking this into account, it is now in order to turn to the laws of the host countries that affected their operations during this second Euro-dollar operating phase.

2. Host Country Laws

a. France

It will be recalled that in January 1966 the French banking law was considerably modified so as to allow *banques de dépôts* to take longer-term deposits.[155] A companion *décret* appearing on the same date modified some of the elements which the Commission de Contrôle des Banques takes into account in supervising the solvency and liquidity of banks in France. Notably, the Commission was empowered to require that banks maintain certain ratios between their own capital, combined with their long- and medium-term credits plus certain of their short-term and demand assets, on the one hand and their real estate investments together with their long- and medium-term advances on the other.[156] The changing asset-liability structure of the banks in France was thus taken into account as longer-term credit operations were becoming more important to the *banques de dépôts*. In the same order of events there followed in May 1966 a change in the minimum capital requirement for *banques de dépôts*, which was doubled from FF 1 million (approx. $200,000) to FF 2 million (approx. $400,000).[157]

Of greater importance, however, was a switch from the monetary control of credit to the control of the money supply by a *décret* issued in January 1967 requiring that banks in France maintain minimum reserves on deposit at the Banque de France. The reserves are calculated as a percentage of the banks' demand and time liabilities, and bear no interest.[158] The following day the Ministère des Finances issued an *avis* setting forth a list of the types of assets and liabilities to be taken into account in calculating the minimum reserves,[159] accompanied by an

155. *Décret* no. 66-81, p. 208, note 28.

156. Ministère de l'Economie et des Finances, *Décret*, no. 66-82, art. 8; *Journal officiel*, February 1, 1966, pp. 913-14.

157. Ministère de l'Economie et des Finances, *Décret* of May 26, 1966; *Journal officiel*, May 28, 1966, p. 4287.

158. Ministère, *Décret* no. 67-27 of January 6, 1967; art. 1; *Journal officiel*, January 10, 1967, pp. 453-54. The treasury coefficient (see page 185, note 135) which required *banques de dépôts* to maintain 35% of their deposits in medium-term paper and Treasury bills was terminated when the minimum reserve requirement went into effect.

159. *Id.*, *Avis* (Décision de caractère général no. 67-01 of January 10, 1967), arts. 1 and 2; *Journal officiel*, January 12, 1967, pp. 546-47. In March 1971 the minimum reserve ratios were lowered from 7.5% to 7.25% on demand deposits and likewise lowered from 2.5% to 2.25% on time deposits. This change was made in conjunction with the setting of reserve requirements on banks' advances as well as

instruction which indicated, *inter alia,* that liabilities concerned are those denominated in French francs.[160] In other words, banks in France were able to avoid the sterilization of a portion of the dollar deposits which could be attracted when the exchange control system was modified in January 1967.[161]

The easing of the rules affecting the taking of dollar deposits, dealt with earlier in the present Chapter, was not, however, reflected in the new exchange control regulations with regard to lending. The revised French exchange control law was not designed to provide total freedom from restriction. Rather it called for freer movement within prescribed bounds. As one official source described the new regime, perhaps somewhat euphemistically, "without prejudice to the convertibility of the franc, control is exercised ... over a limited number of capital movements. This control is not over the transfers which, in any event, are completely free, but over the transactions themselves".[162]

Notably, dollar loans could be made to non-residents; but the details of these transactions had to be reported to the Banque de France.[163] Residents, as pointed out earlier,[164] could borrow from non-resident sources without permission only where direct overseas investment was involved, where the funds were for the direct financing of foreign trade, or where the amounts did not exceed FF 2 million (approx. $400,000).[165] Accordingly the revised exchange control rules meant on the one hand that banks were obliged to report the details of all advances made to foreign borrowers, and on the other that they could lend dollars to their largest

---

on their deposits, so as to cause a wash operation from the banks' standpoint when the second set of reserves had to be created. See page 272, note 262. The reserve requirements were twice raised by 1% in May and by another 1% in July 1971 to 10.25% on demand deposits and 5.25% on time deposits. I.M.F., 23 *International Financiel News Survey* 154, 226 (1971).

160. *Id., Instruction* no. 63 of January 10, 1967; *Journal officiel,* January 12, 1967, p. 547.

161. See pp. 209-10.

162. I.M.F., *(Eighteenth) Exchange Restrictions,* 1967, p. 230.

163. *Décret* no. 67-78, art. 9, and *Arrêté* of January 27, 1967, art. 11 (2), page 209, note 33. As a result of complaints (by the E.E.C. Commission) that this was not in line with the Treaty of Rome, this requirement imposed on foreign borrowers was modified by a decree of February 22, 1971, which exempts E.E.C. member state companies from the advance permission requirement. A second decree issued the same day, however, puts these borrowers back under exchange control.

164. See p. 209.

165. As we have seen, banks themselves had a privileged status with regard to borrowing abroad. *Ibid.* This privilege extended to French branches and subsidiaries of foreign banks. See Roger Pinto, "Le régime juridique des investissements étrangers en France", 94 *Journal du Droit International* 235-64, especially pp. 257-58 (1967).

group of potential customers, i.e., those situated locally, only under certain conditions.

It may be argued that in itself this need not have constituted an insurmountable barrier to effective Euro-dollar operations, and in fact, that banks in France now enjoyed greater liberty than at any time since 1939.[166] Nonetheless, it constituted evidence of the continuing surveillance that was being exercised by the French government.[167] Also, as in the case of the status which U.S. branch banks enjoyed with regard to (Federal Reserve) Regulation Q, the privilege consisted of an exception to a generally restrictive measure rather than a positive right set forth in a law or regulation. Operationally this distinction might not have been significant, but in legal terms it was.[168]

b. *Great Britain*

As indicated in Chapter Four, Euro-dollar lending operations within the British regulatory framework can be divided for analysis into four categories, comprised either of the lending of dollars directly, or the lending of sterling converted from dollars, to residents or to non-residents of the sterling area respectively. It will be recalled that during the first Euro-dollar operating phase from 1959 to mid-1963 only the lending of non-residents' dollar deposits to other non-residents was free from exchange and credit controls.

166. For instance, they had received on September 15, 1966 the power to grant guarantees to non-residents of the French franc zone with regard to exports to non-zone countries. I.M.F., *(Eighteenth) Exchange Restrictions, supra*, p. 228. Later that year the period for which they could extend franc overdraft facilities to non-residents was raised from six months to one year. *Id.*, p. 229.

167. For an interesting analysis of the bearing of the new law on foreign direct investments in France, see Pinto, *supra*. See also Le Monde, January 31, 1967, p. 18, col. 1 (final edition); Mitchell Brock, "The Reform of French Exchange Controls", 22 *The Business Lawyer* 985-990 (1967); and Pierre Jasinski, "The Control of Capital Movements in France", 3 *Journal of World Trade Law* 209-18 (1969).

168. Since the close of the specific period under study there have been several pertinent changes in the French law. On May 29, 1968 exchange control was reinstated, after which it was relaxed in September, only to be reintroduced in November 1968. (See p. 210, note 36). Under this regime, which is currently in force, authorized banks are allowed to advance foreign currencies to non-residents for short-term placement abroad as long as the lending banks remain within their assigned exchange positions. They can also lend to residents to finance foreign trade transactions, and to merchanting houses for international merchanting operations (defined as "consisting only of transactions involving the purchase abroad of a specified parcel of goods and the sale abroad of the same parcel or of an equivalent parcel acquired previously under the same conditons"). I.M.F., *(Twentieth) Exchange Restrictions*, 1969, p. 163. Banks' assigned exchange positions were modified in January 1969, since when they have been required to maintain negative or balanced positions, or to make one-month renewable deposits of dollars with the Banque de France. I.M.F., *(Twenty-first) Exchange Restrictions*, 1970, p. 176.

During the second phase from mid-1963 through the end of 1967, dollar loans to residents continued to come under the exchange control rules. In July 1965 the Bank of England announced that dollars and other foreign currencies would no longer be made available for overseas investments, and that residents thenceforth would have to obtain funds from the investment dollar pool (and pay the premium) for that purpose.[169] This was tightened further when in May 1966 the Bank made it known that investment dollars could be used only if certain criteria were met, especially that the investment be likely to produce immediately positive results for the balance of payments.[170]

At the same time that the official supply of foreign exchange was cut off for resident borrowers in July 1965 the Bank of England also withdrew the blanket permission[171] under which sterling credits could be extended at the lending banks' discretion to resident corporations controlled by non-resident interests.[172] It was stated officially that this move had been partially motivated by the desire to ensure that foreigners would finance their acquisitions of or participations in British companies by exchanging hard currencies rather than by raising sterling through borrowing locally in Great Britain.[173] Thus the U.S. branch banks in London could continue to switch or swap dollars into pounds but could not lend them, beyond amounts needed for normal working balances, to U.S. corporate subsidiaries in Great Britain without exchange control permission from the Bank of England.[174]

No less important, perhaps, was a credit control measure covering sterling loans to residents. These loans did not require exchange control authorization; but from December 1964 onwards all banks in Great Britain were put on notice that it was "now the aim of official policy

169. Bank of England, 7 *Quarterly Bulletin* 258 (1967). See also N.Y. Times, July 28, 1965, p. 1, col. 5 (late city edition). See p. 211, note 41.

170. 7 *Quarterly Bulletin* 258 (1967).

171. See p. 130.

172. 4 *Quarterly Bulletin* 217 (1964). This did not affect advances to banks controlled by non-residents. See I.M.F., *(Seventeenth) Exchange Restrictions,* 1966, pp. 587-88.

173. 7 *Quarterly Bulletin,* 259 (1967). The French authorities have been no less concerned about this issue.

174. It was announced that the Bank of England intended to exercise "more uniform control" when foreign-controlled firms sought to borrow. "[I]n effect, long-established companies will now be subject to the same scrutiny as those more recently established when they wish to raise finance in this country." 5 *Id.* 217 (1965). In January 1971 the Treasury acted to limit severely short-term Euro-dollar borrowing by residents, by announcing that the Bank of England would grant permission only for credits of at least five years. See *Financial Times,* January 12, 1971, p. 1, col. 3.

that the rate of growth of bank advances should decline ..."[175] This was followed by the announcement on April 29, 1965, that the Special Deposit Scheme[176] was being reinstated for the clearing banks and Scottish banks.[177] The U.S. branch banks were again unaffected by this measure;[178] but on May 5, 1965 the Governor of the Bank of England wrote to the Chairman of the London Clearing Bankers as well as to the other major banking associations asking that loans by *all* banks to the private sector not exceed 105% of the amount outstanding on March 31, 1965.[179]

A further letter of July 27, 1965 reiterated the aims of the monetary authorities and emphasized the need for preferential treatment for export financing.[180] On July 12, 1966 it was announced that the 105% level would remain in force at least through the following March. Two days later a second call for Special Deposits was issued,[181] followed by a press release on August 9, 1966 to the effect that the needs of priority borrowers (those seeking funds for export finance and for productive agricultural or industrial investments) were to fit within the 105% limit. A second statement made to the press on November 1, 1966 pointed out that banks were expected to remain sufficiently below the 105% limit so that surges in demand for credit from legitimate borrowers would not put them over that level.[182]

On April 11, 1967 the Bank of England issued a notice discontinuing the 105% limitation for the clearing banks and Scottish banks as well as for the discount houses, but leaving it in force for the other types of banks in Great Britain, including the U.S. branch banks.[183] For the latter the 105% rule had two particularly important effects. First, some of the newer arrivals had very few loans outstanding as of March 31, 1965 or had none whatsoever. So that these branch banks would not be effectively barred from lending sterling locally, an arrangement was

175. Letter from the Governor of the Bank of England to the Chairman of the London Clearing Bankers, dated December 8, 1964. The text of this letter is reproduced at 4 *Quarterly Bulletin* 263 (1964).
176. See pp. 126 and 189, note 156.
177. 5 *Quarterly Bulletin* 111 (1965).
178. It was reported that in April 1967 the Governor of the Bank of England had proposed that similar requirements be placed on the branches of foreign banks and on the merchant banks in London. See *Business Week,* September 30, 1967, p. 150.
179. 5 *Quarterly Bulletin* 111 (1965).
180. *Id.* 217 (1965). See also 6 *Id.* 3 (1966).
181. 6 *Id.* 207 (1966) and 7 *Id.* 124 (1967).
182. 7 *Id.* 10 (1967). This was particularly aimed at advances for private borrowers' year-end "window dressing".
183. The text of this notice is reproduced at 7 *Id.* 164-65 (1967). Sterling lending remained subject to the Borrowing (Control and Guarantees) Act, 1946 (see pp. 126-28) throughout the period under consideration, as it still does.

reported to have been made so that the figure would apply to loans outstanding plus firm credit committments as of the key date. Second, the 105% rule served as an added incentive for lending to local authority borrowers in Great Britain, who were outside the private sector and hence not affected by the limitation. In the past these advances had provided an effective temporary outlet for dollars during those periods when the demand for them had slackened.[184] Increasingly during the second Euro-dollar operating phase local authority loans became a concomitant feature of the other techniques used by the U.S. branch banks in London.

The final sector, that of marrying non-residents' dollar deposits with other non-residents' needs for dollar loans was not affected by any changes in the British regulations. Even when sterling was devalued by one-seventh from $2.80 to $2.40 on November 18, in the closing days of the second Euro-dollar operating phase, the Euro-dollar market was left unfettered. The result was that dollar advances to non-residents continued to rise during that period.[185] For the U.S. branch banks this was extremely important, since as we shall see, they were lending more and more heavily to their head offices, which were non-resident borrowers.[186]

184. See 3 *Id*. 5 (1963) and 4 *Id*. 267 (1964). Moreover, advances to local authorities offer an easy method for lending in a remunerative market free of credit risk.

185. 7 *Id*. 224 (1967). They continued to rise thereafter. *Cf*. 10 *Id*. 448-51 (1970).

186. Since the end of 1967 there have been several pertinent changes in the British law. On February 8, 1968 the Bank of England instituted a Cash Deposits scheme for banks in Great Britain other than the clearers and the Scottish Banks (which had been subject to the on-again off-again Special Deposits scheme since April 1960—see page 189, note 156). Under this (never activated) Cash Deposits scheme banks, including the U.S. branch banks, with sterling deposits in excess of £ 3 million (approx. $7.2 million) were subject to compulsory deposits with the Bank of England on which the current Treasury Bill rate of interest was to be paid. Their Euro-dollar operations were to be unaffected "except to the extent that [foreign] currency deposits may have been 'switched' into employment in sterling assets". 8 *Quarterly Bulletin* 167 (1968).

In May 1968 the Bank of England set a lending limit of 104% of the November 1967 total outstanding for all banks. Early in 1969, in an effort to restrict credit even further, a lending ceiling was set at 98% of that figure. When the clearing banks' figures made it apparent that they were not performing as requested, the Bank of England decided to halve the interest rate paid on the clearers' Special Deposits, which represented 2% of their total sterling deposits at that time. See Bank of England, *Press Announcement* dated May 31, 1969, 9 *Id*. 145 (1969). In April 1970 the credit controls were relaxed to the extent that the clearers and Scottish banks were asked over the next twelve months to stay within 105% of their mid-March 1970 loans outstanding. For the other types of banks, whose performance had been more acceptable in terms of staying within the limit, the figure was set at 107%. The clearers' Special Deposits were raised to 2$1/2$% but the normal Treasury bill rate of interest payable on these funds was restored. In July 1970 the clearing banks were reminded to toe the line. *Cf*. 10 *Id*. 327 (1970); but matters progressed

c. *Switzerland*

In examining the Swiss law governing lending operations during the U.S. branch banks' second Euro-dollar operating phase, it is appropriate to take account of the lending pattern of Swiss banks generally.

The Federal Banking Law provides that banks in Switzerland must maintain certain prescribed capital and liquidity ratios.[187] The ratios are set in a Regulation issued by the Federal Council, which also designates the types of assets and liabilities which qualify for or are subject to the various percentages.[188] These solvency requirements apply to all banks operating in Switzerland, including specifically the Swiss branches of foreign banks.[189]

By and large, banks in Switzerland had not developed the practice of longer-term lending by mid-1963. One reason for this lay in the 27% withholding tax mentioned earlier[190] and a 3% stamp duty,[191] both of which until the end of 1966 were levied on certain types of transactions, including commercial loans exceeding SF 30,000 (approx. $7,500) if they extended for longer than two years. This caused borrowers to obtain credit for an undefined period while retaining the right to repay the loan at any time. It was only after January 1, 1967 that the coupon tax was abolished and the withholding tax (the rate of which was raised to 30%) made applicable to certain types of earnings, but not including interest on commercial loans.[192]

There are more basic reasons, however, underlying the tendency for

---

such that in October 1970 the Bank of England raised the clearers' Special Deposits to 3^1/$_2$% and those of the Scottish banks to 1¾%.

None of the above changes have affected the U.S. branch banks' Euro-dollar operations directly. It is noteworthy, however, that in October 1968 permission was withdrawn from banks generally for the financing of non-sterling area transactions in sterling, a move reminiscent of that in 1957.

See I.M.F., *(Twentieth) Exchange Restrictions,* 1969, pp. 493-94. Euro-dollar financing was not curtailed by this move. In fact, eligible borrowers unable to finance in sterling have turned to Euro-dollars, as was the case in the late 1950's at the dawning of the Euro-dollar market. As noted earlier, the Bank of England instituted a new credit control mechanism in September 1971 when all banks were made subject to reserve requirements and calls for Special Deposits. See Bank of England, 11 *Quarterly Bulletin* 189-93 (1971).

187. Switzerland, Federal Banking Law of 1934, as amended, art. 4. This provision of the Law does not apply to private banks which do not publicly seek deposits.

188. Federal Council Regulation of August 31, 1961, arts. 9-17.

189. Federal Banking Law of 1934, as amended, art. 2.

190. Federal Anticipatory Tax Order of September 1, 1943, art. 11 (1) (c). See p. 215, note 55.

191. Federal Tax Stamp Act, art. 5.

192. I.M.F. *(Eighteenth) Exchange Restrictions,* 1967, p. 576.

248

very short-term lending by banks in Switzerland. One of these has certainly been the absence of generally available credit risk information.[193] More fundamental still is the public orientation toward thrift, already noted in Chapter Two, which is reflected in a relatively high degree of liquidity among Swiss firms generally. Dividend policies tend to be conservative, permitting the accumulation of reserves for self-financing many operations, quite apart from cash flow techniques that many firms in Switzerland have either mistrusted or ignored. It is noteworthy, then, that by mid-1963 longer-term commercial lending was not a well developed practice locally, meaning that the indigenous borrowers and lenders in the host country banking sector had neither the incentive nor the expertise to follow the increasing tendency toward longer-term financing in the Euro-dollar sector.

It is appropriate to examine, then, how the existence of foreign borrowers affected this. Although as we found earlier in the present Chapter Switzerland has not maintained exchange controls for lack of foreign reserves, a distinction is made between lending to residents and to non-residents similar to that made between taking residents' and non-residents' deposits. In Chapter Two it was noted that all banks in Switzerland, including those (mostly private) banks which do not solicit publicly for deposits, must notify the central bank before lending abroad if the amount is SF 10 million (approx. $2.5 million) or more.[194] There have also been restrictions on lending to non-residents for certain specified purposes, a credit control measure forming part of the anti-inflationary program of the 1960's. For instance, during certain periods banks in Switzerland have not been able to lend to non-residents seeking to finance purchases of Swiss real estate or securities. Although technically a credit control device, these restrictions tend to operate in this context very much like exchange control measures.

Another set of credit controls was also in force in Switzerland during the U.S. branch banks' second Euro-dollar operating phase. In 1962 a gentlemen's agreement between the banks and the central bank checked the expansion of credit, which had risen greatly in 1960 and 1961. The agreement provided that new loans could be extended as a percentage of the increase in 1960 and 1961, 108% for mortgage loans and 82% for

---

193. *Cf.*, Sayers and Linder, "Switzerland", *in* R. S. Sayers (ed.), *Banking in Western Europe*, p. 56, note 119, at p. 185. This is not to suggest that credit information cannot be obtained. There is a consumer-credit information clearing-house in Zurich run by a number of banks. Also, it has been reported that since 1971 a joint reporting system for foreign "bad debts" has been maintained by four of the "big banks" whereby debtors are not identified but the amounts are classified by country. Still, such efforts fall far short of the French or U.S. systems.

194. Federal Banking Law of 1934, art. 8.

other types of advances.[195] After renewal in 1963 this gentlemen's agreement became law in June 1964.[196] From January 1, 1967 the 1964 measure was replaced by a Circular Letter from the Swiss National Bank asking banks during 1967 not to exceed their base loans outstanding figure as of December 31, 1966 by more than 7%.[197] These ceilings have not applied to loans to non-residents or to residents who certify that the funds will be used abroad and who ask the lending bank to transfer them outside Switzerland.

There has been a fairly wide spread between the local Swiss debtor and creditor rates and the lending and deposit rates prevailing in the Euro-dollar market. Swiss banks have been committed to lending host currency locally at a margin of only slightly over 1% above the local deposit rates. One of the reported points of friction between Swiss banks and some foreign-controlled banks in Switzerland has been the possibility of taking Swiss francs locally for deposit at, say 4½% and then by swaps placing them at, say 7% or higher in dollar deposits in London.[198] Another potential problem arose when some borrowers sought Swiss francs at the local (lower) rate so that they could swap or switch into dollars for placement abroad, or simply place Swiss francs in Euro-Swiss franc deposits outside the host country.[199]

It is now appropriate to examine dollar lending in Switzerland during the period from mid-1963 through 1967. Earlier in this Chapter we saw that banks in Switzerland carry dollar working balances for some of their customers and for other banks, and that one can place dollars in London

195. Bank for International Settlements, *Eight European Central Banks,* p. 61, note 139, at p. 300.

196. Switzerland, Federal Council, Order of June 1, 1964, *Recueil officiel suisse* 1964, p. 517. See also *Id.,* pp. 518-21. This order was based on an earlier Federal Assembly Order giving the Federal Council the power to render obligatory any informal agreements concerning the control of credit. Federal Assembly, Order of March 13, 1964, *Id.,* pp. 209-12.

197. See Journal de Genève, December 28, 1966, p. 2, col. 1. Subsequent developments have been as follows: In September 1969 the expansion of credit was limited (by the gentlemen's agreement which was substituted for the "Instrumentarium" which had been proposed for the central bank—see p. 83, note 234) to 109% of the total amount outstanding as of August 31, 1969. On October 29, 1969 the base date was moved back from August 31 to July 31, 1969. On January 21, 1970 the credit expansion figure was lowered to 107.65% of the (July 31, 1969) base date figure, at which it currently stands. See Erbe, p. 83, note 234. The limitation was to remain in force at least through July 1972.

198. See 221 (6431) *The Economist,* Banking Supplement, p. xxx (November 26, 1966).

199. See p. 217, note 63. Since early in 1969 some banks in Switzerland have shown a growing preference for placing any spare funds themselves in the London market at the higher yields available, rather than lending to borrowers who can themselves place funds there. See p. 217, note 64.

250

through the fiduciary placement accounts, the earnings on which are not subject to the Swiss federal withholding tax. Even though banks in Switzerland profess to control large amounts of the Euro-dollars on deposit,[200] funds deposited in Swiss banks themselves in demand or relatively short-term time deposit accounts cannot provide the basis for effective longer-term lending of Euro-dollars.

On the other hand, very short-term dollar lending has become an important activity of banks in Switzerland, especially to other banks there and abroad, whose creditworthiness is already known or can be readily verified. In a country where the principal indigenous borrowers self-finance many of their operations, and where a large portion of the dollars controlled by indigenous banks and locally established foreign branch banks are held on a current or relatively short-term basis, it has made good sense to advance very short-term funds in this fashion. The margin of profits to be made is small; but the volume has been large and the costs relatively low. Moreover, this fits well within the cautious approach followed by most Swiss bankers.

It is not surprising, then, that a call money market in dollars has developed in Switzerland[201] and that the international money market or Euro-dollar market in particular has lain behind this development. The presence of U.S. branch banks operating in Switzerland, using the highly efficient Euro-dollar brokerage facilities in Geneva, Lausanne, and Zurich, has been especially significant in this latter respect. In Chapter Three we saw that the lack of an adequate host currency deposit base means that U.S. branch banks tend always to be in the local money market. In the Swiss case, where the absence of exchange controls as normally conceived has removed the distinction between host and most other currencies, the U.S. branch banks have nearly always been ready takers of dollars, which can usually be placed in London at sister branches or in any event in the head office bank.

Earlier, the absence of a formal money market structure in Switzerland tended to dissipate many of the advantages of a fully convertible host currency. In fact, although foreign banks have regularly borrowed dollars from Swiss banks, as noted above, not many foreign non-bank borrowers have thus been accommodated. Those that have borrowed dollars from banks in Switzerland have usually been accommodated through the intermediary of a foreign bank. The presence of a locally established foreign—and especially U.S.—branch bank has meant that banks in Switzerland with temporarily excess dollar funds have been able to lend them at very short-term, in fact as call money, to a local (albeit foreign-con-

200. See p. 217, note 62.
201. *Cf.* Bär, p. 79, note 212, at p. 77.

trolled) bank and thus maintain the fiction of keeping their funds in the indigenous market. Actually, most of these funds have been placed abroad at once, subject to immediate recall, so to speak.

If the U.S. branch banks in Switzerland could not participate as actively in the steadily growing tendency toward longer-term lending and borrowing of Euro-dollars generally, they were nevertheless not isolated completely from it during the second Euro-dollar operating phase. Also, since the removal of federal coupon and withholding taxes from commercial bank loans in 1967, it has been possible to arrange genuine longer-term financing for foreign and Swiss borrowers in an indigenous banking sector rendered more flexible in this respect.[202]

B. *Lending Techniques in the Second Euro-dollar Operating Phase*

By early 1967 Euro-dollar advances of up to eighteen months were occurring[203] and a trend to even longer-term maturities was evident. Having examined the U.S. and host country laws that affected the second phase Euro-dollar operations of the U.S. branch banks, it is now in order to analyse several of the techniques which they have used to provide longer-term Euro-dollar credits to their customers while attempting to satisfy the growing short-term credit needs of their head office banks in the United States.

1. *Euro-dollar Lending Consortia*

In Chapter Four it was noted that each bank or branch bank in the Euro-dollar market sets a limit on the amount of outstanding advances that it will extend to any single bank or non-bank borrower. As end-user borrowers' needs for longer-term Euro-dollar credits increased after mid-1963 the lending banks became increasingly interested in such limits because the end-users are almost always anonymous except to the last bank at the end of the inter-bank lending chain.

Thus, a bank may be able to limit the amounts outstanding to each of

202. In addition to the 1971 amendment to the (1934) Federal Banking Law, since the end of 1967 there have been other pertinent changes in the Swiss law affecting the operations of U.S. branch banks. Of particular importance, on January 18, 1968 the Federal Banking Commission revised the (1936) Ordinance covering Swiss branches of banks chartered abroad. See p. 23, note 8. Two important features of the new rules are: (1) capital allocated to a Swiss bank must be invested in Switzerland, and (2) any liabilities of a Swiss branch to the head office bank are not counted as liabilities whereas amounts due the Swiss branch from the head office must be matched by assets held in Switzerland.

203. See Altman, "What Does it Really Mean? Euro-Dollars", p. 161, note 23, at p. 11.

several bank borrowers in the inter-bank market, whereas in fact the latter themselves might be extending credit to the same or related end-users. The risk to the first bank is allayed to the extent that its debtors are fellow participants in the inter-bank market. This could prove to be of little comfort, however, in the event of a massive inability to pay on the part of one or several large end-user borrowers. Understandably the banks and branch banks have been interested in protecting themselves from being caught in a turmoil of conflicting claims against assets that are rapidly disappearing or have vanished altogether.[204]

One protective method has been to set up an *ad hoc* consortium to accommodate a large end-user borrower. Each participating bank provides an amount of the total advance that corresponds to its own limit to the end-user borrower in question. Also, it attempts to fit the participation into the cadence of maturities in its own Euro-dollar "book" so as to keep this as nearly in phase as possible.

Such consortia for large loans have been known in the host country banking sectors as well as in the United States. The new element in the U.S. branch banks' second Euro-dollar operating phase was that they were particularly free to enter such consortia. In fact, they were even encouraged implicitly to do so when the borrower was an overseas subsidiary of an American corporation. The U.S. balance of payments Guidelines for Banks served as a stimulant for direct action on the part of the U.S. branch banks in dealing with the foreign borrowers, rather than having the loan stem from the head office bank in the United States. Concomitant with the Guidelines was a statutory anti-trust law exemption that had been enacted at the request of the U.S. President in February 1965[205] to "make possible the cooperation of American banks" in support of the balance of payments program.[206] Accordingly the U.S. branch banks were free to pool their efforts with local bankers and with other U.S. branch banks.

2. *Euro-dollar Term Loans*

A natural development in the lengthening of the maturities in the Euro-dollar market has been the Euro-dollar term loan. Long familiar with term loans, U.S.-trained bankers have had little difficulty in adapting to the lengthening maturities in the new international money market. U.S.

204. The danger has not been purely theoretical, as the highly publicized "vegetable oil scandal" of 1963 proved. See Bank of England, 4 *Quarterly Bulletin* 7 (1964).
205. In his balance of payments message to the Congress. See p. 230, note 114.
206. The anti-trust law exemption is contained in Pub. Law 89-175; 31 U.S.C. § 932 (c).

corporate subsidiaries, too, have found that Euro-dollar term loans fit well within the overall financial scheme of their companies' operations.

During their second Euro-dollar operating phase the U.S. branch banks began making term loans in Euro-dollars, with maturities running for periods from three to five years, with interest rates fixed in advance, sometimes with allowance for a revision of the rate every 180 days if necessary.[207] In the latter case the borrower normally has paid a slightly lower interest rate initially than in the former, since with periodically revised rates the lending banks can more easily employ short-term deposits to make the periodic advances to the term loan customer. Of course, in the term loan where rates are not subject to periodic revision, the borrower has an assurance of the exact interest charges that will have to be paid over the life of the loan, and can plan accordingly.

3. *Revolving Euro-dollar Credits*

Perhaps the most interesting developments in the longer-term Euro-dollar market has been the establishing of Euro-dollar credit lines. Known as revolving credits, the first of this type was a $35 million Euro-dollar line granted to a U.S. corporate subsidiary in the spring of 1966,[208] which was followed several months later by a reported $19.2 million line accorded to another large U.S. corporate subsidiary overseas.[209] In each instance, the lines were to have been for approximately four years during which the borrowing corporation could draw 90-day Euro-dollar advances at interest rates determined in accordance with a pre-set formula which took into account prevailing Euro-dollar rates at the time of any drawing. A commitment fee, e.g., ½% on the $35 million revolving Euro-dollar credit mentioned above, was paid on the unused credit during the duration of the line. Eventually, lines of up to $50 million were reported.

Although the revolving Euro-dollar credits are not, strictly speaking, longer-term advances, they assure borrowers that funds will definitely be made available for their operations outside the United States. One major U.S. commercial bank has offered eligible borrowers an alternative arrangement whereby a revolving Euro-dollar credit[210] is established, under

207. In 1971 several New York City banks instituted a fluctuating prime rate calculated to rise and fall with money market rates. Note the distinction.

208. In May 1966 I.B.M. World Trade Corporation was reported to have arranged a $35 million Euro-dollar credit line with a group of fourteen branches or affiliates of U.S. commercial banks. See N.Y. Times, May 25, 1966, p. 62, col. 1 (late city edition).

209. Chas. Phyzer & Co., Inc., from a consortium of sixteen banks. See N.Y. Times, November 14, 1966, p. 65, col. 2 (late city edition).

210. Referred to as an "umbrella host currency/Euro-dollar revolving credit".

which the borrower can have the sequential aspect of the line eliminated, transforming the credit into a host currency term loan for up to four years with a predetermined interest rate.

4. Advances to U.S. Head Office Banks

The tightness of money in the United States during and after the second Euro-dollar phase has meant that banks there have had to compete vigorously with each other and with non-bank lenders for scarce short-term funds. Since 1921 the so-called Federal Funds market had become a medium in which banks not wishing to avail themselves of official rediscount facilities could borrow other banks' temporarily unneeded excess reserves for short periods, usually overnight or over a weekend.[211] U.S. commercial banks with London branches soon found, however, that the Euro-dollar deposits at these branches were often a cheaper source of very short-term money than either the Federal Funds market[212] or the rediscount facilities[213] of the Federal Reserve for two reasons.

First, the dollars deposited in a London branch bank did not (until 1969) come under the compulsory reserve requirement related to domestic deposits. Second, Federal Deposit Insurance requirements do not apply to such balances,[214] meaning that insurance charges (one-twelfth of 1% p.a.) are not incurred.[215]

The overnight advance technique is simple. No actual transfer of funds is required, since the ultimate deposits are in the head office bank in any case. The London branch bank must merely forego lending the Euro-dollars onward to another bank or branch bank in the Euro-dollar market or to an end-user of Euro-dollars, and notifies the head office bank that the funds are available to it.

At first the major U.S. commercial banks with London branches varied considerably in their use of the overnight Euro-dollar facilities. Some banks employed them only in periods of extremely tight money to make

211. See Federal Reserve Bank of Boston, *The Federal Funds Market*, by Parker B. Willis, Boston, 1964.
212. An interesting appraisal of this interrelationship is Alfredo Vernucci, "The Impact of the U.S.A. Federal Funds Market on the International Exchange Market", Banca Nazionale del Lavoro, 19 *Quarterly Review* 346-61 (1966).
213. It was reported that on September 1, 1967 the Board of Governors of the Federal Reserve System wrote a letter to member banks requesting that they "voluntarily limit their liquidation of marketable securities and brake their rate of expansion in business loans" and promising that "banks cooperating in this attempt... could expect discount accommodation for longer periods than would be needed ordinarily". First National City Bank, *Monthly Economic Letter*, November 1967, p. 126.
214. See p. 121, note 102.
215. 12 U.S.C. § 1817 (b) (1). See also § 1817 (a) (1957 edition).

up for temporary gaps as they occurred, while others regularly relied on the Euro-dollars on deposit at their London branches as an alternative source of lendable funds. By mid-1966 when interest rates were reaching what proved to be a temporary peak most of the banks were taking constant advantage of this technique. By then wide use was being made of refinements such as the three-day count for Friday balances:

> "An important use of the Euro-dollar market as a tool of short-term reserve management is for the financing of weekend reserve positions. In fact, most of the banks with [foreign] branches employ overnight deposits each Thursday as a partial substitute for Federal funds purchases on Friday. Because of New York check-clearing practices, overnight borrowing in the Euro-dollar market value-Thursday for repayment on Friday can serve as bank reserves for three days—from Friday through Sunday. Euro-dollar transactions are generally settled through checks on New York banks. Unlike Federal funds transactions, which are recorded in Federal Reserve accounts immediately, these checks must pass through the New York Clearing House, and it is not until the following business day that they become balances in the Federal Reserve accounts of member banks. Thus, a check drawn on bank Y and deposited on Friday in bank B in repayment of a Euro-dollar deposit does not draw down A's reserves until Monday; the same applies if the check is deposited on the day before a holiday."[216]

The U.S. branch banks' advances to their head offices take on added significance in light of the fact that Euro-dollar transactions are normally unsecured. Here we have a situation where the "lender" steering the Euro-dollar deposit out of the interbank market is dealing with itself, so to speak. In this sense the advance is hardly unsecured, if it can even be considered a loan at all. As for the security—if any—provided by the end-user of the funds, this would depend upon the identity of the borrower (from the U.S. head office bank) and upon the type of advance. This factor has unquestionably given an intrinsic advantage to the U.S. branch banks in their Euro-dollar operations.

By taking Euro-dollar deposits and transferring them to accounts for the use of the head office banks in the United States, the U.S. branch banks were officially reported to have accounted for almost all of the $1.3 billion increase in the U.S. short-term liabilities to banks abroad for the twelve month period ending July 1966.[217] By the end of 1967 U.S. commercial banks' liabilities to their foreign branches had risen to $4.2 bil-

---

216. Federal Reserve Bank of New York, 50 *Monthly Review,* 133-34 (1968). A similar phenomenon was reflected in the observation that "dollars sold against sterling for value Friday are not effectively debited in New York until Monday, although the sterling is received on Friday. Thus those selling dollars on Wednesday will have the use of both sterling and dollars over the weekend". Bank of England, 5 *Quarterly Bulletin* 106-107 (1965).

217. 52 Federal *Reserve Bulletin* 1284 (1966).

lion;[218] and the Euro-dollar portion of the Euro-currency market had grown to about $16 billion.[219]

IV. ROLE OF THE U.S. BRANCH BANKS

Having examined the legal framework within which the U.S. branch banks in France, Great Britain, and Switzerland took and placed Euro-dollar deposits during the second phase of their operations in that medium, we are now in a position to analyse their role in a changing Euro-dollar market.

A. *Changing Nature of the Euro-dollar Market*

It is evident that the Euro-dollar market was evolving during the period from mid-1963 through the end of 1967. New techniques and refinements were being developed; and new competitors were entering the field. Both qualitative and quantitative changes were occurring. We shall first examine the impact of the changing qualitative nature of the market.

1. *Impact of the Changing Qualitative Nature of the Market*

In the emergence of an international money market there were new elements relevant to the operations of the U.S. branch banks and their role in that market. These were the fact that maturities were lengthening generally, that odd-dated maturities and lower denominations were being introduced and accommodated in the secondary market for London dollar c.d.'s, the interrelationship between the Euro-dollar and Eurobond markets, and the fungibility of Euro-dollars and dollars in general.

a. *Lengthening Maturities Generally*

Commercial bank lending is normally considered to be short-term in nature, based largely upon funds to which commercial banks have temporary access. Providing short-term, self-liquidating credit in the Euro-dollar market would have occasioned a change of medium without any

---

218. 57 *Id.* A 86 (February 1971). In mid-October 1969 this figure peaked out at $15.4 billion. Federal Reserve Bank of New York, 52 *Monthly Review* 249-50 (1970).

219. Bank for International Settlements, *Thirty-eighth Annual Report*, Basle, 1968, p. 154. Other Euro-currencies amounted to an additional $3 billion. *Ibid.* As of the end of 1970 it was estimated that Euro-dollars amounted to about $46 billion and other Euro-currencies about $11 billion. *Id., Forty-first Annual Report*, Basle, 1971, p. 157.

essential modification in the role of the institution vis à vis other participants in the market, borrowers and lenders alike.

Lengthening maturities in the Euro-dollar market, however, caused concern among some critics of an increasing tendency towards "borrowing short and lending long". In fact, rather than "borrowing short and lending long", many participants in the Euro-dollar market were borrowing short—but also somewhat longer than previously, in order to lend short—and also somewhat longer than had earlier been their practice. Nonetheless, traditional caution sometimes seemed foresworn in favor of practices that might have been considered cavalier. How, it was asked, could responsible institutions base their three to five year advances or guarantees of credit on deposits that could be whisked away in one year, or 180 days, or 90 days, or less?

Proponents of the longer-term operations in the Euro-dollar market countered these warnings by pointing out that commercial lenders always extend credit for terms longer than those for which the mass of their deposits can be retained. Furthermore, it was argued, deposit-taking institutions can rely on a hard core of "lazy" deposits that remain on deposit in customers' working balances regardless of their being technically payable on demand.[220] As there is no official lender-of-last-resort in the Euro-dollar market, however, this argument must be qualified to the extent that central banks would be unwilling or unable to prevent serious market distortion. In light of the furious Euro-dollar trading in the spring of 1971 and the resulting proposals for harmonizing central banks' own use of the market, it may well be that a lender-of-last-resort would step in after all—officially or otherwise, alone or in concert. Of course, there might well be differences of opinion as to when one had arrived at the last resort.

U.S. branch banks[221] were largely making very short-term loans to their head office banks in the United States. Thus they knew the identity of the

220. When discussing the current accounts of the London clearing banks, the Radcliffe Committee stated the following: "Looking at these current account deposits from the point of view of the banks themselves, the quality traditionally stressed by bankers is their repayability on demand, from which an inference commonly drawn is that the banker should be especially cautious in his 'use' of these deposits. This theoretical mobility of the current account deposit has at times been invoked in support of the practice of making overdrafts formally repayable on demand and of the policy of confining bank lending to highly liquid purposes. This consideration has, no doubt, great force when banks are small and insecure, but firmly established banks as large as the present English banks can, we think, safely regard their demand liabilities in total as containing a hard core of permanent resources." (Radcliffe) Committee, *Report,* Cmnd. 827, p. 43, par. 130.

221. By December 1966 the rate for 3 months Euro-dollar deposits reached 7⅛%, an extremely high figure, even taking into account the fact that year-end "window dressing" operations always tend to raise the figure. It should be noted that the 3 month rate nearly reached 13% in the summer of 1969.

end-user as far as the Euro-dollar market was concerned, and usually had a far better knowledge of the ultimate use to which the funds were put. Moreover, for them there was no exchange risk. Furthermore they were relatively more liquid than most Euro-dollar lenders in that they had nearly immediate access to dollars on deposit in these head office banks.[222] Sudden calls by Euro-dollar depositors for their funds could certainly have worked hardships on the U.S. branch and head office banks; but is is likely that funds would have been made available immediately, if necessary with indirect help from the U.S. government.

Such official assistance might have been necessary either because a bank's overall liquidity position was not sufficient or because under the Guidelines it could not freely channel additional funds to a branch bank abroad. It is unlikely, however, that the U.S. monetary authorities would allow a major U.S. commercial bank to renege on a Euro-dollar deposit debt, an act that would seriously disrupt a market that works fundamentally in favor of the United States. In any analysis of the Euro-dollar market itself or of the role played by any participating institution, it must be kept in mind that the very existence of Euro-dollars is evidence of foreign-held U.S. dollars that are not being presented at the U.S. Treasury for conversion into gold or foreign exchange from official reserves.[223]

b. *Odd-dated Maturities and Lower Denominations in the London Dollar Negotiable C.D. Secondary Market*

The longer-term deposits helped to smoothen out some of the otherwise more erratic swings in the flow of funds in the market. Odd-dated maturities in the secondary market for London dollar negotiable c.d.'s contributed in this respect, too. In addition, the lower denomination deposits accommodated through the c.d.'s as well as the willingness of some interbank operators to deal in smaller round lots (as low as $100,000 in some instances)[224] meant that more individual decisions directly affected the Euro-dollar market. Theretofore, a moderate amount did not enter the market until it had been combined with other funds to bring the total up to the minimum round lot sum. Now smaller companies and many indi-

---

222. Authoritative spokesmen for several U.S. branch banks reported that prior to the Guidelines for Banks they had standing instructions to draw such funds immediately if needed to cover Euro-dollar deposits. It was their understanding that after the Guidelines went into effect there would be no less willingness on the part of the head offices to augment the branch banks' liquidity in an emergency.

223. *Cf.* Pierre Biacabe, "Le marché international du dollar en Europe", 80 [French] *Revue d'Economie Politique* 548-69 (1970), who notes that "... du point de vue des Etats-Unis ... ces dépôts d'euro-dollars constituent la meilleure protection de leur stock d'or". *Id.*, at p. 565.

224. Paul Einzig, *The Euro-dollar System: Practice and Theory of International Interest Rates*, 3d edition, London, 1967, p. 24.

viduals could decide for themselves whether to place such a sum in the Euro-dollar stream as an alternative to other short- or medium-term placement possibilities.

c. *Interrelationship between Euro-dollars and Eurobonds*

In 1963 a new aspect was given to a sector of the international long-term capital market which has come to be called the "Eurobond" market.[225] Eurobonds are obligations issued in monetary units other than the national currency of the place of issue. For example, a U.S. dollar obligation issued in Switzerland by a Swiss-, French-, or U.S.-controlled borrower would properly be called a Eurobond, whereas a Swiss franc obligation issued there by any of these would not.[226]

Eurobonds are sometimes referred to as "Euro-dollar bonds" although this designation has some misleading characteristics.[227] Undeniably, how-

225. See David Williams, "Foreign Currency Issues on European Security Markets", International Monetary Fund, 14 *Staff Papers* 47 (1967).

226. Some Eurobonds are also issued in "European Units of Accounts". This imaginary unit is composed of 17 currencies, designed to make it as stable as the most stable among them. The unit is calculated to make it equivalent to the U.S. dollar at the date of issue, but offers some protection against devaluation in that the gold value of the unit is to be reduced only to the extent of the devaluation of the currency which has dropped the least with respect to gold. In November 1970 the European Coal and Steel Community made the first issue in "European Monetary Units" which are similar (covering the six member currencies, EMU 1 = $1) but more significant in that the official sanction of the European Communities is behind the transaction. This EMU 50 million public offering issued at 8% and for 15 years was followed in December 1970 by an EMU 10 million private placement at 7.75% and for 10 years by Eurofima. In both instances bondholders can select the member currency in which they wish each interest payment to be made. As this allows them to take advantage of any revaluations it is likely that the international monetary disruptions in the spring of 1971 will considerably dampen any official enthusiasm for future loans containing this feature. For a recent appraisal of certain legal aspects of the subject generally, see Pierre A. Lalive, "Dépréciation monétaire et contrats en droit international privé" *in XIe Journée juridique, Faculté de droit (1971)*, Geneva, Georg, 1972.

227. Some references to Eurobonds as "Euro-dollar bonds" appear to have been made on the supposition that these bonds are only purchased with Euro-dollars. In practice Eurobonds are usually purchased with Euro-dollars: buyers draw on dollar deposits located in banks outside the United States, or they borrow in the Euro-dollar market to finance the purchase. Prior to the U.S. balance of payments measures, however, Eurobonds could have been acquired freely by U.S. citizens and residents drawing dollars from accounts inside or outside the United States. Since the U.S. balance of payments program took effect, a "U.S. person" has been required to pay the Interest Equalization Tax. The purchase, notwithstanding, would still be feasible. Moreover, no U.S. law prevents non-"U.S. persons" from purchasing dollar-denominated Eurobonds or others by drawing dollars from bank accounts in the United States, although the U.S. banks would now be required to report outward movements exceeding $5,000. See p. 78, note 21 and p. 181, note 119.

260

ever, there is a link between the Euro-dollar and Eurobond markets. Eurobond issuers frequently "garage" excess dollar borrowings in short-term Euro-dollar deposits to await their expected expenditure. Underwriters of Eurobond issues sometimes use borrowed Euro-dollars to help nurse along a slowly moving issue; and Eurobond traders often obtain short-term credit for acquiring Eurobonds by borrowing in the Euro-dollar market.

This double link became more important after mid-1963 as rising interest rates caused corporate borrowers to look increasingly to longer-term commercial bank loans. The U.S. branch banks, especially by means of Euro-dollar term loans and Euro-dollar credit lines, were able to attract to the longer end of the Euro-dollar market corporate borrowers that otherwise would have sought recourse in the shorter end of the Eurobond market, especially after the U.S. corporate guidelines made it imperative that the U.S.-controlled borrowers seek funds outside the New York City capital market. It is difficult to consider the longer-term Euro-dollar market as a "money" market when borrowers have been using it frequently to satisfy some of their fixed capital requirements. Nonetheless, Euro-dollar term loans, the larger ones handled via consortia, have effectively kept some borrowing in the Euro-dollar market and out of the Eurobond market.

During the second Euro-dollar operating phase the Euro-dollar-Eurobond link had added significance for those major U.S. commercial banks for which a London "window" for taking Euro-dollar deposits was not enough. They had developed or were developing overseas networks of branch banks, banking subsidiaries, affiliated banks, and representative offices in varying combinations. Also, some of them had Edge Act or agreement subsidiaries or affiliated banks that participated in Eurobond underwriting syndicates. The U.S. branch banks themselves have been prohibited by U.S. federal banking law from dealing in securities other than obligations of the national government of the host country,[228] a provision that carries into the overseas operation of U.S. commercial banks the same strict division between commercial and investment banking that exists in the United States.[229] The combination of the Edge Act or agreement subsidiary (for underwriting) coupled with the branch bank (for short- and medium-term financing) has meant, however, that these banks have been able to offer a nearly complete range of loan and deposit services overseas to eligible clients.[230] For these banks, multinational opera-

228. (Federal Reserve) Regulation M, 12 C.F.R. § 213.3 (b)(4) as added by 28 Fed. Reg. 8361, August 15, 1963.
229. United States, Banking Act of June 16, 1933, chap. 89, §§ 20 and 21, 48 Stat. 188 and 189, as amended; 12 U.S.C. §§ 377-78.
230. Some of the major U.S. banks have evolved new working techniques because

tions have implied the harmonious interplay of the facilities offered by the various types of overseas units, with correspondents called in if needed.

Being able to perform truly multinational banking operations depends upon being alert to—and capable of servicing—corporate borrowers' actual and potential needs for short- and longer-term credit as well as finding or providing profitable methods for placing temporarily excess liquidity. It is essential in multi-national banking to be capable of offering a wide range of services (in a variety of currencies) sought by large corporate customers operating in many countries and frequently dealing in a great number of products or services.

d. *Fungibility of Euro-dollars with Dollars Generally*

In the earlier stages of the Euro-dollar market there was room for serious discussion as to whether and how Euro-dollars were intrinsically different from U.S. dollars. Before there came to be general agreement on what a Euro-dollar was—or was not—it was difficult to claim that they were fungible with other dollars.

It became clear, however, that the dollars on deposit in an overseas branch of a U.S. bank, or in any bank located outside the United States, could be used to buttress the deposits of banks in the United States. When overnight and weekend advances are made to head office banks in the United States, the origin of the deposits makes little real difference. For instance, the credit needs of a domestic U.S. borrower can be met by a U.S. commercial bank by drawing temporarily on dollars deposited in an overseas branch bank, if it maintains one, or in a foreign bank which is willing to advance the funds to the bank in the United States.[231] The original depositor of those Euro-dollars might even be a firm or individual in the same U.S. city as the borrower.[232]

---

of other facets of U.S. federal law. For instance, Morgan Guaranty Trust Co.'s Paris subsidiary Morgan et Cie S.A. was reported to have been hindered in its underwriting operations because the Federal Trust Indenture Act of 1939 prevented it from underwriting issues of corporations for which the head office bank acted as trustee. This was said to have been one factor leading to the creation of Morgan & Cie Internationale S.A. in conjunction with Morgan Stanley & Co., the investment house. See N.Y. Times, December 22, 1966, p. 59, col. 4 (late city edition).

231. This is the case even if a reserve requirement exists. Since 1969 there has in fact been a marginal reserve requirement. See p. 273.

232. Prior to the U.S. balance of payments measures there was nothing to prevent U.S. resident individuals or firms from depositing funds in banks overseas, including U.S. branch banks. It appears that after the Guidelines went into effect in 1965 some of the U.S. branch banks abroad were reluctant to accept deposits stemming from within the United States, preferring that these funds be deposited in the head office bank or in a branch in the United States. It would be difficult, however, to measure the effectiveness of this. Moreover, a U.S. resident individual or

This fungibility, as seen from the viewpoint of the head office U.S. commercial bank, has proved to be a remarkable advantage to those U.S. banks with branches overseas taking dollars on deposit, just as it proved eventually to be a problem for U.S. (and other) monetary authorities bent on controlling the amount of credit available in an inflationary period.

2. Impact of New Competition

a. Larger and More Versatile Indigenous Banks

Very few, if any, of the major indigenous banks in the host countries remained outside the Euro-dollar market, directly or indirectly, by the mid-1960's. Although London had definitely become the center of this market, banks in Paris and in the Swiss banking centers were dealing in greater or lesser degrees in Euro-dollars, on behalf of their eligible customers and/or for the banks' own accounts. The presence of the U.S. branch banks, if it had not caused consternation earlier, could not now be overlooked in light of the vigorous nature of the U.S. branch banks' participation in the Euro-dollar market. Partially in response, there have occurred in the host country banking sectors two types of changes, those of size and composition, and those of nature or function.

As for the changes of size and composition, larger borrowers' ever increasing demands on the Euro-dollar market have placed the smaller and medium-sized indigenous banks at a disadvantage. The leading indigenous banks have been larger than the largest foreign branch banks present, to be sure; but it is striking to note on closer inspection that in

---

corporation could have deposited the funds in a non-U.S. bank overseas, which then might have redeposited them in a U.S. branch bank, or advanced them to the U.S. bank making the loan. It has been reported that in 1965 the Euro-dollar deposits of U.S. residents declined by $0.2 billion, but rose by $1 billion in 1966 and 1967. Bank for International Settlements, *Thirty-ninth Annual Report*, Basle, 1969, pp. 150-51. As the spread between Euro-dollar and domestic U.S. interest rates paid on deposits became even wider the outflow of dollars from the United States into deposits overseas continued and was estimated at $1.5 billion in 1968. *Id., Fortieth Annual Report*, Basle, 1970, p. 157. This prompted the Board of Governors of the Federal Reserve System to circulate a letter in June 1969 to all member banks with foreign branches, calling attention to the restrictive monetary policy in effect and reiterating the policy of the Federal Reserve System of discouraging U.S. residents from depositing funds at U.S. branch banks abroad unless needed for a definite purpose outside the United States. This meant that U.S. commercial banks were to use their branches overseas for their own international business, but neither for shifting deposits from their domestic branches or head offices nor for diverting funds that would otherwise be deposited there. This approach was strikingly similar to some examples of moral suasion treated elsewhere in this study. The outflow in 1969 was estimated at $0.6 billion. Bank for International Settlements, *Fortieth Annual Report, supra*.

their Euro-dollar deposit-loan structure, the well established U.S. branch banks compared favorably with all but the largest local institutions. One observer estimated that the U.S. branch banks did about one-third of the Euro-dollar financing in the City of London.[233] It is evident that some of the U.S. branch banks have not only come to be in a position to offer stiff competition, but competition on a large scale as well.

Not surprisingly, mergers have occurred among locally controlled banks, just as certain other sectors of Western European industry have witnessed a coalescence of smaller into larger units, partly to cope with increased competition from U.S.-controlled firms. In France the third and fourth largest *banques de dépôts* merged in 1966 to constitute the country's largest commercial bank, making it the sixteenth largest commercial bank in the world at that time.[234] In Great Britain merger negotiations began among three of the "Big Five" clearing banks.[235] In Switzerland, one of the three largest deposit banks, for a number of reasons, merged with a non-banking institution, thereby acquiring the latter's cash reserves and expanding its lending base.[236]

Other types of host country banks have followed different paths. In France and Great Britain some of the *banques d'affaires* or merchant banks entered into associations with major U.S. commercial banks whereby the latter acquired non-controlling stock interests in the European institutions.[237] In Great Britain, one non-clearer made an arrangement in which the U.S. bank in question purchased nearly 15% of the voting stock of the British bank with an option to buy an additional 10%.[238]

As for the second type of change, that of nature or function, the strict division of banks into various categories in France and Great Britain was proving to be a competitive hindrance. In France, indigenous bankers both in the *banque de dépôts* and in the *banque d'affaires* banking sectors were finding the limits to their assigned activities increasingly arbitrary in light of the newly emerging possiblities which the essentially unregu-

233. 219 (6408) *The Economist* p. x (supplement) (1966).
234. This was the merger of the Banque Nationale pour le Commerce et l'Industrie with the Comptoir National d'Escompte de Paris to form the Banque Nationale de Paris, effective July 1, 1966. See Ministère de l'Economie et des Finances, *Décret* of May 26, 1966; *Journal officiel,* May 28, 1966, pp. 4286-87.
235. See p. 64, note 148.
236. This was the merger of the Union Bank of Switzerland with Interhandel.
237. For example, Bankers Trust Co. took a participation in l'Union des Mines— La Hénin. First National City Bank acquired a minority interest in Hill Samuel, that subsequently was terminated.
238. Mellon National Bank & Trust Co. later exercised this option to increase its minority interest in the Bank of London and South America (known as "Bolsa"). In 1970 this arrangement was somewhat modified to take account of the proposed Lloyds-Bolsa plans concerning Lloyds Bank, Europe. See p. 65, note 153.

lated Euro-dollar market offered. Serious contemplation of *"la banque universelle"*[239] was not uncommon. As industrial and commercial credit needs were becoming more complex, institutions catering to these needs could not remain inflexible, save at the risk of finding themselves excluded from active participation in a rapidly evolving medium.

In Great Britain, too, changes occurred. Finding that the flow of acceptances had slackened in direct proportion to the impact of open account credit transactions[240] coupled with Euro-dollar facilities increasingly offered by the deposit banks, certain London discount houses entered the Euro-dollar arena. It was only in Switzerland, where the major banks already come close to being *banques universelles,* that structural changes appeared less necessary.

It is not suggested that the U.S. branch banks were themselves alone responsible for these changes. It is evident, though, that there have been two interrelated stimuli. On the one hand, the very presence of these foreign-controlled branch banks has had an undeniably stimulating effect. Had there been no Euro-dollar market, however, fewer of them would have been established in the host countries. Accordingly, the magnitude of the stimulation has been a function of the existence of that market. On the other hand, the vigorous Euro-dollar activities of the U.S. branch banks have constituted an additional element which has brought into question the need for larger and more versatile indigenous institutions. Had the U.S. branch banks merely been present but only moderately active, this need would have been less acutely felt. Thus, the magnitude of the stimulating effect has also been a function of their high degree of activity.

b. *Third Wave U.S. Branch Banks*

Heretofore mention has been made of the first wave and second wave U.S. branch banks in the host countries. During the second phase of the Euro-dollar market a new wave of U.S. branch banks were coming onto the scene. Whereas the second wave had been established in order to serve their overseas customers more directly, conscious of—but not motivated principally by—the existence of the Euro-dollar market, the third wave branch banks were established primarily because it had become

---

239. I.e., a bank competent in all fields. See p. 73, note 186.

240. Open account credit was being granted more frequently as suppliers gained increasing confidence in purchasers' ability and willingness to pay promptly. Partly this was due to the increased use of swifter transportation facilities, including air freight, and to lower risk methods of cargo handling, notably the introduction of container ships. Moreover, there were more frequent open account transactions among various subsidiaries of one corporate entity or between subsidiary and parent corporation, where the credit transaction is essentially a matter of internal accounting.

necessary for these banks to enter the Euro-dollar market directly. Moreover, for these banks a London branch was essential.

The establishment of the third wave branch banks[241] was primarily motivated by two factors: (a) the need for an overseas office that could deal directly with foreign borrowers, in order to comply with the spirit of the U.S. balance of payments program; and (b) the need for a "window" for taking Euro-dollar deposits that could be used for lending to these borrowers, and ultimately for transfer overnight to the head office when money market conditions became extremely tight.

In Chapter One it was stated that until the mid-1960's branch bank activities abroad were taken up as additional, supplementary activities, outside the U.S. banks' normal domestic pattern of operations.[242] The pressing need for a London "window" was not an additional, supplementary activity, however, but rather a direct extension of a bank's normal domestic pattern of operations, necessitated by the ever-increasing difficulty in obtaining sufficient deposits domestically in the United States. U.S. monetary policy had made the Euro-dollar market a marginal part of the New York City money market. The establishment of one third wave branch bank was accompanied by the frank announcement that the head office bank wanted "access to the London money market and, in particular, to the Euro-dollar market".[243]

By the end of 1967 the number of U.S. branch banks in the three host countries had grown to five in France, fifteen in Great Britain,[244] and two in Switzerland, with a total of fourteen U.S. commercial banks involved.

c. *Newly-Created Multinational Medium-Term Lending Institutions*

Earlier it was pointed out that the terminology "longer-term" has been adopted in the present study to describe operations that are longer than those normally associated with any particular sector of the borrowing-lending operations taking place in Western Europe. A purposely neutral term, it has been used to avoid semantic complications.

Nevertheless, it is evident that in the case of the "longer-term" Euro-dollar operations under analysis, reference more often than not is unmistakably made to what is generally called "medium-term" credit in both the United States and in Western Europe. By entering the longer-term Euro-dollar field, the U.S. branch banks and other short-term lending in-

241. These were established by The Bank of New York, The First National Bank of Boston, The First National Bank of Chicago, Irving Trust Co., Marine-Midland Grace Trust Co. and Mellon National Bank and Trust Co. in London. First National City Bank established second wave branches in Geneva and Zurich.
242. See p. 10, text cited to note 11.
243. 117 *The Banker* 351-52 (1967).
244. Not including West End sub-branches, but including "second generation" branches in cities other than principal financial centers. They are listed at p. 17.

266

stitutions were clearly entering what had theretofore been the strict domain of other institutions in Western Europe. In France, as was noted in Chapter Two, there are special institutions whose sole task is to deal with the medium-term credit needs of borrowers as defined in the French laws. In Great Britain, accepting houses and merchant banks are well ensconced in the medium-term field. Once again, only in Switzerland, where the major deposit banks can indirectly fulfill the roles of medium-term lending institutions, have the U.S. branch banks not encroached on the territory of another special type of indigenous institution by operating in the longer-term Euro-dollar sector.

Whereas the U.S. branch banks had formerly operated only in the sector reserved for short-term institutions, except for their host currency term loans, during their second Euro-dollar operating phase they were regularly encountering competition from—and affecting—the operations of a different group of institutions, such as *banques d'affaires,* merchant banks, and insurance companies, as well as certain pension funds and investment companies.

It is also important to take account of the fact that the major U.S. commercial banks have increasingly faced competition from and joined in with[245] newly-created multinational units designed to deal primarily in the medium-term lending field by means of Euro-dollar credits, and in particular to deal in medium-term negotiable Euro-dollar notes of large industrial borrowers on a private offering basis. In this case, each participating institution is supposed to be the specialist with regard to borrowers and risk most closely associated with its normal areas of operation, with the group as a whole spreading the risks and providing larger Euro-dollar facilities for customers than any of the banks is prepared singly to undertake. Institutions of this type are probably the nearest examples of joint-ventures in the Euro-dollar field.

B. *Implications for the U.S. Branch Banks' Operations*

1. *Inclusion of Retail and Smaller Wholesale Transactions*

The liquid dollar holdings of U.S. corporate subsidiaries were finding their way into the Euro-dollar market during the second phase of the U.S. branch banks' operations.[246] Particularly helpful in channeling these funds into deposits were the London dollar c.d.'s, which the U.S. branch banks and other banks issued during the latter part of that phase. With the introduction of smaller denominations, it was possible to attract dollars

245. For example, see p. 28, note 16.
246. *Cf.* Bank of England, 4 *Quarterly Bulletin* 105 (1964).

from smaller firms and individuals seeking placement opportunities. Although no small savers' funds were being sought in the ordinary sense of the term,[247] these lower denomination instruments reflected a move to include more than the strictly wholesale part of the Euro-dollar market.

In addition, some U.S. banks maintained or opened "second generation" branches in the host countries, i.e., units in non-money market cities like Birmingham or Marseilles. Also sub-branches were operating in the principal financial center cities, such as the West End branches in London. In a sense, this paralleled the moves of some major banks in the United States which had formerly been strictly wholesale institutions, but which decided to establish or acquire branch networks in their home territory.

2. Skewed Stance

In their borrowing and lending operations, it was seen in Chapter Four that the advent of the Euro-dollar market permitted the U.S. branch banks to acquire a position more nearly in equilibrium, both with regard to the inter-bank host currency money markets and with regard to original depositors and end-users.

During the second phase of their Euro-dollar operations, under conditions of high interest rates and the voluntary balance of payments Guidelines, the U.S. branch banks assumed a different stance altogether, similar in some respects and different in others from those in the past.

In their Euro-dollar operations, they were always in the (inter-bank) market as consistent takers of deposits, lending "locally" only those funds which the head office could not profitably use. In a sense this was similar to their position in the host currency money markets in the pre-Euro-dollar period, the difference being that the amounts sought in the market were now used more to satisfy head office needs than for advances to local borrowers.

In their dealings with original depositors and end-users of dollars, however, their stance was skewed in a sense exactly opposite to that in the pre-Euro-dollar host currency operations. Whereas they had formerly been lenders more often than takers of original host currency deposits, in the second phase of their Euro-dollar operations they became heavy takers of dollar original deposits but only occasionally lenders to end-users, preferring to make the dollars thus obtained available to the head office banks in the United States.[248]

With regard to operations in the host currencies during the second

247. The smaller denomination c.d.'s were rarely issued for face amounts of less than $25,000; but see p. 216, note 61.
248. *Cf.* 223 (6459) *The Economist* p. xix (supplement) (1967).

268

phase of the U.S. branch banks' Euro-dollar operations they still had the relatively small deposit base noted earlier. Host currency lending operations, many of which were implemented by swaps out of Euro-dollars prior to the tight money conditions, frequently had to be foregone. The stance of the U.S. branch banks returned, in this sector, to that of the pre-Euro-dollar period.

The consistent thread in the foregoing is that the U.S. branch banks have invariably been more willing than other commercial banking institutions present to take dollars on deposit from original depositors or in the inter-bank market, regardless of the tightness of money or impediments to the free eastward flow of funds from the U.S. head office banks to the branches. Of course, the dollar's convertibility has been partly responsible for this willingness; but this factor influenced indigenous commercial banks as well as other foreign branch banks.

The special interest of the U.S. branch banks is twofold: First, the dollar is the working medium of the head office bank and can nearly always be used profitably there. Second, it is in the long-run interest of the U.S. banks to have their branches maintain confidence in the dollar by being willing at all times to take it on deposit. If the local management of a U.S. branch bank finds itself in a period of temporary excess of liquidity it can elect to bid less aggressively for deposits of dollars, but it will stay in the market, without any exchange risk. Accordingly, if the U.S. branch banks have had a part of their stance "built-in" it is the tendency toward being consistent takers of dollars. Analytically this fact must be used to interpret their operations.

3. Offshore Operations

The Euro-dollar operations of the major U.S. commercial banks have been sufficiently arcane to make it difficult for U.S.-based personnel to decide accurately or rapidly enough on all of the multitude of questions that arise in connection with these transactions. Accordingly, there has been a fundamental "interior" force, i.e., arising out of the medium itself, in favor of a larger degree of autonomous branch bank decision-making once the Euro-dollar market became clearly defined.

Previously it has been noted that many of the important decisions connected with financial operations between U.S. branch banks and foreign borrowers are taken in the United States or elsewhere in the network of a bank or corporation, and not necessarily at the U.S. branch bank making the actual loan. One effect of the voluntary balance of payment Guidelines for banks was that U.S. branch banks were encouraged to deal directly with foreign borrowers, both foreign corporations and the foreign subsidiaries of U.S. corporations.

269

With official encouragement of direct contact at this level, more autonomy of decision making was being forced upon the personnel of the branch bank during the second Euro-dollar operating phase. In fact, after the Guidelines went into effect some of the major U.S. commercial banks discouraged their U.S.-based employees from dealing directly with personnel of U.S. parent corporations when loans for their overseas subsidiaries were contemplated, instructing these employees to refer such loan requests to the appropriate overseas branch bank in their networks. Major decisions were certainly taken in the head office banks and parent corporations in the United States; but the autonomy of the foreign branch bank was augmented by this "exterior" force.[249]

The result of these "interior" and "exterior" forces was an appreciable increase in the independence of the U.S. branch banks, which contributed to the development of genuine offshore operations. Coupled with this phenomenon was the fact that the Guidelines channeled borrowers located outside the United States, or domestic U.S. borrowers needing funds for use abroad, toward credit based upon funds which were themselves on deposit outside the United States. Prior to the Guidelines these borrowers could have been supplied with credit by the outward transfer of U.S.-based liquid assets. After the voluntary program went into effect, however, this alternative was drastically reduced.

The U.S. branch banks were faced with the need to acquire or generate their own funds outside the United States. Moreover, they could no longer rely as freely on head office funds being made available for meeting sudden deposit withdrawals. As a result, in addition to being more on their own in the sense that more decision-making autonamy lay with them, the branch banks were more on their own financially.

C. Developments after 1968

On January 1, 1968 the nature of the U.S. balance of payments program changed fundamentally as the voluntary Guidelines, which since 1965 had been aimed at reducing the outflow of funds from the United States, were replaced by those designed to cause a net inflow of funds, backed by authority to control certain types of capital movements. This closed an era by arresting the continued permissiveness which theretofore had charac-

---

249. Greater autonomy in decision-making was also being brought onto the personnel of U.S. overseas corporate subsidiaries for similar reasons. The Euro-dollar operations of the treasurers of these units have been no less mysterious to many financial officers in the parent corporations than when seen from the banks' viewpoint. The U.S. corporate guidelines were exerting a parallel force, *mutatis mutandis,* on these subsidiaries in a fashion similar to that found in the Guidelines for Banks.

terized the U.S. laws affecting the U.S. branch banks' operations, and simultaneously marked the end of the second phase of their Euro-dollar operations which had started in mid-1963.

Although as a result events transpiring since 1968 have been set in a fundamentally different structure, they are nevertheless of interest, as are certain mutations in the home and host country laws.

1. *Influx of Additional U.S. Branch Banks*

The movement of the major U.S. commercial banks to establish branches in the three host countries—and especially in London—did not cease at the end of the second Euro-dollar operating phase. Newcomers, i.e., banks which previously had no branches in France, Great Britain, or Switzerland, have set up London branches since 1968 primarily for taking Euro-dollar deposits, while those U.S. banks which had already established one or more branches in the three host countries by the end of 1967 have continued to expand their networks there. In 1968 seven newcomer banks[250] set up London branches and one already established bank[251] set up a sub-branch in Paris. The following year saw five more newcomer banks[252] setting up London branches while two already established banks[253] were opening branches in Paris, another[254] opening branches in Manchester, Lyons, and Zurich, another[255] opening branches in Nice as well as in Lugano, Switzerland, and still another[256] opening a branch in Zurich. The pace slackened in 1970, but there were still four newcomer banks[257] which set up branches in London while one already established bank[258] set up a branch in Paris, and another already established bank opened one in Lausanne.[259] In 1971 one already established bank received permission to

---

250. City National Bank of Detroit, First Pennsylvania Bank (Philadelphia), First Wisconsin National Bank of Milwaukee, Girard Trust Bank (Philadelphia), The National Bank of Commerce of Seattle, National Bank of Detroit, and United California Bank (Los Angeles).

251. First National City Bank (New York City).

252. American National Bank and Trust Co. of Chicago, Crocker-Citizens National Bank (San Francisco), The Detroit Bank & Trust Co., The Northern Trust Co. (Chicago), and Security Pacific National Bank (Los Angeles).

253. Bankers Trust Co. (New York City) and Continental Illinois National Bank and Trust Co. of Chicago.

254. Bank of America, N.T. & S.A. (San Francisco).

255. First National City Bank (New York City).

256. Morgan Guaranty Trust Co. of New York.

257. First National Bank in Dallas, Harris Trust and Savings Bank (Chicago), Republic National Bank of Dallas, and Wells Fargo Bank, N.A. (San Francisco).

258. The First National Bank of Chicago.

259. First National City Bank (New York City).

open a Zurich branch,[260] and another already established bank opened one in Geneva.[261]

2. *Changes in the Laws*

In the host countries there have been several pertinent changes in the laws affecting U.S. branch banks' operations since 1968, as previously noted. In sum, the French exchange control system reinstated in 1968 has been a revival of that in effect prior to 1967. Quantitative credit controls were removed in October 1970, at which time an important addition was made to the French monetary policy tools, namely the introduction of reserve requirements on banks' loans outstanding.[262] The British exchange control measures have been somewhat more relaxed, whereas the need to limit credit has continued to be critical as witnessed by the system in use since September 1971, which is far more than a revamping of the earlier ceilings. In Switzerland the selective control of certain types of capital movements has been based on the need to throttle back the inward flow of non-Swiss funds. Credit controls have been applied against a backdrop of parliamentary efforts to grant more power to the central bank and moves to facilitate the changing of the parity of the Swiss franc.[263]

With regard to the changes in the home country laws, the U.S. balance of payments measures since 1968 have continued to be called Guidelines despite the intrinsic change in their nature. There have not been many changes from the arrangements put into force in 1968.[264] One worthy of note was the decision to provide from December 1, 1969 a separate ceiling for credits for one year or longer in amounts of $250,000 or more for the financing of U.S. exports. This was known as the "export term-loan ceiling" and was separate from and in addition to the "general ceil-

260. Chemical Bank (New York City), which was also reported to be planning the establishment of a branch bank in Paris.

261. The First National Bank of Chicago.

262. It will be recalled that reserve requirements on banks' deposits were put in effect in January 1967. See p. 242, note 158. In February 1971 the Conseil National de Crédit was given the authority to fix these new reserve ratios (*Journal officiel*, February 24, 1971, p. 1865), which in March 1971 were set at 0.8% on the portion of banks' advances exceeding 80% of their level as of January 5, 1971. See Le Monde, March 30, 1971, p. 40, col. 5.

263. The parity changing hindrance was not the result of an obligation with respect to the International Monetary Fund (since Switzerland is not a member, just as it is not a member of the United Nations), but rather an internal requirement that the Federal Parliament take action on any change of this kind. Since the end of March 1971 this power has resided with the Federal Council, which acted on May 9, 1971 to revalue the Swiss franc by slightly over 7%.

264. See p. 238, note 150.

ing".[265] In a later revision for 1971, however, export credits have since been made exempt from a separate ceiling.

Directly affecting the Euro-dollar operations of the U.S. branch banks have been changes in two home country regulations in 1969 and 1970. The first of these was the decision in August 1969 to make Euro-dollar deposits subject to marginal reserve requirements.[266] This change in (Federal Reserve) Regulation M placed a 10% (then 20%)[267] requirement as from October 16, 1969 against member banks' borrowings from their foreign branches and against head office assets (i.e., loan participations) acquired by their foreign branches in excess of a base figure, set at the average weekly amounts during the four week period ending May 28, 1969. If these amounts fall below the reserve-free base figure then the latter is reduced accordingly. A corresponding change was made to Regulation D to provide like treatment for similar transactions with foreign banks.[268]

In June 1970 the Board of Governors acted again, this time to remove the Regulation Q interest rate ceilings from 30 to 89 day deposits in banks in the United States in amounts of $100,000 or more.[269]

Of course, the announcement by President Nixon on August 15, 1971 that the dollar would no longer be freely convertible into gold (as it had not been on a *de facto* basis for several years) brought new forces to bear on the legal structure within which the U.S. branch banks have operated.

3. *Effect on the U.S. Branch Banks' Operations*

The changes in the host country laws since 1968 have not altered fundamentally the operating medium of the U.S. branch banks. The 1967 relaxation of the French exchange controls could have been expected to have stimulated multinational banking operations by banks and branch banks there; but the 1968 reintroduction of the controls nipped this prospect in the bud. The growing stability of the pound sterling has been overshadowed to a large extent by the renewed negotiations for British entry into the European Communities. In any event, the City of London definitely continues to be the center for Euro-dollar operations and, if any-

265. 56 *Federal Reserve Bulletin* 13 (1970).
266. United States, Board of Governors of the Federal Reserve System, Regulation M, 12 C.F.R. § 213.7, 34 Fed. Reg. 13409, August 20, 1969. See p. 121, note 104.
267. See material cited to note 271 *infra*.
268. See p. 121, note 104.
269. Regulation Q, 12 C.F.R. § 217.7 (a)(1). See 56 *Federal Reserve Bulletin* 581 (1970). The motivation here was more domestic, in that the Penn-Central financial crisis triggered this change. *Cf.* Federal Reserve Bank of New York, 52 *Monthly Review* 289 (1970).

thing, would gain rather than lose from the strengthened ties with the Common Market. The changes in the Swiss laws reflect a continuing desire to insulate the domestic banking sector from perturbations arising abroad, while at the same time attempting to maximize the yield from what constitutes a major local industry.

The 1969 and 1970 U.S. regulatory changes have directly affected one aspect of the U.S. branch banks' operations, namely the lending of Euro-dollar-backed credits to head office banks for onlending there. This had gained momentum in 1966, causing U.S. banks' liabilities to their foreign branches to double from nearly $2 billion to about $4 billion during that year, the level near which they stood (with some fluctuations) through 1967. After 1968, however, continually rising interest rates put increasing pressure on the (Federal Reserve) Regulation Q ceilings, causing funds to flow out of large denomination certificates of deposit in the United States and partly into Euro-dollar deposits. Lending these funds to their head office banks came to constitute almost the sole *raison d'être* for many of the newcomers' branch banks in London. Although this alone could hardly be called multinational banking it nevertheless must be recognized as an important function.

The reserve requirement imposed in 1969 has reduced some of the appeal of Euro-dollar credits compared with other alternatives for U.S. banks (e.g., Federal Funds). It partially contributed to a decline of U.S. banks' liabilities to their foreign branches from about $15 billion in mid-1969 to about $11 billion the following summer when the Regulation Q lid was raised from large denomination c.d.'s.[270] This second regulatory change has hastened the movement of credits from the head office banks back toward the foreign branches. In fact, some U.S. banks have willingly let their reserve-free base erode as they have been able to increase their deposits in the United States with the large denomination c.d.'s that have become strongly competitive with Euro-dollar deposits for many depositors. In an effort to check the "outbound" Euro-dollar drain, i.e., to encourage U.S. banks to maintain their bases, the Board of Governors of the Federal Reserve System raised the 10% marginal reserve requirement to 20% to take effect as of December 23, 1970.[271] Further pressure was added when Regulation M was amended as of January 15, 1971 to "allow" certain U.S. Export-Import Bank obligations purchased by U.S. branch banks to be included in the head office banks' reserve-free base,[272]

270. Another factor reducing banks' reliance on Euro-dollar credits was increasing resort to bank-related commercial paper during this period. In August 1970 this, too, was made subject to reserve requirements.

271. United States, Board of Governors of the Federal Reserve System, *Press Release,* November 30, 1970.

272. (Federal Reserve) Regulation M, as amended: 12 C.F.R. 213.7 (a). See 57 *Federal Reserve Bulletin* 121-22 (1971).

and again amended as of April 1, 1971 to provide similarly for special U.S. Treasury certificates of indebtedness.[273] By spring 1972 member banks' liabilities to their foreign branches stood near $1 billion, appearing to have passed the nadir.

These U.S. regulatory changes have affected the operations of the U.S. branch banks in proportion to the importance which lending to head office banks has had in relation to their operations taken as a whole. Accordingly those branch banks with varied activities in the host countries, and especially ones which form part of networks outside the United States, have been affected differently from those branch banks whose primary if not sole function has been to serve as an additional deposit-taking window for the head office bank. That is, branch banks engaged in multinational banking must be distinguished from those which are not.

In conclusion, the developments since 1968—and particularly those following the setting of new international currency parities ("central rates") in December 1971[274]—are of interest because of the additional light they shed on the period through the end of 1967. In return, an understanding of that period will prove to be a key to many of the developments in the field of multinational banking in the 1970's and the years beyond. At this stage, then, it is in order to re-examine the thesis set forth in Chapter One, testing it against our analysis and drawing therefrom the conclusions that emerge from the present study.

It is to this final task that we now turn.

---

273. *Id.,* p. 328. These steps were tantamount to offshore mopping-up operations, i.e., an international open market technique. In the autumn of 1971 these certificates were allowed to expire.

274. These were FF 5.1157 and SF 3.84 to $1.00, and $2.6057 to £1.00.

Chapter Six

"CONCLUSIONS"

I. SUMMING UP

From mid-1945 through 1967 there was a steady evolution in the operations of the U.S. branch banks in the three host countries. The first wave, those which had been established or re-established shortly after the end of World War II, were faced with strict foreign exchange controls in the early post-war period. The severe shortage of hard currencies, especially dollars, was only partially alleviated by measures such as the Marshall Plan. Relatively few U.S. corporate subsidiaries were as yet established in or near the host countries.

By the end of 1958 Western Europe had witnessed a gradual economic recovery. The Berlin air-lift and the Korean War had taken place, shattering hopes for a post-war period of "peaceful coexistence". Many of the French and British colonies were moving toward or had already obtained political—if not economic—independence; and another Franco-German halocoust seemed less likely as plans for a common market in Western Europe were taking form. The dollar shortage appeared to be easing as some non-residents of the United States began to acquire net balances of U.S. currency not earmarked for immediate use for purchasing vital capital and consumer goods in the United States. By the end of 1958 ten U.S. branch banks had been established in France and Great Britain.

As the year 1959 got underway the new European Monetary Agreement came into force. In one sense this change was symptomatic, for it attested to the level of recovery, and especially to the newly regained self-confidence, returning to the participating countries. In another sense it was one fundamental element in the new economic expansion which was to follow in the next decade,[1] for it opened the flow of current payments for goods and services. Moreover, it became possible under certain circumstances to take non-residents' funds for deposit and to lend them to other

1. Another element, no less important, was the rising level of import demand which was stimulated by the lowering of trade barriers. See General Agreement on Tariffs and Trade (GATT), *International Trade 1968*, Geneva, 1969, pp. 1-7 and 11-14 as well as appendix table G following p. 305.

276

non-residents. The European Economic Community came into being, followed by the European Free Trade Association, albeit along a different path.

The new economic and political climate in Western Europe attracted U.S. corporate subsidiaries seeking to establish themselves in what appeared to have the potential of a domestic market even larger than that of the already long-since-established common market inside the United States. A second wave of branches appeared as some of the major U.S. commercial banks recognized their utility in handling the affairs of important U.S. corporate customers which might otherwise turn to rival U.S. banks with offices already established in the host or other countries. This second wave included one from a bank headquartered in Chicago.

The overseas dollar shortage was ending. Indeed, heavy U.S. expenditure and investment abroad, reflected in the balance of payments deficit, was feeding even greater amounts of temporarily unneeded dollars into a pool that was accumulating outside the United States. More holders of these dollars were following the earlier example of certain Eastern European state banks and others in placing their funds on deposit outside the United States. Banks taking these deposits were finding it profitable to use them for short-term advances to borrowers who could not or did not choose to borrow in the United States. The Euro-dollar market was taking form.

Gradually the first and second wave U.S. branch banks were caught up in it, some earlier than others and some more actively and imaginatively. In fact, whereas host currency deposits had always been in short supply for these non-indigenous commercial banking institutions, a new source of lendable funds appeared to be accumulating.[2] By the mid-summer of 1963 there were twelve U.S. branch banks in France and Great Britain, and one about to be established in Switzerland.

Then, in July 1963, President Kennedy requested retroactive legislation to dampen the U.S. capital outflow in the form of the Interest Equalization Tax. A levy designed to lower the effective yield of foreign securities to U.S. citizen and resident investors, the measure was also aimed at U.S. lending abroad. The following year President Johnson announced that non-legislative steps were to be taken in the form of voluntary Guidelines which U.S. corporations and lenders, including commercial banks, were to follow in their overseas operations.

2. It will be recalled that a "major" U.S. commercial bank for the purposes of the present study has been defined as one with deposits of at least $1 billion at some time between mid-1945 and the end of 1967. It is noteworthy that some U.S. commercial banks have accumulated that amount on deposit at their overseas branches alone.

At the same time that the free flow of dollars from the United States (including U.S. head office banks) was thus pinched, more and more U.S. corporations were flocking to Western Europe to establish new subsidiaries or acquire locally-owned firms. The supply of lendable funds in all the major Western currencies was increasingly unable to meet the demand, causing interest rates in the major money markets to begin a climb that was to put them at what were to seem like record levels by the autumn of 1966. The United States was becoming deeply involved in a controversial war in Southeast Asia that already was having repercussions in a society faced with critical domestic problems of poverty and racial inequality. Exchange rate stability was threatened as speculators sought profits in gold and foreign currency operations, financing much of their activity by means of Euro-dollar credits. By late 1967 the British government was forced to devalue the pound sterling as other currencies, including the French franc and the dollar, came under pressure. Tight money conditions in the United States caused some U.S. commercial banks without overseas branches to establish a third wave, whose primary task was to take Euro-dollar deposits. In addition, second wave branches were established in Switzerland, bringing the total number of branch banks in the host countries to twenty-two by the end of 1967.

It was against this background that President Johnson announced on January 1, 1968 that the voluntary measures adopted theretofore were being replaced by hard and fast rules to be administered by new federal machinery. U.S. branch banks could still be established in the host countries and elsewhere abroad; but the operating medium changed fundamentally. All but minor outward capital flows from the United States have since been subject to controls under the home country laws. Whereas the host country controls were progressively, if not steadily,[3] relaxed, from mid-1963 the trend in the U.S. controls has been the opposite. Although a squeeze was already being felt when the first U.S. measures were put into effect as of mid-1963, the U.S. branch banks' operations were specifically exempted from hindrances in the Interest Equalization Tax and in the voluntary Guidelines. At the end of 1967, however, the clamp was applied. It is here that we have stopped to look back.

3. Exchange controls in Great Britain waxed and waned, but their overall trend was in the direction of greater freedom. In France this seemed to be the case until 1968.

II. RESTATEMENT OF THE THESIS

Taking the foregoing into account, it is now appropriate to restate the thesis posed in Chapter One.[4]

A. *U.S. Branch Banks Have Engaged in Multinational Banking*

We have stated that many of the U.S. branch banks in France, Great Britain, and Switzerland have engaged in multinational banking.

In fact, some have more than others; and different techniques have been employed. A single branch in London, established primarily to take Euro-dollar deposits, is not in a position to conduct multinational banking operations alone, unlike one with sister branches in several foreign countries. A multitude of branches is not the key requirement, however, for a single London branch bank can engage effectively in multinational banking by using strategically placed representative offices or other units there or elsewhere. For example, a single U.S. branch bank in London operating in harmony with an affiliated local bank, that is itself oriented toward multinational operations, can very definitely engage in multinational banking. This is to say that in addition to certain physical or material facilities, a particular frame of mind or outlook is required.

The U.S. branch banks have had their own style of operation, collectively and individually. Taken as a group they tend to be more aggressive than their host country counterparts, and they work effectively as a team. By and large they have been inventive and flexible, devising or copying new ideas or techniques, and adapting their pace and the structure of their networks to cope with novel situations or changed circumstances. Taken individually, the activities of the U.S. branch banks have reflected different philosophies and styles of operation. One major U.S. commercial bank has followed the policy of establishing a branch wherever host country laws have permitted, following a theory that this gives the head office bank maximum control over the overseas establishment's activities. Another equally important bank has tried to tailor the local establishment according to its appraisal of the particular type of unit that fits best into the host country environment, opting for a branch bank or other type of unit depending upon the circumstances. Accordingly, although the U.S. branch banks have exhibited certain group characteristics they have not formed a homogenous mass in this respect. It is in order therefore to re-examine the reasons lying behind the estab-

4. See p. 18.

lishment of a foreign branch bank instead of another type of unit.

First, there is the argument that a branch bank puts the entire asset structure and net worth of the head office bank and domestic branches behind deposits as a guarantee. Doubtlessly this is of importance to the large institutional depositor, but it probably has little impact on the smaller institutional or individual depositor in a host country. In addition, in the second phase of their Euro-dollar operations the U.S. branch banks' ability to marshall U.S.-based funds was curtailed by the voluntary Guidelines. However, as noted in Chapter Five, it was unlikely that the Guidelines would have been used to prohibit a major U.S. commercial bank from meeting its debts abroad when this would have seriously undermined the structure of the Euro-dollar market. In sum, this first argument is essentially sound, insofar as it applies to wholesale operations.

The second reason for selecting a branch bank is to attract large corporate borrowers by promoting the idea that greater sums can be made available to meet their needs for funds. Since the U.S. branch banks have been primarily interested in the wholesale market this line of reasoning is pertinent to the present study. It could be equally well used in supporting the establishment of a banking subsidiary, however. Also, the Guidelines hinderance mentioned in the preceding paragraph would cut against the argument, for even if the Guidelines would probably not have been used to prevent a major U.S. bank from meeting its debts overseas, this does not suggest that U.S.-based funds would have been freed for new lending abroad. Indeed, this was precisely what the Guidelines were designed to prevent. With a constriction of the supply of home country funds this second proposition fails to stand.

It might also be argued that a U.S. branch bank could have marshalled other funds located outside the United States without running counter to the Guidelines; but this takes the branch bank as a separate entity, operating with its own and other funds outside the United States rather than as an integral part of the head office bank—particularly with regard to its assets. Conceptually it is more akin to the operating structure of a banking subsidiary than of a branch bank. This second argument, that more funds can be made available for lending, is realistic and is pertinent to the thesis; but it would not have special relevance to a branch rather than a subsidiary, and it is valid only under certain circumstances.

Third, there is the argument that a U.S. head office bank can exercise maximum effective control over a branch. This would no doubt be true to the extent that local or other non-head office management interests can be ignored, since there are none. (Whether they should be ignored is, of course, another question.) Also, even the maximum effective control might not be sufficient in some cases,[5] or even desirable, especially when the branch banks' operations are fairly esoteric in nature as in the Euro-dollar field. Here the factors tending towards greater autonomy at the branch bank, examined earlier, make it more like a subsidiary in some respects, or at least, less like a branch. The control argument, too, must be qualified.

Finally, there is a fourth reason, namely that a bank is following a "traditional" pattern overseas. It is difficult to assess whether this is a genuine reason or simply an appraisal of a state of affairs. It is true, however, that some of the major U.S. commercial banks and their legal advisers have developed expertise in meeting the home and foreign host country legal requirements for establishing and using branch banks overseas. At first glance this might seem to be a superficial reason; but effective multinational banking operations depend upon keeping surprises—especially legal ones—at a minimum. As some U.S. banks have acquired the "feel" for wielding an overseas network, even a small one, where one or more branch banks play a key role, it is not surprising that they have tended to continue using the same type of unit wherever possible. Particularly this would be so where the home legal requirements are continually permissive to a large degree, as in the period under study, and where the host country laws are not altered to discourage the operations of branch banks.

Seen in retrospect this might seem to emerge as a traditional pattern. As with many traditions, however, the component acts frequently appear preferable for rather simple, straightforward reasons when seen prospectively. If a major U.S. commercial bank were to have decided to establish a branch bank abroad without too much aforethought this traditional pattern argument might be valid. There is no evidence, however, that any of the U.S. banks have gone about the process in this fashion. Indeed, the case is clearly the contrary. Except as a make-weight, then, the traditional pattern argument is difficult to accept.

B. *Legal Aspects: Causal Relationship*

We have contended that the U.S. branch banks have been able to engage in multinational banking because of the existence of certain types of laws and practices and the absence of others. Also, their multinational banking operations have evolved within and alongside a legal frame-

---

5. For example, one bank which has been a major proponent of the maximum-control-via-branches-wherever-possible argument was reported to have incurred an estimated loss of $8 million (or $4 million net loss after taxes) in 1965 as the result of unauthorized foreign exchange operations by an employee at one of its branch banks abroad. See New York Times, July 21, 1965, p. 47, col. 4 (late city edition).

work that has itself evolved, partially causing and partially reflecting those operations.

In a sense, it might be said that ultimately all aspects of the U.S. branch banks' operations in the host countries are legal, since without the necessary legal structure there can be no multinational banking. The present study has not been prompted by this, however, but rather by the questions of how and why the legal aspects are relevant. We now can assess the laws' effect on the operations, and conversely, how and why the latter in turn affect the operations of the U.S. branch banks. In so doing it must be borne in mind that these are legal measures in some instances and paralegal in others.

1. Effect of the Laws on the U.S. Branch Banks' Multinational Banking Operations

In comparing the effect of the relevant elements of the banking, credit control, and exchange control laws we conclude that a certain threshold of minimum permissiveness is required in all three legal areas. If the right to establish branch banks or to conduct normal banking transactions is too severely restricted, if credit controls bear too heavily on deposit-taking or lending operations, or if exchange controls cut down the flow of foreign exchange to a mere trickle, a U.S. commercial bank might still consider it worthwhile to put or keep a foreign branch bank in operation; but the latter would be unable to engage in multinational banking.

Of the three legal categories, banking laws present the most open-or-shut case. In the home and three host countries these laws are essentially similar since commercial banking transactions are based on common fundamental principles. In all cases a branch bank acts as an intermediary for depositors and borrowers alike in the local market, and eventually in one that has extended beyond national frontiers. The home and host country banking laws reflect social, political, and economic philosophies that have not been conceptually adverse to what we have defined as multinational banking. Since these philosophies did not undergo fundamental change during the period under study the laws themselves remained essentially permissive.

As for the legal and paralegal measures limiting credit, the issue is more complex, for in two of the host countries the U.S. branch banks have encountered a situation quite unlike their home environment.[6]

6. Strictly speaking, the voluntary Guidelines on overseas bank lending were credit measures. In the context of this study, however, they operated to limit the movement of funds abroad rather than the extension of credit as such. Compare with the Swiss measures at pp. 249-50.

Host country credit control measures have not, however, borne more heavily on these guest banking institutions than on indigenous banks. For instance, the U.S. branch banks were among those exempted from the 1946 British cash and liquidity ratios and from the 1958 and 1965 "invitations" to place Special Deposits with the Bank of England. Or again, the 105% lending limit set in 1965 in Great Britain required that all banking institutions throttle back the expansion of their lending activities, not any particular group of banks. New arrivals among the U.S. branch banks not having a previously established lending base on which to apply the percentage were even assigned a hypothetical figure so that they would not be rendered inoperative.[7] In both France and Great Britain these measures have been aimed primarily at restricting the expansion of credit in the local markets, not at hampering advances to non-residents from other non-residents' deposited funds. This latter activity, which became an essential part of the U.S. branch banks' Eurodollar operations, has been conducted in an essentially unregulated field.

In the third legal category, exchange control measures, the situation is quite different from that in the first two. Before the advent of external convertibility near the end of 1958 multinational banking was impossible. Without the ability to transmit large quantities of purchasing power legally across national boundaries—at a profit—banks and branch banks in the host countries were constrained to operating in the separate national boxes or compartments where they were located. For the first wave branch banks this might not have been discouraging, for they had been established or re-established to operate primarily in conjunction with their head office banks in the United States rather than in coordination with other branch banks or foreign units abroad.

When it became possible to advance some non-residents' funds to certain other non-residents, however, a new phase began for them. Foreign in origin and outlook, they and the two succeeding waves were far more hindered or helped than were indigenous banks by exchange control measures, because the foreign sector was so much more important—both quantitatively and qualitatively.

With regard to exchange control measures, finding and using legally permissible channels in the barriers is a key element in conducting multinational banking operations. The wider the channels the more vigorous and varied are the activities, as pent-up demand for funds is unleashed. Had external convertibility been suspended after 1959, how-

7. The new British credit control policy adopted in 1971, whereby minimum reserve requirements and Special Deposit requirements (applying to all banks) have replaced credit ceilings, should not alter fundamentally the U.S. branch banks' operations there, although unquestionably they are thus blended even more firmly into the local setting while adapting to the new regime.

ever, the situation would have altered overnight. Looking ahead, the new elements introduced since 1971, when the dollar was cut loose from gold and new parities set, have cast a new light on the issue; but they will enhance the U.S. branch banks' multinational banking operations in the long run if the result tends to disuade further U.S. measures to control capital movements.

Taking the three categories of laws together during the period under study, the home and host country measures were more or less stringent depending upon the desired goal. In both home and host cases the desirability of allowing multinational banking to develop was evident, for as long as internal policies were not thrown askew (an aspect to which we shall return), a well-ordered and active international financial machinery was of benefit to borrowers and lenders alike in all the participating countries. There was no apparent concern over the U.S. branch banks' escaping host or home country supervision. As far as the host country authorities were concerned, these U.S. branch banks were guests and were present by sufferance. As for the U.S. authorities, it was evident that if the U.S. branch banks were kept out of multinational banking then other banks, not subject to the Federal Reserve System or the Comptroller of the Currency, would eventually occupy the field in one way or another.

Summing up, multinational banking is inversely proportional to the legal density, the operations becoming more numerous and varied as the legal hindrances diminish. The effects of the home and host country banking laws and credit control measures are important; but that of the exchange controls is crucial.

2. *Effect of the U.S. Branch Banks' Multinational Banking Operations on the Laws*

A more difficult task is to assay the effect of the U.S. branch banks' multinational operations on the laws. Had these institutions abused their status there would certainly have occurred a sharp change in both home and host countries, an event which did not occur. There was, however, an evolution in all four legal systems, the effects of which began to be felt before the end of the period under study.

In France the most striking aspect of this was the 1966 move toward according broader powers to French banking institutions. With the passage of time it was becoming increasingly apparent that banks strictly limited to the *banque de dépôts* and *banque d'affaires* categories would have difficulties in structuring their deposit-taking and lending activities so as to satisfy the larger and more complex banking needs of their major institutional customers. It is not suggested that the restructuring

284

of the French law towards universal banking was triggered by the operations of the U.S. branch banks alone nor by their structure. Indeed, the same fears which had caused earlier French lawmakers to prevent *banques de dépôts* from making longer-term advances were clearly evident in the similarly strict division found in the U.S. banking laws between commercial and investment banking houses. Nevertheless, the implications of the operations of the U.S. branch banks were not lost on indigenous French banks or borrowers. This was partially reflected in the changed operating rules for them and their local counterparts.

In Great Britain the U.S. branch banks' operations appear to have contributed indirectly to a similar change in another legal sector. This has been the evident need to stimulate competition among banks, as noted in the conclusions and recommendations of the National (Jones) Board on Prices and Incomes Report in 1967.[8] The U.S branch banks have by no means been held up as paragons in this respect. In fact, taken as a group U.S.-trained bankers, whether they be U.S. nationals or not, are often considered rather too agressive by British standards. Nonetheless, the rigid fixing of the LDR and the refusal to attract depositing or borrowing customers through the price mechanism came to seem increasingly out-of-date to many observers, including borrowers in favor of a more competitive group of local lenders.

Another instance, more clearly reflecting the influence of U.S. branch banks' operations, occurred in connection with the Special Deposit requirements reimposed by the Bank of England in 1965. Although the U.S. branch banks had been among the institutions exempted from the earlier invitation to maintain Special Deposits there was serious consideration of including them in the 1965 measure. Moreover, when the 105% loan ceiling was lifted for the clearers in 1967 it remained in force with respect to some categories of banks, including the U.S. branch banks.[9] These and other foreign controlled banking institutions were now being taken more seriously than in 1959 when the Radcliffe Committee noted the overseas and foreign banks' "relative unimportance in the domestic financial scene".[10] This development was not surprising, for by the later years of the period under study the U.S. branch banks' advances to local borrowers, including local public authorities, could hardly be ignored. This is a case of their operations having a direct influence on the internal scene. Such a state of affairs cannot be taken

---

8. National (Jones) Board, *Report,* Cmnd. 3292, pp. 60-62, especially pars. 182-86 and 189-90.

9. As noted earlier, the U.S. branch banks eventually were made subject to compulsory Cash Deposit requirements in 1968, which remained inoperative.

10. See p. 154.

as tolerantly as when foreign branch banks' operations appear to be related almost solely to the external sector.[11]

Swiss laws were less subject to being particularly influenced by the U.S. branch banks' operations. In fact, some legislative changes that might have seemed likely never occurred. For instance, there was no change in the Swiss tax requirement that effectively kept its financial centers from being Euro-dollar market centers.[12] This can partially be explained by the lack of any need being felt to duplicate locally what was being performed effectively in London. Banks and branch banks in Switzerland have had access to the Euro-dollar facilities there in any event. Also it reflects the desire to isolate the Swiss internal market.

With respect to another type of evolution it is again difficult to establish a direct link with the U.S. branch banks' operations. This is related to the growing sentiment in Switzerland during the late 1960's that stricter admission and operating requirements might have to be imposed on foreign controlled banking institutions. It is more likely that the large number and great variety of foreign branch banks and banking subsidiaries in the country, and those seeking or likely to seek admission in the future, caused greater concern than the operations of the U.S. branch banks already established. If anything, the latter were relatively desirable guests since they were arms of responsible institutions from a country which had many financial and trade ties with the host country. Indirectly, however, there was a causal relationship since there was some apprehension as to how the U.S. authorities might react if too many U.S. banks sought to establish branches or other units in Switzerland.

Turning from host to home country laws through 1967, the operations of the U.S. branch banks influenced the evolution of U.S. laws consistently in one direction—towards permissiveness. As we have seen, the 1963 revision of (Federal Reserve) Regulation M allowed the establishment of second generation branches after thirty days' notice to the Federal Reserve Board. The Euro-dollar and other deposits of the U.S. branch banks remained exempt from the reserve requirements set by Regulation D and from the interest limitations imposed by Regulation Q until 1969 and 1970 respectively. Moreover, in 1966 earnings

11. Perhaps the best evidence of the changed atmosphere is found in the Bank of England's 1971 move to stimulate competition and restructure the banking system in many important respects. These have included abandonment of the LDR (see p. 90) and the clearers' practice of tying lending rates closely to Bank rate, the imposition of reserve requirements on all banks, and the use of Special Deposits or their equivalent "across the whole of the banking system". See Bank of England, 11 *Quarterly Bulletin* 189-93 (1971).

12. In fact, subsequent changes have made certain types of Euro-dollar operations more difficult. See p. 252, note 202.

from these deposits were made exempt from U.S. federal income tax when the law was changed so that this no longer constituted U.S.-source income. Regulation M was greatly modified in 1963 to put U.S. branch banks on a better competitive footing with other banks abroad. Neither the Interest Equalization Tax nor the voluntary Guidelines were used to hamper their multinational banking operations.

Indeed, only when it became apparent that a massive balance of payments problem was developing were the U.S. branch banks' operations made subject to obligatory rules in this respect. Even so, the measures that went into effect in January 1968 were not aimed primarily at the U.S. branch banks, which were necessarily included within their scope. Their operations had not brought about the change. In fact, had they refused to follow the voluntary program their exempt status would certainly have been terminated much earlier.

Thus, up to the end of the period under study, the U.S. regulatory authorities had borrowed a leaf from the book of the British and Swiss: moral suasion. Of course, this tool had been used many times in the past in the United States, but with respect to the foreign branch operations of the U.S. banks it proved particularly effective.

C. Role of the U.S. Branch Banks

We have stated that some branch banks have different roles than others, and that taken collectively their role has undergone modifications.

Geographically the situs of a U.S. branch bank has a bearing on its assigned task, and vice versa. A branch bank in London can normally handle transactions involving the sterling area better than one in Switzerland, which is, for example, better situated for dealing with East-West trade matters. A Paris branch bank can expect to have greater contact with French-speaking African customers than would a London branch, which would find contact with Commonwealth customers more usual. Of course, second generation branches in the host countries have a different type of role than their progenitors, except in Switzerland where the existence of more than one financial center makes operations complementary in many respects.

This geographical variety has been set against a dynamic evolution of the role of the U.S. branch banks generally, as the three waves were composed of units set up for different purposes. It might be said that the first wave branch banks were there because of past experience and the needs of their established customers. For these branches, being established in London or Paris was a normal state of affairs. Indeed, it would have been no easier for a bank with first wave branches to decide to remove one, than for an inexperienced U.S. bank to decide to establish its first overseas branch.

The second wave branch banks have reflected the need of some banks to keep pace. In fact, had the war and its aftermath, in the United States as well as in the host countries, not delayed matters these banks would probably have established Paris or London branches much earlier. The second wave branch banks in Switzerland filled lacunae in the networks of banks that already were using first and second wave branches in France and Great Britain. The setting up of these Swiss branches, even though occurring while third wave branch banks were going into London, was not for the same purpose as the latter since the Swiss cities are not Euro-dollar market centers.

To all three waves Euro-dollar operations became inceasingly important. Whereas for the third wave this was a primary operation, the first and second wave branch banks wove it into their own operating patterns. By the end of the period under study there evolved a single international money market to which many important borrowers and lenders have had access. This market has been parallel to the local money markets, which have continued to function and to which borrowers and lenders or depositors have been confined for legal or other reasons. The international or parallel market has been vital to the U.S. branch banks because of their relatively small host currency deposit base. Moreover, those which have been part of a well coordinated network have had their own intramural money market, and they have been able to shuttle funds and match maturities globally, reducing expenses and commissions payable to outsiders.

This evolution of the role of the U.S. branch banks in adapting Euro-dollar techniques for their operations has been accompanied by developments in the international and local money markets, too. In the former there was the introduction of the London dollar c.d. (which has ultimately been followed by a sterling c.d. in London). Another factor has been the increasing resort to intra-corporate transactions where parent and subsidiary, or two subsidiaries, trade with each other and make payment by means of a ledger entry in a set of books maintained by one of them or by a third subsidiary located where there are fiscal advantages for doing so. These intra-corporate transactions have reduced the amount of marketable paper, especially acceptances, which has had an effect on the local money markets.

Along with the temporal evolution in connection with the international money market there has been another that is worthy of note. Although most of the first and second wave branch banks were avowedly established to help meet the foreign trade financing needs of their U.S. corporate customers, many found that with Euro-dollars or swaps they

288

could satisfy the fixed and working capital requirements of U.S. corporate subsidiaries in the host countries and eventually those of some indigenous concerns as well.

Thus, the U.S. branch banks' role generally has evolved in two respects. First, where previously they operated relatively isolated from other overseas units prior to the end of 1958 they came to function as links in a chain, the size and composition of which have depended upon the policy of the particular U.S. commercial bank and the stage of evolution of its multinational banking operations or aspirations. Second, with the passage of time many of the U.S. branch banks have become more locally oriented and have catered to indigenous as well as to U.S. and other foreign customers. The setting up of second generation branch banks outside the financial centers is evidence of a growing contact with smaller indigenous concerns and individuals. Affirmations that they are established solely "to help meet the foreign trade financing needs of their U.S. corporate customers" have been less frequently heard. In short—the U.S. branch banks as a group have begun to blend into an international banking system and into the host country sectors as well.

D. *Transfer of Technology*

There has been a transfer of technology in two directions, i.e., both to and from the home and host country banking sectors. Here the technology is comprised of two factors: particular tools as well as know-how related to banking activities, and the appreciation of a particular working medium.

With regard to the tools or know-how, U.S.-trained bankers have demonstrated the use of the term loan as it is known in the United States. In return they have been exposed to the theory and techniques of overdraft lending, which have been adopted for the operations of the U.S. branch banks, and with which commercial banks in the United States have begun experimenting domestically.

As for the appreciation of a working medium, U.S.-trained bankers have caused their hosts to reflect on some of the valuable aspects of competition in the banking industry. Indigenous institutions did not rush out to engage in a competitive melee; but it has not been lost on some local bankers and lawmakers that a carefully measured dose of competition might not cause any harm and might even be beneficial. In return, the U.S.-trained bankers have acquired two elements of appreciation. One consists of operating in and near banking systems where exchange controls are critically important. Another—significant in the long run and of juridical interest—is the experience gained in contact with banking systems where there are fewer compulsory and more persuasive devices employed by the regulatory authorities.[13] Some U.S.-trained bankers and their legal advisers have learned that an absence or scarcity of laws means neither chaos nor benign permissiveness.

E. *New Chapter in International Finance*

Finally, we have stated that the development of multinational banking marks a new chapter in the history of international finance, in that it is the response to a certain combination of stimuli to which neither the major U.S. commercial banks nor their host country counterparts have heretofore been exposed. The new stimuli have included a massive increase in international trade, a growing dollar surplus outside the United States, increasingly tight money market conditions in all the major financial centers, and a keener awareness of the new economic power represented by Western Europe taken as a whole.

Let us draw forth the essential elements which lie behind and have accounted for the U.S. branch banks' particular version of multinational banking:

1. the absence of capital movements controls in the home country;
2. a relatively stable, completely convertible home currency;[14]
3. externally or completely convertible host currencies;
4. the presence of home country corporate subsidiaries in the host countries;
5. the establishment of at least a branch bank in London, with one or more other units in the host countries, plus using these as a network; and
6. a particular frame of mind which includes inventiveness, flexibility, patience, a desire to compete, and a sense of teamwork.

The U.S. branch banks have had no monopoly on all of the elements. In fact, many of these or equivalent factors have been accessible to financial institutions from other countries. For instance, should the major Swiss banks decide to increase their own operations abroad there are certain elements favoring the development of a Swiss style of multinational banking just as in the case of the U.S. branch banks. For example, the natural advantage enjoyed by the U.S. institutions in having the principal Euro-currency closely related to their home currency has had

13. It is interesting to note that in July 1969 it was reported that the U.S. Secretary of the Treasury convened a meeting of the heads of the twenty-five largest U.S. commercial banks "to discuss ways in which the public and private sectors can work harmoniously together to bring inflation under control". New York Times, July 4, 1969, p. 27, col. 1 (late city edition).

14. Floating currencies as opposed to fixed international parities should not have an adverse effect as long as the home currency remains relatively stable with respect to the other principal currencies.

as a counterpart the natural association made between Swiss banking generally and banking across frontiers. Bankers from other countries, too, have possessed greater or lesser degrees of elements comparable to those listed above.

One factor merits special attention. Earlier in this Chapter and again in the list above it is stated that a certain frame of mind is required for multinational banking as conducted by many of the U.S. branch banks. It must be added that this outlook is one inducing operations as if there are no boundaries or frontiers whatsoever to impede the flow of purchasing power. This might be explained away by stating simply that the U.S. branch banks have chosen to conduct their multinational operations only where the exchange control laws have been permissive or non-existent, and that ipso facto there have been no barriers. This does not account for the fact, however, that some other institutions which might have been expected to do likewise failed to do so, notably some of the indigenous banks in the host countries as well as branches and subsidiaries of non-U.S. non-host country banks, which apparently have been more conscious of (or inhibited by) the barriers than have the U.S. branch banks.

In effect, the trait displayed by the latter is not that the frontiers are unseen, but rather that they are not seen as barriers. Perhaps this is particularly due to the fact that a U.S. branch bank is on foreign territory in any of the host countries, whereas the indigenous institutions in each country are not. Accordingly the indigenous institutions are always looking outwards while the U.S. branch banks are already outside, and are—both figuratively and actually—surveying their new environment. Another likely reason is that coming from a home country where boundaries between states have not prevented the flow of funds, even though banks are forbidden by law to establish branches outside their home states, the U.S.-trained bankers are not used to barriers and tend to carry this habit—or lack of one—with them to the host countries. This has been reinforced by the fact that they have most frequently been dealing in currency which does not seem foreign, and with many customers who are or who emulate U.S. corporations.

During the evolution of its role the U.S. branch bank has become remarkably independent. By the end of the period under study it was no longer a mere extension of the head office bank but was acting and dealing in an environment with which it was far more familiar than was the head office. The introduction of the U.S. voluntary Guidelines made genuine offshore operations more necessary; and the recondite characteristics of the Euro-dollar market operations meant that the head office could not have the decisive influence that otherwise it might have had.

Paradoxically, the U.S. branch bank has become operationally less an integral part and more like a separate entity, even though its legal structure has remained unchanged. That structure depends, however, on laws which themselves contain the divisive element. For instance, the host country laws require separate local accounts and what amounts to the equivalent of capital allocation to the branch as if it were a subsidiary. The British exchange controls treat a branch bank as if it were a resident corporation, albeit foreign-controlled. The Swiss banking laws do not permit the free flow of information normally present between a head office and a branch bank. It is only the U.S. law that has really carried the branch philosophy overseas, making it clear that a branch is a branch wherever located. Even this, however, has been weakened by the nature of the Euro-dollar operations and by the Guidelines, as it would *a fortiori* be weakened by home country laws controlling capital movements.

The legal aspects are not, then, mere structural lines which are once laid out and then forgotten while the institutions operate. The laws, and the philosophy behind them permeate through to the very core of what we have called multinational banking. Static laws do not prevent an evolution, for in the background lie deeper social, political, and economic factors which themselves evolve.

The intermeshing of the legal and financial aspects of the U.S. branch banks' multinational operations have not merely produced a new pattern formed of old materials. The result has been a new fabric, which in the future may be rewoven in various designs, but which can be expected to bear a kindred relationship to the type of multinational banking that has been developed by many of the U.S. branch banks, which have served as the forerunners.

Appendix

U.S. BRANCH BANKS IN FRANCE, GREAT BRITAIN, AND SWITZERLAND (AS OF JUNE 30, 1971)

Bank	France	Great Britain	Switzerland
1. American National Bank and Trust Co. of Chicago		London	
2. Bank of America, N.T. & S.A. (San Francisco)	Lyons Marseilles Paris	Birming- ham London* Manchester	Zurich
3. (The) Bank of New York		London	
4. Bankers Trust Co. (New York City)	Paris	London*	
5. (The) Chase Manhattan Bank, N.A. (New York City)	Lyons Paris	London*	
6. Chemical Bank (New York City)		London*	Zurich
7. City National Bank of Detroit		London	
8. Continental Illinois National Bank and Trust Co. of Chicago	Paris	London*	
9. Crocker-Citizens National Bank (San Francisco)		London	
10. (The) Detroit Bank & Trust Co.		London	
11. First National Bank in Dallas		London	
12. (The) First National Bank of Boston		London	
13. (The) First National Bank of Chicago	Paris	London	Geneva
14. First National City Bank (New York City)	Nice Paris**	London*	Geneva Lausanne Lugano Zurich
15. First Pennsylvania Banking and Trust Co. (Philadelphia)		London	

Bank	France	Great Britain	Switzerland
16. First Wisconsin National Bank of Milwaukee		London	
17. Girard Trust Bank (Philadelphia)		London	
18. Harris Trust and Savings Bank (Chicago)		London	
19. Irving Trust Co. (New York City)		London	
20. Manufacturers Hanover Trust Co. (New York City)		London*	
21. Marine Midland Bank (New York City)		London	
22. Mellon National Bank and Trust Co. (Pittsburgh)		London	
23. Morgan Guaranty Trust Co. of New York	Paris**	London*	Zurich
24. (The) National Bank of Commerce of Seattle		London	
25. National Bank of Detroit		London	
26. (The) Northern Trust Co. (Chicago)		London	
27. Republic National Bank of Dallas		London	
28. Security Pacific National Bank (Los Angeles)		London	
29. United California Bank (Los Angeles)		London	
30. Wells Fargo Bank, N.A. (San Francisco)		London	

* Also West End branch in London
** Also suburban branch in Paris
Source: Compiled from information supplied by the Federal Reserve Bank of New York and by individual banks.

SELECTED BIBLIOGRAPHY

OFFICIAL PUBLICATIONS

International Organizations

United Nations:
Treaty Series (U.N.T.S.)
International Bank for Reconstruction and Development ("World Bank"):
Finance and Development—quarterly (published jointly with the International Monetary Fund). (See also "Periodicals").
International Monetary Fund:
Annual Report
Central Banking Legislation, Hans Aufricht (ed.). 2 vols, 1961 and 1967.
Schedule of Par Values (through 50th Issue, 1970).
First [et seq.] Annual Report on Exchange Restrictions, 1950-
Staff Papers. (See also "Periodicals").
Finance and Development—quarterly (published jointly with the International Bank for Reconstruction and Development). (See also "Periodicals").
International Financial News Survey—weekly.
General Agreements on Tariffs and Trade (GATT):
International Trade—annual.
Organisation for Economic Co-operation and Development:
Code of Liberalisation of Current Invisible Operations, 1964.
Code of Liberalisation of Capital Movements, 1965.
Economic Survey: [member country]—annual.
Council of Europe:
European Yearbook.
Bank for International Settlements:
Annual Report
Foreign Exchange Restrictions in [France, Great Britain, Switzerland, United States], 1950-1958.
Eight European Central Banks, London, George Allen and Unwin, 1963.

Countries

France:
Code de Commerce (Dalloz)
Journal officiel de la République française
Commission de Contrôle des Banques, *Rapport [year], Bilan des Banques inscrites*

295

Banque de France, *Compte Rendu des Opérations*—annual
Commissariat Général du Plan d'Equipement et de la Productivité, *Ve Plan, 1966-1970*, 2 vols., Paris, Documentation Française (M.494), 1966.
Great Britain:
The Public General Acts, 1939-
Statutory Rules and Orders (S.R. & O.), 1939-1948.
Statutory Instruments (S.I.), 1949-
Index to the Statutes in Force
Papers by Command (Cmnd.) 1956-
Command Papers (Cmd.), 1919-1956.
Bank of England, *Report*—annual.
Bank of England, *Quarterly Bulletin*
Bank of England, *A Guide to United Kingdom Exchange Control*, 1968.
Central Office of Information, *United Kingdom Financial Institutions*, 1960.
Central Office of Information, *The British Banking System*, 1964.
Switzerland:
Recueil officiel des lois et ordonnances de la Confédération suisse
Recueil systématique des lois et ordonnances, 1848-1947
Bureau Fédéral de Statistique, *Annuaire statistique de la Suisse*
Swiss National Bank, Mitteilungen der Volkswirtschaftlichen und Statistischen Abteilung der Schweizerischen Nationalbank, *Das schweizerische Bankwesen im Jahre* [year]
Swiss National Bank, *Monatsbericht—Bulletin mensuel—monthly*
United States:
Federal:
United States Statutes at Large (Stat.)
United States Treaties and Other International Agreements (U.S.T.)
Treaty Series (T.S.)
Treaties and Other International Acts (TIAS)
Treaties, Conventions, International Acts, Protocols, and Agreements between the United States of America and Other Powers, 1776-1909 (Malloy)
United States Code (U.S.C.)
Code of Federal Regulations (C.F.R.)
Federal Register (Fed. Reg.)
Congressional Record
Congress, Senate, Banking and Currency Committee, *Reports*
Congress, Senate, Finance Committee, *Reports*
Congress, House of Representatives, Banking and Currency Committee, *Reports*
Congress, House of Representatives, Ways and Means Committee, *Reports*
Congress, Senate-House of Representatives Conference Committee, *Reports*
Congress, Joint Economic Committee, *Reports*
Department of State, *Digest of International Law*, by Green H. Hackworth, 8 vols., 1940-1944.
Department of State, *Digest of International Law*, by Marjorie M. Whiteman, 13 vols., 1963-
Department of State, *The State Department Bulletin*.
Department of State, *Treaties in Force*—annual.
Department of Commerce, Bureau of Foreign Commerce, *World Trade Information Service*.
Department of the Treasury, Office of the Comptroller of the Currency, *The American Banker*—monthly.
Board of Governors of the Federal Reserve System, *Annual Report*

Board of Governors of the Federal Reserve System, *Federal Reserve Bulletin*—monthly. (See also "Periodicals").

Board of Governors of the Federal Reserve System, *Press Releases*

Federal Reserve Bank of Boston, *The Federal Funds Market,* by Parker B. Willis, 1964.

Federal Reserve Bank of New York, *Foreign Central Banking: the Instruments of Monetary Policy,* by Peter Fousek, New York, 1957.

Federal Reserve Bank of New York, *Annual Report*

Federal Reserve Bank of New York, *Monthly Review* (See also "Periodicals").

States:

California: *Statutes and Amendments to the Code of California: Financial Code*

Illinois: *Illinois Revised Statutes: Banking Act*

Massachusetts: *Acts and Resolves Passed by the General Court of Massachusetts: General Laws* (Banking Companies and Trust Companies)

New York: *Laws of the State of New York: Banking Law*

New York: *Banking Board Regulations*

New York: *Civil Practice Laws and Rules*

Pennsylvania: *Banking Code of 1965*

BOOKS

Ardant, Henri. *Technique de la banque.* Paris: Presses Universitaires de France, 1953.

Auburn, H. W. (ed.). *Comparative Banking.* 3d ed. Dunstable: Waterlow, 1966.

Aufricht, Hans. *Comparative Survey of Central Bank Law.* London: Stevens, 1965.

Bär, Hans J. *The Banking System of Switzerland.* 3d ed. revised. Zurich: Schulthess, 1964.

Barazzetti, P. *Le régime des banques étrangères dans les principales législations.* Paris: Rousseau, 1923.

Baudhuin, Fernand. *Crédit et banque.* 2d ed. Paris: Librairie Générale de Droit et de Jurisprudence, 1949.

Beckhart, Benjamin Haggott (ed). *Banking Systems.* New York: Columbia University Press, 1954.

Béguin, Jean-Pierre. *Les entreprises conjointes internationales dans les pays en voie de développement; Le régime des participations.* Geneva: Graduate Institute of International Studies, University of Geneva, 1972.

Bener, Hans-Rudolph. *La fusion des sociétés anonymes en droit privé.* Geneva: Société Générale d'Imprimerie, 1967.

Branger, Jacques. *Traité d'économie bancaire.* 2 vols. Paris: Presses Universitaires de France, 1966 and 1968.

Braucher, Robert, and Sutherland, Arthur E., Jr. *Commercial Transactions.* Brooklyn: Foundation Press, 1958.

Chalmers, Eric B. (ed). *Readings in the Euro-dollar.* London: W. P. Griffith, 1969.

Chamas, Samy. *L'Etat et les systèmes bancaires contemporains.* Paris: Sirey, 1965.

Cochran, John A. *Money, Banking and the Economy.* New York: Macmillan, and London: Collier-Macmillan, 1967.

Colomes, Marcel. *Comment fonder et gérer une entreprise en France.* 2d ed. Paris: J. Delmas, 1966.

Dairaines, Serge. *Les étrangers et les sociétés étrangères en France; statut juridique, fiscal et social immunités.* Paris: Villefort, 1957.

Delaume, Georges R. *American-French Private International Law.* 2d ed. New York: Oceana (Columbia University, Parker School of Comparative and Foreign Law), 1961.

Dupont, P. *Le contrôle des banques et la direction du crédit en France.* Paris: Dunod, 1952.

Einzig, Paul. *The Euro-dollar System: Practice and Theory of International Interest Rates.* 4th ed. London and New York: Macmillan, 1970.

Einzig, Paul. *A Textbook on Foreign Exchange.* London: Macmillan, 1966.

Federation of British Industries. *Taxation in Western Europe, 1963.* 5th ed. revised. London: 1963.

Fehrenbach, T. R. *The Swiss Banks.* New York, London, Toronto: McGraw-Hill, 1966.

Foster, Major B., and Rodgers, Raymond (eds). *Money and Banking.* 3d ed. New York: Prentice-Hall, 1947.

Friedmann, Wolfgang G., and Kalmanoff, George (eds). *Joint International Business Ventures.* New York: Columbia University Press, 1961.

Graham, Benjamin, Dodd, David L., and Cottle, Sidney. *Security Analysis, Principles and Technique.* 4th ed. New York: McGraw-Hill, 1962.

Guggenheim, Paul. *Traité de droit international public.* 2 vols. Geneva: Georg, 1953.

Hirsch, Fred. *Money International.* London: A. Lane (Penguin), 1967.

Katz, Milton, and Brewster, Kingman. *The Law of International Transactions and Relations.* Brooklyn: Foundation Press and London: Stevens, 1960.

Lalive, Pierre A. *The Transfer of Chattels in the Conflict of Laws.* Oxford: Clarendon Press, 1955.

Mann, F. A. *The Legal Aspect of Money.* 2d ed. revised. Oxford: Clarendon Press, 1953.

Marchal, Jean. *Monnaie et crédit.* Paris: Cujas, 1964.

Meynaud, Jean, and Sidjanski, Dusan. *L'Europe des affaires.* Paris: Payot, 1967.

Nussbaum, Arthur. *American-Swiss Private International Law.* 2d ed. New York: Oceana (Columbia University, Parker School of Comparative and Foreign Law), 1958.

Nussbaum, Arthur. *Money in the Law—National and International.* Brooklyn: Foundation Press, 1950.

Oppenheim, L. *International Law.* 2 vols. 8th ed. (H. Lauterpacht, ed). London: Longmans, 1955.

Phelps, Clyde William. *The Foreign Expansion of American Banks—American Branch Banking Abroad.* New York: Ronald Press, 1927.

Prochnow, Herbert V. (ed). *The Federal Reserve System.* New York: Harper, 1960.

Rabel, Ernst. *The Conflict of Laws.* 4 vols. Ann Arbor: University of Michigan Law School, 1947.

Reimann, Guenther, and Wigglesworth, Edwin F. (eds). *The Challenge of International Finance.* New York: McGraw-Hill, 1966.

Reimann, Robert. *Kommentar zum Bundesgesetz über die Banken und Sparkassen vom 8. November 1934.* Zurich: Polygraphischer Verlag, 1963.

Samuelson, Paul A. *Economics.* 6th ed. New York: McGraw-Hill, 1964.

Sayers, Richard Sidney. *Banking in Western Europe.* Oxford: Clarendon Press, 1962.

Schwarzenberger, Georg. *A Manual of International Law.* 5th ed. London: Stevens, 1967.

Servan-Schreiber, Jean-Jacques. *The American Challenge.* New York: Atheneum, 1969.

Servan-Schreiber, Jean-Jacques. *Le défi américain*. Paris, Denoël, 1967.
Sheldon, Herbert Percival, and Drover, C. B. *The Practice and Law of Banking*. 9th ed. revised. London: Macdonald & Evans, 1962.
Spero, Herbert. *Money and Banking*. 2d ed. New York: Barnes & Noble, 1953.
Stein, Eric, and Nicholson, Thomas L. (eds). *American Enterprise in the Common Market; A Legal Profile*. 2 vols. Ann Arbor: University of Michigan Law School, 1960.
Topham, Alfred Frank (ed). *Palmer's Company Law*. 19th ed. London: Stevens, 1949.
Tschopp, Peter. *Inflation et politique monétaire, le cas de la Suisse*. Geneva: Editions Générales, 1967.
Wasserman, Max J., Hultman, Charles W., and Zsoldos, Laszlo. *International Finance*. New York: Simmons-Boardman, 1963.
Whittlesey, Charles Raymond. *Principles and Practices of Money and Banking*. New York: Macmillan, 1948.
Wilson, J. S. G. *French Banking Structure and Credit Policy*. London: G. Bell (University of London, The London School of Economic and Political Science), 1957.

MONOGRAPHS, ADDRESSES, COURSES, AND CONTRIBUTIONS TO COLLECTIONS

Allen, Harvey & Ross, Ltd. *This is Bill-broking*, London: 1965.
Bishop. "General Course of Public International Law" in Academy of International Law (The Hague), *Recueil des cours*, vol. 115, 1966, pp. 151-467.
Boyd, William, Jr. "The Development of United States Banking Services to Meet Customers' Needs Abroad" in National Foreign Trade Council, Inc., *Proceedings of the Fifty-Sixth National Foreign Trade Convention* (New York City, November 1969), New York: National Foreign Trade Council, Inc., 1970.
Brinkhorst, L. J. "European Law as a Legal Reality" in L. J. Brinkhorst and J. D. B. Mitchell, *European Law and Institutions*, Edinburgh: University Press, 1969, pp. 7-29.
District Bank, Ltd., *Digest of the United Kingdom Exchange Regulations*, 9th ed., London, 1951.
Einzig, Paul. "London" in Guenther Reimann and Edwin F. Wigglesworth (eds), *The Challenge of International Finance*, New York: McGraw-Hill, 1966, pp. 243-54.
Farley, Terrence M. *The "Edge Act" and United States International Banking and Finance*, New York: Brown Brothers Harriman & Co., 1962, p. 89.
Fournier, H. "Les institutions et mécanismes bancaires en France" in *Institutions et mécanismes bancaires dans les pays de la Communauté économique européenne*, Paris: Dunod, 1969, pp. 67-194.
Furth, J. Herbert. "International Relations and the Federal Reserve System" in Herbert v. Prochnow (ed), *The Federal Reserve System*, New York: Harper, 1960, pp. 273-94.
Germain-Martin, Henry. "France" in Benjamin Haggott Beckhart (ed), *Banking Systems*, New York: Columbia University Press, 1954, pp. 225-310.
Grossmann, Eugen. "Switzerland" in Benjamin Haggott Beckhart (ed), *Banking Systems*, New York: Columbia University Press, 1954, pp. 693-732.
Guggenheim, Paul. "Traités d'établissement", *Fiches Juridiques Suisses*, no. 662, Geneva, 1943.
Jeantet, Fernand Charles. "Exchange Control Regulations in France" in Eric Stein

299

and Thomas L. Nicholson (eds), *American Enterprise in the Common Market; a legal Profile,* 2 vols, Ann Arbor: University of Michigan Law School, 1960.

Jennings, R. Y. "General Course on Principles of International Law" in Academy of International Law (The Hague), *Recueil des cours,* vol. 121, 1967, pp. 327-600.

Johnson, Norris O. *Eurodollars in the New International Money Market,* New York: First National City Bank, 1964.

Lalive, Pierre A. "Harmonization et rapprochement de législations européennes" in *L'intégration européenne,* Geneva: Georg, 1964, pp. 45-77.

Lalive, Pierre A. "Dépréciation monétaire et contrats en droit international privé" in *XIe Journée juridique, Faculté de droit (1971),* Geneva: Georg, 1972.

Lando, Arturo. "Euro-dollar", Address delivered at the Institute of Studies for Economic Development, Naples, second academic year, 1963-1964 (translation from the original), Naples: L'Arte Tipografica Napoli, 1964.

Loussouarn, Yvon. "La condition des personnes morales en droit international privé" in Academy of International Law (The Hague), *Recueil des cours,* vol. 96, 1959, pp. 447-550.

Machlup, Fritz. *Euro-Dollar Creation: A Mystery Story,* Princeton: Princeton University Press (Reprints in International Finance, no. 16), 1970. (See also "Periodicals").

McQuade, Lawrence C. "Corporate Voluntary Balance of Payments Program and the Lawyer" in Southwestern Legal Foundation, *Private Investors Abroad, Structures and Safeguards,* Albany: Matthew Bender, 1966, pp. 205-26.

Oetterli, Max. "The History, Structure and Function of Banking in Switzerland", Address delivered at the Volkshochschule, Zurich, April 25, 1968.

Revell, Jack. *Changes in British Banking; the Growth of a Secondary Banking System,* London: Hill, Samuel & Co., Ltd., 1968.

Sayers, Richard Sidney, and Linder, W. "Switzerland" in Richard Sidney Sayers (ed), *Banking in Western Europe,* Oxford: Clarendon Press, 1962, pp. 174-96.

Schaefer, A. "The Importance of the Swiss Banks' Foreign Business", Address delivered at the ordinary general meeting of the Union Bank of Switzerland, Zurich, March 10, 1967.

Swoboda, Alexander K. *The Euro-Dollar Market: an Interpretation,* Princeton: Princeton University Press (Essays in International Finance, no. 64), 1968.

Thompson, Dennis. *The Proposal for a European Company,* London: Chatham House, 1969.

Wadsworth, John Edwin. "United Kingdom of Great Britain and Northern Ireland" in Benjamin Haggott Beckhart (ed), *Banking Systems,* New York: Columbia University Press, 1954, pp. 769-837.

Wilson, J. S. G. "France" in Richard Sidney Sayers (ed), *Banking in Western Europe,* Oxford: Clarendon Press, 1962, pp. 1-52.

PERIODICALS

Articles

In official publications:

Altman, Oscar L. "Canadian Markets for U.S. Dollars", International Monetary Fund, *Staff Papers,* vol. 9, pp. 297-316 (1962).

Altman, Oscar L. "Euro-Dollars: Some Further Comments", *Id.,* vol. 12, pp. 1-15 (1965).

Altman, Oscar L. "Foreign Markets for Dollars, Sterling, and other Currencies", *Id.,* vol. 8, pp. 313-52 (1960-1961).

Altman, Oscar L. "Recent Developments in Foreign Markets for Dollars and other Currencies", *Id.,* vol. 10, pp. 48-96 (1963).

Altman, Oscar L. "What Does it Really Mean? Euro-Dollars?" International Monetary Fund and International Bank for Reconstruction and Development, *Finance and Development,* vol. 4, pp. 9-16 (1967).

Chandavarkar, Anand G. "Unused Bank Overdrafts: Their Implications for Monetary Analysis and Policy", International Monetary Fund, *Staff Papers,* vol. 15, pp. 491-530 (1968).

Hirschman, Albert O. and Rosa [sic], Robert V. "Postwar Credit Controls in France", Board of Governors of the Federal Reserve System, *Federal Reserve Bulletin,* vol. 35, pp. 348-60 (1949).

Klopstock, Fred H., "Money Creation in the Euro-Dollar Market—A Note on Professor Friedman's Views", Federal Reserve Bank of New York, *Monthly Review,* vol. 52, pp. 12-15 (1970).

Tamagna, Frank M. and Willis, Parker B. "United States Banking Organization Abroad", Board of Governors of the Federal Reserve System, Federal Reserve Bulletin, vol. 42, pp. 1284-99 (1956).

Williams, David. "Foreign Currency Issues on European Security Markets", International Monetary Fund, *Staff Papers,* vol. 14, pp. 43-79 (1967).

In other publications:

Aubert, Maurice. "Portée du secret des banques envers le pouvoir judiciare", [Swiss] *Semaine Judiciare",* no. 39, December 1967, pp. 609-52.

Aubert, Maurice. "Secret et responsabilité des banques suisses envers les héritiers", [Swiss] *Id.,* no. 39, December 1964, pp. 1-46.

Beitzke, Günther. "Les conflits de lois en matière de fusion de sociétés (droit communautaire et droit international privé)", *Revue Critique de Droit International Privé,* vol. 56, 1967, pp. 1-22.

Biacabe, Pierre. "Le marché international du dollar en Europe", [French] *Revue d'Economie Politique,* vol. 80, 1970, pp. 548-69.

Branger, Jacques. "The French Banking System", *Journal of the Institute of Bankers,* vol. 85, 1964, pp. 184-95.

Brock, Mitchell. "The Reform of French Exchange Controls", *The Business Lawyer,* vol. 22, 1967, pp. 985-90.

Caflish, Lucius. "La nationalité des sociétés commerciales en droit international privé", *Schweizerisches Jahrbuch für Internationales Recht/Annuaire suisse de droit international,* vol. 24, 1967, pp. 119-60.

Campet, Charles. "Le Marché commun bancaire", *Revue du Marché Commun,* no. 137, 1970, pp. 441-46.

Christie, H. "Eurodollars and the Balance of Payments", *The Banker,* vol. 117, 1967, pp. 34-45.

Craig, W. L. "Application of the Trading with the Enemy Act to Foreign Corporations owned by Americans—Reflections on *Fruehauf* v. *Massardy*", *Harvard Law Review,* vol. 83, 1970, pp. 579-601.

Crane, Burton. "Invisible Pound Reigns in Trade", New York Times, March 23, 1958, § 3, p. 1, col. 5 (late city edition).

Dach, Joseph. "Legal Nature of the Euro-Dollar", *American Journal of Comparative Law,* vol. 13, 1964, pp. 30-43.

De La Giroday, J. B. "The Effects of the European Economic Community on the Banking Business within It", *The Business Lawyer,* vol. 18, 1963, pp. 1025-54.

Effros, Robert C. "The Whys and Wherefores of Eurodollars", *The Business Lawyer,* vol. 23, 1968, pp. 629-44.

Einzig, Paul. "Dollar Deposits in London", *The Banker,* vol. 110, 1960, pp. 23-27.

Erbe, René. "Instruments of Monetary Policy in Switzerland", *Journal of World Trade Law,* vol. 5, 1971, pp. 209-14.

Fordham, Jefferson B. "Branch Banks as Separate Entities", *Columbia Law Review,* vol. 31, 1931, pp. 975-95.

Friedman, Milton. "The Euro-Dollar Market: Some First Principles", Morgan Guaranty Trust Co., *The Morgan Guaranty Survey,* October 1969, pp. 4-14.

Grahame-Parker, J. "The Nationalisation of the French Banking System", *The Banker,* vol. 77, 1946, pp. 18-21.

Hackley, Howard H. "Our Baffling Banking System", *Virginia Law Review,* vol. 52, 1966, pp. 565 and 771.

Jasinski, Pierre. "The Control of Capital Movements in France", *Journal of World Trade Law,* vol. 3, 1969, pp. 209-18.

Jasinski, Pierre. "Export Financing in France", *Id.,* vol. 4, 1970, pp. 426-46.

Machlup, Fritz. "Euro-Dollar Creation: A Mystery Story", Banca Nazionale del Lavoro, *Quarterly Review,* vol. 94, 1970, pp. 219-60. (See also "Monographs").

Mann, F. A. "Exchange Restrictions in England", *Modern Law Review,* vol. 3, 1940, pp. 202-14.

Mann, F. A. "The Exchange Control Act, 1947", *Id.,* vol. 10, 1947, pp. 411-19.

Mast, Hans J. "International Issues in Europe", *Opera Mundi Europe,* nos. 368 and 369, August 4 and 11, 1966.

Oetterli, Max. "The New Legislation on Foreign Banks in Switzerland", *The Banker,* vol. 120, 1970, pp. 78-81.

Pinto, Roger. "Le régime juridique des investissements étrangers en France", *Journal du Droit International,* vol. 94, 1967, pp. 235-64.

Schwamm, Henri. "Banks and Industrial Concentration", International Credit Bank, *Quarterly Review,* vol. 7, no. 2, 1969, pp. 16-28.

Schwamm, Henri. "Swiss Industrial Penetration in the Common Market", *Id.,* vol. 8, no. 3, 1970, pp. 9-17.

Swoboda, Alexander K. "Multinational Banking, the Euro-dollar Market and Economic Policy", *Journal of World Trade Law,* vol. 5, 1971, pp. 121-30.

Vernucci, Alfredo. "The Impact of the U.S.A. Federal Funds Market on the International Exchange Market", Banca Nazionale del Lavoro, *Quarterly Review,* vol. 19, 1966, pp. 346-61.

Willatt, Norris. "The Overdraft Comes to America", *The Banker,* vol. 117, 1967, pp. 428-433.

Woodland, Don L. "Foreign Subsidiaries of American Commercial Banks", *University of Houston Business Review,* vol. 10, 1963, pp. 1-80.

—. "Le franc suisse et la politique monétaire et financière de la Suisse depuis 1960," [French] *Notes et Etudes Documentaires,* September 5, 1966, pp. 1-37.

—. *Texas Law Review,* vol. 47, 1969, pp. 703-707.

Periodicals used and/or otherwise cited:

Newspapers:
Financial Times (London)
International Herald Tribune (Paris)
Journal de Genève (Geneva)
Le Monde, final edition (Paris)
The New York Times, late city edition (New York City)
The Wall Street Journal, Eastern edition (New York City)

Other periodicals:
American Bar Association Journal (Chicago)
Business Week (New York City)
The Economist (London)
Entreprise (Paris)
First National City Bank, *Monthly Economic Letter*
Forbes Magazine (New York City)

Other Publications

American Law Institute. *Restatement (2d), Foreign Relations Law of the United States*, St. Paul, American Law Institute Publishers, 1965.
American Society of International Law. *International Legal Materials*—quarterly.
Black, Henry Campbell. *Black's Law Dictionary*, 4th ed. St. Paul, West, 1951.
Fédération Bancaire de la Communauté Economique Européenne, *Rapport*, 1968-1970, Brussels 1971.
Halsbury's Laws of England, 3d ed.
International Bureau of Fiscal Documentation. *European Taxation*—monthly.
Juris-Classeur Commercial (Paris).
Uniform Commercial Code.
United States Code Annotated.
United States Code Congressional and Administrative News—monthly. (Compiled annually).

INDEX

Acceptance financing 21, 130, 134 n, 135-37, 152, 183-84, 265
Acceptances (bankers') 191 n, 216 n, 288
Accepting house: *see* Merchant bank (Great Britain)
Accepting House Committee (London) 62
Acclimatization 149-51, 283 n, 289
Advances in current account (overdrafts) 88, 95, 117, 132-33, 137, 146-47, 244 n, 258 n, 289
Affiliated bank 4, 19-20, 25-29, 196-97, 221, 225, 235, 261, 264, 279
Afghan National Bank 65
Agence (France, Switzerland) 32
Agency 32
Agreement corporation 16 n, 26 n, 30, 40, 42 n, 225, 261
Agreements: *see* Gentlemen's agreements
Agricultural Mortgage Corporation Ltd. (Great Britain) 63
Air Finance Ltd. (Great Britain) 63
Allen, Harvey & Ross, Ltd. 221 n
Allocation of capital to branch bank abroad 58-59, 85, 103, 122, 185, 236, 252 n, 292
Alternative maturities, deposits with 109 n, 218-19
American Express Co. 28 n, 38
American National Bank and Trust Co. of Chicago 44 n, 271 n, 293
Anti-trust laws 65 n, 170 n
  Exemption from U.S. 253
  Within E.E.C. 158
Arbitrageurs 195
Argentina 111 n
Asset structure of U.S. bank standing behind deposits in foreign branches: *see* Deposits in foreign branch bank, U.S. bank assets as guarantee
Associated bank: *see* Affiliated bank
Association of Swiss Private Bankers 75
Association Professionnelle des Banques (France) 55-57, 59, 67

Association Suisse des Banquiers 81 n
  see also Swiss Bankers Association
Associazione Svizzera dei Banchieri 81 n
  see also Swiss Bankers Association
Australia and New Zealand Bank 65
Authorised banks and authorised dealers (Great Britain) 70-71, 149, 188
Autonomy (of branch bank) 7, 74, 184-85, 269-70, 281, 291-92

"Backdoor" subsidiaries (Great Britain) 63 n
Balance of payments
  Great Britain 127-28, 187, 245
  United States 40 n, 161, 199, 205 n, 226, 228-31, 234-35, 239, 253, 260 n, 262 n, 266, 277, 287
Banca Leu e Cia 73 n
  see also Bank Leu & Co., A.G.
Banca Nazionale Svizzera (Switzerland) 79 n
  see also Swiss National Bank
Banca Popolare Svizzera 73 n
  see also Swiss Popular Bank
Banco de Ponce 106 n
Bank Firestone, A.G. 240 n
Bank for International Settlements 212
Bank Leu & Co., A.G. 73
Bank of America, N.T. & S.A. 15, 17, 24 n, 28 n, 38, 40 n, 58 n, 71 n, 198 n, 220 n, 271 n, 293
Bank of England 62-63, 65-67, 70-71, 100, 125-26, 128-30, 134 n, 150-51, 187-89, 196, 210 n, 211 n, 221, 240, 245-46, 247 n, 283, 285, 286 n
Bank of France: *see* Banque de France
Bank of London and South America 65, 220 n, 264 n
Bank of New York, The 16-17, 38, 266 n, 293
Bank of Scotland 223 n
Bank of the Manhattan Co. 119 n
  see also Chase Manhattan Bank,

N.A., The
Bank Rate (Great Britain): *see under* Rediscount
Banker viii, 2, 8, 62, 66 n, 75, 104-105
U.S.-trained 11, 26, 139, 142, 146-47, 149-50, 193, 218, 289-91
Bankers' acceptances: *see* Acceptances (bankers')
Bankers Trust Co. 15, 17, 24 n, 28 n, 30 n, 38, 71 n, 198 n, 220 n, 264 n, 271 n, 293
Banking affiliate: *see* Affiliated bank
Banking correspondent: *see* Correspondent banking relationship
Banking laws generally 282, 284,
Within E.E.C. 158
Banking secret 170 n
Switzerland 6 n, 77-79, 292
Banking subsidiary 4, 12, 19, 23 n, 24 n, 25 n, 28-31, 45, 57-58, 84, 85 n, 99, 235, 241, 261, 280-81, 292
Implications of Omar case 203 n
Of host country bank in United States 13, 179 n, 227
Banque agréée (France): *see Intermédiaire agréé* (France)
Banque commerciale ix
Banque Commerciale pour l'Europe du Nord 164
Banque d'affaires (France) 30, 51, 53, 122, 201 n, 208, 264, 267, 284
Banque de dépôts (France) ix, 31, 50-53, 57-58, 63, 73, 95, 116 n, 121-22, 150, 207-208, 242, 264, 284-85
Banque de France 50-55, 58, 120 n, 122, 132 n, 134, 137-38, 173, 176 n, 209 n, 242-43, 244 n
Banque de l'Indochine 71 n, 223 n
Banque de l'Union Parisienne 53
Banque de Paris et des Pays-Bas 53
Banque de Suez et de l'Union des Mines 53, 264 n
Banque d'épargne (France) 51
Banque Française du Commerce Extérieur (BFCE) 136 n, 138 n
Banque inscrite (France) 50, 54, 56-58
Banque Lazard Frères 53
Banque Leu & Cie S.A. 73 n
see also Bank Leu & Co., A.G.
Banque Nationale de Paris 52, 264 n
Banque Nationale pour le Commerce et l'Industrie 52, 264 n
see also Banque Nationale de Paris

Banque Nationale Suisse (Switzerland) 79 n
see also Swiss National Bank
Banque Neuflize Schlumberger et Mallet 53
Banque Populaire Suisse 73 n
see also Swiss Popular Bank
Banque Suisse et Française 52 n
Banque universelle 201 n, 265
see also Universal banking
Banque Worms 53
Bär, Julius & Co. 75 n
Barclays Bank (D.C.O.) Ltd. 64
Barclays Bank Ltd. 64, 65 n
Berlin airlift 276
"Big Four" (Great Britain) 52, 64
Bill broker: *see* Discount house (Great Britain)
Bills: *see* Discounting drafts or bills and notes
Blocked accounts 90, 102, 113, 164, 180, 204, 205 n
Board of Trade (Great Britain) 63 n, 68 n, 136 n
see also Department of Trade and Industry (Great Britain)
Bon de caisse
France 90, 95
Switzerland 73 n, 90, 95 n
Bon de Trésor (France): *see under* Treasury bill
"Bona fide banking business" (Great Britain) 71 n
Bordier & Cie 75 n
Borrower of last resort 218
see also Lender of last resort
Borrowing short and lending long 258
Branch bank
Distinguished 19-20, 23 n, 28-32, 45, 59, 84, 99, 152, 197, 203-204, 235, 241, 261, 279-81, 291-92
Of host country bank in United States 13, 179 n, 227
Branch banks (U.S.) established in the host countries
as of December 31, 1967 17
as of June 30, 1971 293-94
British and French Bank (for Commerce and Industry) Ltd. 71 n
British Bank of the Middle East 65
British Overseas Banks Association 64
Brokers in Euro-dollars: *see under* Euro-dollar

Bundesrat (Switzerland) 72 n
see also Federal Council (Switzerland)

C.D.: see Certificate of deposit (c.d.)
Caisse d'épargne (France, Switzerland) 51, 75 n
Caisse de Dépôts et Consignations (France) 51, 138
Caisse Nationale des Marchés de l'Etat (France) 51
California, (state) law 43, 116
Cantonal Bank of Bern 74 n
Cantonal Bank of Zurich 74 n
Cantonal banks (Switzerland) 74, 79
Capital allocation: see Allocation of capital to branch bank abroad
Capital Issues Committee (Great Britain) 67, 127-28, 138
Capital movements controls 158, 290, 292
    France 243
    Switzerland 272
    United States 15, 78 n, 150, 181, 238, 240, 260 n, 270, 278, 284, 287
    Within E.E.C. 157-59, 243 n
    see also Exchange control
Capital requirements
    France 242
    Switzerland 248
Carte de commerçant (France) 59
Cartel arrangements 74 n, 90, 158 n, 220
    see also Anti-trust laws
    see also Gentlemen's agreements
Cash Deposits (Great Britain) 247 n, 285 n
Cash flow 147, 249
Cash ratio 125, 283
Casse di risparmio (Switzerland) 75 n
Cater, Ryder & Co. 221 n
Ceilings on interest rates payable: see under Interest paid on deposits
Central Hanover Bank and Trust Co. 15, 71 n
    see also Manufacturers Hanover Trust Co.
Central rates 275
Certificat de trésorerie (France) 123 n
Certificate of deposit (c.d.)
    In the United States 90, 95 n, 139 n, 216 n, 219, 274
    London dollar negotiable

certificate of deposit 219-24, 257, 259-60, 267-68, 288
    Sterling certificate of deposit 222, 288
    Swiss National Bank (proposed) 83 n
    see also Secondary market for London dollar c.d.'s
Chartered Bank Ltd. 65 n
Chase Bank 16, 58 n
    see also Chase Manhattan Bank, N.A., The
Chase Manhattan Bank, N.A., The 15 n, 17, 30 n, 38, 40 n, 58 n, 65 n, 198 n, 293
Chase National Bank of the City of New York 15, 71 n, 119 n, 120 n
    see also Chase Manhattan Bank, N.A., The
Chemical Bank 16 n, 17, 38, 272 n, 293
Chemical Bank New York Trust Co. 16, 38 n, 198, 220 n
    see also Chemical Bank
City National Bank of Detroit 271 n, 293
City of London 17, 62, 65, 67, 82, 151, 197, 264, 273
Clearing banks (Great Britain) 62, 64, 67, 109 n, 125-26, 152, 179, 189-90, 191 n, 220, 246, 247 n, 258 n, 264, 285, 286 n
Comity 33
Commercial bank distinguished ix n, 22, **29, 31, 50,** 62-64, 72, 87, 131, 139, **142, 285**
Commercial paper (United States) 134, 192, 216 n, 219, 274 n
Commission de Contrôle des Banques (France) 55, 59, 67, 242
Commission Fédérale des Banques (Switzerland) 72 **n**
    see also Federal Banking Commission (Switzerland)
Commissione Federale per le Banche (Switzerland) 72 n
    see also Federal Banking Commission (Switzerland)
Committee on the Working of the Monetary System (Great Britain) ("Radcliffe Committee") 63-64, 126, 152-54, 233, 258 n, 285
Common Market: see European Economic Community (E.E.C.)
Commonwealth Development Finance

306

308

N.A. (abbreviation): *see* National Association (United States)

Napoleon Bonaparte 53

National and Grindlays Bank Ltd. 65

National Association (United States) 38 n

National Bank Ltd., The 64 n

National Bank of Commerce of Seattle, The 271 n, 294

National Bank of Detroit 271 n, 294

National banks (United States) 36-44, 46-48, 92, 117, 182-83, 225

National City Bank of New York 15, 58 n, 71 n
see also First National City Bank

National City Bank of the City of New York (France), S.A. 16
see also First National City Bank

National Giro (Great Britain) 63 n, 114 n
see also Giro systems

National (Jones) Board on Prices and Income (Great Britain) 285

National Provincial and Rothschild (London) 221 n

National Provincial Bank Ltd. 64

National treatment 35

National Westminster Bank Ltd. 65 n

Nationalization 52-55, 107, 116 n, 122, 143, 150

Nesbitt, Thomson and Co. 221 n

Network operations 91, 112-13, 144, 148, 156, 192, 195-96, 225, 261, 268, 270-71, 275, 279, 281, 283, 288-90

New York, (state) law 32, 43, 48-49, 116 n, 153 n, 171, 203

New York Clearing House 256

Nixon, U.S. President Richard M. 273

Nominee companies (Great Britain) 30, 220 n

Northern Trust Co., The 44 n, 271 n, 294

Notes, promissory: *see under* Eurodollar
see also Discounting drafts or bills and notes

Nouveau franc (NF) 122 n, 176, 186

Numbered account (Switzerland) 79
see also Banking secret

O.E.C.D.: *see* Organisation for Economic Co-operation and Development (O.E.C.D.)

Office des Changes (France) 54, 95-96, 124, 172-75, 176 n, 186 n

Office of Foreign Direct Investments (United States) 238 n

Official foreign (non-U.S.) time deposits 167, 202 n

Offshore operations 236, 269-70, 275 n, 291

One-bank holding companies (United States) ix-x, 73 n

Open account transactions 265

Open market operations
Great Britain 150
Switzerland 80, 83 n
United States 150, 275 n

Operations Account countries viii
see also French franc area

Oral agreements:
see under Gentlemen's agreements

"Ordinary course" of business 126, 150, 227, 229, 231

Orelli im Thalhof 75 n

Organisation for Economic Co-operation and Development (O.E.C.D.) 6 n, 230 n

Original depositor (of Euro-dollars): *see under* Euro-dollar

"Outbound" Euro-dollar drain 274

Overdrafts: *see* Advances in current account (overdrafts)

Overnight advances 179, 255-56, 262, 266

"Overseas branch" (Great Britain) 70 n

Papier commercial (France) 134 n

Papier financier (France) 134 n

Parallel money market: *see* International money market

Patman, U.S. Representative Wright 78 n

Payment of interest on deposits: *see* Interest paid on deposits

Penn-Central financial crisis 273 n

Pennsylvania, (state) law 44, 116 n

Personal loans 63 n, 119-20, 142

Personne morale 171

Philippines 10

Phyzer, Chas. & Co., Inc. 254 n

Pictet & Cie 75 n

"Pipelining" head office bank funds 236, 241, 259, 270, 278, 280

Plafond (France) 123 n

Plancher (France) 123 n, 185 n

313

Plans, development (France) 122-23, 138, 207
Post Office Savings Bank (Great Britain) 63, 114 n
Powers of U.S. branch banks abroad, 1963 expansion in 182-85
Premium dollars
see Investment dollars (Great Britain)
Primary deposits 87-89
Prime rate, fluctuating 254 n
Private bank (France, Switzerland) 53, 74-75, 77, 248 n, 249
Profit margins 82 n, 87, 118, 145-46, 148, 186-88, 193, 211, 217, 250-51, 283

Radcliffe Committee Report (Great Britain): *see* Committee on the Working of the Monetary System (Great Britain) ("Radcliffe Committee")
Rahn & Bodmer 75 n
Raiffeisen banks (Switzerland) 76
Rates of interest: *see* Interest rates
Records of U.S. branch bank abroad 30 n, 46, 59, 69, 84, 122, 125, 169-71, 292
Rediscount 88, 134
France 122 n, 123, 132 n, 138
Great Britain (Bank Rate) 66, 137, 150, 151 n, 286 n
Switzerland 80, 134
United States 255
Registre de commerce (France, Switzerland) 23 n, 57, 59, 84
Regulation M (U.S. Federal Reserve) 26 n, 40-41, 47-48, 92, 121, 169, 184-85, 201 n, 225, 261, 273-74, 286-87
Regulation Q (U.S. Federal Reserve) 89, 93, 109 n, 166-68, 202, 207, 218 n, 244, 273-74, 286
Regulatory style: *see* Style of regulation
Representative office 3-4, 19-20, 22-25, 28, 91, 144, 196-97, 241, 261, 279
Republic National Bank of Dallas 271 n, 294
Reserve requirements 88, 262 n
France 210 n, 242-43, 272
Great Britain 125, 247 n, 283 n, 286 n
Switzerland 77, 80, 83 n, 214 n
United States 121, 135, 150, 169, 255, 262 n, 273-74, 286
Retail banking operations 63 n, 73 n, 119-20, 141-42, 145, 221, 267-68

see also Wholesale banking operations
Revaluation 109 n, 260 n
French franc 275 n
Pound sterling 275 n
Swiss franc 73 n, 272 n, 275 n
see also Devaluation
Revolving Euro-dollar credits: *see under* Euro-dollar
Rolling over loans at maturity ix, 128, 137, 192, 234
Royal Bank of Scotland 64 n

St. Lawrence Seaway 198
Sassoon Banking Co., E.D. 65
Savings bank 51, 63, 75-76, 215 n
Scheduled Territories (sterling area) viii, 98-102, 128-30, 156, 163, 177-78, 188, 211-12, 244, 247 n, 287
Schweizerische Bankgesellschaft 73 n
see also Union Bank of Switzerland
Schweizerische Bankvereinigung (Switzerland) 81 n
see also Swiss Bankers Association
Schweizerische Kreditanstalt 73 n
see also Swiss Credit Bank
Schweizerische Nationalbank (Switzerland) 79 n
see also Swiss National Bank
Schweizerische Volksbank 73 n
see also Swiss Popular Bank
Schweizerischer Bankverein 73 n
see also Swiss Bank Corporation
Scottish banks 64, 126, 189 n, 246, 247 n
Second generation branch banks 16-17, 41, 85 n, 266 n, 268, 287, 289
Second wave branch banks 16, 104 n, 105, 106 n, 109 n, 111, 119, 145, 197-98, 265, 277-78, 283, 287-88
Secondary market for London dollar c.d.'s 220-22, 257, 259-60
Secrecy: *see* Banking secret
Security dollars: *see* Investment dollars (Great Britain)
Security or switch sterling (Great Britain) 102
Security Pacific National Bank 271 n, 294
Self-financing 139 n, 200, 249, 251
Senate (U.S.), Finance Committee 168, 226 n, 227-29, 231-32
Senate-House (U.S.) Conference Committee 228

315

Third wave branch banks 16, 104 n, 106 n, 109 n, 111, 119, 265-66, 278, 283, 287-88
Tight money conditions 139, 211, 218, 241, 255-56, 266, 268-69, 278, 290
see also Interest rates
Time deposit account 64, 87 n, 90-91, 109-10, 113, 139 n, 141, 165, 168, 179, 207-208, 218-19
see also Certificate of deposit (c.d.)
Trade: *see* International trade
Tradition
  Banker-customer relationship 110, 143, 149, 201-202
  Effect on adopting new techniques 147-48
  Motive for establishing branch bank 31, 281
Transfer of technology: *see under* Technology
Transferable sterling 101-102, 157
Travelers cheques 3, 22 n, 38 n, 223
Treasury, H. M. (Great Britain) 66-67, 71, 98, 100, 127, 138, 151, 178, 245 n
Treasury bill
  France *(bon de trésor)* 123, 242 n
  Great Britain 66, 125 n, 130, 247 n
  United States 165, 191 n, 192, 216 n, 219, 221
Treasury coefficient (France) 123 n, 185 n, 242 n
Treasury Department (United States) 29 n, 114 n, 117, 183, 224, 234, 259, 290 n
  Office of the Comptroller of the Currency 11, 22 n, 39, 41-42, 46-47, 92, 284
  Certificates of indebtedness 275
Treaties 6, 33-36, 78 n
  see also Double taxation, treaties to reduce
Treaty of Rome 155, 157-60, 243 n
Treaty of Stockholm 159-60
Trustee Savings Banks Association (Great Britain) 63

Umbrella host currency Euro-dollar revolving credits 254 n
Underwriting: *see* Investment banking operations
Uniform Commercial Code 45
Union Bank of Switzerland 73, 76, 264 n

Union de Banques Suisses 73 n
  see also Union Bank of Switzerland
Unione di Banche Svizzere 73 n
  see also Union Bank of Switzerland
Unit trusts 63, 76
  see also Mutual funds (open-end investment companies)
United California Bank 271 n, 294
United Nations 272 n
Universal banking 73, 76, 284-85
  see also Banque universelle

"Vegetable oil scandal" 253 n
Vehicle currencies 163
Virgin Islands, U.S. 163 n
Viscosity of outbound head office funds 236, 241, 259, 270, 278
  see also Deposits in foreign branch bank, U.S. bank assets as guarantee
Voluntary Foreign Credit Restraint Program, U.S. (Guidelines) 40 n, 120 n, 200, 230 n, 234-42, 253, 259, 262 n, 268-70, 272, 277-78, 280, 282 n, 287, 291-92
  see also Corporate guidelines (U.S. balance of payments)
Vontobel, J. & Co. 75 n

Wegelin & Co. 75 n
Wells Fargo Bank, N.A. 271 n, 294
Westminster Bank Ltd. 64
Westminster Foreign Bank Ltd. 65
White, Weld and Co. 221 n, 222 n
Wholesale banking operations 119 n, 121, 141-44, 146, 148, 190, 192-93, 221-22, 267-68, 280
  see also Retail banking operations
Williams & Glyn's Bank Ltd. 64 n
Williams Deacon's Bank 64 n
Window dressing ix, 192, 246 n, 258 n
Withdrawal before maturity: *see* Alternative maturities, deposits with
Withholding tax: *see under* Taxes and taxation
Working balances 103-104, 213, 216, 219, 236, 245, 250, 258

Yield 214-15, 226-28, 236, 250 n, 277
  Defined 165 n
  On U.S. securities and bank deposits 165-67
  see also Profit margins

Zivnostenska Banka 65

316